The Chinese Approach
to
International Commercial Arbitration

The Chinese Approach
to
International Commercial Arbitration

Steve K Ngo

Published by
RUSSELL SQUARE PUBLISHING LIMITED
6 Manorside, Barnet, London EN5 2LD, United Kingdom
www.RussellSquarePublishing.com
Russell Square Publishing Limited was founded with
the objective of furthering legal research and scholarship
by publishing in
LONDON NEW YORK SINGAPORE THE HAGUE

RUSSELL SQUARE®

Russell Square® is a registered trademark of Russell Square Publishing Limited

Published in the United Kingdom by Russell Square Publishing Limited

Re-published in 2017 by WPublications Limited under licence

First published 2016

British Library Cataloguing in Publication Data
Data Available

Typeset by Araba Phoenix SRL Limited, Gibraltar
Printed in the United Kingdom

ISBN: 978-1-912142-07-1

Cover illustration:
'Zhong Kui, the legendary Demon Queller', by Ren Yi (also known as Ren Bonian) (1883)
Hanging scroll: ink and colour on paper, in the collection of the Metropolitan Museum of Art,
New York, USA. Zhong Kui appears here as an elegant, if somewhat eccentric, scholar.
His sword sheathed and a blossom stuck in his hair, he sits reading decorously beside a table
laid out with archaic bronzes filled with flowers and fruits, an image that suggests
it was the Chinese scholars' command of their cultural heritage rather than
their military prowess that set them apart from their Manchu overlords.

For Tristan.

About the Author

Professor Steve Ngo MCIArb is a practitioner of international arbitration and dispute resolution where he has acted as international consultant and arbitrator.

Professor Ngo has advised public and private entities not only on post-dispute matters but negotiation, mediation and dispute management. Over the past decade, he has focused on Indonesia and China, the two key growth economies of Asia and South East Asia. He has been involved in oil and gas, energy, investment, joint venture, telecommunications, shipping, mining, financial services, international trade and engineering. Professor Ngo has extensive experience dealing with parties from all over the world, bringing strong cross-cultural proficiency to international dispute resolution processes and strategizing.

Professor Ngo has been involved in matters involving arbitration rules of, among others, CIETAC, LMAA, SAC, ICC, SIAC, PCA, UNCITRAL, ICSID, HKIAC, BANI and KLRCA. In addition to international commercial arbitration, he has been consulted on potential investor-state arbitrations, evaluating cases against and for the state party.

He also has vast experience in design and delivery of arbitration professional training programmes and postgraduate courses throughout Asia. With previous professional experience in the higher education sector, Professor Ngo has special interest in the pedagogy and methodology of education. In addition to lectures and talks at academic institutions in the region, he has also lectured on dispute resolution at the Ministry of Energy and Mineral Resources Indonesia, Guangxi Lawyers' Association, Singapore Law Society, Malaysian Bar Council, Taipei Bar Association and the Permanent Court of Arbitration, The Hague.

Professor Ngo has been appointed to positions at a number of universities, including Honorary Professor of Law, National

Law University, Delhi; Part-time Professor at the School of Law, Guangxi University for Nationalities, Nanning; Guest Professor at the East China University of Politics and Law, Shanghai; and Foundation Professor in International Arbitration, Saint Martin's School of Law, Malta.

In addition, he is an Adviser/Foreign Representative of the Shanghai Arbitration Court of International Shipping and Adviser of the University of London International Programmes, Postgraduate Law Programmes.

Professor Ngo has written and published on subjects relating to arbitration and dispute resolution.

Abbreviations

AA 1996	English Arbitration Act 1996 Cap. 23
ADR	Alternative Dispute Resolution
ASEAN	Association of South East Asian Nations
BAC	Beijing Arbitration Commission
CAL	China Arbitration Law
CIETAC	China International Economic and Trade Arbitration Commission
CPL	China Civil Procedure Law
FIE	Foreign-Invested Entity
FTZ	Free Trade Zone
HKIAC	Hong Kong International Arbitration Centre
IAA	Singapore International Arbitration Act Cap. 143A
ICC	International Chamber of Commerce

ICSID	International Centre for Settlement of Investment Disputes
New York Convention	United Nations Convention on the Recognition and Enforcement of Foreign Arbitral Awards
OBOR	'One Belt, One Road'
PRC	People's Republic of China
RMB	Chinese Renminbi
SAC	Shanghai Arbitration Commission
SACIS	Shanghai Arbitration Court of International Shipping
SAR	Special Administrative Region
SIAC	Singapore International Arbitration Centre
SPC	Supreme People's Court
SPC's Circular	Circular of Supreme People's Court on Implementing Convention on the Recognition and Enforcement of Foreign Arbitral Awards Entered by China

UK	United Kingdom
UNCITRAL Model Law	UNCITRAL Model Law on International Commercial Arbitration
UNCITRAL	United Nations Commission on International Trade Law
US$	United States Dollar
USA	United States of America
WFOE	Wholly Foreign-Owned Enterprise

Foreword by
Professor Derek Roebuck[1]

After more than fifty years of trying to comprehend China and the Chinese way of doing things, I can state only one opinion with confidence: there are no such things. The most scientific, the most meticulous, the most labourious research will lead every scholar, Chinese as well as foreign, to the conclusion: too big, too varied.

That is not to say that the terms 'China' and 'Chinese' have no purpose. China is one vast country, with an enormous population. If it is to be governed as one, it is politically necessary that its peoples share an identity. They speak many quite distinct languages, some mutually incomprehensible. Politically, however, whatever linguistic science may say, it is essential as a matter of policy that there should be only one Chinese language, the written form. It would be impolite to ask what an illiterate person was speaking.

And so the only conclusion an honest foreign scholar can come to starts as a confession of ignorance – but not of despair. The realm of dispute resolution provides good examples. If the primary sources are searched, they will reveal the most exciting insights for the comparatist. If the research is focussed on an expressed time and place, all those lazy assumptions are seen for what they are: that the Chinese have something intrinsic in their culture throughout history which makes them readier to settle their disputes, while Western cultures – whatever that means – have always been litigious.

1 Former Editor-in-chief of *Arbitration: The Journal of the Chartered Institute of Arbitrators*; taught and practised law in England, New Zealand, Australia, Papua New Guinea and Hong Kong; Senior Associate Research Fellow at the Institute of Advanced Legal Studies, London; Guest Professor at the People's University of China; written over 50 books including Editor of the seven volume Peking University Press bilingual texts on Hong Kong contract, criminal law and procedure.

Steve Ngo's comprehensive study makes no such false assumptions. In his Preface he writes: 'nothing conclusive can be said about an intriguingly diverse China'. For the foreign reader, though, there is plenty to learn. Ngo reveals many insights just from his choice of subject-matter, his own approach and his own rich experience.

He is right to stress the Chinese openness to adopt, adapt and exploit ideas from abroad, particularly new technology. I had to smile as I read: 'For instance, Lenovo acquired IBM's personal computer business and has clearly become a globally accepted and leading computer brand' on my Lenovo computer screen.

Ngo's explanations of *guanxi* and *mianzi* are down-to-earth and essential preparation for the beginner. Forget old wives' tales: if there is a profit in it, there will be no problem in holding a meeting at 4.44pm on 4 April, whatever superstitions are supposed to flow from 4 = death. Just the explanation of why a lawyer's office may be dingy and approached through a passage festooned with washing is worth the price of this book. Remember! Dentons took US$ 450 million in fees in 2015.

Ngo's clear exposition of the policies of the present Government and of future prospects has all the clarity to be expected from a Singaporean disciple of Lee Kuan Yew.

All of this book is illuminated with insights from personal experience, of which Ngo provides many examples. And there is evidence of wide learning, too, from Confucius to 'From Mao to Mozart: Isaac Stern in China'.

Those of us who speak English-English should remember that we are now in a minority. English is now spoken by more people in China than in England. The language of this book is the vibrant, muscular language of Singapore, and all the more enjoyable for that. Indeed, this book is not only constantly revealing and challenging, sensible and up to the minute. It is genuinely fun to read.

Derek Roebuck
Senior Associate Research Fellow
Institute of Advanced Legal Studies, University of London
Visiting Professor, People's University of China
November 2016

Foreword by Jimmy Yim SC, PBM[2]

Professor Steve Ngo's book is a must-read for all who are interested in international commercial arbitration in the People's Republic of China. It neatly compacts the two complex subjects of international commercial arbitration and China into seven tightly-written chapters. Like good modern vitamin supplements, it packs plenty of goodness in the form of insightful observations and actual experiences of the author in a small area.

China, a vast and ancient country of more than one billion people, is the largest foreign creditor of the United States today. This awakened dragon is fast catching up in all areas of development and modernisation. In fact, through its sheer size and population and trade demographics, China has more commercial arbitrations conducted there than any other country in the world.

The book's first two chapters on China and the Chinese client provide a good foundational overview of the unique characteristics of the Chinese. The reader is then brought through four illuminating chapters on international arbitration in China.

In the rapidly growing areas of international commercial business and trade with China, understanding and applying the correct dispute resolution mechanism can prove to be one of the most important tools for the international businessman or lawyer alike. I commend Professor Ngo for this excellent

---

2 Partner and Managing Director of Drew & Napier (Singapore) Dispute Resolution practice. He has over 33 years of experience in civil and commercial law, criminal law and international commercial arbitration. His experience in international arbitration ranges from disputes concerning energy projects, building construction, pharmaceutical contracts, distributorship agreements and joint-venture contracts. He has acted as lead counsel or arbitrator in numerous disputes and international arbitrations under the rules of the Singapore International Arbitration Centre (SIAC), International Chamber of Commerce (ICC) and United Nations Commission on International Trade Law (UNCITRAL).

book, which I recommend as essential reading either in the office whilst preparing to depart, or inflight whilst bound, for the amazing land of China.

Jimmy Yim, SC, PBM, FSIArb
Partner and Managing Director Dispute Resolution,
Drew & Napier (Singapore)
November 2016

Foreword by Huo Zhengmei

推荐函

目前的中国仲裁，起源于 1995 年 9 月 1 日实施的《中华人民共和国仲裁法》。随着中国市场经济的不断深化，仲裁在多元化纠纷解决机制中，正在发挥着积极地作用。上海仲裁委员会从 1995 年 9 月 18 日设立至今 20 余年，受理中外当事人的仲裁案件的数量年均增幅达 20%，2015 年裁决争议金额是刚起步时的 150 倍。这只是中国仲裁发展的一个缩影。

当前中国经济正在不断融入世界市场，中国仲裁也随之被越来越多的法律界、企业界和学者们所认识和研究。本书作者吴伟伟先生，作为上海仲裁委员会国际航运仲裁院的海外顾问专家，用己所学专长，十分用心的研究中国仲裁法律制度，并对上海仲裁的发展提出积极的建议。借此机会，我代表上海国际航运仲裁院表示衷心地感谢！

随着“一带一路”中国战略的推进，可以预见今后将会有越来越多的外国当事人出现在中国的国际商事仲裁中。本书所阐述的国际商业仲裁的中国道路，会有助于读者了解中国在处理涉外仲裁过程中的特征及特点，并对执业律师和学者们大有裨益。

霍正美

上海国际航运仲裁院院长

2016 年 11 月 3 日

The current situation of arbitration in China originated on 1 September 1995 with the implementation of the 'People's Republic of China Arbitration Law'. With the deepening of China's market economy, arbitration as a diversification of dispute resolution mechanisms is playing an active role. Since the establishment of the Shanghai Arbitration Commission on 18 September 1995, the number of arbitration cases conducted by Chinese and foreign parties has increased by 20% annually, and in 2015, the disputed amount is 150 times that at the beginning. This is only a microcosm of China's arbitration development.

At present, China's economy is being integrated into the world market, and Chinese arbitration has been recognised and studied by more and more legal circles, enterprises and scholars. The author of this book, Mr Steve Ngo, as the Shanghai Arbitration Commission's Shanghai Arbitration Court of International Shipping overseas adviser, through his own expertise, has written a very careful study of the Chinese arbitration legal system and the positive development of arbitration in Shanghai. I would like to take this opportunity to express my heartfelt thanks on behalf of the Shanghai Arbitration Court of International Shipping!

With the advancement of China's strategy of 'One belt, one road', it is foreseeable that increasingly more foreign parties will appear in China's international commercial arbitration in the future. The Chinese road to international commercial arbitration described in this book will help readers understand the characteristics of China in handling foreign-related arbitration, and it is of great benefit to practicing lawyers and scholars.

Huo Zhengmei
President,
Shanghai Arbitration Court of
International Shipping
November 2016

Preface

It is commonly said that, in a light-hearted way, the prevalent question these days is not about 'what is made in China' but rather 'what is not made in China'. Similarly in the academy, the corresponding question would be 'what has not yet been written about China?' This question holds true when looking at the massive amount of publications relating to the subject of law, business and management involving China. Publications on the subject of China are proliferating, offering various opinions and comments. However, the subject of China should best be described as 'work in progress' because nothing conclusive can be said about an intriguingly diverse China which is also evolving. It is a country that is always learning and is transforming. As I recall my first visit to China many years ago, I can only conclude that today it was not a particularly 'memorable' trip simply because I can no longer recollect most of the sights, sounds and smell of the places from my first visit; they have all transformed and are unrecognisable today. This is not a negative review or sentiment but a reflection of the changing China, signifying that there is certainly hope for change for the better.

The co-star with China in this book is international dispute settlement and commercial arbitration. Conflicts between people and commercial disputes are unavoidable in reality. Of course, from the standpoint of management, while professionals have crafted phrases such as 'dispute avoidance' and 'conflict management', cynics consider these as 'palliative' by nature and sceptics think that disputes are generally unavoidable. My grandmother often said that 'even your teeth can bite your own tongue; surely there will be conflicts or disputes among men'. It is nearly a fallacy to say that disputes can all be generally avoided but it would not be a fantasy to occasionally arrest disputes specifically. It is all a treatment process.

It is vital to explain the key aims of this book, what it is not as well as what it is all about. It is not a textbook on China arbitration law and practice; no doubt in this book there are discussions about the theories and fundamental legal concepts of arbitration but it is essentially a study on how the Chinese parties think, perceive or behave when involved in international disputes involving foreign parties. Foreign companies doing business with Chinese companies have been reluctant to submit to Chinese courts and this is rightfully so due to the many advantageous features international commercial arbitration has to offer to parties involved in cross-border disputes. In dealing with the Chinese, it is useful and pivotal to understand how Chinese companies react to and conduct themselves in international commercial arbitrations. A common assumption is that Chinese in every nook and cranny of China all think alike but nothing could be farther than the truth. However, there is also no doubt that there are commonalities among the Chinese in such aspects as basic national culture, common societal values and beliefs as well as Confucianism. This book attempts to balance the contemporary attitude of Chinese with inherent cultural values as well as their behaviour in handling commercial disputes, so that the book is as objective as it can be in terms of scholarship.

In recent times, many Chinese have been educated in the West and were heavily influenced by what they have learnt. They were no doubt eager to apply their new-found knowledge at home but this is not always meant to be. Some of them have had to abandon their ideals and reverted to doing it the way every other Chinese person within that society does it. There can be many determining factors at play, such as the nature of the profession and industry, but changes take time. It is often interesting to see the pragmatism of Chinese people in action in a situation like this and it is not possible to stereotype them.

This book is based on experiences, observations and interviews. The study of cultures, past and present, underpins the foundation of this book and its research. At times, there is a thin line between stereotypes and widely held views, therefore the careful approach is to ensure objectivity so that it offers readers the opportunity to form their own conclusion by also taking into account their own unique experiences on the same subject. As mentioned throughout the book, China and the Chinese most of the time can be described as befitting the parable of the blind men and an elephant, each touching different parts of the same animal but experiencing it rather differently. We can generally agree that China is an important global trading and economic country today and it is hoped that readers who are involved in business and dispute resolution with China and Chinese parties will find this book useful and enlightening.

In writing this book, so much gratitude is owed to so many for their service and assistance. For all your support and assistance, I sincerely thank you. Whether they answered my questions, pointed me to the correct sources of information or caused me more uncertainty that I had to think deeper, I thank them. I have made it a point in this book to not mention anyone by name because I would most certainly risk missing out some names inadvertently. I have also gained my inspiration and information from the many strangers and 'unsung heroes' I have met throughout my 'China life': from the stall-keeper with whom I haggled the price of some souvenirs but never bargained for her life's story then suddenly the sale was concluded at the lowest imaginable price all because I was her 'first' or 'last' customer of the day, to the furious group of passengers I was stranded together with in a Chinese airport due to a domestic flight delay. I have learnt so many things, regardless of whether I agree or disagree, but the point is so many have inspired me meaningfully resulting in this book. With some part of this book written when I was in

China, needless to say, the feeling is phenomenal and beyond motivation.

Finally, this book was completed on my son's birthday. I hope he will look back in life with gratitude for what he has and not what he does not have. I pray that he will grow up to be a useful person to others and inspired to attain all of his dreams and heart's desire.

Steve Ngo
Singapore
22 September 2016

Explanatory Notes

Throughout this book, certain terminologies are used and they denote specific meaning. The definition of 'China' refers to the People's Republic of China (PRC). Nothing in this book talks about Taiwan. Whenever Hong Kong is mentioned, it is referred to as the Special Administrative Region (SAR) of the PRC.

'Chinese' or 'Chinese people' in this book refers to PRC nationals. Whilst Chinese can also refer to people of Chinese ethnicity at large or a diaspora, here they are referred to as 'overseas Chinese' or '华侨' (*huáqiáo*) for the purpose of describing people who have left China and adopted another country as their home, such as those in South East Asia. Some commentators have suggested that *huáqiáo* denotes one who still retains PRC citizenship thus loyalty to China but this book will not get involved in the unnecessary politicising and complicating of this terminology. Instead of describing 'Singaporean Chinese' or 'Indonesian Chinese', for the purpose of this book they are collectively described as overseas Chinese.

The use of the terms 'foreigners', 'foreign investors' and 'foreign parties' throughout this book refers to non-Chinese parties. This is not a racial or ethnic study. This book does not suggest that the attitude to the handling of international disputes and conduct of commercial arbitrations is wholly dictated by ethnicities and nationalities.

This book uses the simplified Chinese (简化字) (*jiǎnhuàzì*) which is officially used in the PRC. There are four tones of Mandarin and the *Hanyu Pinyin* in this book uses diacritics to denote the four tones, in aid of non-native Chinese language readers. Words importing one gender include all genders.

Finally, with the sanctity of confidentiality and privacy paramount, sensitive information or specific details pertaining to, or that could potentially lead to the revelation of cases and/or parties, have been given the necessary editorial treatment to ensure that their identities will never be known and readers can still benefit from the substance of the various case studies.

All web urls were checked on 11 November 2016.

The Chinese Approach
to
International Commercial Arbitration

Chapter 1

China and Chinese

1.1. Introduction

The concise history and origin of China have been very widely researched, written and published, not requiring another attempt to venture into that subject by this book. Looking at China today, one cannot be oblivious to the fact that this unique country and its people have a civilisation dating back a very long time with the past continuing to influence many parts of modern life today. The lifestyles of overseas Chinese who have settled all over the world from the predominant South East Asia region to other parts of Asia, Africa, Europe and the Americas mainly still retain a good part of basic Chinese ethnic culture if not remnants of it. What constitutes Chinese ethnic culture, as will be discussed later in this book, is no doubt a complex subject which can be elusive yet amusing, perhaps similar to saying that 'chicken tikka masala' is an Indian dish when it is arguably British. In modern times, Chinese culture has been monetized by opportunists quick to jump onto the Chinese ethnicity bandwagon, which unfortunately does not do justice to the truth. It is all but entertaining and amusing to read stories about supposedly Chinese parenting or management skills, attaching names of real and mythological animals on Chinese people.[3]

American statesman Henry Kissinger wrote that 'a special feature of Chinese civilisation is that it seems to have no beginning'.[4] Kissinger went further to describe how some present aspects of the Chinese is a legacy of the past:

3 For example, Amy Chua, *Battle Hymn of the Tiger Mother* (Penguin Books 2011).

4 Henry Kissinger, *Henry Kissinger on China* (Penguin Books 2012) 5.

> When Chinese written characters first evolved, during the Shang Dynasty in the second millennium B.C., ancient Egypt was at the height of its glory. The great city-states of classical Greece had not yet emerged, and Rome was millennia away. Yet the direct descendant of the Shang writing system is still used by well over a billion people today.[5]

The Chinese civilisation is undoubtedly an old one, with many of its ancient trade ties with the world such as the Silk Road well documented and evidenced. Diplomatic ties were established during imperial times, cementing relationships between China and the outside world including the western powers. In ancient times, the Chinese travelled far for trade and commerce but, unlike the English, Arabs, Spanish, Portuguese or Dutch, colonisation and spreading of religion was not exactly on their agenda; they were contented in just trading and prospering with the outside world. While the ancient Chinese who had subscribed to the strict teachings of Confucianism were not commanded to 'go forth and multiply',[6] Confucius taught the Chinese to respect others and live in harmony together, as well as ascribing to the mantra 'Do not impose on others what you yourself do not desire'.[7]

And so the Chinese people have developed skills and knowledge in cross-border trade and commerce, in other words, a proclivity for business and making money. Such skills, memories and knowledge have been passed on from generation to generation among the Chinese people including overseas Chinese. To this day, the Chinese culture is steeped in financial prosperity whereby being financially able is a blessing whereas the opposite, a curse. For illustration purposes, Italian mothers and families would have been very proud to talk

5 *Ibid* 6.

6 *Genesis* 1:28.

7 Confucius (trans DC Lau), *The Analects* (Penguin Books 1979) XV:24, at 135. See also *Matthew* 7:12.

about have their sons who are clergy of the Roman Catholic Church and likely to be immensely proud to trace their family genealogies of Bishops, Cardinals and maybe Popes. In the Chinese family, however, they are proud of their sons and daughters who are highly educated (denoting that they are intellectually superior and not peasants) therefore likely to be successful in their career. Or above all, how well off they are financially as successful businessmen or entrepreneurs; or their daughters married off to rich husbands.

In the Chinese culture, flaunting of wealth is not exactly *chutzpah* but instead the lack of wealth is humiliating and a mark a failure, consequently most Chinese were brought up subscribing to the notion that success is mostly measured by one's wealth. Accumulation of wealth through working for someone and rising up the ranks is also thought to be a slow and arduous process which may likely fail due to fierce talent competition. Despite the many risks attached to doing business, being an entrepreneur is still perceived to be the quickest route to becoming successful and wealthy in China. The idea of one becoming his own boss is partly a symbol of success due to the ability to employ people, being the employer, and, of course, making money.

But the unpleasant face of the Chinese belief in prosperity is that many times money is viewed as the ultimate solution to many issues; to resolve a conflict, one compensates and almost everything becomes quantifiable. Flaunting is rarely thought to be in bad taste, nevertheless the younger generation from wealthy families, also commonly known as '*fù'èrdài*' (富二代), meaning 'second generation of the rich', have been increasingly criticised and despised for their excessive show of wealth which is perceived as mocking the less fortunate, given the widening income gap in China these days.

Meanwhile, westerners who are unaccustomed to the Chinese culture would find it awkward, for instance, being part of a conversation discussing how much one earns or the number of properties owned including the price paid. To the Chinese, these are pertinent matters as part of peer review and emulation, flaunting by the haves and motivation to the have-nots to succeed. For example, two university mates from similar humble background graduated at the same time. The first is an employee but the other, an entrepreneur. Supposed they have agreed to meet for lunch and the entrepreneur arrived in a luxurious continental car compared to the employee friend. He will most likely talk about his overseas trips, regular visits to Shanghai and Beijing; the expensive timepiece he is wearing, his clothing and very likely pick up the tab for the lavish lunch. The less successful of the two would have been very keen to know his friend made it despite coming from the same background; 'what is the secret of his success?' he will ask himself. Whilst the Chinese culture espouses virtues of humility, it is a thin line when it comes to humility and gaining peer/societal recognition.

In the Chinese culture, enduring hardship and going through struggle without shortcuts in life are among the common mantras. Some from among the numerous idioms handed down from parents to children include '水滴石穿' (*shuǐ dī shí chuān*) meaning 'unceasing efforts will bring success' or '一分耕耘，一分收获' (*yī fēn gēngyún, yī fēn shōuhuò*) or 'the more one works at something, the better the results'. No doubt many Chinese people, on the other hand, have made their mark in areas like sports, music, science and the arts globally. Even among families of overseas Chinese, children are brought up to work hard to achieve results.

This purpose of this introductory chapter is to explore and discuss the anatomy of contemporary observed cultures of China and the Chinese, thus laying the foundation of this book as to how certain values might affect the Chinese approach to international dispute resolution and arbitration.

1.2. Chinese catching-up: 'Arise, ye who refuse to be slaves!'

The title to this heading incorporates the first stanza of China national anthem, 'March of the Volunteers'[8] which was officially adopted as the national anthem of China only in 1982. The undoubtedly rousing lyrics of the anthem are a call to prevail over past setbacks and for unity as well as progress by the people. With the end of the Cultural Revolution and the beginning of a new era in China's economic and political progress, the March of the Volunteers was an auspicious anthem of solidarity to motivate the people forward. Chaos and wars have been destructive towards China's past progress. When Adam Smith wrote *The Wealth of Nations*[9] first published in 1776, China was described as 'long one of the richest, that is, one of the most fertile, best cultivated, most industrious, and most populous countries in the world'.[10] But Smith also said that the country's development seemed to 'have been long stationary' when he compared Marco Polo's observation 500 years ago with what travellers to China in 'present times' had described the state of China to be in the same terms.[11] According to commentators, Smith's authority on China was probably Jean-Bapiste Du Halde[12] who published a work on China in 1735.[13] This would have been during the rule of Kangxi or Yongzheng Emperors (from 1661-1735) of the Qing Dynasty. During these times, both Emperors had experienced battles and unrest which might suggest that the tumultuous era would have caused the country's progress to stall.

---

8 See English translation on the State Council of the People's Republic of China website at <www.gov.cn/english/2005-08/16/content_23523.htm>.

9 Adam Smith, *The Wealth of Nations* (Oxford University Press reissued 2008).

10 *Ibid* 70-1.

11 *Ibid* 71.

12 A French Jesuit historian who specialised in China.

13 See Smith (n 10) 481-2.

After the Second World War and China's civil war, China and the Chinese were determined to catch up economically, especially after the last setback from the Cultural Revolution (1966 to 1976). When Deng Xiaoping took over leadership,[14] he led the country through economic reforms which has proven to be monumental in the opening up of China to the global world, setting the foundations for what the country is today. There is very little to dispute the significance of Deng's contribution in this respect; noteworthy in the context of this book, it was during Deng's time that China became a member state of the United Nations Convention on the Recognition and Enforcement of Foreign Arbitral Awards, in 1987. The Chinese government have also been constantly learning and on the lookout for ideas that can continue to ensure that the country maintains its momentum in terms of economic growth and prosperity so that there can be stability; when people are doing well and happy, there is peace. In the economic and commerce front, when China embarked on manufacturing for the world it became the world's factory and now it is looking at progressing to the next level by evolving from being a mere mass production centre to producing high technology and precision products. China and Chinese will never be content to be average.

In terms of the lifestyle of Chinese people, progress has improved by leaps and bounds. Migrant Chinese workers can now afford mobile phones to call home; gone are the days when they could only rely on letters to communicate back home. The middle and upper classes today can afford many material things including European branded products[15] which

---

14 Although, Deng was paramount leader he never held official position as head of state or government.

15 It is reported that Chinese shoppers account for nearly half of the global luxury market. China's luxury spending in 2015 was reported to have totalled $16.8 billion, up 9 percent, year on year. 'China remains largest market for luxury goods', *China Daily* (Beijing 8 Apr 2016), <www.chinadaily.com.cn/business/2016-04/08/content_24372744.htm>. Chinese

previously their peers could only dream of having. The rapid rise of ultra-wealthy and super rich is perhaps unprecedented, created by the demand of the people and caught in the whirlwind of economic explosion and prosperity boom.[16] It is an ecosystem of prosperity where one class will benefit the other.

One simple illustration is a person who started a small factory making cheap plastic buttons to be exported globally. By all means, this is not a sophisticated or high technology product but it created jobs for hundreds of workers. As export increased, the factory expanded and hundreds more workers were employed. In due course, clients overseas suggested to the owner to make clothing labels and zippers since it is much more convenient for them to procure from one source, and so he did and expanded to setting up a garment factory doing contract manufacturing for international brands. From driving a beaten up used car, the company now owns a fleet of luxurious cars that are used to ferry overseas clients to the factory for meetings and inspections. At the same time in the beginning, a man set up a small stall outside the small factory to sell cigarettes, snacks and Chinese medications to the factory workers. As the factory expanded with more headcount, product demand from the stall also increased; now the stall is rebuilt into a small shop equipped with a payphone to cater to homesick workers to call home. The now-shop owner rode the manufacturing boom, prospered and went downtown to set up a restaurant; he invested in real estate and started owning hotels and went into other investments.

---

accounted for 46 per cent of worldwide sales of luxury goods as reported in 2015. 'China shoppers tipped to remain world's biggest luxury spenders' *South China Morning Post* (Hong Kong 25 Nov 2015) <www.scmp.com/news/china/money-wealth/article/1883079/chinese-shoppers-tipped-remain-worlds-biggest-luxury>.

16 The story of Zhang Zhifeng, a Chinese home-grown fashion designer who came from a poor family background, is an example of people in China trying to create expensive and luxury brands to cater to the booming market of newly rich people, 'Asian shoppers thirst for luxury' *BBC Global Business* (London 24 Jan 2011) <www.bbc.com/news/business-12251712>.

There are many success stories in China of entrepreneurs who are almost all entirely self-made and previously coming from humble backgrounds with no connections whatsoever. In a country with more than one billion population, it is not too difficult to imagine the possibility of multiplying effects. The rich have become societal role models where everyone dreams of becoming rich as the memories of hardship and poverty have not faded from the memories of the people. There are still survivors from those times of adversity who are living reminders to the current generation of that tumultuous era in China.

Chinese people are disciplined enough to separate themselves according to roles, ranks and responsibilities. The teaching of Confucianism permeates the people's way of life and government. Once, Confucius was asked about government to which he answered:

> 'Let the ruler be a ruler, the subject a subject, the father a father, the son a son'. The Duke said. 'Splendid! Truly, if the ruler be not a ruler, the subject not a subject, the father not a father, the son not a son, then even if there be grain, would I get to it?'[17]

The above quote is thought to interpret the teachings regarding duties and obligations of each and every Chinese. Everyone is required to carry out their duties according to their roles and responsibilities as well as be expected to do well at it. Arguably this describes the current dichotomous state of affairs in China whereby the government will do its job and the people support the government whilst free to pursue their own happiness. Politics are not in the mainstream interest of the ordinary people and the Chinese can be very pragmatic about this; if it is in their best interest to be successful, why meddle in the affairs of the country? People who want to

17 Confucius, *The Analects* XII:11, at 114.

serve the country enter the government consciously whereas people who do not will stay out of it.

Lastly, Chinese people are increasingly pursuing higher education and learning abroad. Many of these have also entered academia and chosen to remain overseas but many have also returned to their home country, some at the invitation of the government to spur the Chinese talent market.[18] The economic boom in China has also resulted in career opportunities arising back at home for Chinese intellectuals and academics with impressive credentials. Not just that they will return home to make their contribution to their country but to some extent the slowing western economy has also made it practical for them to go where the action is: China.

1.3. Chinese behaviour in dilemma

Local cultures are vast in China and many people still speak dialects among themselves locally. Some behaviours are associated with where they come from in China and how to speak Chinese language or *Putonghua* ('普通话' *pǔtōnghuà)* literally meaning 'common language' commonly referred to in English as Mandarin. At times, how one speaks may affect the first impression; some people coming from bigger cities like Beijing and Shanghai may at times be dismissive of people coming from the rural areas basing on the way they speak, perceiving them as 'people from small town' or '小地方人' (*xiǎo dìfāng rén*) which is considered derogatory. It is a good experience when travelling domestically in China, traversing from one province to another, to observe noticeable changing local behaviours between Chinese from different parts of China. In drawing a parallel with the English language, one can expect someone from Beijing speaking in

18 See 'A matter of honours: China is trying to reverse its brain drain', *Economist* (London 22 Nov 2014).

refined *Putonghua* like the 'Queen's English' compared to someone probably form the south who speaks less fluent or 'classy' Chinese language. People from the southern part of China tend to be more rugged and robust. Whilst there is no social caste system in China, people do form opinion about someone from the way he or she speaks and behaves.

In the light of people prospering rather rapidly and increased mobility in terms of air travel, more Chinese are now able to travel and visit overseas countries. Chinese tourists have been reportedly misbehaving[20] in foreign countries prompting the Chinese government to plan to set up a database of bad behaving Chinese travellers which will include travellers with a record of misbehaviour to receive messages 'reminding them to behave themselves'.[19] According to the same report, the Chinese civil aviation authority is similarly considering such a blacklisting[20] as can be seen from many social media platforms sharing viral videos of unruly Chinese air travellers.[21] There is also a lack of education and understanding regarding proper decorum and conduct; for instance, cutlery provided on board flights is not meant to be taken home but to be reused by airlines or that touching historical artefacts is forbidden because this can expedite its deterioration.[22] There is the much talked about subject of Chinese air travellers gone berserk at airports due to

---

19 See <www.youtube.com/watch?v=6j9bLIg84XM>.

20 See 'China plans database of bad-behaving tourists', *China Daily Asia* (Hong Kong 16 Jan 2015) <www.chinadailyasia.com/nation/2015-01/16/content_15215278.html>. See also 'Tourists Behaving Badly: Name-and-Shame Effort Fails to Fix China's Image', *New York Times* (New York 10 Oct 2016) <www.nytimes.com/2016/10/11/world/asia/bad-manners-china-tourism-blacklist.html>.

21 'Chinese airlines to start "blacklist" unruly passengers', *Independent* (London 2 Feb 2016) <www.independent.co.uk/news/world/asia/five-chinese-airlines-introduce-new-rules-to-blacklist-unruly-passengers-a6848521.html>.

22 'Shocking moment a group of unruly passengers hit, slap and throw food on airline staff after their flight was delayed', *Daily Mail* (London 26 Apr 16) <www.dailymail.co.uk/news/peoplesdaily/article-3559065/

flight delays or cancellations, much to the amusement and chagrin of travellers overseas but also domestically.[23] This behaviour is a combination of many factors but chief among them is a sense of self-entitlement and the attitude that one must get exactly what had been paid for. Bearing in mind that many Chinese people used to be poor but now that they have made it, they have high expectations to get the service they have paid for using their hard-earned money. Other common grievances about Chinese behaviours such as not queuing up, littering, not flushing the toilet after using and talking loudly in public are largely attributed to lack of education. While this is increasingly something of the past, occasionally television commercials on Chinese network can be still be seen educating people about proper behaviour and conduct.

There are staggering numbers of *nouveau riche* who have certainly changed the economic and social landscape of China. How the newly wealthy people conduct themselves in business and international trade may always be consistent with their contemporaries elsewhere. For example, a consultant who has spent many years involved in business consulting in China once stated to the author:

> There are many wealthy Chinese businessmen who will not bat an eyelid spending $1 million at a casino, a night. Yet to invest the same amount of money in a business, these businessmen tend to ask a lot of questions and think it through over and over again before committing.

Shocking-moment-group-unruly-passengers-hit-slap-throw-food-airline-staff-flight-delayed.html>; <www.youtube.com/watch?v=WaoKap4vEK4>; <www.youtube.com/watch?v=4M7396iuIcw>; <www.youtube.com/watch?v=XnolhqBTrAs>.

23 In a 2013 news report, a Chinese teenager was reported to have defaced a stone sculpture in an ancient Egyptian temple with graffiti. 'Netizen outrage after Chinese tourist defaces Egyptian Temple', *CNN* (Atlanta 29 May 2013) <http://edition.cnn.com/2013/05/27/travel/china-egypt/>.

Perhaps when people get rich too suddenly and too quickly, there is still some catching up in terms of learning how to manage wealth cleverly and develop the proper etiquette and social graces.

1.4. Focussing on self-interest

In the words of Chinese people themselves, they tend to display the characteristic of focussing on self-interests, that is putting their own interests before others. Being in this state leads to one being concerned with oneself, leading to the lack of trust in others, thus relying on their own judgement. The result is that if people behave in this matter, then in a situation of 'you or me', one is likely to act in the interest of 'me' instead of 'you'. The lack of trust is a natural reaction to the realisation that everyone is self-centred, hence why trust another when they are likely to serve their own interest and not yours? In an example given by a learned, senior government official during a conversation with the author:

> In a traffic hold up at a traffic light junction, you will find other drivers outwit, outmanoeuvring other cars to get ahead. Also, another interesting observation is when a car approaches a road with a roadside that says 'Road closure - under construction'. The driver instead of turning around might think 'I will find out for myself if this is true, maybe this was put up a while ago'. When he reached a dead end, he will willingly make a U-turn, now he is satisfied that he has verified it for himself the veracity of the situation. He trusted his own judgement and he will not easily take 'no' for an answer.

It is also observed that the pursuit of 'truth' to satisfy one's own judgement gives rise to a behavioural pattern of not giving up too easily and an inquisitive mind. But not giving up can be perceived as determined or, at worst, demanding or quarrelsome. For example, one can walk into a half-empty restaurant and ask for a table but told that the restaurant is full. Possibly one will just walk away but a Chinese will likely question how the restaurant can be full if he can see empty tables. Perhaps the empty tables have been reserved but he may even negotiate for an alternative solution, whether he can dine now since the guests have not arrived. A Chinese is unlikely to give up too easily.

If a Chinese is inclined to be promoting self-interest, how would this operate in a corporation or governmental system? The answer can be found in the characteristics of the Chinese being people who work in unity and work as a group, instead of basing on the individual decision. Therefore, when this is transposed into a group scale people work towards achieving a beneficial outcome and results for the group, in other words, collective self-interest.

Though a general observation, such a fascinating pattern in modern Chinese culture may well be nothing shocking because in a country with an enormous population, competition is very stiff in numerous aspects of Chinese life, giving no room to be too generous when it comes to self-interest. In all fairness, there are other cultures that are observed to be not easily trusting or even suspicious. As mentioned earlier, the Chinese culture of not giving up too easily also gives rise to challenging conventions and testing the limit which is also the same Chinese spirit that has given rise to the rapid growth and transformation in China, which no doubt have also benefited the world.

1.5. Eager to learn, swift in implementing

Predominant values of Chinese society are said to be found in the teachings of Confucius[24] with learning being important in a Confucian society.[25] But learning is also a motivation for some key outcomes; for example, learning to prepare for exams so that obtaining a qualification allows one a good or better career prospect or even in the case of Chinese corporation[26] to achieve their corporate ambitions. Simply put, the culture of the Chinese people is one that never thinks there is a limit to learning and this is admirable. This attitude is even observed at the government level. From the author's own experiences, the Chinese government is one example of knowledge absorption; no knowledge is too much for them. Even if something is already not new to them, they are glad to listen and validate their understanding or compare it against what they already know; if their understanding seemed to differ, they will inquire further. Such is the general mechanics of the Chinese learning attitude.

The Cultural Revolution that lasted for about a decade took the Chinese economy and society backwards. China today recognises that it has to catch up for the lost years and they have to work harder, faster. Many wonder what would be the situation in China today if there had been no Cultural Revolution. Shenzhen Special Economic Zone is the first special economic zone in China, established in 1980,

---

24 See Kissinger (n 5) 13.

25 See *ibid* 14.

26 The journalist was seated in a plane next to a Chinese engineer on the flight from San Francisco to Beijing. Both discussed how different countries have skills in certain type of business of which the Chinese engineer said that even Chinese companies excel in learning. Discussing Lenovo's acquisition of IBM's personal computer division, it was observed that Lenovo wanted to enter the world stage and to achieve their ambition and they are learning from around them. See 'A hunger for knowledge is China's real secret weapon', *Financial Times* (London 5 Oct 2005) <www.ft.com/intl/cms/s/0/210bf4fe-353d-11da-9e12-00000e2511c8.html#axzz46ZR5uqUM>.

as a result of Deng Xiaoping's economic reform, turning Shenzhen from a sleepy backwater into a bustling metropolis today. Dr Goh Keng Swee, a former Deputy Prime Minister of Singapore, was appointed China's first foreign adviser after he left Singapore politics, contributing to China's economic reform.[27] Notwithstanding all there is to criticise about China's political and government system, it is far from the common perception of a bureaucratically and hierarchically inefficient government machinery. Instead, it is prepared to listen, learn, adopt and apply, without taking a long time to decide. In this instance, China's pragmatism and the need for success somewhat overwhelms the inherent culture of 'face saving' to the extent that they will not escape from the truth but implement, leaving no stone unturned if it is for the overall benefit of the country and people. The former Singapore Prime Minister, the late Lee Kuan Yew, recounted a conversation with Deng who had congratulated him when being impressed by Singapore during his visit, to which Lee replied that whatever Singapore does, China can do better.[28] Indeed subsequently Deng would say to his leadership to learn from the world, particularly Singapore, and do better than them.[29]

For the Chinese private sector, the success of its companies and industries can be said to be quite spectacular. China's homegrown information technology and telecommunication industries today are forces to be reckoned with. In the race for 'speed,' the Chinese are conscious of high-quality products, global market and branding and they do not want to settle for second best. For instance, Lenovo acquired IBM's personal computer business and has clearly become a globally accepted and leading computer brand. Other Chinese companies such

---

27 'Dr Goh helped shape China's economy: Zhao Ziyang's son', *The Straits Times* (Singapore 19 May 2010) <http://news.asiaone.com/News/the+Straits+Times/Story/A1Story20100519-217043.html>.

28 Lee Kuan Yew, *One Man's View of the World* (Straits Times Press 2013) 30.

29 *Ibid.*

as Huawei and Xiaomi are making their marks overseas. As for the automobile industries, local Chinese car manufacturer Geely acquired the renowned Swedish marque, Volvo, and iconic London Taxi Company. China also enjoys a large, well-trained and low-cost pool of scientific and engineering talent who are eager for challenge and career advancement.[30] Such a talent pool can be expected to contribute to the research and development of companies as can already be seen through global market penetration of home-grown Chinese products.

According to the ancient Chinese military strategist Sun Tzu, speed was given prominence in waging war:[31]

> In War,
> Victory should be
> Swift.
> If victory is slow,
> Men tire,
> Morale sags.
>
> I have heard that in war
> Haste can be
> Folly
> But have never seen
> Delay that was
> Wise.

From the author's own experience in cross-border dealings, China stands out from the rest. For example, one is invited to a meeting or to give a presentation at a government department or private entity. It takes place in a conference room attended by a team of people from the Chinese party. Copious amounts

30 Anil K Gupta & Haiyan Wang, *Getting China and India Right* (Jossey-Bass 2009) 18.

31 Sun Tzu (trans John Minford), *The Art of War* (Penguin Books 2002) 7-8.

of notes will be taken and plenty of questions asked and one can be expected to be asked searching questions. Out of courtesy, the guest speaker will likely compliment the audience and say that he believes the Chinese will achieve what they aim for should they put their heart and mind to it. The Chinese will, though a matter of time, make changes and achieve what the guest had exactly said. The likelihood is by the time the guest returns, changes will have taken place. For instance, from the author's visit to a Chinese law firm twice in a span of one and a half year, he found himself sitting in a modern, opulent conference room totally different from that of his first visit. The law firm principal partner in the meeting thanked the author for his previous suggestions and believe in the firm that they have managed to grow substantially and move towards internationalisation of their firm, including the massive makeover of the firm's office.

What is different between the Chinese and elsewhere is that in the same scenario given above, changes may not yet have taken place after years or possibly never. Similarly, the author recalled another engagement in another country where the same agenda has been discussed for years but never implemented; in fact even in the same meeting room where the discussion took place, a faint shoeprint on a section of the meeting room wall still remained after so many years, uncleaned.

In China, it is not about all talk only; they are determined to make a difference.[32] In a 1967 interview with Lee Kuan Yew, journalist Seymour Topping of the *New York Times* asked what he thought about the future of China in the light of people (then) saying that China was politically divided and whether the country will unite in which case will it be a threat to South East Asia. Lee said:

> I would say they are determined, as a people, to unify and build a modern, powerful, wealthy

32 For interesting knowledge, see the award-winning documentary *From Mao to Mozart: Isaac Stern in China* (Docu Rama 1979).

> Chinese nation and I say good luck to them. And I think the moment they get prosperous, good luck to me, because I will be much safer.[33]

Not just that China as a country has achieved tremendous success today but the Chinese people through their determination have tasted personal and individual success. China as a country can achieve so much success within a remarkably short period of time through harmonious coexistence and productive efforts between the people and the government.

With the 'never give up' spirit and determined attitude ingrained in the Chinese culture, many entrepreneurial initiatives by creative people have found solutions to their particular circumstances. For example, Youku was created because of the inability of internet users in China to access YouTube, whereas others, including WeChat, SinaWeibo and Alibaba, have all become successful companies established in recent times by Chinese entrepreneurs, all with humble beginnings. Call them imitators but they are successful and have seized on golden opportunities available to them which were also available to all others. Incidentally, Indians have a concept called '*jugaad*' which similarly espouses workarounds for solutions in some of life's challenges. In big countries where people face stiff competition, they tend to be able to think out of the box. They may be severely constrained in terms of resources, financial support or even lacking in terms of personal educational qualifications to do something 'big', but, evidently, discoveries and breakthroughs do not come from perfect circumstances or settings.

---

33 'Meet the Press' (22 Oct 1967). Transcript available from the National Archive of Singapore online <www.nas.gov.sg/archivesonline/data/pdfdoc/lky19671022.pdf>.

1.6. Crouching *mianzi*, hidden *guanxi*

Discussing about the Chinese will not be complete without mentioning two quintessential Chinese cultural characteristics, the overused *guanxi* (关系) and *mianzi* (面子). The general meaning of *guanxi* refers to relationship/ties whereas *mianzi* is about one's 'face': his honour, prestige and dignity. There are numerous interpretations on, and definition of, *guanxi* and *mianzi*, ranging from books on doing business in China to doctorate theses but in this book, without going into complex dissection and classifying different types of it, the general aspects of the two characteristics will be dealt with in a nutshell.

First is *mianzi*; the common example of it is one loses face when rejected, embarrassed or looked down upon. It can also be a reciprocal concept, in failing to give 'face' to another person, one is also dishonouring himself, hence losing face. As an example, if you acted disproportionately to someone publicly, you are of course making him embarrassed and 'losing face' but in turn, the public may also condemn you for your high-handedness and lack of restraint, consequently you could lose face.

There is no written code for *mianzi*, only abstract guides mostly passed on from generation to generation, dictated by one's society. It is complicated and complex. To give someone face or make someone lose face can be based on a broad combination of actions and expressions (with examples in each bracket) such as speech (disparaging someone), mannerism (intentional act of ignoring someone as a slight), nuances (indirect speech or insinuation about someone) or expression of emotions (confrontation and showing anger). Among Chinese people including overseas Chinese, the concept of *mianzi* is still central in their lives. To restrain oneself from doing or saying something is the most basic form and example of 'giving face'. It is also for the sake of preserving future relationships, a form of compromise which may or may not be entirely linked to forgiveness but a show of magnanimity. To some Chinese, *mianzi* is also about pride and pretending to be someone he is not for sake of face value; for example, for wanting to be seen as successful, a person could go to the extent of incurring massive personal debts to purchase an expensive car and wear expensive jewellery so that neighbours, peers and friends will hold the person in a favourable light.

There is also an obscure downside of *mianzi* in that by giving 'face' one can actually cause more harm than good. For instance, someone may have an erroneous understanding about something but this was not corrected by someone who knew and heard it, for not wanting to make him lose face. But with the mistake not corrected, the person continues retaining the incorrect understanding until one day something happens and he suffers a major embarrassment. It is not uncommon to hear one saying 'Don't correct him lest he will lose face. Let him find out for himself' but if no one will ever correct him because of *mianzi*, then he might learn it the *very* hard way. In short, *mianzi* is described here as 'crouching' as it befits what it is: staying low, subtle, indirect expression usually operate by hints and nuances. Being direct can be hurtful and causes someone to lose face.

Coming to *guanxi*, it is about relationships between people usually having attained a certain degree of camaraderie or friendship, beyond just normal acquaintances or mere casual connection. *Guanxi* is a very old concept and forms an integral part of the lives of Chinese and their culture. Arguably, there is nothing sinister about this because even in the western world, people connect with each other through professional or social networks. To create *guanxi* one must first create a relationship, then the relationship will have to be developed leading to a higher degree of connection or friendship. There will be time and investment going into showing one's sincerity and the building of the relationship. The more one gets to know another and keeping in regular contact helps tremendously in creating *guanxi* which can be achieved through dining, drinking and song. Undoubtedly with technology such as instant messaging using handheld devices, keeping in touch these days can still achieve closeness without meeting often face to face.

It is also said that nurturing *guanxi* takes place at the dining table. It is from lunching and dining that people let their hair down and talks openly and casually about their family, current trend, jokes, gossips or perhaps even serious business. It is almost certain that refusing lunch or dinner invitations paves the way to not establishing *guanxi*. The Chinese culture is very steep in eating together. A foreigner recounted to the author how after a hectic meeting, he declined to join the Chinese delegation for dinner until the leader of the Chinese delegation sent someone to talk to him to enquire if there was anything wrong or if there was anything he was displeased about. After China, he was in Delhi where he was surprised that meetings arranged to take place almost at lunch time and dinner time did not continue with invitations to meals. That is the norm in India and does not imply anything adverse about the relationship.

There is also a much-quoted phrase '我说你行，你就行' (*wǒ shuō nǐ xíng, nǐ jiùxíng*) which translates to: 'If I say you can, then you can' which implies the hierarchical system in China where the leader makes the edict but this phrase also denotes connection-based outcome where one also need *guanxi* to make things happen.

In addition, *guanxi* can sometimes be used to intercede for someone. For example, you require assistance in Nanning, but do not know anyone there. However, one of your close friend knows many people there. He agrees to help you and, through his *guanxi*, you are able to receive the help required. This is the quickest method for you to get help without having direct connection or 'secondary *guanxi*'.

Guanxi is mostly hidden from plain sight since it is not exactly something that is written on one's forehead. These days it is also treated with care and sensitivity due to concern of accusations relating to favouritism especially for government officials. At times *mianzi* and *guanxi* are intertwined, with the former an enabler of the latter. In a relationship or *guanxi*, acceding to a request is giving face or *mianzi*. If I were to go to you for a favour using our relationship, by turning me down, you are not 'giving me face'. Yet in an evolving society and culture like China, it would not be correct to say that even *guanxi* and *mianzi* have been unaffected by the changing world. Values of pragmatism and self-interest that are creeping into the Chinese culture today may no longer see *mianzi* and *guanxi* in its strict sense.

1.7. Chinese people's art of *guanxi* and *mianzi*

Chinese people have certainly developed an interesting paradigm of behaviour, way of life and treatment of others along the principles of *guanxi* and *mianzi*. Here is an anecdote of them in action. A delegation of foreign lawyers visited a city in China to meet local law firms and lawyers' association leadership. In one of the meeting, a senior lawyer told the foreign guests that she would like to introduce them to a local lawyer, who used to be her mentee. Phone numbers were exchanged and a breakfast meeting on a Saturday morning was arranged. The foreign guests were invited to breakfast at an impressive Chinese restaurant. The décor and food were spectacular. After breakfast, the hosts suggested a slow walk down the road along a scenic lake-park, from the restaurant to their office. It was no doubt a breath-taking view. During the walk, the hosts pointed to several tall buildings in the horizon and explained that they belonged to some of his clients. They continued walking through the park where locals can be seen stretching out and kids running about happily. It was a sight of carefree and tranquillity. Soon, the guests and hosts emerged out of the park into the civilisation and arrived at the Chinese's law firm. It was located in a tired low rise building directly next an old dwelling apartment. The dingy office was spartan but functional and the host explained that they have been in this location for a decade and mostly work out of clients' office. There is nothing wrong at all about not having opulent office[34] but the change in sight and environment were not unnoticed. Here, an aspect of *mianzi* was at play. In compensating for their inadequacy, the hosts deployed other alternative treatment to impress the guests. To be fair, it is also typical of the Chinese good hospitality to entertain guests well but in the mind of every Chinese, they want to impress and give a good first impression; indeed, it is about face value or *mianzi*. Other example involved someone who splurged at least a month's wages on dinner, hiring a private room in a karaoke lounge, then ordered a bottle of pricey Scottish single malt whisky.

Such is the Chinese people's art of *mianzi*. To the uninitiated, it would be prudent to be sensitive to such cultural 'performance' so as not to be insensitively critical of the host, leading to embarrassment. To some extent, one should go along with it and appreciate the gesture behind it, sometimes even exaggerated. However, be careful not to fall prey to sinister schemes disguised as good hospitality of the Chinese people. Exercise good judgment and discernment. Use *guanxi* as 'due diligence' to ensure obtaining good and reliable contacts in China.

1.8. Self-beating to the finishing line

Chinese people can be ironic in the sense that when winning is sweet, success is blissful and experience is eternal,

---

34 It is generally the case that in China, lawyers will visit clients instead. Lavish and opulent offices can potentially scare clients due to the

they tend to beat themselves too much too unnecessarily. Specifically, there is a deep-seated belief and tendency to deny oneself praise and recognition but to leave it to others to do so. If a foreigner has ever been invited to a Chinese home for dinner, be prepared to be offered an apology from your host that it is a humble abode or the meal is a simple one. Such comments must not be taken too literally or seriously; the correct answers will be to reply in disagreement but to compliment the host. Do not agree that indeed the food is simple because it is very rare for a Chinese host to invite someone to meal without offering nothing short of a lavish spread, as it is *mianzi*.

This no doubt these characteristics have their roots in Confucianism but they also exist in some other cultures. In the Christian Bible, it was also taught that when invited to a feast, do not take your seat in the place of honour because someone more distinguished could have been invited and one would suffer the embarrassment of having to move to the lowest place, however should you take the lowest seat then asked by your guest to move up higher, everyone will see that the person is honoured, thus a lesson on humility.[35] In fact and in truth, at any Chinese banquet, the seating plan at the dining table is always carefully considered. For example, the seat directly facing the door to the private dining room is reserved for the most esteemed person at the table. Expect to first resist accepting the esteemed seat when offered, to show humility and denial of honour.

---

prospect of high fees. Litigators tend to work out of, or set up office in, apartment units which is more cost economical since they spend most of their time at courts or at the client's location. It can be a hilarious sight having to walk through apartment units, seeing among others, laundry hanging to dry outside or other common 'domestic' sights, to reach a law firm. Nevertheless, multi-service large law firms in Shanghai, Beijing or other major cities have spectacular, designer offices that can easily rival those of 'magic circle' law firms' offices in London, New York, Hong Kong or Singapore.

35 *Luke* 14:7-13.

The 'self-beating' practiced by the Chinese people can sometimes cause regrets later on, for example in the narration of a New York Chinese:

> I was once in a situation whereby I was to be elected the Chairman of a certain organisation. Indeed I have been with the organisation long enough and have attained the seniority befitting this position. However, during the meeting to discuss my election, my name was put up for election but I said perhaps I am not ready yet to be the Chairman. The next person on the line of succession asked 'are you sure you don't want this position? Fine then, in that case I am willing to take up the Chairmanship. I now convene our first meeting as the new Chairman'. I thoroughly regretted my action as I should have accepted the appointment.

A Chinese person is no doubt influenced by this programming and such nature is still evident in many overseas Chinese although of varying degrees of subtleness depending on where they are located (in eastern or western countries). Instead of highlighting their own strengths, the Chinese are inclined to tell success stories such as how others find them useful or helpful therefore indirectly telling the listener how good, successful or smart they are. In the words of a successful lawyer, 'even if I am good, I cannot say so about myself. It is for others to say that I am good because no one should say that they themselves are good'.

What could be the consequences of such attributes? To be denied due recognition can be painful but can also drive a person to want to achieve more so that he can eventually be recognised. But it can be frustrating and emotionally draining, sometimes leading to burnouts.

1.9. China Chinese vis-à-vis overseas Chinese

It is an intriguing question to ask if Chinese people in China are different from overseas Chinese and, if so, how much different are they? In the first instance, what constitute overseas Chinese? The origin of overseas Chinese is said to date back to the 15th century time of the Ming Dynasty eunuch Admiral Zheng He's voyages to South East Asia.[36] The *Peranakan*[37] or Straits Chinese are descendants of Chinese migrants who came to the Malay Archipelago where they intermarried with local Malays and developed unique local cultures. The Peranakan retains Chinese ethnic surnames, speaks a distinct language which is a mix of Malay language and Chinese dialect, and developed their own cuisine which is expectedly a mix of local and Chinese. They have also developed their own customs and spiritual beliefs (though many are Christians) which still retain much of the Confucianism influence even after so many centuries. They do not have links to China anymore and have limited interest in the affairs of China. Given the assimilation they have gone through for a very long period of time, they are not likely to consider themselves the archetypal example of people of Chinese ethnicity.

The term overseas Chinese has been subject to debate as it is alleged that this term denotes one who may still be a citizen of China. As mentioned earlier, for the purpose of this book it is not necessary to further complicate the definition and, for simplicity purposes, overseas Chinese will be construed as generally people of Chinese ethnicity or whose parents or grandparents were Chinese migrants who had left China

---

36 See also Gavin Menzies, *1421: The Year China Discovered the World* (Bantam Press 2001).

37 Tommy Koh et al (eds), *Singapore: The Encyclopedia* (Didier Millet 2007) 410.

especially in the last century.[38] Historically, many Chinese people left China in search of a better life by migrating all over the world but a large number ended up in South East Asia, for example the Chinese who came to work in the mines, rubber plantations and farms in Malaya. Because of the large population of Chinese migrants in this region, they are able to sustain their population continuity through marrying within the group, thus preserving their cultures.

Those who left China during this era brought with them memories and programming of the Chinese culture of that time. They brought with them old Chinese cultures[39] of those days which were imprinted in their mind indelibly, considering most of them did not leave China willingly or gladly but to search for a better life.[40] Also, they retain the rituals, spiritual beliefs, family values and cuisine from their home of origin. Generally overseas Chinese are less likely to possess all the contemporary cultures and characteristics of Chinese people today given that many were born overseas and might no longer maintain contacts with relatives in China, if any still exists. Their culture is likely to be orthodox, strict and rigid hierarchical Chinese cultures of the 19th till early or mid-20th century 'Victorian' China. As an example, children must obey their parents and sometimes are not permitted to talk to their fathers directly. Daughters can be expected to be married off in their late teens with no prospects of education whatsoever. Modern Chinese parents

38 There is still Chinese immigration in present times to Singapore, for example, due to better career and business opportunities, taking up citizenship in the city-state, or to Africa or South America, where investment opportunities are fresh. For the purpose of this book, discussion of overseas Chinese generally refers to migrant Chinese who left China during the time of hardship, political turmoil and unrest from the late 19th till early or mid-20th century and their descendants.

39 A parallel example would be the Quebec people of French descent.

40 Whilst many were hoping to return to their motherland after succeeding or making enough money; most ended up never returning to China.

today enjoy rather liberal relationship with their children as compared to some overseas Chinese today. In fact, even the strict segregation between the old and young as well as the superior and subordinate are no longer the culture today in China where collaborative interactions are rather common, whenever appropriate. For many years now, women in China can pursue higher education, evidencing how China today has good female representation in the government, politics, academia or private sectors.

The way we think, feel or potentially behave are basing on experiences gained throughout one's lifetime. According to renowned Dutch social psychologist Geert Hofstede, there are three levels of uniqueness in mental programming. These are human nature which is largely inherited, culture which is learn and not innate which derives from 'one's social environment rather than one's genes'[41] and personality which is partly inherited 'within individual's unique set of genes and partly learned'.[42] People of Chinese ethnicity are steeped in traditions and rituals, their memories and programming of Chinese cultures cannot be completely purged in their lifetime and they are also likely to pass on their knowledge to their children and subsequent generations but as time goes by, memories can expect to gradually fade and culture values be diluted.[43] This is particularly so for overseas Chinese living further away from Asia such as in Europe and the USA where being a minority, there is a natural instinct to assimilate with

---

41 Geert Hofstede, Gert Jan Hofstede & Michael Minkov, *Cultures and Organizations: Software of the Mind* (McGraw-Hill Education 3rd edn 2010) 6.

42 *Ibid* 7.

43 Countries like Singapore can continue to retain its Chinese foundation among the young as Chinese language is compulsory for Singapore citizens or Permanent Residents in Singapore schools to study their respective mother tongue language.

the culture of the majority and their adopted country.[44] The overseas Chinese were only able to keep themselves abreast from a distance (for example through written communications with relatives in China or relying on newspaper reports), which was much more challenging before the advent of modern technology. One is not influenced by cultural changes nor keep up with them from reading about them but when immerse in them

Today, many overseas Chinese are reconnecting with their roots. This is not particularly challenging (especially for those living near to China) because the Chinese ethnicity is a very large population dispersed all over the world. It is evidently not an obscure race or a population which is going into extinction. In fact, the Chinese government have established a governmental body called the Overseas Chinese Affairs Office which seek to, among other things, engage overseas Chinese with a view to establishing cooperation, investment and cultural development. Indeed, China and Chinese culture are enjoying a revival in this recent decade.[45] Chinese today are living in a golden era of economic progress and social stability. In an ironic twist of fate, many overseas Chinese are now going to China in search of business or economic opportunities. Some of the older generation of overseas Chinese who are detached from (and obviously also uninformed about) modern China are bewildered why people are going to China when the memories of their fathers having left China 'in search of better opportunities overseas' are still fresh in their consciousness.

---

44 Perhaps Chinese migrants did not need to change their names to mask their ethnic identity unlike some Jewish people in Europe or the USA who felt the need to do so in order not to be discriminated against. Clearly though, Chinese people are unable to 'hide' from their obvious physical appearances.

45 China is becoming a popular international tourist destination in addition to it already being an important country for global business and investment. In recent times, many foreigners are also going to China for academic purposes where many of its universities and academic institutions are becoming world renowned.

Chinese today are very well travelled also because they are financially able. Many are able to go overseas in search of career opportunities but they tend to do so because of better income and not so much because of extreme poverty back at home. Chinese professionals and intellectuals are also going places where they are sought after, unlike centuries ago where they were only coolies. Unfortunately, in recent times Chinese people have also become the subject of dislike or are unwelcomed, paradoxically even in places where the population is predominantly of Chinese ethnicity. One common reasons is that the Chinese (often also referred to as 'Mainlanders') do not fit into the local culture and/or refuse to assimilate, which interestingly validates the theory earlier that there are cultural differences between Chinese and overseas Chinese. Critics are quick to condemn Chinese demeanour and behaviours which are said to be not in conformity to generally acceptable local cultures and conduct overseas (such as talking loudly in public, personal hygiene, excessive flaunting of wealth and so forth). A few years ago, Singapore[46] had experienced rather strong feelings against Chinese people but this have abated substantially whereas Hong Kong[47] is still grappling with this issue. Each of the affected governments has been taking conscientious efforts to eradicate such misconceptions and prejudices, although the situation in Hong Kong is more political than xenophobic or

46 Singapore's Prime Minister Lee Hsien Loong in his National Day Rally 2012 speech (English) touched on the subject of urging Singaporeans to be big-hearted in embracing immigrants and foreign workers. 'It reflects badly on us, it damages our international reputation. People think that Singapore is anti-foreigner, xenophobic ... It does not do us good. But more fundamentally than that, apart from our reputation, it speaks poorly of what sort of people we are. I mean, what sort of people do we want to be? We need to be people who are proud of ourselves, who have a heart, who can feel for other fellow human beings, who will be courteous, respectful and behave with others as we would like others to behave to us.' See <www.pmo.gov.sg/mediacentre/prime-minister-lee-hsien-loongs-national-day-rally-2012-speech-english>.

47 Although largely attributed to political discontent of Hong Kongers, this has metamorphosed into dislike for Mainland Chinese

racial, since the majority of Hong Kongers themselves are of Chinese ethnicity and Hong Kong is part of China. Similarly, most Singaporeans are ethnic Chinese and the city-state is a country of immigrants.

Despite modernisation and 'cultural evolution', Chinese will continue to retain some or many of the values that define them, which will not disappear from the face of the earth. In turn, overseas Chinese are of the same genetic and DNA pool as people from China but were separated by historical events and, these days, citizenships, political ideologies, local cultures as well as customs. Yet, cultural gaps can exist also in a vast country like China, between Chinese people of different cities or provinces. As Hofstede put it, cultures are learned. People adapt to the changing world so that they do not retrograde and to ensure their existence. As Newman put it: 'In a higher world it is otherwise; but here below to live is to change, and to be perfect is to have changed often'.[48]

1.10. Looking at China today

China is not all fully developed with regard to modern and advanced infrastructure which is not surprising for a country of it scale. Major cities such as Shanghai, Beijing, Chengdu, Shenzhen or Guangzhou would impress anyone visiting them. Other cities are developing or catching up and the China growth story is real and not a Potemkin village. But every now and then, there are public concerns such as ethical

---

people. This have been widely reported. See 'Hong Kong must have zero tolerance for anti-mainlander hate campaigns', *South China Morning Post* (Hong Kong 6 Mar 2014) <www.scmp.com/comment/insight-opinion/article/1441654/hong-kong-must-have-zero-tolerance-anti-mainlander-hate> and 'Hong Kong may amend its race hate law to protect mainland visitors', *South China Morning Post* (Hong Kong 20 Feb 2014) <www.scmp.com/news/hong-kong/article/1432229/hong-kong-may-amend-its-race-hate-law-protect-mainland-visitors>.

48 John Henry Cardinal Newman, *An Essay on the Development of Christian Doctrine* (James Toovey 1845) 39.

conduct affecting the general population at large. According to a Chinese 2013 news report, 904 people were arrested over 'meat-related crimes' such as producing fake beef and mutton from rat, mink and fox.[49] The fake and harmful meat were subjected to chemical treatment to disguise the misdeeds. There was the scandal involving infant formula adulterated with harmful melamine which resulted in the death and injury of thousands of children across China.[50] In 2016, Chinese state media reported that half of the country's food safety testers were not certified.[51] The subject of ethics or the lack of it exists across a broad spectrum of industries. Even among professionals, some may not bother to do things professionally and responsibly. It is not that they are unqualified but rather, as it would seem, a case of resting on laurels and taking the easy way out.

China has come a long way to be where it is today and undeniably the scepticism and prejudices about China one used to hear in the past are abating and are less apparent in recent times. Of course, it is common to hear racial jokes not just of Chinese people but others, however it warrants concern when remarks about races are made by public figures. Towards the end of 2016, a Commissioner of the European Union[52] in a speech to business leaders in Hamburg referred to the Chinese as 'slitty-eyed rascals'[53] and 'sly

---

49 'Over 900 arrested in China for meat-related crimes', *Xinhua* (Beijing 2 May 2013) <http://news.xinhuanet.com/english/china/2013-05/02/c_132355301.htm>.

50 'Tainted-Baby-Milk Scandal in China', *Time* (New York 16 Sept 2008) <http://content.time.com/time/world/article/0,8599,1841535,00.html>.

51 'Half of country's food safety testers not certified', *China Daily* (Beijing 1 July 2016) <www.chinadaily.com.cn/china/2016-07/01/content_25928206.htm>.

52 Günther Oettinger, of Germany, then European Commissioner for Digital Economy and Society.

53 'EU commissioner Oettinger in "racism" row over China speech', *BBC* (London 31 Oct 2016) <www.bbc.com/news/world-europe-37822419>.

dogs'.[54] Although this official later tried to explain that 'slitty-eyed rascals' 'was in no way meant to be disrespectful to the Chinese',[55] the remark made is universally derogatory, and to describe Chinese people as 'dogs' is the lowest dishonour one can accord to Chinese. This incident will likely be overlooked in due course and dismissed as purely a public speech mishap but such attitudes, if often dismissed, could tilt the balance of the scale of racist behaviour (regardless of races).

There are people who have yet to visit China and still hold prejudiced views about China, thinking that it is a socialist country that is backwards but nothing can be further than the truth. A Chinese professor once had a conversation with the author and asked about the perception of foreigners towards the Chinese then animatedly emphasised in English whether people call them 'communist people!' To use the term 'communist' with regard to Chinese people these days can be come across as a slight or at best insinuating nothing flattering. Deng Xiaoping in an interview with American journalist Mike Wallace in 1986 said that during the Cultural Revolution 'there was a view that poor communism was preferable to rich capitalism'. Deng disagreed and said that:

> There can be no communism with pauperism, or socialism with pauperism. So to get rich is no sin. However, what we mean by getting rich is different from what you mean. Wealth in a socialist society belongs to the people. To get rich in a socialist society means prosperity for the entire people.[56]

---

54 Melissa Eddy & James Kanter, 'German E.U. Official Is in Trouble Over Remarks About Chinese', *New York Times* (New York 31 Oct 2016) <www.nytimes.com/2016/11/01/world/europe/eu-official-insults-chinese.html>.

55 *Ibid.*

56 'Deng Xiaoping, "Interview with Mike Wallace of 60 Minutes"' (2 Sept 1986) USC Annenberg US-China Institute <http://china.usc.edu/deng-xiaoping-interview-mike-wallace-60-minutes-sept-2-1986>.

Lee Kuan Yew described China and the Communist Party of China as 'no longer communist in the strict sense of the word' and that the political structures of China predates communism.[57] Lee also said that communism in China is like 'an old label on an old bottle into which new wine has been poured'.[58] The contemporary Chinese political commentator Eric X. Li argued that the Communist Party 'happens to be one of the most meritocratic political institutions in the world today' and that there is not only one way to govern countries:

> China's political system will never supplant electoral democracy because unlike the latter, it doesn't pretend to be universal. It cannot be exported ... The significance of China's example is not that it provides an alternative, but the demonstration that alternatives exist.[59]

As China grows to become the largest economy in the world, it is probably a unique success story of how a country with almost 1.4 billion people who need not be involved in politics can contribute to the success of the country and themselves. It operates via a mutually convenient cooperation system in a country where there is a dichotomy between the public and private worlds. They are people who are determined to make China and their own lives better, each with its own motivations towards achieving their own aims.

Even towards the end of his life, Singapore Statesman Lee Kuan Yew, who was recognised as the world's pre-eminent authority on China, was consistently sought for his views on China by world leaders, including the USA. In a 2011 interview

---

57 Lee Kuan Yew, *One Man's View of the World* (Straits Times Press 2013) 21.

58 *Ibid* 21.

59 Eric X Li, 'A tale of two political systems', TEDTalks (1 July 2013) <www.youtube.com/watch?v=soYjL9rZyRo>.

by American journalist Charlie Rose about China, Lee had the following to say:[60]

> They do not like the established order to be tinkered with. If it's working, fine, leave it. And everybody, if there's something good, will borrow it and test it out. Why take the risk? Their attitude is let's play it safe. If you let 1.3 billion smart guys experimenting, you'd have near chaos.[61]
>
> ...
>
> The Chinese fear of any government is '*Luan*' it means chaos. It's a huge country and you cannot control everything. You cannot micro control it, so you just stop it.[62]

In China, laws play a major role in the shaping and governance of the Chinese, like in any other countries. What is particularly challenging for a country like China is the magnitude of the country's geography and demography. If the country's leadership lets their hair down, it could potentially lead to catastrophic outcomes which could spell disaster for the world's economic powerhouse. In the unlikely event of a chaotic China in modern times, it would certainly do no good to the world economy or security at large. Thankfully, the Chinese people are pragmatic enough today to comprehend that revolution rarely ended up with achieving the ideals of the revolutionaries, which usually remain as ideals only. So it is said: 'don't kill the goose which lays the golden eggs';[63] if it works, why risk it? In fact, why even meddle with it since a working machinery brings abundance of benefits to all. It is not selfishness and apathy but to the Chinese how does bringing about change benefit them individually? The

---

60 Charlie Rose interview with Lee Kuan Yew (28 Mar 2011). See transcription and video at <charlierose.com/videos/18935#>.

61 *Ibid*, transcription/video at 24:08 min.

62 *Ibid*, transcription/video at 25:56 min.

63 See *Aesop's Fables*, number 87.

Chinese government system, whilst never claiming to be perfect, has acted as catalyst for both national and people's growth. After all, in the mind of every Chinese they want to be successful and want to improve their destiny.

1.11. China and Chinese tomorrow

A strong leadership ensures the future of China. For a very long time, the Chinese believed that the country is secure and safe only when the centre is strong and, conversely, when the centre is strong, it leads to peaceful and prosperous China.[64] As it is, China has a very strong leadership and control, this being the case for decades now. In turn, the country is doing spectacularly well economically and people are undoubtedly benefitting from China's success with no logical reason why the pragmatic Chinese people would want to 'rock the boat'. Should a Golden Goose that laid golden eggs be given to a Chinese couple like in the *Aesop's Fables*, chances are the goose will not be killed but instead they might think of ways to reproduce and multiply the goose. Economically as a country, China will only grow bigger although at a different pace because there is no other way but to grow. Must the 'balloon burst' at some stage? Not everything must necessarily fall when it rises too high, in the case of a country, unless something so unimaginable disastrous of apocalyptic proportion happened in China. China will want to displace the USA as the number one power in the world. China is already on the right track to attaining this due to the momentum of its growth, even if they do not wish to, this is bearing in mind that they have transformed a poor society by an economic miracle to now become the second-largest economy.[65] Also, for them to become

64 See Lee (n 59) 13.

65 Graham Allison, Robert D Blackwill & Ali Wyne, *Lee Kuan Yew: The Grand Master's Insights on China, the United States, and the World* (MIT Press 2013) 2.

the world's number one or two is crucial to continuously strengthening their centre which in turn secures their future and stability.

Will China ever become a liberal democracy, or a western style democracy, where 1.3 billion people will vote for their leaders and a president when there is apparently no need to? If the Chinese system works very well, indeed though nothing is perfect, why change it? Why introduce liberal democracy just to gratify or give satisfaction to the wider world? The population is not suffering and the country is not swamped by corruption, so there is no reason for 1.3 billion people to demand to go to the polls.[66]

1.12. Summary

This chapter does not pretend to be authoritative on the subject of China and the Chinese. Experience with China and Chinese people can be described by the story of the blind men and an elephant; each of them touched an elephant at different parts and ended up disagreeing with the others' views of what an elephant is, when comparing notes. Whilst it is thought to be not possible to conclusively sum up China, in this chapter the observations and various commentaries on contemporary China and Chinese culture, as well as an attempt to understand Chinese mindset, act as the narrative that sets the landscape for further discussion and analysis about the attitude and approaches of the Chinese towards international dispute resolution.

It is likely that those who have had dealings with China and Chinese may have their own version of experiences regarding the cultural aspects of the Chinese, after all, as it has already been said, China is a big country and rich in diversity. Harmony

66 'I don't believe the Chinese people themselves believe that with 1.3 billion people you can have one man, one vote for a president. It's not workable'. Lee (n 59) 27.

is also the central theme that binds everything together in making Chinese and China a success story, now and in the future. The word for Harmony in Chinese is '*hé*' (和) which is made up of '禾' or '*hé*', which means 'grain', and '口' '*kǒu*', which means 'mouth'. This has it origin in past Chinese agrarian society and also nourishment where food and its sufficiency is 'sacred' in the life of Chinese people, thereby suggesting that in harmony, there will be sufficiency for all.

Is China finding itself growing too quickly at breakneck speed with limited opportunity to attend to some areas so that it grows up properly? Accelerated growth can bring dilemmas, of course. Are Chinese legal professionals and arbitration users prepared and adequately equipped in terms of global knowledge and know-how? This will be further examined in the subsequent chapters.

Chapter 2

The Chinese Client and Lawyer

2.1. Chinese clients

This subchapter will explain some of the common characteristics of Chinese clients and how they interact with their lawyers and legal advisers in the context of international disputes. The Chinese clients' attitude and treatment towards legal professionals are not similar to other countries where the relationship between clients-professionals to a greater extent enjoys a considerably high level of respect and recognition. The experience will be useful for foreign professionals making an initial foray into the China market and the first-time handling of Chinese clients.

2.1.1. Conduct of legal affairs

Foreign lawyers and professionals are likely to be called upon to provide services to Chinese clients who are individuals or private companies. Chinese state-owned companies would typically appoint local Chinese lawyers who in turn may engage foreign lawyers if there are foreign elements involved, such as in matters involving international commercial arbitration. However, it is also widely observed that many private Chinese companies are serviced by local lawyers (including on retainer basis), hence in the event of disputes or matters involving foreign elements, usually the local lawyers will seek the service of, and recommend potential foreign lawyers to the Chinese clients.

Most Chinese multinational corporations are large enough in terms of volume of work to justify have their own in-house legal departments to attend to all legal-related affairs of the companies If not, companies tend to employ legally qualified personnel to manage the commercial affairs of the company in the form of 'fused' roles such as managers or directors in the contracts, finance, procurement or asset management departments. This should not come as a surprise given that the work in the stated departments are legal-related. However, in recent times as large corporations in China are evolving and modernising, they have started to take on best foreign management practices, resulting in Chinese corporations adopting structures and set ups emulating management structure of western entities. Increasingly, titles commonly seen in the western world such as 'General Counsel' or 'Vice President of Legal' are proliferating in the structure of modern day Chinese corporations. Still, the majority of Chinese companies are run in the Chinese style and they continue to retain the typical characteristics of control and administration as influenced by the unique Chinese management culture.

Usually, it is not widespread for the parties to engage lawyers to participate in business negotiation and contracts formulation which are handled internally by the Chinese companies themselves. It is sometimes thought that matters involving business deals are matters involving businesspeople. The negotiation process could have involved a series of discussion, face to face meetings and dining between the company leaders, where it is thought that the involvement of lawyers would be inconvenient or impractical. Furthermore, there is still a culture of self-drafting contracts or agreements which could be linked to the 'old' behaviour of treating contracts as just a mere formality, leaving crucial details open to further discussion and negotiation as it comes along, on account of trust. As such, very little thought could be given in the writing of self-drafted agreements. However, as many Chinese modernise in their business conduct compounded by the multitude of cross-border transactions and the need for certainty as well as profitability, business contracts in China are taken as final and binding on the parties. Even if they are not, the content of the contracts may say otherwise and the courts or arbitral tribunal will duly interpret them, in the event of disputes. Another possible reason that drafting contracts does not always involve lawyers is because the lawyering culture and tradition in China is a contemporary phenomenon, which did not exist too long ago. Hence there is lack of urge or desire to retain a lawyer in a business negotiation process. While in the case of contracts within China and agreements in the Chinese language, decisions to go without lawyers can be understandable, what could be alarming is the similar attitude adopted when it comes to international contracts in the English language. Consequently, this has resulted in poorly or erroneously drafted agreements with international parties, in English. Given that many of these contracts are of substantial value, there is good reason to believe that it is not merely about saving legal fees but could be the mindset.

Nevertheless, there is also the possibility that Chinese parties negotiating a business deal find it 'inauspicious' to anticipate or talk about future disputes. It is common that in business negotiations not even in China, dispute resolution clauses are treated with the least importance, therefore, it is not unsurprising that, say, arbitration clauses may contain more ambiguities compared to other commercial provisions within the same agreement.

In spite of what has been said about the Chinese attitude, it is worth noting that Chinese parties do typically take written and signed contracts seriously, although absolute compliance and performance are something else. In international contracts, Chinese parties do often also rely on them to sue against foreign parties. Also, it is sometimes said that doing business with Chinese can be difficult because they renege on contracts or are always seeking to 'screw' foreign parties. This is but a generalisation and stereotyping as many Chinese parties have experienced their fair share of contractual breach or default committed by foreign parties.

2.1.2. Chinese clients' attitude towards legal process

To be further discussed in a later chapter, in short, Chinese people do not like to be embroiled in legal proceedings, whether litigation or arbitration. Their first preference is to resolve commercial disputes amicably. This does not mean that Chinese people are pushovers, and negotiation can be a long and arduous process. In this part, we will look at the situation after a dispute has arisen with negotiations already taken place and there is no prospect of amicable settlement other than to go to arbitration. The issue that will be right on top of everything else is legal fees and how to recover money without having to spend anything; if not, as little as possible.

The single most common Chinese client-lawyer arrangement in handling contentious matter is contingency fee arrangement, meaning 'no win, no pay'. Chinese clients also tend to 'distrust' their lawyers in paying them professional fees with no guaranteed outcome and they do not want their lawyers to be enriched by their misfortune. The popular western saying that lawyers tend to be the biggest winner in any legal proceedings certainly does not apply in China for Chinese clients expect commitment and sharing of risk by their lawyers. It is also thought that contingency fee arrangement will motivate the lawyers to work harder. Below is an excerpt of a discussion between the author and a senior lawyer practising with a major law firm in China on the question of contingency fee arrangement:

> Lawyer: Clients only believe in 'no cure, no pay'. They think that if their problem is not resolved, why should they pay? There is no positive outcome.
>
> Author: In the same vein, can these clients then tell their surgeons that if the surgery was not successful, they will not pay the doctor's fees. Or if they see a doctor because of ailment but did

not recover, can they then ask for contingency fee basis?

Lawyer: Yes, indeed, this has happened before with doctors.

According to Chinese lawyers, Chinese parties do approach them with an offer of 'cooperation' in resolving their disputes and commencing of legal actions rather than the attitude of approaching a trusted professional for service to cure his problem. The more senior lawyers are content with attending to corporate legal work, therefore less inclined to accept litigation or arbitration cases in view of the time and sharing of risk, however they sometimes find themselves obliged to accept such cases on account of existing client relationship or due to the large value of the disputes. In any case, there are many litigation or arbitration lawyers who specialise in the handling of contentious cases to the extent that the expenses and 'operational' fees collected are sufficient to keep them going for an entire year, covering their time costs and expenses.

According to local Chinese lawyers, the perception of the lawyering profession in China is yet to reach the level elsewhere in western countries or even in developed Asian territories like Hong Kong, Singapore, Japan or South Korea. It is said that Chinese clients treat lawyers as just another service provider, tasked to handle their legal disputes and legal services are considered to be 'intangible' products unlike buying something one can feel and touch.

2.1.2.1. Contingency fee arrangement as claimant

Under contingency fee arrangement in China, lawyers can potentially gain lucrative earnings from the profit-sharing arrangement of arbitration cases handled, but this is restricted to a maximum of 30% according to Chinese regulation.[67] Usually, under contingency fee arrangement, lawyers will request some payment to cover operational and actual expenses especially given that some cases may take a long time to conclude. Such 'operational fees' when and if agreed to be given by the client, can merely be a token sum. The very senior and prominent lawyers are said to be able to command premium 'operational fees' of sometimes between US$ 5,000 and US$ 10,000 from their clients. New lawyers or lawyers keen to make a name have been said to have taken work with no prior payment and even 'investing' their own money to cover actual expenses incurred with no guarantee of success in the cases handled. It is said that even Chinese lawyers find it frustrating in trying to convince Chinese clients that there are overheads, staff costs and expenses to be paid, hence the need for at least some decent payment for the lawyers' expenses.

The contingency fee preference may not always work for the Chinese clients when involved in international disputes, at least in jurisdictions like Singapore and Hong Kong where a lot of Chinese cross-border contracts have governing laws and place of arbitration clauses stipulating the abovementioned jurisdictions, as the legal profession regulations there do not allow contingency fee arrangements.

Sometimes in contingency fee arrangement, the client may work out a certain basis for pay out. For instance, following a protracted negotiation between the client and the other party, he may have been offered a certain sum of money as settlement but this was not accepted, for the purpose

67 Promulgated by the National Development and Reform Commission and Ministry of Justice, which took effect on 1 December 2006. '律师服务收费管理办法' (*lùshī fúwù shōufèi guǎnlǐ bànfǎ*) or 'Measures on the management of lawyers' service fees' under Article 13, it is stated that contingency fees charged shall not exceed 30% of the damages claimed or awarded (实行风险代理收费，最高收费金额不得高于收费合同约定标的额的30%) (*shíxíng fēngxiǎn dàilǐ shōufèi, zuìgāo shōufèi jīn'é bùdé gāo yú shōufèi hétóng yuēdìng biāodì é de*). See <www.moj.gov.cn/lsgzgzzds/content/2008-07/21/content_905383.htm?node=278>.

of illustration, say RMB 5 million. Therefore, if the client were to initiate arbitration, he may tell his lawyer that even without going to arbitration, he would have received RMB 5 million. His original demand was RMB 20 million therefore the contingency fee would only be based on any amount obtained above RMB 5 million only. The likelihood of lawyers not getting anything at the end of it all is real. As such lawyers sometimes feel that they are being squeezed by clients and ending up as losers. Furthermore, it is common for clients to revisit the agreed terms of the contingency fee arrangement. Even after obtaining a favourable arbitration award or court judgement, clients may potentially ask for discount citing all sorts of financial reasons or because the case dragged on for too long; ironically, the lawyers who had been unpaid and banking on the contingency fee have also been waiting for a long time to get paid.

2.1.2.2. Contingency fee – as defendant

Many have asked how contingency arrangement work in China in instances of defending claims. The immediate reaction would be how do Chinese lawyers get paid by contingency fee arrangement when defending a claim? Where is the profit to split in the case of defending claim since there is no money to make? Some Chinese lawyers have shed light on the *modus operandi* of this arrangement, which might be one of the best-kept secrets, in the esoteric world of contingency fee arrangement.

The answer lies in a rather innovative arrangement where the lawyer will get a percentage from savings. To illustrate this, say a party is claimed against for a sum of US$ 1 million in an arbitration proceedings and the client will expect his lawyer to vigorously defend the claim. Assuming if the defendant was adjudged to be liable to pay to the claimant a sum of US$ 500,000 there is a savings of US$ 500,000. As agreed at the outset between the client and his lawyer under a contingency fee arrangement, the lawyer is entitled to a percentage of the savings of US$ 500,000. Of course, the more savings obtained by the client, the more the lawyer will get paid. Mathematically, even if the agreed percentage to be paid to the lawyer is 20% of savings, obtained, this works out to US$ 100,000 and adding to the amount the respondent is liable to pay would be US$ 600,000 and this is still considered a major savings compared to the claim amount of US$ 1 million.

Although a contingency arrangement for defending a claim is not rare, Chinese lawyers are said to be reluctant to accept contingency fee arrangement for such, compared to acting for claimants. Taking up cases for defendant on contingency fee are largely influenced by relationship factor with the clients (such as long term or high-value clients) or unless there are grounds for counter-claims.

2.1.3. Chinese clients and foreign lawyers

Chinese clients tend to transpose their domestic dispute resolution attitude to the international context, although this is observed to be more prevalent among local Chinese companies with limited or no international exposure. Depending on the jurisdictions where their disputes are involved or located, they would need to seek legal assistance from that geographical location instead of relying on their domestic Chinese lawyers. Singapore and Hong Kong remain the popular juridical seats for international arbitration as well as the use of its laws as governing laws of Chinese contracts. In these two jurisdictions, lawyers are prohibited from contingency fee arrangements but even if they were permitted, the foreign lawyers are less likely to agree to such an arrangement because of the risk of non-payment by the Chinese client. How to recover such unpaid fees or if the fee amount is disputed by the Chinese party? Imagine the hassle of having to 'sue' the Chinese client just to recover unpaid fees, in China. Imagine having to resort to arbitration to recover monies due arising from services rendered for an arbitration.

In recent times, Chinese clients are beginning to understand that foreign lawyers do not subscribe to some of their 'values' but they (Chinese client) will still try without giving up too easily. They will either bargain for very low initial professional fees with its bulk to be paid only after a favourable outcome obtained or expect the lawyer to be able to assure them of a favourable outcome. Sometimes it is also ludicrous that some Chinese clients can be insistent on a contingency fee basis in the light of a low value dispute (even at times when the Chinese claimant has questionable chances of winning), or with large value dispute where there will be substantial amount of work incurred from commencement to completion of arbitration proceedings, yet they may still attempt to negotiate for contingency fee arrangement with foreign lawyers.

In international arbitrations, even if the foreign lawyers are permitted to accept the matter on contingency fee basis, they may be constrained from agreeing because the arbitration proceedings is likely to involve an enormous amount of work especially for complex disputes. Legal research must be conducted, correspondence, statement of claims, responding to counter-claims, formulation of strategies, oral arguments before the tribunal and so forth. Bills must be paid, salary of supporting lawyers to be paid whereas time costs of the handling by senior lawyers must be justified. The problem is some Chinese clients think that they are not 'buying' tangible, real goods from their lawyers and the argument that the lawyers' time spent is money will be countered with the answer that a shop owner will only be paid for his goods sold and not for his time in the shop making sales.

Chinese clients also expected to bargain and negotiate over fees. This requires patience and tenacity as such process is arguably unproductive amidst the on-going dispute. For the lawyers, having preliminary reviewed the case, they are likely to be attracted to taking up the case but Chinese clients could instead be preoccupied with negotiation over fees, sometimes oblivious to the urgency of the matter. Some foreign lawyers can find it rather trying when fees are agreed at the eleventh hour, leaving them with very little time especially when a deadline for response or submission is due shortly. To the clients, they have agreed on the fees and how the lawyers are going to do it is not their problem. But payment of fees is not without its challenges since payment delays are to be expected which can be due to reasonable grounds such as remitting funds overseas from China which require a process to be followed as required by regulations. The process to agree on fees tends to be 'easier' when the Chinese client is a respondent party which in substance is a disadvantageous position, however there is always exception. From the experience of the author, a legal team was summoned to China to meet the client over an arbitration commenced against him by a foreign party. Upon reaching the destination, it became apparent to the legal team that the potential client had been served with a notice of arbitration months ago but had yet to appoint lawyers to represent him. Although behind the scenes negotiations were taking place, the notice of arbitration remained and the timeline for the arbitration proceedings had officially commenced. There was a grave sense of urgency and criticality amongst the legal team that at any time now an *ex parte* proceeding could be commenced against the Chinese party. Yet, during the meeting the Chinese party was engrossed in relating his emotional disappointment and complaints over the claimant. Then he started expressing his disappointment as to why the lawyers did not advise him about counter-claiming against the other party to which the lawyers explained that they did not yet have the opportunity to review the case properly. The foreign lawyers returned home without securing the case. This type of behaviour is nothing short of 'playing' it dangerously.

Chinese clients approach foreign lawyers for the obvious reason that their dispute requires foreign legal assistance. The innovative and resourceful Chinese would have explored other avenues locally before resorting to engaging foreign lawyers. On the other hand, local Chinese lawyers did not take up the case because they were unable to, due to limitations of their expertise or experience in handling international and foreign related matters. But what are some of the observed characteristics of Chinese clients, from the lens of foreign professionals? For instance, in the usual western lawyering practice, clients will need to be consulted and their approval obtained before responding to the counterparty or certain decision regarding the matter. Some Chinese parties tend to consider it the lawyer's responsibilities to think of the appropriate solutions and answers for them. Partly a client's personnel when asked for clarification might find it awkward to ask the superiors questions or because they do not have the answers themselves. They are also likely to think that 'we are paying you to act for us, so you tell us what we should do or figure out the solution for us'.

The above may be misunderstood as being difficult, unsophisticated or rude; to the Chinese client, they have paid for someone to take care of the matter, whereas for the lawyer, they need the clients to fill in so many facts and also to obtain their instruction. Foreign lawyers handling Chinese clients will need to be aware of some factors at play here; if English is used in the communications, it is to be understood that it is not their first language of business conduct. Chances are, the Chinese will have an interpreter to do English translations but translations have their severe limitations especially matters involving cultural elements. Likewise, many English phrases or jargon cannot be fully translated and may thus result in misunderstanding and communication breakdown. In order to cure this problem, it may take longer time and patience to get the complete and correct message across before the foreign lawyers finally get the necessary answer. Large international law firms in and outside China have Chinese qualified lawyers who are bilingual in English and Chinese specifically to handle cross-border work involving Chinese parties. While this will not offer a perfect solution, it will help solve some of the problems.

2.2. Chinese lawyers

It is increasingly becoming necessary for foreign lawyers to cooperate with Chinese lawyers, therefore there is a need to understand how Chinese lawyers function and their culture. Chinese clients with matters involving foreign jurisdictions will no doubt require the assistance of foreign lawyers but unless the clients/foreign lawyers already know each other through past and present relationships, the Chinese party will almost certainly first approach his local Chinese lawyer. In turn, the Chinese lawyer will source suitable foreign lawyers to be involved thus they play an important role as intermediaries. Some Chinese law firms are set up to handle cross-border work particularly international arbitration, where they are generally allowed by foreign jurisdictions to represent Chinese parties in arbitration proceedings conducted there. Due to the complexity and diversity of international commercial arbitration work, foreign lawyers do often find themselves having to work together with Chinese law firms and vice versa. With increasingly more foreign law firms setting up partnerships with local Chinese firms in China, they are poised to provide 'one-stop' services to Chinese clients with foreign related matters. However, many Chinese clients do still give work on account of relationship and *guanxi*, not law firm brand or reputation. As already described, dealing with the Chinese involves establishing ties and trust more so than merely how distinguished one is. After all, in the words of a Chinese client 'what good is it if you are very good as a lawyer but we cannot get along'.

2.2.1. Background to lawyering in China

According to Bodde and Morris, the Chinese traditional society was not legally oriented and the 'penal emphasis' of the law meant that:

> matters of a civil nature were either ignored by it entirely (for example, contracts), or were given only limited treatment within its penal format (for example, property rights, inheritance, marriage). The law was only secondarily interested in defending the rights - especially the economic rights - of one individual or group against another individual or group and not at all in defending such rights against the state.[68]

In Imperial China, the law was viewed primarily as a 'governmental instrument applied from above to punish infractions of the social and political order, rather than as a means theoretically, at least, within the reach of anyone wishing to assert a claim against someone else or against the government itself'.[69] This is not particularly difficult to comprehend in a large country where its society and people were influenced by Confucian values, premising their way of life on harmonious living and compromise without being hostile and contentious. There was no formally recognised legal profession and occasionally in rural China, some individuals would come along, with or without fees, assist to prepare a legal petition or accusation for a relative, friend or client, thus the 'sordid' business of litigation began. They are referred to as 'litigation tricksters' and were considered as troublemakers and 'corruptors of the simple country folk'.[70]

68 Derk Bodde & Clarence Morris, *Law in Imperial China* (Harvard University Press 1967) 4.

69 *Ibid* 413.

70 *Ibid.*

These 'litigation trickster' would not be spared punishment[71] which could be in the form of exile with varying banishment distances and could also include fine and whipping.[72]

In 1949, the People's Republic of China came into being and laws promulgated under the Nationalist Government were abolished.[73] China issued a circular banning 'Evil-Minded Lawyers' and 'Pettifoggers' which outlawed lawyering activities from the Nationalist era,[74] in 1950. The existence of lawyers was not recognised or was thought to be uncertain until China's first constitution in 1954 which mentioned that accused in criminal cases can retain a lawyer for their defence.[75] But the good times unfortunately did not last too long for in 1957 the anti-rightist movement brought the provisional start of lawyering to a sudden stop.[76]

Post-Cultural Revolution, with China's economic reform and development under the leadership of Deng Xiaoping, Deng realised that lawyers are integral to economic plans and reforms. Firstly, lawyers were required to be involved in drafting legislation in the transformation efforts of the economy and secondly, to be advisers and drafters of contracts and other legal documents to state-owned-enterprises and other entities.[77] However, weakened by the anti-rightist movement and then the Cultural Revolution, the lawyering

---

71 *Ibid* 414. 'In order to escape punishment as a "litigation trickster," one should be a close relative of, and therefore have a legitimate interest in, the person for whom or about whom one initiates legal action.' Also, 'as few as six or seven legal petitions written for as many persons are enough to make one punishable as a professional litigation trickster.'

72 *Ibid* 551-2.

73 Timothy A Gelatt, 'Lawyers in China: The Past Decade and Beyond', (1991) 23 *New York University Journal of International Law & Politics* 751, 752.

74 Chen Youxi, 'A Tale of Two Cities: The Legal Profession in China', (Mar 2013) Thematic Papers No 2 *International Bar Association's Human Rights Institute (IBAHRI)* 4.

75 See Gelatt (n 75) 752.

76 See *ibid* 753.

77 Randall Peerenboom, *China's Long March Toward Rule of Law* (Cambridge University Press 2002) 348.

profession in China was left broken, with either poorly trained or aging lawyers[78] in any case not up to mark in fulfilling the needs of Deng's economic reform. Legal education was re-established[79] and in the beginning, liberal dispensations were accorded in the interest of promoting rapid expansion of the legal work force such as minimal and flexible qualification requirements, as well as lawyers being exempted from taking a bar exam as a requirement to practice law.[80] All these were for the obvious reason of urgently satisfying the demand for lawyers.[81]

And so 'Lawyers' re-emerge and make a comeback in China, this time with a promising future and the right to a defence lawyer returned to the Chinese Constitution in 1978.[82] In 1980, the Interim Regulations of the People's Republic of China on Lawyers[83] (which took effect only on 1 January 1982) defined lawyers as 'state legal workers' or '*guójiā de fǎlǜ gōngzuò zhě*') (国家的法律工作者):

> whose task is to give legal assistance to state organs, enterprises and institutions, public organisations, people's communes and citizens in order to ensure the correct implementation of the law and protect the interests of the state and collectives as well as the lawful rights and interests of citizens.[84]

Formal testing of lawyers' qualification was finally introduced with a semi-annual nationwide bar examination

78 *Ibid.*

79 *Ibid.*

80 *Ibid.*

81 *Ibid.*

82 See Gelatt (n 75) 755.

83 中华人民共和国律师暂行条例 (*zhōnghuá rénmín gònghéguó lǜshī zhànxíng tiáolì)* (Interim Regulations).

84 Interim Regulations, cap 1, 'The Task and Rights of Lawyers, art 1. See also <en.pkulaw.cn/display.aspx?cgid=785&lib=law>.

in 1986.[85] More changes to lawyering regulations took place alongside China's economic reform and liberalisation, most significantly in the 1990s where law firms could now organise themselves as private partnerships with many 'state-owned law firms' converting into such partnerships.[86] This has given rise to the Chinese legal profession modelled after practices in the West and paved the way for the current mergers and combination with western law firms. In 1996, the Law of the People's Republic of China on Lawyers was enacted to replace the 1980 Interim Regulation, and a considerably landmark amendment to the Chinese Lawyers Law passed on 28 October 2007 (effective on I June 2008)[87], introducing various measures that 'make life easier for lawyers'[88] but in essence reflecting steps in creating an independent and efficient legal profession in China. As the saying goes, the rest is history and the Chinese lawyering industry has developed rapidly, as will be explained later in this chapter.

Evidently, the modern lawyering profession in China is relatively young and recent. But the awakening of China as an economic giant has also given rise Chinese lawyers 'growing up' ahead of their time, finding themselves in international trade facing foreign lawyers as equal in standing but not likely to be equal in terms of legal culture and tradition, where foreign lawyers like the English or American can trace back their modern legal profession through centuries.

---

85 See Gelatt (n 75) 9.

86 See Chen (n 76) 6.

87 See English text from the National People's Congress of the People's Republic of China <www.npc.gov.cn/englishnpc/Law/2009-02/20/content_1471604.htm>.

88 See 'China amends law to make life easier for lawyers', *Xinhua* (Beijing 28 Oct 2007) <http://news.xinhuanet.com/english/2007-10/28/content_6966548.htm>.

2.2.2. Observations about Chinese lawyering

2.2.2.1. Current state of Chinese law firms

Already mentioned earlier, the modernisation of Chinese lawyering regulations has led to liberalisation of legal practice in China. There are increasingly big Chinese law firms merging or combining with foreign law firms under mutually beneficial arrangements such as adopting the 'Swiss Verein' structure. Many foreign law firms have wanted to establish themselves in China as it is a wise business decision to do so, given that the market is still growing and also China being such a large country. The Chinese legal industry is a real opportunity and not just in theory; India is only recently contemplating liberalising some parts of its legal industry to allow foreign law firms into the country. Also, the standard of lawyers and lawyering in China still has room for improvement, unlike in India where leading and national law schools have been producing brilliant law graduates, where they emulate the esteemed English legal tradition.

Any form of cooperation or merger between foreign law firms and reputable Chinese firms means potential access to upcoming Chinese cities in provinces other than Shanghai, Beijing, Shenzhen and Guangzhou. It also presents a win-win situation for Chinese firms which will also benefit from foreign/international branding and transfer of knowledge. As it is, big Chinese law firms tend to be attractive to ambitious law graduates particularly those from *crème de la crème* law schools in China or those who went overseas to complete their postgraduate law qualifications. They in turn add to China's legal job market by offering an 'elite' option of smart, overseas exposed and highly qualified young professionals. However, professional experience is something else.

The largest firm in China in terms of headcount, Dacheng, merged with western-centric law firm Dentons to now form the biggest law firm in the world.[89] Even before the merger, Dacheng was the largest in China (in terms of headcount). In the early days of its establishment, Dacheng's model was more like 'a confederation of English barristers' chambers than a typical full-scale law firm; lawyers worked in autonomous offices and kept the bulk of their earnings.[90] Most Chinese law firms still subscribe to a 'commission-based model whereby each partner is an individual profit centre' and the partners pay a percentage of their fees obtained (or commission) to the firm whilst they will usually be responsible for their own associates; in some firms, the partners may get to keep between 90 and 95 percent of their fees but could drop to 75 percent if there are centralised resource sharing and marketing costs in the particular firm.[91] This is the common model among Chinese law firms which no doubt yields the best revenue and profit for the partners.

Inter-branch cross referral of work or between partners from different branches may be elusive. Whilst in theory they are expected to, in reality this can be challenging in a culture like China where trust and *guanxi* are paramount. Moreover, in a large law firm structure, someone for instance in Wuhan, Hubei province branch, may not know who exactly to refer his client to, about 2,300 km away in its Harbin, Heilongjiang branch (further than the distance from London, Britain to Sarajevo, Bosnia and Herzegovina). For the sake of argument, even if the Wuhan lawyer can avail himself of the firm's online directory, he may not be sure if the lawyer in Harbin can be trusted to handle to the matter, whether from the standpoint of qualification, experience or personality. Moreover *guanxi* may play some part whereby a firm partner may for various

89 'Chinese legal mergers: Rules and laws', *Economist* (London 31 Jan 2015).

90 *Ibid.*

91 Anna Zhang, 'How do Chinese law firms operate?', *Asian Lawyer* (New York 6 June 2016) <www.international.law.com/id=1202759347077/How-Do-Chinese-Law-Firms-Operate?mcode=0&curindex=0&curpage=1>.

reasons refer a work to, for instance, a well-known lawyer in his area of practice or a good friend from another firm and not necessarily cooperating with other partners from the same firm.[92] As opposed to the corporation model, the commission-based system is simply individualistic and any cross-referral most certainly involves the question of self-interest as to what is the benefit for a work be referred to someone and how it will benefit the referrer.[93]

Nevertheless, Chinese-foreign law firm arrangements do have some obvious advantages. In theory, foreign investors going to China now have the convenience of dealing with just one firm, for instance using the investor's trusted and existing global law firm in his home country, which in turn could link up formally, directly or indirectly, with the global firm's China branch. Vice versa, Chinese clients venturing overseas could no doubt utilise the services of Chinese-foreign law firms whereby, say, the Shanghai branch of the firm would introduce the client to their Singapore office. However, the idea of lawyering profession as *intuitu personae* meaning personal service holds true in a society like China where work can be given on account of *guanxi* and basis of trust. Moreover, from the example above, the foreign investor may find that the Chinese lawyer although from the same international law firm, fell short of his expectation. This is likely to occur; after all, local cultures and the professionals all over the world are different. The law firm structure cannot be equated with global fast food brands where all the burgers in McDonald's

---

92 Shangjing Li, 'Wu Mingde of Allbright Law Offices: Corporate structure not the future for law firms in China' *Asian Legal Business* (20 Apr 2016) <www.legalbusinessonline.com/features/wu-mingde-allbright-law-offices-corporate-structure-not-future-law-firms-china/72132>. In an interview, Wu Mingde, Managing Partner of Allbright Law Offices, one of the leading Shanghai law firm, was quoted as saying that law firms in the USA and Europe are more cooperative by nature compared to Chinese firms. Corporate structure for law firms does not stir enthusiasm among the Chinese.

93 There is an (in)famous common Chinese saying, '对我有什么好处?' (*dui wo you she me haochu*?) meaning 'What is in it for me?'

chain from Singapore to Siberia will taste the same, even so there is always exception, as the fast-food company's India outlets do not sell beef due to religious reasons.

2.2.2.2. Chinese lawyers – An examination

It is reported that the number of lawyers in China exceeds 230,000 (2013) compared to only 2,000 less than 30 years ago.[94] Mathematically, this equates to about 1 lawyer per over 6,000 people. For comparative purposes, according to the American Bar Association, there were about 1.3 million licensed lawyers in the USA in 2015[95] (about 1 lawyer per 244 people) or in a country of comparable population India, it is said that there about 1.3 million lawyers in 2011[96] (about 1 lawyer per 960 people). Whilst it may appear that the number of lawyers in China is rather low relative to the size of the population, general sentiments among lawyers in China is that competition is stiff at the very top of the pyramid to secure major clients and deals. It is also likely that the better lawyers (in terms of experience and qualifications) are concentrated in the major commercial cities of China, given that the head office of large Chinese corporations are based there, where high value work and cases are likely to originate. The Chinese situation may not be peculiar given that, as in many countries in the world, business competition can be intense and law firms are competing for the coveted international arbitration cases or clients.[97]

94 See Chen (n 76) 3.

95 See generally American Bar Association Lawyer Demographics for 2015 at <www.americanbar.org/content/dam/aba/administrative/market_research/lawyer-demographics-tables-2015.authcheckdam.pdf>.

96 See Kian Ganz, 'RTI reveals: 1.3m advocates; 1 in 300 Delhi-ites a lawyer; Maharashtra lawyers 'richest'; Jharkand, Assam, J&K fastest', *Legally India* (Mumbai 18 Feb 2013) <www.legallyindia.com/201302183448/Bar-Bench-Litigation/rti-reveals-number-of-lawyers-india>.

97 For instance, in the arbitration case of *Yukos Universal Limited (Isle of Man) v The Russian Federation* (2014) at the Permanent Court of Arbitration,

In a country where remnants of the ancient Mandarin system still remain in the cultural DNA of the Chinese people, academic qualifications and credentials are key. Many lawyers are expected to have such honours and 'decorations' to impress their clients. Increasingly many Chinese lawyers have dual Chinese-western or foreign qualifications. Elsewhere in other countries, successful and highly sought after lawyers tend to be streetwise rather than merely possessing strings of academic qualifications however Chinese lawyers could be in possession of Doctorate degrees obtained in succession after undergraduate degree. Many young Chinese lawyers have also sought and obtained work internship overseas with the hope of eventually returning to practice in China with 'superior' experience than the rest of their peers as well as mastering the English language.

Obviously the western or foreign qualifications adds to their sophistication and intelligence 'aura' in impressing clients. One such professional qualification gaining widespread popularity in China is the New York Bar qualification. Anyone dealing with such Chinese lawyers, whether the foreign clients or foreign lawyers, can expect to hear the proud introduction of such a credential by a Chinese lawyer who possessed it. The Chinese, who are deft in the art of examinations since ancient times, have in modern times proved themselves successful in getting admission to the New York Bar which is obtained by examinations only[98] which has become a 'must have' qualification, currently in vogue in China.

Communicating in English with Chinese lawyers can be challenging. Whilst many Chinese lawyers are taking English language courses, many are still handicapped in terms of the language. It is observed that because lawyers in Shanghai

---

claimant's professional legal fees totalled more than US$ 62 million, a 'dream case' for many arbitration practitioners and aspirants but, in all fairness, the case was not a walk in the park but still it was a rewarding and fulfilling walk. See 'Final Award' 568-9 <http://pcacases.com/web/sendAttach/420>.

98 In an interview of a Chinese law student participating in a scheme to 'sample life' in London's top barristers' chambers, the Chinese

are accustomed to foreign and cross border elements, thus they tend to be able to communicate in English but the same cannot be said with lawyers from other parts of China. Even senior and prominent lawyers do not necessarily speak English since they were either from the older generation of lawyers entirely educated in China or, due to their seniority, they do not believe it necessary to learn English. Even among some Chinese lawyers who have spent years studying in, and obtained postgraduate qualifications from, English-speaking countries, they are still not eloquent and articulate in the language.

The following is an interesting experience by the author dealing with a matter involving Chinese lawyers and parties. A meeting was arranged by Chinese lawyers to meet a client involved in an arbitration matter with a foreign party. Upon arrival at the Chinese lawyer's modern and impressive office, everyone was ushered into the meeting room. Given that all the parties met for the first time face to face, the lawyer introduced herself and mentioned that she is also a 'New York lawyer'. In front of her was a laptop computer of a ubiquitous American brand so popular these days and she informed everyone present that she will do a presentation. However, the next five to ten minutes were spent doing technical troubleshooting because the large flat screen television could not receive wireless transmission from her laptop. Finally, the screen worked and what appeared on the screen were slides of direct excerpts from the agreements and documents all entirely in English with no Chinese translation, as already distributed at the start of the meeting. The Chinese client clearly appeared not to be

law student said about the English legal system that he was 'frustrated by England's "more closed" system of legal education where the requirement that law school graduates complete a training contract or pupillage to become fully-fledged lawyers makes it "harder to qualify" than in the US, where there is no such barrier to practise'. See Alex Aldridge, 'English Lawyers have nothing on China's legal pomp and ceremony', *The Guardian* (London 25 July 2012) <www.theguardian.com/law/2012/jul/25/training-to-be-a-barrister-training-to-be-a-solicitor>.

proficient in the English language. The Chinese clients were possibly embarrassed to admit that they do not understand what was shown and merely nodded in agreement but seemed to be intensely reading from the screen. The Chinese lawyer then proceeded to explain about the background of the case in the Chinese language, but never failing to raise her voice to repeatedly emphasise two words in English: 'contract' and 'arbitration'. Nevertheless, it was an obvious attempt at impressing the client and in demonstrating that the matter was complex and difficult served her purpose well indeed.

The expectations and level of satisfaction for a foreign lawyer or investor dealing with Chinese lawyers cannot be the same as lawyers from their home country (assuming from established jurisdictions like United Kingdom, USA, France or Germany) or even from Singapore or Hong Kong. As was covered earlier in this chapter, the rapid economic progress of China and the urgent demand for Chinese lawyers may have compromise quality.[99] Young lawyers and junior associates working with the senior lawyers are often not given formal training but are expected to learn on the job. This is because the seniors are typically busy sourcing for work and handling customers, leaving them with little time to sit down and tutor the apprentices. On the other hand, the myriad of business deals encountered by lawyers through existing clients or networks can sometimes blur the line between legal and consulting work, for instance, a client asking to source for foreign investors for a certain prospective venture in China. This is compounded by work which is unfamiliar to the lawyers such as international dispute resolution and arbitration matters. Given also that the senior lawyers themselves have not been trained by their seniors when they were young lawyers, it would appear that generally lawyers in China are not exactly practising lawyering as a fine craft of intellect. It was said by a commentator that to a considerable extent, Chinese lawyers 'have had to figure out

99 See Peerenboom (n 79) 364.

for themselves what it means to be a lawyer'.[100] Knowledge of the laws and improving legal skills can sometimes be secondary in an industry where deals come first, resulting in that attitude being carried over by younger lawyers eager to strike it out on their own or moving to another firm for pay's sake but this will not do much good to the quality of the profession.[101] When all is said and done, there are always exceptions and these can largely be found in the many Chinese-foreign firms set to rejuvenate the lawyering scene in China which have certainly identified the strengths and opportunities available.

Already mentioned above, some Chinese lawyers, particularly younger practitioners who have had some exposure working with foreign law firms and have returned to Chinese firms, attempt to conduct business according to 'international standards'. Unfortunately, most of the time they are still beholden to local culture and their Chinese clients who still view lawyers as 'bothersome transaction cost rather than trusted advisers'.[102] To secure Chinese clients may involve considerable efforts at rainmaking and pitching for work. A senior Chinese lawyer with years of experience working for an Australian law firm lamented about a Chinese client's insistence on a contingency fee arrangement for an arbitration matter, calling it 'the Chinese mindset'.

It is also observed that a many times, engaging a lawyer in China is on the basis of the lawyer as individual and not necessarily because of the firm's hallmark. A 'disappointed' businessperson recounted an unpleasant experience engaging a lawyer from a renowned Shanghai law firm. As it turned out, this person walked into the firm in Shanghai without recommendations or appointments and was referred to and attended by a relatively inexperienced lawyer who was at the desk in the office. When this was related to a senior lawyer from the same firm, he commented that:

100 *Ibid* 366.

101 *Ibid* 364-6.

102 See 'Chinese legal mergers' (n 91).

> All the good and senior lawyers are usually not in the office but out there with clients. There are hundreds of lawyers in our firm. Chances are this person must have been attended by a young lawyer sitting idle in the office: evidently not a very sought after lawyer.

It is a fact that many busy and reputable Chinese lawyers operate outside their office. One such senior lawyer from a reputable firm in Shanghai practically spent all day long meeting and talking to clients, communicating through mobile phones and his laptop computer, sometimes stopping at hotels to utilise the lobbies or coffee lounges and in between meetings to check his e-mails and doing some work.[103]

Finally, foreign lawyers dealing with their Chinese counterparts can expect unequal bargain, sometimes of frustrating proportions. As mentioned earlier, Chinese lawyers contacting a foreign lawyer about a foreign arbitration involving their client will typically begin on the premise that the case will be remunerated on the basis of contingency fees. However, when foreign lawyers approach Chinese lawyers for matters involving China, they can expect to be quoted very high professional fees sometimes devoid of basis or reasoning. In the first instance, any mention of a contingency fee will be avoided. Even if a contingency fee arrangement is eventually negotiated, the Chinese lawyers will likely request substantial upfront fees. But Confucianism propagates 'Do not impose on others what you yourself do not desire'.[104]

2.2.2.3. The money is good

The legal profession is not only considered prestigious in China today but it is also perceived to be financially

103 See Zhang (n 93).

104 See n 7.

rewarding by those entering law schools.[105] Available statistics do not suggest that there is an oversupply of lawyers in China; if anything, there appears to be room to accommodate increasing number of lawyers considering the ratio of lawyers to population. It was also reported that China's legal sector has plenty of room to grow, generating US$ 7.6 billion in annual revenues or just 0.1% of its GDP, compared with more than 1% in major European countries.[106] It was reported that the average 'business incomes' of a lawyer in Beijing was RMB 0.4 million yuan (about $60,000 according to late 2016 exchange rate, not taking into account inflation) in 2003, which was considered to be 'a relatively high income among the industries all over the country'.[107]

Likewise, in an article in *The Economist*[108] comparing selected major law firms in China in 2013, Tiantong topped the chart with revenue of US$ 667,000 per lawyer, King & Wood Mallesons at US$ 453,000 revenue per lawyer, Fangda at US$ 310,000 per lawyer, Jun He at US$ 285,000 per lawyer, Dacheng (now part of Dentons, forming the biggest law firm in the world) recorded US$ 88,000 per lawyer and Yingke at US$ 42,000 per lawyer. Compare this with China's GDP per capita of US$ 14,300 (2015)[109] and President Xi Jinping reported earnings of US$ 22,256 per year.[110]

---

105 Mary Szto, 'Gender and the Chinese Legal Profession: From Heaven and Earth to Rule of Woman?', (2009) 18 *Texas Journal of Women & Law* 195.

106 See 'Chinese legal mergers' (n 91).

107 Cui Yuqing, 'China has a strong demand for lawyers', *China Economic Net* (Beijing 11 Oct 2005) <http://en.ce.cn/Insight/200510/11/t20051011_4902926.shtml>.

108 See 'Chinese legal mergers' (n 91).

109 CIA, 'The World Factbook: China – Economy' <www.cia.gov/library/publications/the-world-factbook/geos/ch.html>.

110 Lucy Hornby, 'Xi Jinping's pay far behind global peers even after 62% rise', *Financial Times* (London 20 Jan 2015) <www.ft.com/cms/s/0/5860726a-a084-11e4-9aee-00144feab7de.html#axzz4AX8eSFPb>.

In addition, according to a news report the average salary (assumed to be monthly salary) among 32 major cities in China is RMB 6,070 yuan (about US$ 909 or US$ 10,908 per year) for job vacancies posted online for the winter of 2015, with Beijing at RMB 9,227 (about US$ 1,380 or US$ 16,560 per year), Shanghai RMB 8,664 (about US$ 1,290 or US$ 15,480 per year) and Shenzhen RM 7,728 (about US$ 1,100 or US$ 13,200 per year).[111] Comparing these figures with the earnings of Chinese lawyers, they are clearly the winners and with the expanding legal sector in China there is certainly room for growth in terms of earnings.

2.2.2.4. Shedding dependency on foreign expertise

In recent times, Chinese lawyers are beginning to exert control over cases involving foreign elements, specifically, international arbitration matters. Due to the massive growth of arbitration, many jurisdictions in the world, to promote the conduct of international arbitrations in their countries, have permitted foreign lawyers to appear in international arbitration proceedings. For instance, Singapore is a popular arbitration destination for Chinese parties which include the use of Singapore law as the governing law of their contracts even when the transactions have no connection with Singapore. The driving force behind Chinese lawyers wanting to handle the case themselves entirely can be attributed to fees and evidently the fees in international arbitration proceedings are lucrative.

However, Chinese lawyers can expect to face several challenges should they think that they can bypass foreign lawyers and experts in international proceedings unless, of course, it is a Chinese-foreign law firm which obviously has both local and

111 'Average salary in major Chinese cities is $900 and growing', *China Daily* (Beijing 21 Jan 2016) <www.chinadaily.com.cn/china/2016-01/21/content_23183484.htm>.

international expertise under one roof. First, many Chinese lawyers are likely to encounter an English language barrier and proficiency issues when drafting a statement of claims/ defence, pleadings or even at oral proceedings. Second, Chinese lawyers often lack experience, familiarity or finesse when it comes to international commercial arbitration. This could be due to many reasons, among others, the vast difference between domestic China and international arbitrations. Also, the international arbitration skills among Chinese lawyers, if any, are not as developed as lawyers from Europe, the USA, Singapore and Hong Kong where professionals have spent many years mastering the laws and practice of arbitration. Finally, there are elements of western litigation tradition often found in arbitration proceedings and this may be totally alien to Chinese lawyers who are accustomed to the totally different Chinese court litigation method.

Chinese clients, on the other hand, may also prefer to deal directly with foreign lawyers when the matter involves foreign elements, cutting out the 'middlemen' Chinese lawyers. Some Chinese clients are also said to be 'nervous' about the level of professionalism of their own Chinese lawyers, hence preferring to hand over their foreign-related arbitration to overseas-based experts. Chinese clients who are established or large multinational corporations are likely to have English speaking senior managers and/or in-house legal counsel who would be able to effectively communicate, engage and deal with foreign lawyers directly.

Given time, Chinese lawyers will emulate lawyers from other jurisdictions in terms of knowledge and professionalism. But the question is: how much time? Meanwhile, Chinese law firms are already merging with law foreign law firms. They want to metamorphose (whilst some already have) into international law firms' worthy set up. Increasingly many law firms in China have selected names 'that might be more comforting than Chinese names to international clients and

Western law firms seeking to affiliate with them'[112] often with amusing results, with names concocted out of thin air. Surely, it is not sufficient to merely imitate international lawyers to become like them. This situation will surely change because the Chinese are fast learners. On this account, the legal world will be watching very closely the developments in China.

2.3. Getting Chinese work

It is of paramount importance for foreign lawyers dealing with Chinese clients or lawyers to understand their perspective and behaviour. Knowing how the Chinese do what they do, gets to the root of all understanding, invests one with the knowledge to better alert to possible warnings and also take advantage of opportunities arising.

2.3.1. Bidding for work

Chinese companies are increasingly resorting to taking legal actions.[113] They are well known to request quotations from several parties or firms, which could either be initiated and coordinated by the Chinese clients directly or Chinese lawyers. In some instances, such as the preparation of a legal due diligence report or foreign legal opinion requested by Chinese lawyer for their client, the foreign lawyer's 'client' would be the Chinese lawyer.

112 Leigh Jones, 'What's in a name? For Chinese law firms, Bright is often right', *Reuters* (New York 8 Feb 2012) <www.reuters.com/article/lawfirms-china-names-idUSL2E8D87Y320120208>.

113 Dan Harris, 'China lawsuits as a growth industry', *Above the Law* (New York 1 Feb 2016) <http://abovethelaw.com/2016/02/china-lawsuits-as-a-growth-industry>. Commenting on the increase in litigation and arbitration between western companies and Chinese parties, the author commented on the 'recent uptick in litigation and arbitration involving Chinese companies is China's economic downturn.' And that 'companies with economic problems tend to be more open to pursuing new ways (like litigation and arbitration) of acquiring funds.'

Whilst there is nothing wrong with doing price comparison, it is about how this is being done which is quite unheard of in the West. Most reproachful of all is when Chinese clients forward the official communication and quote from one firm to another, often complete with e-mail exchanges unredacted between the client and lawyers which include communications regarding fee reduction. Fee reduction is a matter of goodwill and, as a matter of courtesy, it should be treated with dignity and not forwarded to another party for them to match. In one such instance from the author's experience, an international arbitration matter with complex elements of different seats and the governing law of the agreement and parties not related to either seat resulted to quotes being solicited from Hong Kong and Singapore law firms. It mortified the lawyers when they found out that their confidential e-mail transmission comprising of fee quote, pertinent information regarding their services and fee reduction quote were shown to competitors.

One possible explanation for this would be the Chinese client's weak command of English language, therefore they might think that it would be easier to forward 'lock, stock, and barrel' all e-mails and documents to the next lawyer for them to counter-offer a better deal. However, a similar practice occurs even for quotes or proposals already in Chinese language being indiscriminately forwarded to other lawyers. The conclusion that can be summed up is that it is an intentional act to put all parties in a competitive mode so that they will be pressured to come up with a better offer after seeing a real quote by another firm. Where credit is due, some Chinese clients were more discreet and would merely inform a lawyer that they have obtained a better quote from another firm, with the name of the other firm unmentioned.

This reality is an integral aspect for those wanting to do business with the Chinese, given that legal work is increasing. Chinese clients are not reserved in terms of using a quote to bargain for lower fees from another firm, or simply start a 'bidding war' which is not entirely a respectful exercise for law firms because criteria for appointment should not lie with fees alone.

To Chinese clients, it is of little significance if comparing quotes would have started a 'bidding war' between law firms they have approached since, as to them, they want the best deal they can get and the less they pay, the better. To them, in their business, bidding is part and parcel of getting deals. Since it can be argued that in present times, fees for a myriad of professions out there are made available online for all to see and consider, what could be so incorrect to reveal the quotes to all and sundry? Nonetheless, the lawyering profession is nowhere resembling mere sale of goods where one look looks at a list with descriptions and make his pick; one does not do that even when selecting a restaurant at which to entertain clients. Professional services are dynamic and quality varies, and there can be many surprises or unforeseen circumstances in the course of legal proceedings such as arbitration.

2.3.2. Pitch for work at your own cost

Many Chinese clients still expect foreign lawyers (and local lawyers) to come to them with a view of initial discussion about their case with no promise of eventual engagement. Meeting face to face in China, especially with the senior management and decisions makers, is often necessary, certainly when involving substantial international arbitration matters. Attitude do vary among Chinese clients, with some being ethical enough to pay for travel and accommodation expenses, but in the first instance this will not be voluntarily offered by the client. For new, potential clients, it might be prudent to expect the Chinese parties to arrange for the air tickets instead of incurring the expenses first then making an expenses reimbursement claim. One can provide the Chinese party with the passport photo page for air ticket arrangements and indicate preferred airlines and flights arrangement although this may not always be fulfilled. Business Class air travel is very unlikely. On the contrary, discount 'no frills' airline tickets will more likely be provided. Some clients are shrewd enough to deem it the lawyers' expected 'business investment' to meet them to discuss the case, even when knowing that foreign lawyers must travel from overseas.

Part cost-sharing is possible, such as the potential client making hotel arrangements and paying for it. However, accommodation expenses are dwarfed by the professionals' air travel expenses and time costs attending the matter. Foreign law firms keen to secure Chinese deals tend to work with local Chinese lawyers acting as their interface and coordinators, which is a perfectly wise thing to do. However, it is imperative that the Chinese minder be accomplished enough for this role when handling potential case leads or else there can be misunderstanding and mismanaged expectations which could be a total waste of time and resources.

For instance, a local Chinese minder pitching for a large arbitration matter gave a 'green light' to the foreign team to come to China from a great distance only to find themselves having a conversation with the potential client who eventually told them that he preferred another law firm, which was not even invited to meet face to face. The excuse given by the minder was that he thought that the Chinese party had already agreed to engage them. The result was not only was there no case in hand but they had bills to foot on their own for travelling expenses all the way to China just to meet the Chinese party for lunch. It is unsurprising that Chinese parties are known to be shrewd but there is very little excuse for the local minder to misread the local situation.

In practice, when initially approached by a Chinese potential client, it is possible to make enquiries as subtly as possible to find out the *status quo* of the matter and whether it is likely for the foreign lawyers to be eventually engaged. With travelling expenses fully covered at least it is not a total waste of resources to give a potential case a good pitch by travelling to China to meet the potential client. Finally, always insist on full travelling expenses arrangement so that the Chinese party having incurred costs and made some 'investment' themselves will be likely to eventually make the service engagement. Whenever possible, never incur the expenses first and ask for reimbursement later as the situation can get complicated whether intentionally or simply due to difficulties in making the funds transfer out of China.

2.3.3. Keeping the relationship going

Chinese clients value relationship management through regular engagements. Future work comes from the present engagement and the saying 'out of sight, out of mind' holds true. After all, this is consistent with the concept of *guanxi* and in order to benefit from the continuous future relationship, the present must be taken care of. Completing an assignment or work for a client satisfactorily is a good start to a possible long term relationship but subject to some considerations. First, one must be prepared to offer advice free of professional charges from time to time when requested. The responses can be short and simple but attention must be shown in order to demonstrate one's investing in the relationship. Second, in the Chinese business culture, money is central and the client would also look to receive preferential fees on account of the relationship. It is a good argument to the senior management that repeat work is given to a particular lawyer because of previous working relationship and special fees levied. In fact, it is very Chinese culture, somewhat also prevalent among other Asians, to expect special concession from existing relationship. Contrasted this with western values, where friendship and relationship do not mix with business and, in fact, it is thought opportunistic and an abuse of the relationship to expect a fee reduction or discounts.

The jury is out whether there is loyalty or not between Chinese clients and lawyers. Some clients continuously work with a particular law firm where *guanxi* plays some role. However, the evolving Chinese culture also means that pragmatism is creeping in and work may not perpetually stay with one law firm if it is felt that other law firms are preferable.[114] One thing is certain: in a competitive market like in China (and elsewhere), business relationships between the service providers and clients are dynamic and not perpetual; they need to be maintained and worked on constantly.

2.3.4. Getting paid

As mentioned earlier, Chinese parties do take contracts seriously and rely on them to set out the final agreed terms between the parties. Even if a contract is not reneged, getting paid can be a challenging and a fee reduction or discounts is common. The truth is payments do get delayed for genuine reasons. Due to China's capital controls, transferring money out of China to overseas, whilst certainly possible, can involve troublesome approval processes. Paperwork needs to be in order and, at times, many translations in the Chinese language would be required. When all is thought to be in order, an unexpected request for more documentation can come that could range from a copy of agreements, original invoices and all sorts of requests. What frustrates foreign parties is when an approval process seems so much more complicated than a

114 On general Chinese consumer attitude, 'Chinese consumers remain brand conscious but, unlike shoppers elsewhere, they focus on value so intensely that brand loyalty is often secondary.' See Yuval Atsmon, Vinay Dixit, Max Magni & Ian St-Maurice, 'China's new pragmatic consumers', Oct 2010, McKinsey & Company <http://www.mckinsey.com/business-functions/marketing-and-sales/our-insights/chinas-new-pragmatic-consumers>.

payment transfer from another Chinese client which was not as complicated or in fact even seamless.

It is no doubt frustrating and annoying, but admittedly, payment process could vary from business to business or even industries and the short answer is if a firm deals with Chinese clients regularly, do consider hiring someone who understands the Chinese accounting and finance system to liaise with clients in China. But there is always the human factor at play; a client may have other more pressing matters to attend to (such as collecting and chasing for payments owed to them by others) therefore paying can be the last item on their list of priority. Or simply, the client is disgruntled and unwilling to pay, also because there is no urgency for them to do so.

On the other hand, clients can potentially ask for discounts or fee reduction during the course of the work. Common excuses would be how the company is running into financial difficulties or simply splitting hairs over the quality of work already done. As for the latter, the clients or Chinese intermediary lawyers could complain that the work was unsatisfactorily done or has caused 'significant damage to their 'reputation' or 'future relationship with client'. In the Chinese culture, it is not common to write or speak to the senior management or leadership to complain, therefore, if caught in a dispute over payment, future relationship, *guanxi* and *mianzi* must be thought through very seriously and any action planned must be calculated.

Money is a compensating element in China's business world today. To some extent, to appease unhappy clients or parties, compensation in monetary form is the way forward, whether due to a mistake, delay or when a work was not up to expectation. It is said that, whenever possible, seasoned business people dealing with China price a 'disgruntlement' premium into their fee. Unsatisfactory service or quality of work would not suffice with a mere apology. To demonstrate remorse and service recovery, discounts and fee reduction are the norm. Goodwill settlement is usually welcomed. Those subscribing to western values may not necessarily agree with such a practice.

2.4. Summary

There are some important observations and useful takeaways in dealing with Chinese clients and lawyers. First of all, the fast and vastly expanding Chinese economy has led to evolving Chinese culture which changes with time and adapts to global events. Some of the evolving cultures are not necessarily rooted in the West or western values but in the Chinese rediscovering themselves and innovating. Chinese clients or users of legal services look to lawyering as just intangible products they are buying, hence in the same vein attitudes or expectation of foreign lawyers who are accustomed to treatment as an honourable member of the legal fraternity in their home country will need to come to terms to accept different treatment by Chinese clients.

China remains a very important market and it is not possible to ignore its importance. In a recent report of revenues of leadings international Chinese law firms in 2015, King & Wood Mallesons (in China) reportedly had revenue of US$ 350 million, Dentons with US$ 450 million, Zhong Lun with US$ 315 million, both Allbright Law Offices and Grandall Law Firm both with US$ 207 million, Yingke Law Firm with US$ 202 million and JunHe with US$ 186 million[115] are considered not short of wonder, given that these Chinese law firms are recent phenomenon and when compared to Magic Circle firms, their growth can be said to be phenomenal.

On the other hand, Chinese lawyers are in the 'Golden era' of China's legal industry. With foreign lawyers increasing

115 Anna Zhang, 'Revenues climb at China's biggest firms', *American Lawyer* (New York 8 Sept 2016) <www.americanlawyer.com/id=1202766982153/Revenues-Climb-at-Chinas-Biggest-Firms>.

looking to do work for Chinese clients or cooperating with Chinese lawyers, local law firms are strategically positioned to welcome them into China through mutually beneficial cooperation models. With many foreign law firms keen to combine with Chinese firms, some also prefer to work on 'best friend' model first without setting up shop in China yet, until such time the cooperation is fruitful then the next advance step will be looked into. Nonetheless, there is cultural gaps between foreign lawyers and Chinese lawyers, as well as Chinese clients. Bridging the differences is by no means simple but the determination of the Chinese to succeed and motivation of foreign firms to expand into China could result in a mutually beneficial outcome.

Chapter 3

Dispute Settlement

3.1. Negotiations

3.1.1. Introduction – 'Benefits' and 'profits'

Central to any negotiation for dispute settlement, the spoken and unspoken, written and unwritten, direct or indirect central tenet is '对我有什么好处' (*duì wǒ yǒu shé me hǎochù*) meaning 'What are the benefits for me?' or 'What is in it for me?' Any negotiation disregarding profits and benefits will be futile and pointless, in fact, a waste of time to the Chinese parties. It is not a matter of 'principle' but principal in the monetary sense. This may be criticised as mercenary but to the Chinese, it is pragmatism, where business is business. Such pragmatism may have been driven by China's contemporary economic and societal conditions, to work hard and achieve results, expecting no one to help you or give handouts.[116]

Any negotiation in the first instance should not be premised on 'our company's expectation' or 'you must do it this way'. Threats do not go well with the Chinese for it is a blatant act of aggression and also an assault on one's dignity and *mianzi*. The gravity and depth of *mianzi* should not be underestimated because the Chinese tend to have long memory and any past humiliation is not likely to be forgotten too easily. A 'payback' can be expected when the opportunity presents itself for the Chinese party.

116 An example of Chinese pragmatism: billionaire Jack Ma was quoted saying 'The primary responsibility of entrepreneurs is making good investments to create jobs and wealth – blind donations will do no good.' '"It's harder to donate money to Chinese charities than earn it," says Alibaba billionaire Jack Ma', *South China Morning Post* (Hong Kong 16 Sept 2015) <www.scmp.com/news/china/money-wealth/article/1858697/its-harder-donate-money-chinese-charities-earn-it-says>.

Many self-help business books on 'doing business in China' almost all written and published by foreigners will not fail to mention Sun Tzu's *The Art of War*, giving the impression that all Chinese businesspeople and negotiators live and breathe this 'gospel'. Nothing could be further from the truth, in fact, a good number of Chinese today may not have even read the book much less use it as the guiding principle in their life. No doubt the book have many insightful philosophies and some of it may have made its way into the Chinese culture but it is more likely to be considered mostly as a revered work of literature than scripture for Chinese businesspeople, negotiators or lawyers.

In the first instance, Chinese parties in a commercial dispute settlement negotiations will always put their own interest above all and may commence with putting forward what may seem like a totally one-sided proposition. This is only the start of the negotiation process and there is definitely room for discussion. Foreign parties should not be too easily flustered but remain level-headed.

3.1.2. Chinese attitude towards commercial dispute settlement

There is an abundance of written work on Chinese negotiations where each commentator and writer describes and prescribes different techniques they assert to be essentials in negotiations with the Chinese. Some of these techniques or methods are no doubt insightful and helpful but they also bordered on stereotypes or generalisations basing on Sun Tzu or some obscure Chinese culture. Some have also formulated methods according to auspicious numbers in the Chinese culture or to avoid certain inauspicious number such as 'four' in negotiation, for it sounded like 'death' in Chinese language or many other techniques that even the Chinese themselves find perplexing. In reality, the Chinese are pragmatic businesspeople who can be very level headed and not easily cowed when it comes to business negotiation; even if an important negotiation is to take place on 4 April at 4.44pm, the Chinese will be there on the appointed date and time. It is observed that in present Chinese society, superstitions have very little or limited impact on the Chinese people's life especially in situations where there are important agendas on hand.

Rather, negotiation in China and with the Chinese in present times are largely influenced by a combination of values which is part old culture (which has been around for millennial) and part contemporary values (such as those influenced by recent and global events) though it is also thought that the dominant values of Chinese culture still take centre stage in the event of 'ambiguity'. The Chinese can be understanding and accommodating, for example in the author's experience there were instances whereby the visiting guests have strict religious dietary requirements, and the Chinese host/ receiving hosts were completely natural about the requests and accommodated the needs seamlessly. We are talking about a culture that has established international trade and diplomatic relations with the outside world for a very long time now.

What are the key common features of Chinese people and culture when involved in negotiation? First of all, the Chinese tend to be curious, detailed and sceptical to the extent of being perceived as distrustful. A lot of questions will be asked. Chinese negotiators are typically polite in the demeanour even though they are insistent about having their questions answered but once the queries are answered, they will move on. At times, the other party may refuse to provide a direct answer to a question or evade a question; the Chinese parties can be sensitive enough to pick this up and will not continue their 'interrogation'. The Chinese party may reply 'I know' or '*wǒ zhīdào le*' ('我知道了') when clearly a question was not answered but this response could mean that he is going to drop the question even though he is dissatisfied.

Chinese corporations will usually send negotiators with authorities and powers to negotiate on their behalf, therefore it is crucial not to send someone not of equal standing to the negotiation table. It will be perceived not only as a waste of time but also an insult. However, in a hierarchical corporate culture, the negotiator is also likely to report to his leadership (领导) '*lǐngdǎo*' when certain items of the negotiation are beyond his authority or if the negotiator's senior management so requires. In a negotiation process spanning several days, be prepared to face similar questions over and over again. It is not meant to be an attempt to annoy but because they need assurance and confirmation. Chinese parties do make concessions as part of the bargaining process in a negotiation, accordingly, some aspects will need to be deliberated internally as part of collective decision making. This may take time, given that some negotiations take place overseas or, if locally in China, not where all the senior management could attend the meeting. Typically, Chinese management will adopt a peer basis negotiation, meaning they are likely to only send a negotiator of equal position, status or standing as the other party's to conduct negotiation and not someone of much higher office. The Chinese party may delegate an executive of a higher position to conduct negotiation as a show of magnanimity and *mianzi* but not as intimidation. At times, if the negotiation takes place in China, the senior management may drop by during the meeting to momentarily listen to the discussion or to just greet the foreign parties. There have been instances of foreign negotiators interpreting this the wrong way and started behaving defensively, perceiving the Chinese party as putting pressure on them. Unsurprisingly, the outcome was not ideal. Also, Chinese senior management particularly those in state-owned companies may not be free to travel overseas or may even be subjected to overseas travelling restrictions like civil servants, thus a manager of adequate seniority and position may be sent on behalf of the company overseas for the negotiation. The 'emissary' will be given the mandate to discuss and make some decisions on behalf of the company but is still likely to report back to the head office for decision clearance and final approval.

3.1.3. Hofstede's cultural dimensions

Professor Geert Hofstede is the Dutch social psychologist renowned for his pioneering work on cross-culture studies. He developed a cultural dimensions theory comprising six dimensions of national culture that can have a bearing on a negotiation process.[117] The dimensions are: 'Power Distance', 'Individualism', 'Masculinity', 'Uncertainty Avoidance', 'Long Term Orientation' and 'Indulgence'.

According to Hofstede's theory, China scores high in terms of 'Power Distance' which means that individuals accept that not everyone is equal in the society. This is consistent with hierarchical structure in Chinese (as well as other Asian) organisations where there are subordinates and superiors. This can impact upon control and the decision-making process, therefore influencing the negotiator. 'Individualism' or 'collectivism' deals with interdependence among members in the society. In this case, China scores low, signifying a collectivist culture. This can imply that, in a negotiation process, any decisions are likely to be made in the interest of the organisation, taking into account the broader good.

Next is 'Masculinity', indicating competitive nature of the society, driven to achieve results and success. According to Hofstede, China is a 'Masculine' society and this does not come as a surprise given the Chinese people's determination to succeed as can be seen in many different aspects of the society including international sporting events. Therefore, Chinese negotiators can be expected to be serious about achieving results from a negotiation process as well as having the responsibility of showing to senior management that he

117 See Hofstede, Hofstede & Minkov (n 43).

can accomplish results. As a whole, they are also determined to achieve successful outcome for the organisation.

This is followed by 'Uncertainty Avoidance' referring to the society's tolerance for ambiguity and uncertainty. China scores low, meaning they can accept uncertainty. This dimension can imply that in the process of negotiation, they can stomach ambiguity and hardship, thus making them likely to be robust negotiators. Another dimension 'Long Term Orientation' deals with perseverance and pragmatism, also signifying that it is a society that is willing to adapt to changing conditions. In this instance, China scores high which is also not a surprise given the Chinese's ability to adapt their culture to the changing world as well as always planning for the future. In terms of negotiation, this could mean that they may make concessions and are willing to consider future relationship in the resolution of any differences. They are less likely to burn bridges. Finally, with regard to 'Indulgence' the Chinese society scores low on Hofstede's meaning it is a 'restrained' society which puts less emphasis on leisure time and does not have propensity to indulge themselves. In negotiation, it can be expected that the negotiator would be focussed on getting the work done and not allowing pleasure to come before their responsibility.

The above theory is fascinating in attempting to forecast negotiation styles, approach and outcomes but Hofstede's theory is only as good as the negotiator himself. Whether the model is useful when put to use in negotiating with the Chinese will be examined below but it should be used as a reference guide only because there are always exceptions.

In this case study, a Chinese multinational company sent its general manager (who is legally qualified) and technical officer to Europe for a negotiation to resolve late delivery of goods from a European seller. The agenda for the visit included discussing compensation for delay and expedited delivery to make up for lost time. The meeting was scheduled at the office of the manufacturer. On the first day of the negotiation meeting, the European party was represented by its in-house legal counsel and sales manager. The Chinese general manager was visibly surprised and asked if the European's Managing Director will be attending the negotiation meeting, to which the sales manager explained that he has been asked to do the negotiation on behalf of the company. Not entirely satisfied with the explanation, the Chinese remarked that he had the mandate from the senior management to negotiate thus would prefer that the decision-maker from the European side be also present in the discussion.

However, the sales manager assured the Chinese party that should they come to a consensus, their Managing Director will join the meeting at some stage to sign the settlement memorandum, otherwise it would have been a waste of resources.[118] The European appeared to think that this could put pressure on the Chinese to resolve the matter quickly. Little did he know that the meeting had not started on a good footing both because the Chinese felt that they have lost 'face' but, above all, because of their belief that the attendance of the senior management from the European side would result in a better outcome. The Chinese party had been put in a defensive mode and now becoming cautious about the sincerity of the European party.

Nevertheless, the first day's meeting commenced with the Chinese party laying down their terms which totally deviated from the terms offered by the European party in writing before the meeting. The seller had requested a period of four additional months to deliver the goods and would require additional payment for expedited air shipping cost; if not, it could take up to six weeks for normal shipment by sea as per the original contractual terms. The Chinese party nonchalantly requested that the European party deliver the goods in China within a month and would not pay even a

118 Sometimes, it is the 'western pragmatism' at play; too focussed on efficient use of time and resources without considering sensitivities of Asian cultures.

dollar more for expedited shipping since it was the seller's responsibility to comply with the contract. This caused a momentary uproar with the European party but the Chinese buyer was unperturbed and stood their ground. After a short break, both parties returned to the meeting room and the European seller now calmly explained to the buyer that there was no way they can have the goods delivered within a month because they would take at least a month to produce the goods much less to have it delivered to China within a month. The Chinese party replied that they had suffered considerable economic loss due to the delay attributed to the seller but the European pleaded that their manufacturing line needed time to manufacture the goods. The buyer then proposed that the seller can let them have the goods meant for their other customers, after all, either way the European is likely to incur a late delivery penalty, either from the Chinese or the other customers. The Chinese party was not about to give up too easily and they were determined to come and do their job in the interest of the company and face uncertainty they were not going to avoid.

The refusal of the European Managing Director to actively participate in the meetings was reported to the buyer's Shanghai head office and the negotiator was asked to press on with the negotiation. A visit initially planned for two days, the Chinese party notified the European that they will stay for six days, with meetings every day. At first, the European party thought that this was an untenable strategy deployed by the Chinese and perhaps they would give up, pack up and leave for China after a few days but little did they fully understand Chinese culture.

The Chinese party embarked on discussing each and every detail of the production schedule of the European seller's plant and looking into how the production could be expedited. Also, at the end of each meeting day, the previous day's discussion was revisited. It was not a pointless tactic but meticulousness and determination in seeking more clarification. The outcome of every day's meeting was duly reported to the head office's senior leadership for comments and suggestions. This was done each morning in Europe before the general manager went for the meetings.

On some days, the Chinese negotiator would make it clear that they were prepared to take the matter to arbitration and that his senior management had made it clear that legal action was the last option left to them. Days into the daily meetings, the European party was exasperated but by then also rattled by the legal threat of the Chinese party; the protracted negotiations had taken its toll on the Europeans.

On the third day, the European Managing Director finally came in for the morning meeting despite no consensus reached but to assure the Chinese party that a consensus would be in the best interest of all parties. At one stage, a conclusion was reached and was conveyed to the European as 'tentative subject to management approval', only to be partly rejected because one of the senior management personnel, who was not present in the previous days' teleconference, warned that the company would be disadvantaged by agreeing with the latest offer. The Chinese had 'long-term orientation' about the matter and maintained its stamina in the negotiation process, now exhausting the European party. The European party eventually came to a significantly improved offer but could not budge any further, suggesting to the Chinese that they would have wasted their trip to Europe should they go back empty handed. However, the Chinese parties thanked their seller and remarked that it had been a fruitful meeting and they now know the European's attitude towards the matter.

Although the Chinese went back without a final settlement, they did not consider the visit a wasted effort because should they take the European seller to arbitration, they were now better prepared and had gathered some valuable information from the visit. Nevertheless, weeks after the visit and communicating from a distance, the Chinese agreed to accommodate the seller's offer and entered into a settlement agreement. According to the Chinese, the long-term economic loss would have been greater to them should they have insisted on standing their ground and also because the products they were acquiring were only produced by a limited few in Europe, with the European seller under study being one of the more reputable ones.

The above case study seemed to suggest the application of Hofstede's theory rather fittingly. All the dimensions have been identified through this case study, however, there are always exception and examples where most or a minor part of the dimensions are engaged.

3.1.4. Observations about negotiations with Chinese parties

Negotiation experiences with Chinese parties vary and nothing can be said to be uniform and identical. At the start of a negotiation, it is expected that the Chinese party will commence with terms very much benefitting them only and it is common to expect seemingly unreasonable demands at the outset, but that is also the start of a bargaining process. In any negotiation between foreign and Chinese parties, it is inevitable that language plays a major role when English is used. Foreign parties negotiating with Chinese parties should engage the service of good interpreters or intermediaries proficient in the English language. It would be preferable to engage Chinese interpreters proficient in English language instead of foreign interpreters proficient in the Chinese language. The Chinese language itself is one thing but nuances, hints or insinuations are unspoken and it takes one Chinese to detect or observe it from another Chinese, yet nothing can be clear-cut or certain so guessing or conjecture may be necessary. For instance, did it mean anything when the Chinese party said 'we need time to consider your offer'

848483LVX00160BA	CASE	9780521111690	6.00X9.00	Distribution Modulo One and Diophantine A	318	<I>	0.875	GLOSS	(1)
848483LVX00161BA	CASE	9780979610134	6.00X9.00	Medical Billing Networks and Processes - P	312	<H>	0.8125	GLOSS	(1)
848483LVX00162BA	CASE	9780890063712	6.00X9.00	Radar Cross Section Analysis and Control	308	<H>	0.8125	GLOSS	(1)
848483LVX00163BA	CASE	9781764734714	6.00X9.00	Decision Debt: The Real Bottleneck in Softw	306	<H>	0.8125	GLOSS	(1)
848483LVX00164BA	CASE	9781621906308	6.00X9.00	Native Intoxicants of North America	306	<H>	0.8125	GLOSS	(1)
848483LVX00165BA	CASE	9781874267614	6.00X9.00	Environmental and Social Justice in the City:	302	<H>	0.8125	GLOSS	(1)
848483LVX00166BA	CASE	9780313270697	6.00X9.00	Sports Violence: The Interaction Between Pr	300	<H>	0.8125	GLOSS	(1)
848483LVX00167BA	CASE	9781107010512	6.00X9.00	Modern Approaches to the Invariant-Subspa	298	<H>	0.8125	GLOSS	(1)
848483LVX00168BA	CASE	9781593332211	6.00X9.00	A Comparison of Ancient Near Eastern Law	296	<H>	0.8125	GLOSS	(1)
848483LVX00171BA	CASE	9780521867283	6.00X9.00	Random Fragmentation and Coagulation Pro	290	<H>	0.8125	GLOSS	(1)
848483LVX00172BA	CASE	9780198565307	6.00X9.00	Modern Radio Science 1996	288	<H>	0.8125	GLOSS	(1)
848483LVX00183BA	CASE	9781107119130	6.00X9.00	The Theory of Self-Determination	258	<G>	0.75	GLOSS	(1)
848483LVX00184BA	CASE	9780275959487	6.00X9.00	Domestic Constraints and the Breakdown of	256	<G>	0.75	GLOSS	(1)
848483LVX00186BA	CASE	9781604976397	6.00X9.00	Observing Society: Meaning, Communicati	252	<F>	0.6875	GLOSS	(1)
848483LVX00206BA	CASE	9798895887752	6.00X9.00	Life Without Zero : The Power Of Nothing	174	<D>	0.5625	GLOSS	(1)
848483LVX00231BA	CASE	9781804412985	6.14X9.21	Management as Deliberation: On How to Get	280	<G>	0.75	GLOSS	(1)
848483LVX00232BA	CASE	9781804413388	6.14X9.21	Philosophy of Ecology and Capitalism: The T	298	<H>	0.8125	GLOSS	(1)
848483LVX00234BA	CASE	9781804413364	6.14X9.21	From Systems to Actor-Networks: A Paradig	358	<J>	0.9375	GLOSS	(1)
848483LVX00235BA	CASE	9781107168398	6.14X9.21	Essential Stability Theory	368	<J>	0.9375	GLOSS	(1)
848483LVX00236BA	CASE	9781804413302	6.14X9.21	Islamic Wealth Taxation and Financing Publ	384	<K>	1.0	GLOSS	(1)

or when the Chinese negotiator simply lit a cigarette and said nothing in response.

The Chinese party is likely to arrange translation through internal resources in the form of an office staff member who can speak some English. The message is almost certainly pushing their own interests but also be prepared for less than refined quality of translation which could be confusing and at worst, unwittingly conveying the wrong meaning. In one instances, a Chinese party initiating the termination of a product distribution agreement with a foreign party had wanted to convey their views that 'you may not be familiar with your own market with regard to marketing our products' but instead wrote in English language that 'you are not good in selling our products in your own country' leading to misunderstanding. Nevertheless, there is nothing like communicating directly with the Chinese party in the Chinese language but this is likely to be impossible for foreign parties. However, there is no known disadvantage in using interpreters in negotiations. As long as the message is accurately conveyed, the Chinese can be flexible, adaptable and non-prejudicial towards foreigners who cannot speak their language, partly they also realise that they themselves are not proficient in the English language. The presence of female negotiators will not affect any negotiation process because the Chinese society by and large is not known to be sexist.

Dispute resolution negotiations can be different from negotiations to establish business relationships. Negotiation with Chinese parties requires an exchange of ideas, views and thoughts for each other's consideration where each party needs to be given a fair opportunity of presenting their case. Even if a negotiation did not yield any outcome, allow some time to let reality sets in and for the other party to think it through, so that once they have analysed their strengths and weaknesses, a reply will come from them. Unlike other cultures, the Chinese rarely do not know what they want or need to achieve and they are not predisposed to idle discussions.

Not all negotiations are the same. Some Chinese companies adopt an international approach to management with personnel who have vast overseas exposure, hence they could be modern and western in their dealings. Others may simply require face to face interaction and in rare cases, the business owner did not even read his e-mails. There is no one-size-fits-all approach to negotiation in China. In addition, what can be observed among the Chinese is underlying principle of not to burn bridges. It seems that most Chinese people including overseas Chinese have been culturally brought up to be prudent and in case one will cross path with another again in future business dealings therefore the need is to make friends and no enemies.

In China, there is an important culture of dining which is central to the lives of Chines people. Friendly business negotiation almost certainly involves invitation to meals and it must rarely be declined. Intense and contentious dispute negotiation may not involve invitation to meals given the possible awkwardness to both parties but should an invitation be extended, to reject such invitation must be given very serious thought. The Chinese do not by nature engage in hostile dispute resolution negotiation, in fact some discussion can take place during meals. At times, it is when in a relaxed mode and out of a meeting room setting that issues can be better discussed, sometimes with positive or favourable outcome as it is common to talk about non-business related topics during meals and common understanding could be established from such a relaxed setting.

However, such cosy partaking of meal should be avoided when in dispute settlement meetings, as opposed to business discussion where the latter is *de rigueur*. One should be reserved and be guarded when in a dispute situation although civilised and brief lunches or dinners augur no harm. Most of the time, Chinese parties do not talk business at the dining table but if a serious topic creeps into meal conversation, it is fine to politely decline discussing it or by evading the question.

Coming back to meals, food can also be expected to be served in abundance and usually in a serious dining establishments. A variety of food can be expected and foreign guests will be treated to delectable spread for it is *mianzi* for Chinese to treat their guests to a good meal. Foreign business guests attending serious business lunches or dinners have not known to be treated to ridiculous culinary adventure usually heard in urban myths, because if guests were made to look silly, the Chinese hosts will be culpable and lose face. During meal but usually during dinner, liberal partaking of alcohol including strong liquors (e.g. *Baijiu*, in excess of 50% alcohol content) can be expected.

It is from the partaking of alcohol and good food that inexperienced negotiators need to be cautious about not getting caught in the merrymaking and on the spur of the moment. Spontaneity and emotional outburst are not rare. In a case as narrated by a Chinese lawyer, a ship buyer and shipyard owner concluded a large contract for new construction of several large ships earlier in the day and as expected, both parties had a celebratory dinner in the evening. Copious volume of alcohol went round the table that evening and both business owners were high in spirits (both emotion and intoxication), talking happily about the contract by raising their glasses and toasting to each other lavishly in expectation of good business relationship together. Suddenly during the dinner, the buyer in an outburst of emotion and drunken stupor told the shipyard owner that he will make a gift worth several million dollars to the latter to acquire new machineries in order to expedite work at the shipyard due to the new orders. Needless to say, it was a happy ending to the dinner but not quite to the entire story. A while later, the buyer defaulted on its progress payments as required under the contract due to financial difficulties and the shipyard sued him for the payment default including the several million dollars 'gift' promised but never made. Reportedly, despite the dubious circumstances of the promise of the gift and it was never made in writing, the buyer did not dispute the claim. Was it a case of *mianzi*?

Finally, it is also observed that negotiations with the Chinese, whenever possible, combine bargaining and compromising. Thus, the saying 'leave something on the table' so that in an ideal world there is a win-win situation so that harmony, *mianzi* and a mutually beneficial outcome is achieved. In any victory achieved from ruthless negotiation against Chinese parties, be mindful that this could upset some people greatly and they can take it rather personally. If one would continue to do business in China, then be conscious of the Chinese sayings that 'the world is small' and 'people do cross paths'. It would have been very awkward to encounter a competitor who was a former business partner previously ousted.

In closing, always attempt to strike a balance when negotiating with Chinese parties; read up about the companies and individuals one will be negotiating with. Taking a leaf from Sun Tzu, 'know thy enemies' in any 'battle'. Different foreigners will have different experience negotiating with Chinese parties, expectedly ranging from good to bad. There are stories of Chinese parties refusing to sign contracts already negotiated at the last minute, demanding changes to their advantage; or instances of Chinese parties refusing to adhere to contracts signed and wanting to renegotiate terms already agreed. This might not be uniquely and absolutely a Chinese problem and argued to be more of an opportunistic behaviour transcending races or nationalities, although some Chinese business people are still less accustomed to international business decorum and ethics. However, in general the Chinese society today is law abiding and legal contracts are taken seriously.

3.1.5. Why negotiations may not always work and possibly increasing legal actions in China

A Chinese lawyer in a conversation with the author commented that negotiations may not always work in China these days, leading to increasing legal actions but usually involving state-owned companies.

Let us say that a company is owed US$ 1,000,000. A senior executive took the lead in negotiating a settlement and avoided legal actions to have the debtor agreeing to pay US$ 950,000. This may not seem like a bad settlement however he risked being accused by someone in the company for failing to recover whatever was owed. He was then perceived as incapable and did not act in the best interest of the company. Worse, he could be accused of being too lenient to the debtor and perhaps could be receiving kickbacks.

Now let's say that another executive can recover the full amount of US$ 1,000,000 owed, however instead of being congratulated again he could be accused of not acting in the best interest of the company to claim interest. Perhaps the debtor would have been willing to pay interest but he had pocketed the difference?

Now finally even if another executive managed to get the debtor to pay US$ 1,100,000 with interest and late payment charges without commencing legal action. This was an achievement for which he should be congratulated; however, others might say that he could have obtained US$ 1.5 million instead. Was he bribed by the other party? As a result, in order to avoid criticisms and accusations, perhaps it would be best to let legal professionals take charge and negotiate, not the company executives.

The above demonstrates commonplace situations within organisations except that in China allegations of taking kickbacks can lead to very cumbersome consequences even if one is innocent. Worse still, corruption can carry capital punishment in China. Whilst the above example may not be representative of the current situation in China, it would not be unimaginable for the above scenario to occur, particularly with state-owned companies unlike privately held companies, where the question of money can be sensitive and delicate. It is also understandable that no salaried company executives would want to risk his career and future to make thankless decisions. Companies in China including state-owned companies are required to make important decisions and it is likely that there are internal procedures and processes relating to decision making such as in the above example, which would not put the decision in the hands of a sole executive or several personnel, therefore, making them entirely liable and blameworthy.

3.2. Mediation

An attempt at peacemaking in international commercial disputes, in avoidance of arbitration, is common with Chinese parties. In the first instance, Chinese parties are open to the idea of resolving their disputes without going through legal proceedings which can be attributed to Chinese pragmatism of not wanting to prolong a dispute and thus incur legal costs. Alternative dispute resolution (ADR) efforts will be deployed such as negotiation and 'bargaining' though formal methods such as mediation have only gained popularity in recent times.[119] However conciliation was already a feature of the Foreign Economic and Trade Arbitration Commission (FETAC)[120] before it was renamed CIETAC in the late 1980s.

---

119 '[I]n recent years the CCPIT Mediation Center has reportedly experienced an enormous increase in its activity.' Jerome A Cohen, 'Settling International Business Disputes which China: Then and Now', (2014) 47 *Cornell International Law Journal* 560.

120 Tang Houzhi, 'Arbitration: A Method Used by China to Settle Foreign Trade and Economic Disputes', (1984) 4 *Pace Law Review* 521.

Dispute resolution with Chinese parties can involve intense negotiation and bargaining processes, whether or not such a process is carried out by the disputants themselves directly or through formal ADR method such as mediation, all with the ultimate aim of getting disputes resolved.

Chinese parties are generally amiable to mediation, therefore, be open to request for mediation or if not, propose it. Foreign parties should not perceive the willingness of the Chinese to mediate as a sign of weakness. Large Chinese corporations these days can be well advised and are not ignorant of their rights. With the proliferation of international law firms in China, they are not isolated from the global world as well as not short of law firms approaching them to offer their services. Mediation can be a good opportunity for both parties to 'take stock' and for the sake of commercial consideration evaluate the option of a swift resolution of disputes without incurring more time and cost by going to arbitration.[121] Even if Chinese parties were represented by lawyers remunerated on contingency fee basis, the lawyers will likely encourage their clients to settle through mediation because of the quick case 'turnaround' which will benefit them as well.

3.2.1. Current modern mediation practices

Arbitration commissions in China are increasingly offering mediationoptiontodisputants.Thearbitrationrules[122]ofChina International Economic and Trade Arbitration Commission

---

121 'The reasons for using mediation...first, the commercial clientele's disenchantment with the cost and time involved in litigating in national courts and in arbitration; ...secondly, a growing feeling amongst international traders that 'interest-based' solutions may produce better outcomes in the medium or long term than 'rights-based' solutions.' Martin Hunter, 'International Commercial Dispute Resolution: The Challenge of the Twenty-first Century' (2000) 16 *Arbitration International* 383.

122 See Appendices 5 & 6. Effective as of 1 Jan 2015

(CIETAC), one of the major arbitration commission in China, provides for mediation[123] also referred to as 'conciliation' in the English version of the rules.[124] According to the mediation/conciliation provision of the CIETAC Rules, the mediation can be carried out by the arbitral tribunal already constituted, with consent of the parties[125] and if the parties do not want the conciliation to be conducted by the arbitral tribunal, with the consent of the parties CIETAC will assist to mediate/conciliate the dispute 'in a manner and procedure it considers appropriate'.[126] When the parties consent to the arbitral tribunal conciliating the matter for them, again with their consent, the tribunal may conduct it in a manner it deems appropriate.[127]

There is also freedom for the parties to decide on the direction of the mediation, allowing either party to requests the tribunal to terminate the process, or if the tribunal considers that the conciliation efforts will be futile.[128] Finally, the mediation/conciliation provision of the CIETAC arbitration rules are conducted on a 'without prejudice' basis:

> Where conciliation is not successful, neither party may invoke any ...opinion, view or statement, and any proposal or proposition expressing acceptance or opposition by either party or by the arbitral tribunal in the process of conciliation as grounds for any claim, defence or counterclaim in the subsequent arbitral proceedings, judicial proceedings, or any other proceedings.[129]

---

123 Mediation and Conciliation in Chinese are similarly called *tiáojiě* (调解).

124 CIETAC Rules, art 47 – Combination of Conciliation with Arbitration, <www.cietac.org/Uploads/201607/5795f078aa6d5.pdf>.

125 CIETAC Rules, art 47(1).

126 *Ibid* art 47(8).

127 *Ibid* art 47(2).

128 *Ibid* art 47(3).

129 *Ibid* art 47(9).

The Shanghai Arbitration Court of International Shipping (SACIS), an institution established by the Shanghai Arbitration Commission[130] to arbitrate disputes relating to shipping, logistics, maritime affairs and port constructions, has a Mediation Centre which enacts its own mediation rules. As is the case with mediation, it is a voluntary process at the SACIS Mediation Centre[131] as per 'written agreement' of the parties but in the absence of such an agreement, the SACIS Mediation Centre may accept a case at the application of one party and accepted by the other.[132] Mediators can be chosen from SACIS Mediation Centre's Panel of Mediators or those not listed in the Panel. A mediation session at the SACIS Mediation Centre is not open to the public and assures its users of confidentiality including keeping confidential all matters relating to the mediation by the Centre's staff.[133] The mediator will be entrusted to conduct the mediation according to a manner the mediator considers appropriate.[134] In the event of failure to achieve a settlement and the matter is to be referred to arbitration, the mediator shall not be appointed as arbitrator in the subsequent arbitration unless with the agreement of the parties.[135] Any settlement achieved by the parties can be incorporated in a signed settlement agreement, 'mediation agreement'[136] or if 'require a confirmation by an arbitral legal instrument' in other words, an arbitral consent award, by applying to Shanghai Arbitration Commission or SACIS.[137] Finally, the SACIS Mediation Centre's rules adopt 'med-arb' principles as commonly in place in many other international

130 See Appendix 9.

131 Art 4, Mediation Rules of Shanghai Arbitration Commission Arbitration Court of International Shipping, adopted at the Director's Meeting of Shanghai Arbitration Commission on October 15, 2010 and effective as of January 1, 2011 (SACIS Mediation Rules).

132 SACIS Mediation Rules, art 3.

133 *Ibid* art 12.

134 *Ibid* art 13.

135 *Ibid* art 18.

136 *Ibid* art 16.

137 *Ibid* art 17.

dispute resolution centres allowing the parties to submit the disputes that cannot be resolved to mediation to arbitration to SACIS or the Shanghai Arbitration Commission.

In closing, it is encouraging for the international dispute resolution community to see that leading Chinese commissions are receptive to and have adopted international practices and methods of alternative dispute settlement which are consistent with practices outside China and in other key international bodies. Another conclusion that can be drawn is that leading Chinese commissions aspire to become international dispute resolution and arbitration players, leveraging China's global economic status and also drawing from their experiences in Chinese dispute resolution to offer such expertise to foreign parties.[138] However it remains to be seen if foreign parties would confidently and willingly submit to mediation in China before Chinese mediators when involving Chinese parties.[139] Unsurprisingly, a foreign party might be fearful that they may be at disadvantage mediating in a foreign 'territory' before a mediator from the home country of the other disputing party. Because of the need to keep mediation costs low and the process quick, a foreign party may be less inclined to bargain for a mediator from a foreign country to come to China to conduct the mediation, that is, if the other party agrees to such a request. Also, a Chinese mediator will likely prefer a Chinese speaking mediator otherwise a translator would be required but a foreign party may not relish the prospect of

138 CIETAC Working Report of 2011 and Working Plan of 2012, (5 Jan 2012, Beijing) para 1: 'As a comprehensive arbitration institution authorized to accept both domestic cases and international cases, CIETAC has made great endeavors to grow itself into a leading international arbitration institution. The number of foreign-related cases saw an increase' <http://bj.cietac.org/index/aboutUs/workingReport/477b4fd5b387f87f001.cms>.

139 See Cohen (n 121) 559: 'My impression is that in many important disputes with China, as with other countries, foreign firms do not often take formal mediation seriously. If unable to settle matters through bilateral negotiations, they tend to be pessimistic about mediation's prospects for success'.

using a translator to communicate with a Chinese mediator. If mediation takes place overseas, the Chinese party would need to rely on interpreter to communicate with the foreign mediator, who will most likely speak and conduct the mediation in the English language as is the common practice internationally.

3.3. Alternative method of dispute resolution – case studies

3.3.1. Proactive conciliatory judge

A South East Asian commodity seller was embroiled in a dispute with a Chinese buyer. In the sales agreement, the dispute resolution provision provides for arbitration in Singapore. A dispute arose about the quality of the commodity shipped to the Chinese buyer, in which it was claimed that the quality of the commodity shipped upon reaching the designated port in China was below the quality as agreed between the parties in the sales agreement. Part payment had been made by the buyer but the balance of payment was secured by way of a bank guarantee provided to the seller, issued by a Chinese bank. Disputes over the quality of commodities are common, typically with buyers claiming that test results have shown that the products were of substantially lower quality than agreed upon so they would expect substantial price deduction basing on cost calculation methods typically found in the sales and purchase agreement for commodities. On the other hand, sellers typically alleged that it is the buyer's tendency to act in bad faith by wanting to pay nothing or as little as possible.

The seller offered price deduction in the interest of a quick resolution, an amount not thought to be insignificant. Unsurprisingly, the Chinese buyer was not satisfied and wanted a further price reduction. They had also relied on their own shipment surveyor's report in which the buyer averred that the quality of the commodity was way too inferior hence would require a substantial write-off partly as compensation for their inability to use the products for their intended purposes. As no consensus can be reached with the buyer, the seller was prepared to invoke the arbitration clause. Before the arbitration could commence, the buyer was able to obtain a court injunction in China to prevent the seller from calling on the aforesaid bank guarantee. Fraud was alleged as the basis to injunct the bank guarantee for a certain fixed period of time.

Given the recent development, the seller was now in a quandary as they had temporarily lost the opportunity to call on the bank guarantee; the options available to them now would be to contest the injunction on the bank guarantee in a Chinese court, which was clearly not preferred by them and also to commence arbitration proceedings. Although the seller was fairly confident of obtaining an award in their favour by arbitration, the proceedings may take time including enforcement in China, considering the amount was not substantial at all.

Attempts were made at negotiation between the friends of both parties but a settlement still could not be achieved. Meanwhile, through the lawyers of both parties, the option for mediation was on the table but the seller was taking a tough stand, viewing the buyer as unreasonable and wanted their lawyer to aggressively pursue the buyer. Interestingly, the presiding judge who issued the injunction communicated with the lawyers for both parties. He warned the buyer that the injunction of the bank guarantee will be lifted soon and he is unlikely to extend it unless the buyer commenced legal proceedings with the regard to the allegation of fraud made. On the other hand, he told the seller that it might be in their best interest as a foreign party to come to a settlement with the buyer swiftly instead of prolonging it, which will otherwise involve lengthy legal proceedings consider the small amount of dispute. The informal 'mediation' came from the most unexpected party, the Chinese judge who did not meet a representative of both parties at all but only communicated over the telephone. Yet, his advice sunk in with the seller and buyer resulting in them reconsidering their positions very carefully.

Finally, both the seller and buyer were able to reach an amicable settlement. A language barrier was present as the buyer communicated through their own internal interpreter and the seller through their lawyer. However, it was thought that the judge's unexpected conciliatory intervention sealed the deal.

3.3.2. An offer difficult to refuse

A mid-sized South East Asian company entered into a ship purchase agreement with a Shanghai seller. A dispute ensued between the buyer and the shipbuilder due to non-payment issues under the agreement but it was not that simple. According to the buyer, the seller and he were formerly business partners and they enjoyed close business and personal relationship over the years. Given their relationship, they have been helping each other and allegedly some personal loans were extended to the seller which the buyer now claimed had surreptitiously been turned against the buyer resulting in a personal debt being owed by the buyer to the Chinese party. Apparently, legal proceedings commenced in the Shanghai courts which the South East Asia party was awarded against.

The buyer's director then claimed that she was served with notice of repossession of her personal assets in China, due to the dispute. She was said to be in shock as the dispute involved corporate entities and under no circumstances should it implicate the directors/shareholders personally. It was further alleged the Chinese seller was well connected in Shanghai and was privy to many of the director's personal aspects in China. A notice of auction was ostensibly issued against the buyer's director and she was feeling a palpable sense of helplessness as well as outrage. The only positive outcome out of this was the seller being able to pressure the buyer to the negotiation table. The final outcome of the dispute was not known but for the buyer to be reduced to a desperate state with even her personal properties in China at risk of being auctioned off, this was certainly a negotiation which was too difficult to reject.

3.4. Closing

Below is taken from the *Analects* of Confucius which so appropriately describes the approach to dispute resolution:

> There are nine things the gentleman turns his thought to: to seeing clearly when he uses his eyes, to hearing acutely when he uses his ears, to looking cordial when it comes to his countenance, to appearing respectful when it comes to his demeanour, to being conscientious when he speaks, to being reverent when he performs his duties, to seeking advice when he is in doubt, to the consequences when he is enraged, and to what is right at the sight of gain.[140]

Whilst Confucianism by itself is not an absolute characterisation of every Chinese person, some of the values are no doubt part of the Chinese culture since time immemorial which defines the Chinese people. Mastery of the Chinese language by foreigners is just one part but the cultural complexity which is a combination of family values/ upbringing, education (both at school and at home) and influence of the surroundings and society all bear on the way Chinese look at, perceive and handle disputes. Details and

140 See Confucius, *The Analects* XVI:10, at 140-1.

rituals[141] are not to be overlooked as they matter. The common and old popular sayings among Chinese people '和气生财' ('*héqì shēngcái*') meaning 'Harmony brings wealth' and '以和为贵' ('*yǐ hé wéi guì*') meaning 'Harmony is a virtue' are some of the many mantras out there which the Chinese upholds or put in esteem regards. The Chinese culture is a shibboleth.

In the dispute resolution process, it is important not to overlook the signs and hints, which many times can be subtle. They are found in speech and actions, not necessarily difficult to spot though more challenging to interpret. However, the fundamental point is there will always be willingness and readiness to negotiate and make peace; westerners can thus be assured of this even if in the first instance the demand is seemingly unreasonable. Keep emotions at bay and never let them loose. Remember that it is cultural and part and parcel of bargaining, coming from a culture which is consultative and people working as a unit, team, community or a cell rather than individuals. Any good must be for the common good, sometimes sacrificing principles and rights. Be open minded at all times.[142]

---

141 For example, how a guest is seated at the dining table plays an important role in Chinese culture. So too does dining 'diplomacy' in dispute settlement. In the West, it is not uncommon for opposing parties to decline lunch or dinner invitations during a negotiation process. Vigilance is golden no doubt, however the Chinese's motive should not always be viewed with suspicion. Be mindful not to constantly decline any request made out of goodwill or else it could be misunderstood as distrust and rejection.

142 See Confucius, *The Analects* VII:29, at 90. 'Why should we be so exacting? When a man comes after having purified himself, we approve of his purification but cannot vouch for his past.'

Chapter 4

Arbitration

4.1. Chinese's acceptance of arbitration

Those unfamiliar with China often ask if arbitration is used in the country and whether the Chinese know what it is. The answer is unequivocally positive. Business people and corporate entities are at least familiar with domestic arbitration in China if they themselves are not past or current users of arbitration. As it will be explained shortly, domestic arbitrations in China must be administered by Chinese arbitration commissions. There are numerous arbitration commissions in China and their establishment is governed by the Arbitration Law of the People's Republic of China (CAL).[143] This is in contrast with the situation outside China where the establishment of arbitration organisations was not known to be required to comply with any specific legislations regarding the formation of arbitral bodies.[144] Whilst arbitration is widely considered as a private dispute resolution mechanism which enshrines the doctrine of party autonomy, arbitration in China also has a higher purpose of serving the needs of the judiciary in disposing of commercial civil disputes. Thus, the state can look to arbitration commissions as partners in the resolution of disputes, this way reducing caseload and the burden on the state. China in enacting legislation that also deals with the

143 See Appendix 2. Adopted by the 9th Meeting of the Standing Committee of the Eighth National People's Congress on 31 October 1994 and promulgated by the Decree No. 31 of the President of the People's Republic of China on 31 October 1994.

144 Elsewhere arbitration centres or institutions can be freely established by likeminded professionals for the advancement of study and conduct of arbitration. Typically, they are established as associations, societies or companies.

establishment of arbitration commissions is not without its basis.[145]

There are numerous arbitration commissions throughout China, reportedly numbering 225 commissions as of 2013.[146] According to the case statistics of CIETAC,[147] from 2007 to 2015, its caseload was in excess of a thousand annually, with foreign-related cases no less than 300 per annum. For instance, in 2015, 1,531 were domestic cases whereas 437 were foreign-related. In terms of the amount of claims in 2015, CIETAC reported a total claim for all cases at RMB 42.5 billion or in excess of US$ 6.2 billion.[148] Meanwhile caseload at the Shanghai Arbitration Commission, which did not provide a detailed breakdown of domestic and foreign-related cases, reported more than 1,400 cases per year since 2011 recording 2,073 cases alone in 2015.[149] Another commission that should be mentioned is the Beijing Arbitration Commission (BAC)[150] which was established in 1995 and is said to be recognised

145 For example, Singapore maintains a dual regime for arbitration, 'international' and 'domestic'. The Law Reform Committee, Sub-committee on Review of Arbitration Laws, *inter alia*, at para 10 of the Report: 'A greater degree of curial supervision and intervention is, however, generally considered to be more appropriate in the case of domestic arbitration'. Whereas at para 12: 'the Committee considered that a closer involvement by the courts in domestic arbitration is desirable, both for the development of domestic commercial and legal practice, and for a closer supervision of decisions which may affect weaker domestic parties.' <www.sal.org.sg/Lists/Law%20Reform%20Committee%20Reports/Attachments/2/review_of_arbitration_laws.pdf>.

146 Wei Sun & Melanie Willems, *Arbitration in China* (Kluwer Law International 2015) 5.

147 CIETAC Statistics, English version <www.cietac.org/index.php?m=Page&a=index&id=40&l=en>.

148 See CIETAC Statistics Chinese version. Apparently, the English version stated that the claim received for 2015 was RMB 425 billion whereas the Chinese version which was believed to be accurate gave it as RMB 42.5 billion (in excess of US$ 63 billion). Chinese version <www.cietac.org/index.php?m=Page&a=index&id=24>.

149 See Shanghai Arbitration Commission website <www.accsh.org/index.php?m=content&c=index&a=lists&catid=42&menu=6-42->.

150 See Appendix 8: Beijing Arbitration Commission Arbitration Rules.

as 'the only local arbitration commission which meets or surpasses global standards' by the Economic Intelligence Unit.[151] The BAC reportedly accepted 2,944 cases in 2015 which is an increase of 903 cases (44.2%) from the preceding year and reported that amounts in dispute reached RMB 41.1 billion, which is in excess of US$ 6.1 billion.[152] The BAC is said to be offering service 'closest to international standards'[153] and is proud of its independence of which it was said that:

> Independence reflects the core value of arbitration. In some arbitration institutions of developing countries, independence would only be hanging on the wall at the office. At the BAC, however, it comes to life. It has been fully endorsed by the leadership team and well integrated into the BAC's practice.[154]

If caseloads are generally considered high and understandably so at key arbitration commissions or commissions located in major Chinese cities, even the Hainan Arbitration Commission (from likely the smallest province in China) reported that since their inception in 1996 to date of the report on the website (unknown) it had handled 2,000 cases.[155] Between 1999 and 2005, local Chinese arbitration commissions have recorded a combined caseload of more than

---

151 Beijing Arbitration Commission website, 'About us, Introduction' at paragraph 3 <www.bjac.org.cn/english/page/gybh/introduce_index.html>.

152 Beijing Arbitration Commission 2015 Annual Report/ 2015 Work Summary of Beijing Arbitration Commission (BAC) <www.bjac.org.cn/news/view?id=2771>.

153 See Cohen (n 121) 567.

154 Chen Fuyong & Sun Wei, 'Looking Beyond Rules: An Analysing Insight into the Competitive Attractions of BAC', (2014) *LexisNexis Dispute Resolution Law Guide* <http://arbitrator.bjac.org.cn/en/images/20120716/Looking%20Beyond%20Rules.pdf>.

155 Hainan Arbitration Commission website <http://218.77.188.134/wz/143000020/default1.asp?lan=gb&catid=10739>.

150,000 cases with 47,314 cases alone in 2005.[156] Nevertheless, the precise data collection methodology[157] of cases involving Chinese arbitration commissions is not known, for instance whether it is cumulative (pending/on-going and new cases) or purely new cases received in each calendar year.

From another source, Wuhan Arbitration Commission was reported to have accepted 10,608 cases in 2012 and 10,469 cases in 2013. In comparison with the number of cases for other commissions: Beijing Arbitration Commission (BAC) 1,473 (2012) and 1,627 (2013); Shanghai Arbitration Commission 1,415 (2012) and 1,616 (2013); and CIETAC 1,060 (2012) and 1,256 (2013) cases accepted in those two years.[158] It also ranked arbitration commissions by caseloads in 2013 for domestic arbitrations, with Wuhan Arbitration Commission topping the list with 10,469 cases, second place was Guangzhou Arbitration Commission with 5,031 cases, third place was Changchun Arbitration Commission with 3,436 cases, fourth place was Jinan Arbitration Commission with 3,348 and Chongqing Arbitration Commission taking the fifth place with 3,159. BAC is ranked 13 with 1,627 cases, SAC ranked 14 with 1,616 cases and CIETAC at ranking 19 with 1,256 cases.[159] However the data also presented the view that whilst BAC and CIETAC did not rank high in terms of case numbers, they do receive cases of higher dispute value, ranking CIETAC and BAC first and second respectively in 2013 with SAC ranked sixth.[160] Finally, 2% of all arbitrations cases accepted by

---

156 Chen Fuyong, 'Striving for Independence, Competence, and Fairness: A Case Study of the Beijing Arbitration Commission', (2009) 18 *American Review of International Arbitration* 313, 314.

157 For instance, in the same year 2005, ICC International Court of Arbitration recorded only 521 requests for arbitration worldwide but this is in relation to international arbitration, certainly cannot be equated to the volume based domestic arbitrations in China. See <www.iccwbo.org/Products-and-Services/Arbitration-and-ADR/Arbitration/Introduction-to-ICC-Arbitration/Statistics/>.

158 See Sun & Willems (n 148) 5-6.

159 *Ibid.*

160 *Ibid* 6-7.

Chinese institutions in 2012 (that is, 1,512) were 'arbitrations with a foreign element'.[161] The above impressive statistics are convincing evidence substantiating the popularity and wide acceptance of arbitration in China. Furthermore, from enquiries among Chinese business people and legal practitioners, it is generally accepted that arbitration is their accepted method for cross-border commercial disputes instead of litigating in foreign countries.

Separately it is reported that as of March 2016, a total of 14.2 million cases had been filed in Chinese courts which represent a 28.44% increase year-on-year,[162] by any account, staggering statistics. Arbitration as a partner to the judiciary with its primary function as 'private judiciary' where disputants pay for their 'private judges' (arbitrators) as well as cost and expenses of proceedings, are very important elements which do not just relieve case workloads of court judges but also expenditure of the state in maintaining it judicial organs.[163] This cooperation and collaboration between the courts and arbitration are clearly a beneficial symbiosis and the judicial attitude towards ADR and arbitration should never be one that harbours jealousy towards it or even closet anti-arbitration.

In the case of China, the demand for arbitration domestically did not differ much from textbook definitions laying down the key benefits of arbitration compared to litigation: speed, low cost and choice of arbitrators to suit the nature of disputes, whereby such features endear Chinese legal practitioners and users to arbitration. The ability to choose own arbitrators

161 *Ibid* 7.

162 Cao Yin, 'Guideline streamlines China's court case filing process', *China Daily* (Beijing, 10 May 2016) <www.chinadaily.com.cn/china/2016-05/10/content_25186603.htm>.

163 See speech by Chief Justice Sundaresh Menon, 'Judicial Attitudes towards Arbitration and Mediation in Singapore', 25 Oct 2013, Kuala Lumpur, Malaysia <www.supremecourt.gov.sg/docs/default-source/default-document-library/media-room/judicial-attitudes-to-arbitration-and-mediation-in-singapore.pdf>.

further alleviates the fear of corruption in the dispute resolution process and arbitrators with appropriate specialised training, qualification or experience can be appropriately appointed to arbitrate the dispute. Also, the final and binding nature of arbitration in international arbitration is crucial to Chinese users because of certainty as well as confidentiality which fits well into the Chinese *mianzi* culture. In a vast country like China, increasingly sophisticated and complex private commercial disputes as well as difficulties in the hiring of qualified judges pose challenges to the judiciary[164] with the changing landscape of legal careers and industry in China contributing towards judges going into private practice.[165] In private practice, it is likely that those previously in the judiciary will find their training and experience a good fit in handling dispute resolution work including arbitration.

4.2. Foreign perception of doing arbitration in China

Foreign parties doing business in China are almost certain to avoid local Chinese courts for litigation unless of course they are compelled to. As discussed earlier, there are many Chinese arbitration users and amongst them are business people who appreciate the features of arbitration. However, foreign parties would in the first instance probably avoid arbitrating their disputes in China. This also means that foreign parties are reluctant to submit their disputes to a Chinese arbitration commission. However, if it involves a Wholly Foreign-Owned Enterprise (WFOE) in China or an enterprise is considered a 'domestic' Chinese entity, it will be

---

164 See also Benjamin L Liebman, 'China's Courts: Restricted Reform', (2007) 21 *Columbia Journal of Asian Law* 1 (Columbia Public Law Research Paper No. 08-180).

165 'Judging judges', *Economist* (London 26 Sept 2015) <www.economist.com/news/china/21667952-help-build-rule-law-china-demoting-judges-judging-judges>. 'I was tired of it. I did not like the pressure, so I chose freedom,' referring to the resignation of China's court officials to seek better income outside the judiciary.

required that the arbitration be submitted only to a Chinese arbitration commission.

Arbitration seated in and with its juridical base in China would be governed by the underlying arbitration law of China (CAL) and subject to the chosen Chinese arbitration commission. It is understandable for foreign parties in the first instance to be apprehensive about arbitration in China, being subjected to Chinese arbitration law and commission rules especially when reading some less than glowing reports[166] about the morbid and sordid situation of arbitration in China and Chinese arbitration commissions. The fear of the unknown is not particularly surprisingly given the normal suspicion that the Chinese party is thought to be more familiar with his own jurisdiction and 'turf'. More of this will be examined later, which may prove to be a comforting revelation. Second, foreign parties generally lack familiarity of Chinese arbitration law and rules of Chinese arbitration commissions especially the obscure ones. The CAL does not adopt the United Nations Commission on International Trade Law Model Law on International Commercial Arbitration (UNCITRAL Model Law) and not all Chinese arbitration commission rules adopt the UNCITRAL Model Law either. The central purpose of the UNCITRAL Model Law is to promote harmonisation and unification of international trade law, which includes international commercial arbitration law.[167] However, some Chinese arbitration commissions have devised rules which are in line with modern arbitration practice which also adopt some parts of the UNCITRAL Model Law, which is

166 See Cohen (n 121) 562: 'I had become progressively disillusioned by instances of corruption, government influence over decisions, ethical deficiencies, conflicts of interest, bias against foreign companies, faulty methods of selecting arbitrators, ... and other unfair practices'.

167 'The Model Law is designed to assist States in reforming and modernizing their laws on arbitral procedure so as to take into account the particular features and needs of international commercial arbitration'. See <www.uncitral.org/uncitral/en/uncitral_texts/arbitration/1985Model_arbitration.html>.

commendable in trying to attract foreign parties to arbitrate in China.

Thirdly, there is reasonable question as to the quality of local arbitrators, whether they are familiar with disputes involving foreign elements. Is there a reason for their lack of understanding in the theories of international arbitration? With many law schools in China teaching highly competitive syllabus, what could be lacking in terms of their education? It is argued that there is lack of good study materials on international arbitration in Chinese and translated into the Chinese language. There is an abundance of good books, articles and journals published regularly on the subject of international commercial arbitration but they are almost all in English. International arbitration practitioners have the advantage of access to such materials freely including the multitude of academic materials and commentaries by practitioners that can be found on the internet.

There is concern and fear that Chinese arbitrators may be inclined to side with their 'own people', but it is worthwhile considering the possibility that perhaps the lack of understanding of, and familiarity with, the foreign context may be a reason why Chinese arbitrators have made arbitral awards perceived to be unfavourable towards foreign parties. Whilst English might be an issue for Chinese arbitrators, if foreign parties were to conduct arbitration in China in accordance with Chinese law, it is expected they will be represented by Chinese lawyers. It is still possible to conduct arbitration in another language other than Chinese in accordance with the agreement of the parties.[168]

Fourthly, foreign parties will be concerned about the choice of arbitrators. Whilst a foreign arbitrator can be appointed to a tribunal of three arbitrators, generally the feedback is that Chinese arbitrators still make the majority of the tribunal.

---

168 See for example, CIETAC Rules art 81 and BAC Rules art 72.

Also, it is thought that the panels of arbitrators of arbitration commissions are limited in terms of foreign arbitrators and lacking in terms of qualified Chinese arbitrators. A tribunal with a majority of Chinese arbitrators may not suggest anything disadvantageous or sinister except that the foreign party will feel that they do not have foreign representation in the tribunal. Depending on the rules of the arbitration commission chosen, it is generally possible for disputants to nominate arbitrators from outside the panel of arbitration commissions. Foreign parties can also consider nomination of prominent Chinese arbitrators who have international exposure and thought to be able to arbitrate the case satisfactorily. After all, disputants have their say in arbitration proceedings and the constitution of arbitrators is one of the chief feature of this dispute resolution process.

4.3. China arbitration law and practice

4.3.1. Arbitration Law of the People's Republic of China (1994)

For the purpose of comparing and understanding the fundamental features of establishing arbitration according to the CAL, the following key provisions showing notable differences compared to other arbitration laws elsewhere can be seen in Articles 10, 11, 12, 16 and 20:

> Article 10 – Arbitration commissions may be established in municipalities directly under the Central Government and in cities that are the seats of the people's governments of provinces or autonomous regions. They may also be established in other cities divided into districts, according to need. Arbitration commissions shall not be established at each level of the administrative divisions. People's governments of the cities referred to in the preceding paragraph shall

> arrange for the relevant departments and chambers of commerce to organise arbitration commissions in a unified manner. The establishment of an arbitration commission shall be registered with the administrative department of justice of the relevant province, autonomous region or municipality directly under the Central Government.

Notes: The protocol for the establishment of Chinese arbitration commissions is clearly laid out above. It is unsurprisingly a bureaucratic process stipulating when an arbitration commission may or may not be established as well as the registration process. Many arbitration organisations elsewhere are established by private individuals or group of likeminded people for the advancement of common interest in dispute resolution. In most foreign jurisdictions, arbitration organisations are typically established as corporate entities usually with no regulatory approval needed with regard to its conduct of arbitration activities.

> Article 11 – An arbitration commission shall meet the conditions set forth below:
>
> (1) To have its own name, domicile and charter;
>
> (2) To have the necessary property;
>
> (3) To have the personnel that are to form the commission; and
>
> (4) To have appointed arbitrators.
>
> The charter of an arbitration commission shall be formulated in accordance with this Law.

Notes: According to original Chinese wording, Article 11(2) suggests physical presence of the arbitration commission in China, referring to 'property' or in Chinese '财产' (*cáichǎn*). Article 11 basically states the basic requirement of an arbitration commission which is self-explanatory.

> Article 12 – An arbitration commission shall be composed of one chairman, two to four vice chairmen and seven to eleven members. The offices of chairman, vice chairman and members of an arbitration commission shall be held by experts in the field of law, economy and trade and persons with practical working experience. Experts in the field of law, economy and trade shall account for at least two thirds of the people forming an arbitration commission.

Notes: There is prescribed requirements on the composition of office bearers which define a Chinese arbitration commission. The minimum two-thirds requirement seemed to suggest an emphasis on law, finance and commerce leaving open one-third option to those who are not industry experts, perhaps representation from local government. In any case, practitioners still, retain majority composition of arbitration commissions.

> Article 16 – An arbitration agreement shall include arbitration clauses stipulated in the contract and agreements of submission to arbitration that are concluded in other written forms before or after disputes arise.
>
> An arbitration agreement shall contain the following particulars:
>
> (1) an expression of intention to apply for arbitration;
>
> (2) matters for arbitration; and
>
> (3) a designated arbitration commission

Notes: Crucially, Article 16 stipulates the requirement for an arbitration agreement to stipulate an arbitration commission. Contrary to practices in most other countries, minimally drafted arbitration agreements referring to arbitration in accordance with the rules of an arbitration institution is suffice to give effect to it as an arbitration under the said the rules. This is not the case in China and, according to a

Supreme People's Court interpretation,[169] the mention of arbitration rules only and not an arbitration commission is not in compliance with Article 16(3) of the CAL.

> Article 20 – If a party challenges the validity of the arbitration agreement, he may request the arbitration commission to make a decision or apply to the people's court for a ruling. If one party requests the arbitration commission to make a decision and the other party applies to the people's court for a ruling, the people's court shall give a ruling. A party's challenge of the validity of the arbitration agreement shall be raised prior to the arbitration tribunal's first hearing.

Notes: Under the CAL, the arbitral tribunal may not rule on the validity of the arbitration agreement. This is unlike the UNCITRAL Model Law[170] where the arbitral tribunal may rule on its own jurisdiction including any objection in respect of the existence or validity of the arbitration agreement. Some commentators have an issue with Article 20 of the CAL claiming that it does not accord the tribunal with the powers to rule on the validity of the arbitration agreement, implying a lack of power and freedom. Is this entirely true? According to the Singapore International Arbitration Centre Rules (SIAC Rules),[171] any objection to the existence or validity of the arbitration agreement before the constitution of the arbitral tribunal shall be determined by the Registrar if such objection shall be referred to the Court (referring to the Court of Arbitration of SIAC which includes a Committee of the Court) and if so, the Court shall decide if the arbitration shall proceed.[172] In the event that the tribunal has been constituted, then it shall have the power

169 Art 4, Interpretation of the Supreme People's Court concerning Some Issues on Application of the Arbitration Law of the People's Republic of China, came into force on 8 September 2006. See Appendix 5.

170 Art 16(1).

171 See Appendix 13.

172 SIAC Rules 2016, Rule 28.1.

to decide on any objections with respect to the arbitration agreement.[173]

4.3.2. Practice and law of arbitration in China

Without going into a detailed legal analysis of the CAL as this is not an arbitration law textbook, two salient characteristics of Chinese arbitration law must be borne in mind. Arbitration in China is still exposed to some uncertainties as can be seen with the Chinese court decisions in recent times. Firstly, the general rule is that Chinese entities or 'domestic parties' can only arbitrate their disputes in China meaning to say only China seated arbitration and not abroad. Contravention of this by two Chinese entities could lead to refusal of recognition and enforcement in China. What constitutes 'domestic parties', which may be least expected by some foreign investors, and the question of whether 'foreign-related' arbitrations are distinguished from domestic arbitrations will be discussed later in this chapter.

Secondly, it is required for Chinese 'domestic' parties to conduct their arbitrations at Chinese arbitration commissions (constituted under the CAL) so that arbitration awards rendered by ad hoc arbitrations will risk unenforceability in China. This also calls into question if Chinese parties can submit their dispute for arbitration seated in China but referred to foreign arbitration institutions (that is, non-Chinese arbitration commission). Contrary to any misconceptions, if any, Chinese courts do not supervise commercial arbitration proceedings between private parties. Fundamentally, it is not a question of whether one can or cannot conduct arbitration according to their desires. In reality, disputants can do anything they wish but as 'all roads lead to Rome' in the arbitration world, it boils down to the enforceability of arbitral awards.

Chinese 'domestic parties' must submit their disputes to

173 *Ibid* Rule 28.2.

domestic arbitration in China, in other words, arbitration referred to Chinese arbitration commissions. At first glance, it appears irrelevant to foreign parties doing business with Chinese parties until one is told that WFOE is considered a domestic entity. This is not unique to China because, for example, if a Singapore company incorporates a business entity in the United Kingdom with the Singaporean entity being the sole shareholder, it is still a British legal entity. Nevertheless, as WFOEs are considered 'domestic entities', disputes between them and Chinese parties are considered domestic disputes and so would need to be subject to a domestic arbitration regime. Surely this may not be what WFOEs want or agree to but there is very little point in arguing over this requirement. To insist on arbitrating outside these limits would lead to unenforceable arbitral awards, thereby a waste of time, costs and resources for the parties.

The case of *Beijing Chaolaixinsheng Sports and Leisure Co. Ltd v Beijing Suowangzhixin Investment Consulting Co. Ltd* (2014) which was widely reported by commentators mostly in the new media involved a dispute between a Chinese party and a South Korean-owned WFOE. The arbitration reportedly took place offshore in South Korea and an arbitral award was eventually rendered. When enforcement of the award was sought in China, it was refused on the grounds of violation of the domestic rules as both parties were domestic entities (the WFOE though owned by a South Korean was a Chinese entity) and the contract was performed in China as well as its subject matter located in China. The decision by the Chinese court was consistent with the Chinese arbitration law requiring such a dispute to be referred to a Chinese arbitration commission as per the CAL Article 16(3).

There are numerous other Chinese cases reported and commentaries in the form of articles written by law firms in, or with interest in, China. Nevertheless, it is necessary to note the Interpretations of the Supreme People's Court on Several Issues Concerning Application of the Law of the People's

Republic of China on Choice of Law for Foreign-Related Civil Relationships (SPC 2012)[174] elucidating what makes a civil relation 'foreign-related' which defines whether a dispute is 'domestic' or 'foreign-related' in which case a 'foreign dispute' may potentially circumvent the need for domestic arbitration in China. The SPC 2012 at Article 1 states that:

> Where a civil relationship falls under any of the following circumstances, the people's court may determine it as foreign-related civil relationship:
>
> 1. Where either party or both parties are foreign citizens, foreign legal persons or other organisations or stateless persons;
>
> 2. Where the habitual residence of either party or both parties is located outside the territory of the People's Republic of China;
>
> 3. Where the subject matter is outside the territory of the People's Republic of China;
>
> 4. Where the legal fact that leads to establishment, change or termination of civil relationship happens outside the territory of the People's Republic of China; or
>
> 5. Other circumstances under which the civil relationship may be determined as foreign-related civil relationship.

Notwithstanding, a recent case that has been widely celebrated (hopefully not too prematurely) as a monumental step towards reformation of Chinese arbitration: *Siemens International Trading (Shanghai) Co. Ltd v Shanghai Golden Landmark Co. Ltd (2013)*[175] also known as '*Golden Landmark*'.

---

174 Interpretations of the Supreme People's Court on Several Issues Concerning Application of the Law of the People's Republic of China on Choice of Law for Foreign-Related Civil Relationships, Interpretation No. 24 [2012] issued on 28 Dec 2012 and coming into force on 7 Jan 2013. <http://en.pkulaw.cn/display.aspx?cgid=192329&lib=law>.

175 Hu Yi Zhong Min Ren (Wai Zhong) Zi No. 2 (2015) (Shanghai No. 1 Intermediate People's Court).

Both parties are WFOEs which arbitrated their dispute offshore in Singapore. The arbitral award was brought back to China for enforcement as both entities are based there where their assets are located. Shanghai Golden Landmark sought enforcement of the award but was challenged on grounds that the arbitration clause violated the domestic rule hence invalid under Chinese law. However, the court held that there was a 'foreign related' element in the dispute as both parties are WFOEs incorporated in the Shanghai Free Trade Zone (Shanghai FTZ) and the nature of the contract was for international sale of goods involving the Shanghai FTZ. In this instance, the Shanghai No. 1 Intermediate People's Court held that the above factors constituted 'other circumstances' which were regarded as 'foreign-related' therefore satisfying SPC 2012 Article 1(5). As the relationship between the parties was considered foreign and their action to arbitrate abroad in Singapore at the Singapore International Arbitration Centre (SIAC) did not contravene Chinese laws, consequently the arbitral award rendered in Singapore was allowed enforcement.

Whilst some commentators were quick to celebrate the *Golden Landmark* case, hailing it as a development which could spell the dawn of a new era, practitioners should know that no two cases are the same. The case has some unique circumstances which engaged the 'other circumstances' provision under the SPC 2012. Every transaction is fact-sensitive and foreign parties planning to incorporate arbitration clauses providing for arbitration abroad should exercise caution. As a last cautious note, China does not practice the doctrine of *stare decisis*.

Second is the requirement for arbitration seated in China to be referred to Chinese arbitration commissions. In the case of *Züblin International GmbH v. Wuxi Woke General Engineering Rubber Co Ltd* (2004)[176] (*Zublin*) the SPC ruled

176 See <http://en.pkulaw.cn/display.aspx?cgid=1970324837024395&lib=case>.

that an arbitration clause specifying 'Arbitration: ICC Rules, Shanghai shall apply' as invalid, therefore, the enforcement of its award was refused. According to the SPC, the arbitration agreement failed to specify an arbitration commission in accordance with the CAL Article 16(3). Meanwhile, in another case *Duferco S.A. v. Ningbo Arts & Crafts Import and Export Co. Ltd* (2009) (*Ningbo Arts*),[177] where the background of the case was slightly complicated due to differing arbitration clauses between the English and Chinese version, the matter was conducted as an ICC arbitration and concluded with an award rendered. However, the Court in Ningbo agreed to enforce the ICC arbitral award. Whilst this appears to contradict the earlier *Zublin* case, the court upheld the arbitral award in *Ningbo Arts* because the respondent did not question and challenge the validity of the arbitration agreement during arbitration proceedings but only at the enforcement stage. In the CAL at Article 20, 'A party's challenge of the validity of the arbitration agreement shall be raised prior to the arbitration tribunal's first hearing.' However, to rely on the *Ningbo Arts* case absolutely and entirely may be risky since it dealt with a procedural point and did not address the main issue of whether arbitrations seated in China submitted to a foreign rules institution is permitted. Then a case came along several years later: *Anhui Longlide Packaging and Printing Co Ltd v BP Agnati SRL* (2013)[178] (*Longlide*). The contract between BP Agnati, an Italian company, with Anhui Longlide, a Chinese company, contained a provision providing for all disputes arising between them to be settled by arbitration by submitting to the International Chamber of Commerce under its Rules,

177 See (2008) Yong Zhong Jian Zi No. 4, available at <http://newyorkconvention1958.org/index.php?lvl=authperso_see&id=106>. See also Michael J. Moser (ed), *Dispute Resolution in China* (JurisNet LLC 2012) 230-2.

178 The Supreme People's Court [2013] Min Si Ta Zi No. 13. For detailed study and analysis on this and other cases generally see Sun & Willems (n 148).

with the 'place of jurisdiction' in Shanghai.[179] The validity of the arbitration clause was challenged as the ICC was argued not to be a recognised arbitration commission under Chinese law. At the Hefei Court, Longlide's argument was accepted and the arbitration clause was deemed invalid as it was agreed to be not an 'arbitration commission' according to the CAL. However, this was reversed when it was referred to the Anhui High People's Court which held the arbitration agreement to be valid as it contained the required elements under Article 16 of the CAL. This decision was upheld by the SPC. Advocates of the use of non-Chinese arbitration commissions and as well as those championing foreign arbitration institutions in China certainly welcome this decision but is this all there is with regard to the on-going question on the use of foreign arbitral institutions in China?

The binding nature of the *Longlide* case on all future cases and on Chinese courts is not known whereas there are some unanswered questions arising from this case which may not have answered some of the key questions. Article 10 of the CAL states that 'The establishment of an arbitration commission shall be registered with the administrative department of justice of the relevant province, autonomous region or municipality directly under the Central Government.' Can a foreign institution be effectively registered in China in accordance with the relevant provisions under the CAL? Is the CAL designed to include foreign arbitration institutions? If a foreign arbitration institution is not registered as an 'arbitration commission' in accordance with Article 10 of the CAL, will it then satisfy the requirements under Article 16(3)? To err on the side of caution, it would be wise to take a cautious approach when it comes to electing to arbitrate in China using foreign arbitration institutions. Foreign investors need to know what they want and what their concerns are; do they distrust Chinese arbitration commissions? There are increasingly more international influenced arbitration

179 See Sun & Willems (n 148) 64-65, 72-75.

commissions in China which appear to emulate rules, practices, standards and outlooks of foreign arbitration centres. In the spirit of party autonomy in arbitration, foreign parties can decide how their arbitration agreements would be designed; they can implement safeguards such as the requirement for the appointment of foreign arbitrators or choice of language in the proceedings.

Some closing observations: the Chinese courts are not thought to be populist yet they cannot be said to be totally ignorant and disregarding global issues and modern developments in arbitration. They have learned that some changes are necessary but some are not. Perhaps changes may come one day in the form of a revision to the CAL, which may be due for revision after more than two decades in force.

4.4. Chinese's perspective of arbitrating abroad

Many Chinese parties recognise that in the first instance foreign parties do not prefer to arbitrate in China. This does not come as a major surprise because some Chinese parties do agree to arbitrate abroad instead, if it is permissible under the Chinese laws and when involving foreign parties. The preferred seat will usually be in established jurisdictions such as Singapore, Hong Kong, London or Paris. In the case of large contracts, the Chinese parties consider the importance of competent international jurisdictions to conduct arbitrations as some might be concerned if Chinese arbitration commissions are up to the mark when it comes to the conduct of international commercial arbitration. Opting to arbitrate on home ground in China may not necessarily give them any added advantage. The tactical and strategic thinking of the Chinese means they would not rule out any possibility, for example, that the foreign party arbitrating in China may have engaged very influential and capable local Chinese lawyers to represent them.

Chinese parties may agree to arbitrate abroad because it was a condition or demand set by the foreign party at the contract negotiating stage. However, they are seldom sceptical about doing arbitration in foreign jurisdictions as long as the place chosen is reputable and established. But as is the case with the drafting of arbitration agreements, they are called 'midnight clauses' meaning it is the last clause in a commercial contract to be considered, either late at night or in the early hours of the morning[180] whereas in the case of Chinese contracts, it can also be attributed to the Chinese's perception of avoiding dealing with 'inauspicious' matters such as disputes. Their hope is to do business smoothly, harmoniously and profitably. Whilst Chinese business people and professionals are increasingly becoming savvy, nothing suggests that they all necessarily understand the entire mechanics of arbitration laws and practices, such as the interaction between arbitration centre rules and laws, as well as the correct naming of some leading arbitration institutions including the existence of centres named in their arbitration agreements. This is evident from the many pathological arbitration clauses[181] commonly found in Chinese contracts.

At one stage, Stockholm was a very popular choice for the Chinese and this was said to be due to the Swedish policy of neutrality even during the cold war. Several Chinese lawyers questioned by the author also opined that the choice of Stockholm could have been 'cut and paste' arbitration clauses gone viral. It is not unheard of that one lawyer shares with another lawyer sample arbitration clause. In recent years, choice of arbitration in London, Singapore and Hong Kong has been widely seen.

---

180 Nigel Blackaby & Constantine Partasides with Alan Redfern & Martin Hunter, *Redfern and Hunter on International Arbitration* (Oxford University Press 6th edn student ver 2015) 72.

181 See *ibid* 244, noting that a defective arbitration clause that 'fails to provide either for an effective method of constituting the arbitral tribunal or for the place of arbitration may turn out to be inoperable'.

According to an ICC report, Singapore is the number one seat of ICC arbitration in Asia and the fourth most preferred seat of ICC arbitration in the world.[182] Singapore is a popular venue for Chinese to do arbitration and, according to SIAC, China and India have remained strong contributors of its cases over the past five years with China ranked second in terms of foreign users in 2015.[183] Some corporate lawyers in China have said that, in recent times, some Chinese parties have turned to Singapore as a neutral arbitration venue because of anti-Mainland sentiments in Hong Kong. On the other hand, professionals in China and Hong Kong are upbeat about the role of Hong Kong as the legal and dispute resolution arm for China's One Belt One Road (OBOR) initiative.[184] As it is, Hong Kong is a popular venue for arbitration involving Chinese parties. According to the Hong Kong International Arbitration Centre (HKIAC)[185] 2015 case statistics, in terms of nationality of parties, Mainland China is ranked second.[186] In the author's view, both Singapore and Hong Kong each presents its unique value proposition to Chinese (as well as other foreign) arbitration users which need not lead to intense rivalry but healthy competition in the region. With the anticipated growth of Chinese parties taking their international commercial disputes to arbitration due to exponential growth in regional trade volume, there should be enough cases for both venues. Ultimately, it is the choice of arbitration users and there are many factors involved in the choosing of their preferred seats of arbitration, which

---

182 ICC report confirms Singapore as a leading Asia arbitration hub (6 June 2016) <www.iccwbo.org/News/Articles/2016/ICC-report-confirms-Singapore-as-a-leading-Asia-arbitration-hub/>.

183 SIAC Annual Report 2015.

184 'China's one belt, one road initiative set to transform economy by connecting with trading partners along ancient Silk Road', South China Morning Post (Hong Kong 21 June 2016) <www.scmp.com/business/china-business/article/1978450/chinas-one-belt-one-road-initiative-set-transform-economy>.

185 See Appendix 10 for the HKIAC Rules.

186 See HKIAC Statistics <www.hkiac.org/about-us/statistics>.

may or may not be influenced by their lawyers involved in the contracts negotiation and drafting process.

In summary, from the perspective of the author it is not observed that Chinese parties are adamant to only arbitrate in China when transacting with foreign parties. It is yet to be heard that Chinese parties have set a prerequisite to arbitrating in China only or the 'deal is off', in fact it is likely to be the foreign parties that insist on only offshore arbitration and none other.

4.5. Comparative arbitration laws

Already discussed above, disputes between Chinese and foreign entities (not Foreign-Invested Entity (FIEs) or WFOEs) can be arbitrated offshore. Conversely, Chinese and foreign entities can choose to arbitrate in China. It is increasingly popular for disputants to submit their disputes to arbitral institutions as administered arbitrations and when doing so, the procedural aspects (and sometimes more) will be subject to the rules of the arbitration institutions selected by the parties at the outset. Similarly, in the case of post-dispute arbitrations, the submission to arbitration agreements will stipulate the choice of arbitral institutions and its rules, if the choice of the parties is not ad hoc arbitration.

Rules of arbitral institutions are not arbitration laws. An arbitration is governed by the law of the place in which it is held, which is the 'juridical seat' of the arbitration, the law governing the arbitration or '*lex arbitri*'.[187] Choosing a place of arbitration brings with it its own law or *lex arbitri* of that place which must be complied with.[188]

> [A]n English woman who takes her car to France has 'chosen' French traffic law, which will oblige her to

187 See Blackaby, Partasides, Redfern & Hunter (n 182) 171-2.
188 *Ibid* 176.

> drive on the right-hand side of the road... But it would be an odd use of language to say that this notional motorist had opted for 'French traffic law'; rather, she has chosen to go to France—and the applicability of French law then follows automatically. It is not a matter of choice.[189]

If arbitrating in China, then the foreign parties should be familiarised with the CAL. Given that foreign parties are increasingly finding contracts with Chinese parties referring to arbitration in Singapore, it would be useful to understand how the arbitration law works but above all, Singapore's International Arbitration Act Cap. 143A (IAA)[190] which adopts the UNCITRAL Model Law like many other countries. New entrants to international commercial arbitration, including those interested to further the study on this subject, are encouraged to refer to the bibliography section of this book which provides a very useful list of books, articles, journals and publications. Nevertheless, for the purpose of this book, it is useful to highlight the key provisions in each arbitration legislation for simple comparative purposes. Below is a table showing some key provisions of the English Arbitration Act 1996[191] (AA 1996) which does not adopt the UNCITRAL Model Law and Singapore's IAA when juxtaposed against each other. London and Singapore are both popular arbitration venues for Chinese parties, with both locales equally popular for non-Chinese parties.

For a comparison of salient points of AA 1996, IAA and CAL, see Figure 1 on page 193.

In summary, the comparison will prove useful to both Chinese and foreign arbitration users who are likely to arbitrate either in China or offshore. The Chinese perspective

189 *Ibid.*

190 Singapore has dual regime arbitrations with international arbitration coming under the International Arbitration Act Cap. 143A.

191 Arbitration Act 1996 Cap. 23.

on arbitrating offshore would largely be influenced by how protected is their interest. Their natural instinct is to safeguard their position when it comes to arbitrating commercial disputes overseas. The preference of Chinese parties when it comes to arbitrating overseas will be explained later in this chapter.

It is also necessary to mention the Hong Kong Arbitration Ordinance (Cap. 609) which came into effect in 2011, repealing the previous Ordinance (Cap. 341). The Ordinance adopts the UNCITRAL Model Law, making it in line with many other arbitration laws including Singapore's. Whilst Hong Kong is a Special Administrative Region, it is not subject to the CAL's prohibition of ad hoc arbitration, in other words, awards made in Hong Kong consequent to ad hoc arbitration can be enforced in Mainland China.[192]

4.6. Popular choices of overseas arbitration venues by Chinese parties

Some Chinese parties can have an entrenched choice about locations for the conduct of commercial arbitration overseas. As mentioned earlier, sometimes there is no decision to be made *per se*, because the choice of arbitration venue was either consciously chosen by lawyers involved in the contract negotiation process or, in some cases, incorporated without much thought from another contract ('cut and paste'). No doubt Chinese parties do get involved directly in contract drafting, as can be seen in the case of established or large corporations where their in-house counsel or senior personnel take active roles in the drafting stage including of the arbitration clauses. Some contracts may not involve drafting from scratch as it could be a template provided by

192 See reply issued by the SPC to a query from the Secretary of Justice of Hong Kong SAR concerning enforceability of awards of ad hoc arbitrations in Hong Kong <www.hklawsoc.org.hk/mem/download/attachment.asp?issue=07-669a3.pdf>.

the other foreign party, but at times it can become a game of chance if the draft contract was prepared by someone whose first language is not English and the arbitration clause may be a pathological clause. On the other hand, good English language by itself does not guarantee anything, as ambiguously drafted or flawed arbitration clauses can still be found even in contracts originating from English speaking countries and written by lawyers.

The Chinese parties are not particularly adventurous when it comes to choosing arbitration venues despite their bigger business appetite investing all over the world. They would prefer tried and tested choices[193] as well as avoiding jurisdictions which they perceive to be hostile towards them. Not in the order of importance, the following cities abroad are common and popular seat of arbitration involving Chinese parties: Singapore, Hong Kong, London and Paris. Cities in the USA as first choice of venue for arbitration by Chinese parties are rare unless there are compelling underlying reasons for it.[194] In fact the author has never yet personally seen it. Distance plays an important role due to the cost factor and that it would be more challenging to supervise and manage the matter. It is also observed that Chinese parties tend to choose English speaking jurisdictions for the obvious reason that the English language tend to be the only foreign language spoken by the majority of Chinese as well, as to some degree, there is trust and admiration in the time-honoured English/common law system, hence the attraction to arbitrate in places like Singapore, Hong Kong

193 In consulting some Chinese parties about Malta as a possible venue for arbitration, since the Maltese government wanted to establish itself as a potential international arbitration venue, most were reluctant. One senior lawyer who was more vocal said that Chinese parties will not 'use' arbitration 'in unheard of places, they will never agree, so just stick to Singapore or Hong Kong. If to be conducted in Europe, use London or Paris.'

194 For example, perhaps if an American party has a dominant position in the transaction, for example a lending agreement where the lender is a New York financial institution.

and London. But as international commercial arbitration gains momentum in Asia, Singapore and Hong Kong have become popular and trusted arbitration venues to the extent that Chinese parties are said to be excluding London despite how deeply fond they are personally of the historic capital of Britain, in favour of venues nearer to them.

In terms of choice of international arbitration rules when arbitrating abroad, ICC, SIAC, HKIAC and UNCITRAL Rules all have been observed to be selected. Chinese arbitration commission rules also increasingly popular for use by foreign parties for international arbitration but typically seated in China. They are characteristically rules of major Chinese commissions and in major Chinese cities, such as CIETAC, BAC and SAC.

4.7. Choosing arbitrators

In arbitration proceedings, Chinese parties are inclined to choose Chinese arbitrators for the obvious reason of 'trust' but they are also inclined to nominate foreign arbitrators basing on recommendations by their lawyers or industry peers. In other words, they are less inclined to entrust their dispute in the hands of people they cannot figure out. It is unsurprising and not unique to the Chinese parties to be concerned about choosing the 'wrong' arbitrator which might be prejudicial towards their case. The much-quoted French saying comes to mind '*Tant vaut l'arbitre, tant vaut l'arbitrage.*' ('An arbitration is only as good as the arbitrator.')[195]

195 See, for example, Stephen R Bond, 'The International Arbitrator: From the Perspective of the ICC International Court of Arbitration', (1991-2) 12 *Northwestern Journal of International Law & Business* 1.

Cultural prejudice is not unheard of, for instance in the case of *Catalina v Norma* (1938).[196] On the other hand, it will not come as a surprise for some arbitrators to personally prefer arguments which are easier to listen to[197] in the language familiar to them, either by lawyers or even the disputant themselves. If the arbitration proceeding is to be conducted in the English language and the arbitrator is conversant with English, insufficient command of the language can disrupt the oral hearing resulting in difficulties in understanding the arguments put forward. Similarly, in the case of unsatisfactorily written pleadings.

Chinese parties do often enquire if they can nominate arbitrators from among their circle of contacts. Their chief concern is appointing arbitrators whom 'they do not know' but, rather than implying friendship or acquaintanceship, at the least it is intended to simply avoid appointing an arbitrator who might be hostile towards their case. This does not come as a total surprise since arbitration is based on the doctrine of party autonomy where the parties can have some say in the choice of their 'judge', that is, the arbitrators. For instance, a shipyard party in an arbitration would rightfully be cautious about agreeing to the appointment of an arbitrator who is a lawyer often acting successfully against shipyards. Or, as an extreme illustration, the refusal of a Chinese party to the appointment of a person as arbitrator who has made public

196 *Catalina SS (Owners) v Norma (Owners)* [1938] 61 *Lloyd's Law Reports* 360. A very senior and eminent King's Counsel while acting as an arbitrator, was heard to have uttered remarks to the effect that Italians were liars and so were the Portuguese and one of the parties before him was Portuguese.

197 *Fletamentos Maritimos SA v Effjohn International BV (No. 2)* [1997] 2 *Lloyd's Law Reports* 302 as per Morrit LJ: 'It is inevitable that judges and arbitrators will form opinions as to the professional skills and integrity of those who appear before them; they are bound to find some advocates easier to listen to, and likely, therefore, to be more persuasive, than others. But the existence of such views, whether held privately or, as in this case made known to others, cannot, without more, be sufficient to constitute bias against that advocate's client.'

his personal views about his dislike of Chinese corporations. This is different to litigation, where judges are employed by the state and cannot be chosen by the disputants. No doubt judges are not necessarily better qualified and experienced compared to arbitrators, in fact usually not, but the safeguard can be found in the state legal systems which provides for an appellate system. In arbitration, the arbitrator is the first and final adjudicator with no appellate system within arbitration. The arbitrator is therefore expected to be the all-encompassing and 'ultimate judge'.

Finally, a common question among foreign parties/ disputants, especially those opting to arbitrate in China, is regarding the impartiality and neutrality of Chinese arbitrators when arbitrating against Chinese parties. Such concern seems to suggest that, because of *guanxi*, a Chinese party could surreptitiously appoint a friend as arbitrator or simply someone who will be on their side. One commentator who is an international arbitration academic and practitioner alleged[198] about his own personal experience dealing with an arbitration commission and made public his criticism about how the commission functioned, including issues concerning impartiality of arbitrators. This is not likely to be a hazard unique to China. In fact, some Chinese parties are equally concerned if they would be in any less advantageous situation themselves; conversely Chinese parties could be suspicious about foreign parties too who might be able to afford hiring well connected Chinese lawyers who in turn might appoint Chinese arbitrators according to their *guanxi*. It works both ways. Any allegations about impartiality and neutrality of arbitrators are for the parties and disputants to address during the appointment of arbitrator(s) stage, at the commencement of proceedings. In arbitration, the parties are in the driver's seat. It would only be logical not to appoint

198 See generally Jerome A Cohen, 'Time to fix China's arbitration', (Jan 2005) *Far Eastern Economic Review* 31, available at <http://carnegieendowment.org/pdf/2005-04-18/cohen_pub2.pdf>, and Cohen (n 121).

people whose background cannot be known fully or people who are open about their inclination about certain issues which can reasonably raise doubt about neutrality and/or impartiality. Above all, the arbitration laws of any country today provide well established safeguards to protect parties in case of a 'rogue' arbitrator. Arbitrators, on the other hand, are also adequately protected by laws against frivolous and baseless attack on their lack of impartiality or neutrality.

4.8. Closing

As much as foreign investors or disputants would like to understand how the Chinese businessperson thinks and their approach to international commercial arbitration, correspondingly, they would also want to know how outsiders view disputes involving them. Detailed strategising and planning are common these days as the stakes are high in arbitration, compounded by the adversarial nature of the proceedings. Arbitration is never a win-win process. It has always been a battle between people who came together to do business but ended up acrimoniously. For interesting reading, more than six decades ago, a commentator wrote: 'It is probable that the advantages of arbitration have been to some extent underestimated by lawyers and exaggerated by commercial men'.[199] So much has changed since the publication of that commentator's work, in fact it was published before the New York Convention came into being. It is certainly very fascinating to read old writings to understand the sentiments of scholars of that time about arbitration. But many today can certainly agree that arbitration is no longer a choice but a necessity in nearly all instances involving cross-border commercial dispute settlement, owing to the New York Convention. Arbitration is fuelled by international trade

199 G Ellenbogen, 'English Arbitration Practice', (1952) 17 *Law and Contemporary Problems* 656-78.

and transnational business is here to stay and China plays a prominent role in the global economy.

Chapter 5

Arbitration Case Studies

5.1. Arbitration case studies

As mentioned previously, Chinese parties doing arbitration abroad and subjected to foreign arbitration rules would either be represented by foreign or Chinese lawyers, sometimes a combination of both. In the case of representation by Chinese lawyers, it is likely to be from large Chinese firms with international staffing, affiliation or links. With the involvement of foreign lawyers familiar with the conduct of international arbitration, proceedings involving Chinese parties are not thought to be significantly different from those not involving Chinese parties. However, the similarity ends there as Chinese lawyers, although with international exposure, do sometimes still operate according to Chinese culture or perhaps due to pressure by Chinese clients; assuming the Chinese lawyers are of international standards and know what they are doing. Some differences are observed in the way Chinese parties/lawyers react or conduct themselves in international arbitration proceedings which can be attributed to cultural and language factors as well as possibly lack of experience. For example, in an arbitration proceedings, the Chinese lawyer representing the Chinese party in one of their written response to the tribunal began with 'Hello all' and when addressing a member of the tribunal orally, a 'Professor John Smith' as 'Hi, John'. Is this inappropriate conduct? Perhaps there is no offence committed, but it is inappropriate etiquette. A Chinese lawyer in the midst of a highly contentious arbitration proceeding wrote to the respondent's foreign lawyers starting with 'Your letter is well received' ending the letter with 'Thank you and best regards', perhaps unnecessarily too kind.

This chapter contains some interesting case studies on international arbitrations involving Chinese parties. The case studies are not intended as stereotyping the nature and characteristics of Chinese parties. Nevertheless, the cases are selected on the basis that they are observed to reflect some of their common trends and behaviour in international commercial arbitrations involving Chinese parties. In order to preserve the confidentiality of the parties, certain identifiable facts or information regarding the disputes have been altered.

5.1.1. Case No. 1 – Arbitrating it their way

Parties: Chinese investor and Asian mine concession holder

Contract: Cooperation agreement

Arbitration: Arbitration clause providing for SIAC arbitration in Singapore

Nature of dispute: Chinese investment in mining business

In the case under study, the lawyer for the Chinese investor is one Mr Zhang, a senior partner of a major law firm in China with at least 20 years of professional experience who graduated from a prestigious law school in China. The Chinese party is an investment entity which purportedly provided funding of about US$ 70 million to a South East Asian company which held a mining concession in an Asian country. It was the classic account, quite often encountered with China corporations, where it is questioned whether the corporations in making substantial investments or transacting in large deals with overseas parties have carried out their due diligence and, if so, whether the appraisal was comprehensive. It was alleged that after providing the investment, it was discovered the mineral deposits eventually determined at exploration stage would be vastly below the reserves originally represented to the

Chinese party and were now thought not to be economically mineable. It was not known if there was any form of feasibility study, bankable or non-bankable, for that matter. A dispute arose between the parties and the Chinese investor sought to have its investment returned and reserved its rights to claim for all losses incurred consequent to this cooperation. The allegations were denied by the Asian party and discussions as well as negotiations eventually broke down.

The cooperation agreement between the Asian and Chinese parties provided for arbitration in Singapore at SIAC with Chinese governing law and language of proceedings in English. The Chinese company wanted to commence arbitration proceedings to recover their investment but, given the Singapore arbitration component, Mr Zhang approached a firm of Singapore lawyers as part of the preparation prior to commence the arbitration proceedings. The following points and questions were raised by the Chinese parties and Mr Zhang:

1. Can the Singapore lawyers work on the basis of contingency fee basis with no professional fees to be paid?
2. Can foreign counsel be involved in arbitration proceedings seated in Singapore?
3. Mr Zhang would like to take the lead in the arbitration proceedings but he can only present his oral arguments in the Chinese language and be translated into English. Would this be an issue?
4. Whether his client can select a Chinese arbitrator and an arbitrator who is known to them.
5. Whether they can have the arbitration conducted in China instead of Singapore.

Insofar as fees were concerned, the Singapore lawyers declined this on the basis that it is prohibited by the local legal professional regulation. Above all, given the quantum of the claim, a substantial amount of work would be required in preparing and handling the arbitration proceedings, hence time costs need to be accounted for as well as expenses. Purely as an estimate, based on a claim of US$ 70 million and given the complexity of the matter, billable professional fees of US$ 500,000 were the minimum basing on the typical market rate but likely would be more. Mr Zhang was of the view that time cost billing but subject to fee capping was ideal in this case. The client would be expected to pay professional fees notwithstanding the contingency fee restriction given the amount of work all professionals were expected to put in. Although Chinese lawyers can expect to earn more from contingency fee arrangement (in percentage), the reality is some proceedings can take a very long time and compensation will be subject to successful enforcement of the arbitral award, when and if in favour of the Chinese party.

Next would be whether foreign counsel can be involved in arbitration proceedings seated in Singapore. As a pro-arbitration country, Singapore grants disputants the freedom to appoint professionals or any persons they elect to represent them before arbitration proceedings in the country, including foreign counsel. This flexibility is also key in that international disputes are likely to involve multi-jurisdictional and multi-disciplinary issues hence the justification for a combination of professionals. This feature of arbitration was thought to have incurred the displeasure of traditional legal practitioners in the earlier days of modern arbitration practice as they found themselves sometimes displaced in arbitration proceedings with non-lawyers who at times outperformed them. But as arbitration became extensively used for transnational dispute resolution, it became apparent that international arbitration proceedings are characterised by dynamic, multi-approach strategies of dispute settlement. Although influenced by western litigation cultures, arbitration is a methodology of its own today which is 'unselfish'.

The next point was whether Mr Zhang could take the lead in the arbitration proceedings by appearing and making his argument in Chinese instead of English. Evidently he wanted to be the primary counsel and to take control over the matter, not subordinate to the foreign lawyers. He might also be of the view that speaking in the Chinese language would better advance his client's position, especially when there would be a Chinese arbitrator on the tribunal.

The response to this point was not exactly positive. The arbitration would be governed by rules of international arbitration, so it was unlikely that the majority of the three-arbitrator tribunal would be entirely Chinese and there was the distinct possibility that a majority of the tribunal would not even be Chinese language proficient, unless the parties agreed so at the outset, which was unlikely. Another factor to consider was the number of documents in the Chinese and English languages. Assuming that the contract was dual language, it was not known what proportion of other communications between the disputants was in English, but there is a tendency for foreign parties to use the English language. In any case, the agreed language of the proceedings was English. For Mr Zhang to argue the case in Chinese meant a translator would need to be available whereas in the likely event that the other party appointed English speaking lawyers, obviously, they would be speaking directly to the ears of the tribunal, who could be presumed to be English conversant. Consequently, this might not be favourable to the case of the Chinese party, as there could be annoying disruptions to the smooth process of the proceedings. As the majority of the people involved in the arbitration were likely to be proficient in the English language, it would appear that the request to use the Chinese language in the proceedings was mostly for the benefit of Mr Zhang.

On the selection of arbitrator(s) according to the choice of the Chinese party, in the first instance, arbitration does provide for a party to nominate an arbitrator of their choice. However at least two broad criteria must be satisfied: firstly, the arbitrator nominated must pass the neutrality and impartiality tests and, secondly, the nomination and appointment must be in accordance with the agreement of the parties which otherwise will be subject to the procedures according to the rules of arbitration adopted by the parties. What constitute an arbitrator 'known' to the Chinese party requires more clarification. Whilst it is argued to be sensible that parties appoint arbitrators they can depend on and trust to adjudicate their disputes, arbitrators are not an agent of the parties nor can they be secretly fighting for a favourable outcome for the parties who have appointed them. It is particularly interesting to note the current trend, compared to than say, perhaps even as recent as half a decade ago: the tendency to make objections to the choice of arbitrator nominated by one party by the other is becoming less common. Objections made for the sake of doing so is nothing short of annoyance and pointless hostility, generally thought by the more experienced practitioners as an act of naïveté commonly deployed by newer practitioners. The exception that proves the rule of course is when there are grounds to question the impartiality and neutrality of the nominated arbitrator.

To shift the place of the arbitration from Singapore to China warranted serious discussion. In the absence of express provision that Singapore is merely the venue for the oral hearing of the arbitration proceedings, the agreed place of arbitration becomes the juridical seat of the arbitration. It cannot be changed unilaterally except with agreement of all parties. Any attempt to alter the jurisdiction of arbitration would be a serious breach of the arbitration agreement which would almost certainly render the arbitral award rendered consequent to such change in seat without the agreement of the other party to be in breach of the New York Convention. At the outset, the parties had agreed to a Singapore seated arbitration not China, meaning also an arbitral award made in Singapore. Some parties have reasoned that the place where the hearing is to take place should be near the location where most of the documents, evidence pertaining to the dispute or even the matter in dispute were physically located. However, when and if this becomes an issue, the tribunal can always determine if some part of the evidence taking or oral hearing can be held in a geographically convenient place but this is does not mean a change in the juridical seat.

Arbitration enshrines the doctrine of party autonomy but procedurally it is never designed to allow a party to unfairly dominate the entire process. Amidst the many strengths of arbitration and potency of arbitral awards in transnational commercial dispute settlement, there are sufficient safeguards in place to ensure fairness to all parties.

5.1.2. Case No. 2 – Arbitration that is not worthwhile

Parties: Chinese manufacturer and South East Asian buyer

Contract: Sales agreement

Arbitration: Arbitration clause providing for CIETAC arbitration

Nature of dispute: Payment default under sales agreement

The Chinese company Big Dragon entered into a sales agreement with Alpha, a company domiciled in a South East Asian country, for the sale of chemical process plant equipment. The contract value was in excess of US$ 30 million. As part of the contract, Big Dragon required Alpha's parent company to provide a corporate guarantee as surety for repayment under the agreement. It was not known if any due diligence was conducted prior to Big Dragon entering into the agreement.

The equipment was shipped to the project location by Big Dragon and not long after that Alpha defaulted on payment under the agreement. Big Dragon sought payment but failed and they conceded legal action needed to be taken against

Alpha. The English language sales agreement was governed by Chinese law and provide for CIETAC arbitration in China to be conducted in the English language. It is observed that a foreign party making the concession to arbitration in China will in turn request a compromise, in this instance, for proceedings in the English language. Big Dragon approached a Chinese law firm to represent them. However, given that the proceedings were to be conducted in English and the foreign parties and elements involved, a foreign law firm was approached with a view of forming a Chinese-foreign legal team to handle the matter.

Like most Chinese parties, Big Dragon wanted to pay on success basis. However, the foreign lawyers did not agree to such an arrangement. Eventually Big Dragon agreed to fee paying arrangement with the foreign lawyer subject to fee capping. Prior to formal commencement of the arbitration proceedings, Big Dragon wanted the foreign lawyers to conduct a search of the assets of Alpha and its parent company for the purpose of enforcement of arbitral awards should they win. The investigation revealed that Alpha had pending lawsuits against them for various unpaid debts. Furthermore, the principal officer of Alpha was personally subject to legal actions also for debts due. Investigation of the parent company of Alpha did not yield particularly good prospects either. The only property owned by the parent company of Alpha represents only a small fraction of the value of the contract and, even so, was mortgaged to banks. Golden Dragon was dissatisfied with the initial findings and insisted that Alpha and its parent company had assets elsewhere. The foreign lawyers advised Golden Dragon that the prospect of securing the other party's assets was bleak and there were severe limitations to uncovering any further assets of the other parties at that stage (before proceeding were even commenced). Big Dragon's Chinese lawyers informed their counterpart that 'no matter what, they will need to go through arbitration proceedings'. This did not appear unreasonable given that Big Dragon may well have been conducting this arbitration as a corporate debt recovery exercise.

Big Dragon then informed their foreign lawyers that in the course of the discussion, Alpha had advised them that they currently have various on-going projects and therefore accounts receivable. It was unfathomable how, before the formal arbitration proceedings were commenced, much less an arbitral award in favour of Golden Dragon, the lawyers could be expected to contact all the banks on the region to enquire about Alpha's banking relationships with them with a view of identifying their assets. Finally, Golden Dragon told the foreign lawyers that they had been told Alpha and its parent company had stock-in-trade and other assets that could be realised but this seemed to be a task perhaps not even police enforcement investigators would find easy to locate. This was but a desperate effort by Golden Dragon to 'find' some assets to justify bringing the arbitration.

Arbitration is not a panacea for every problem and dispute. Parties entering into contracts must fully understand the need for good due diligence as well as taking reasonable measures to secure their basic rights and interests at the outset, not waiting until disputes have arisen. However, among Chinese business people, it is not unheard of entering into contracts on the basis of trust and taking risk.

5.1.3. Case No. 3 – ICC arbitration it is

Parties: Chinese buyer and Oceania mining technology seller

Contract: Sales agreement

Arbitration: Arbitration clause providing for ICC arbitration (disputed)

Nature of dispute: Contractual default

It is interesting that, notwithstanding how widespread arbitration is around the world, ambiguous and poorly drafted arbitration agreements of all sorts are found in contracts. Worst are pathological arbitration clauses including very unorthodox ones, such as referring disputes to entities that do not get involved in the business of arbitration. Curious arbitration agreements are out there. This cannot be controlled as there are creative drafters who are the product of rising popularity of arbitration who, after attending some seminars or talks on arbitration, took off to start practicing arbitration with insufficient knowledge.[200] On the subject of interesting drafting of arbitration agreement, one must read the case of *Insigma Technology Co Ltd v Alstom Technology Ltd*[201] about 'hybrid' arbitration clause putting two leading arbitration centres together under one clause. The case under study is a slightly different scenario but with a disastrous outcome potentially waiting.

A Chinese buyer entered into an agreement with an Oceania company to purchase mining technology equipment. The Chinese party required the equipment to be delivered on the agreed date as per the agreement however the seller failed to do so. Consequently, the seller suddenly became uncontactable and non-responsive. After months of exhausting all avenues, the Chinese party finally decided to take action and a Chinese lawyer was appointed to represent them. The arbitration clause stated:

---

200 The distinguished arbitration practitioner Professor Pierre Lalive had these harsh words to say when he wrote that with great proportion of writing on arbitration consists of 'trite generalisations and rather mediocre repetitions or compilations' by people eager to enter the industry, young authors pursuing their doctorate degrees or 'underworked attorneys'. Pierre Lalive, 'Towards a Decline of International Arbitration?', (1999) 65 *Arbitration* 252.

201 [2009] 3 Singapore Law Reports 936; [2009] Singapore Court of Appeals 24.

> In the event of dispute it shall be referred to international chamber of commerce for arbitration in Singapore.

Lawyers for the Chinese buyer wanted send out its Notice of Arbitration however upon consultation with their client, it was alleged that they did not want to have anything to do with ICC Paris. They claimed that they have wanted a Singapore arbitration and an arbitration basing on international commerce in Singapore. They were about to nominate their arbitrator candidate but there is certainly a major uncertainty and ambiguity here, given 1) the potential claimant alleged that it was not an ICC Paris arbitration, 2) uncertainty as to how to commence the proceedings and 3) the potential respondent was not to be found. The view of the Chinese party was that the words 'international chamber of commerce' were generic. Their disagreement largely stemmed from the fact that they did not see the need pay ICC Paris to have them administer the arbitration. They then argued that should the original intention had been an ICC Paris arbitration, surely the clause would have reflected wordings from the prescribed ICC arbitration clause which states that disputes will be settled under the '[R]ules of Arbitration of the International Chamber of Commerce'.

There is very little point debating within oneself the intention of the arbitration clause formed previously but it is even worse to interpret it to your present desires unilaterally. The formation of arbitration clause was a matter of *consensus ad idem* between the parties and it takes both parties to jointly and mutually agree to vary the arbitration clause should they now refuse to take the dispute to the ICC. A single party cannot unilaterally push through his own agenda merely to suit his interest. Arbitration does not work on the basis that one party takes a look at the arbitration clause and decides to change it simply because he does not like it. Lawyers for the buyer then formed the idea of commencing an arbitration seated in Singapore as an ad hoc arbitration. Constitution of the tribunal would proceed accordingly if the seller remained non-responsive, therefore being an *ex parte* hearing. There was no need to involve the ICC since they would not know.

But there was no doubt that the line of thought above was risky and problematic should it be pushed through. Altering the arbitration from an ICC one to *ad hoc* could result in the award being rendered not in accordance with the agreement of the parties and giving rise to a violation under the New York Convention.[202] That was also the possibility that at the outset of the proceedings, the tribunal would finds itself not having jurisdiction to hear the matter thus putting an end to this ill-interpreted and wrongly applied arbitration agreement. The plain reading of the clause holds very little doubt that it is an ICC arbitration for there are no other 'international chamber of commerce' except the former. The correct course of action would be for the Chinese party to proceed with a proper ICC arbitration and, assuming the seller continues to be uncontactable, then the tribunal could determine to hold an *ex parte* hearing and proceed as accordingly. There is no point in obtaining an award that eventually cannot be enforced for it would have been a waste of resources and time.

5.1.4. Case No. 4 – A shipping case

Parties: South East Asian claimant and Chinese respondent

Contract: Sales agreement

Arbitration: Foreign seated ad hoc arbitration

Nature of dispute: Commodity dispute

202 Article V (1) (d): 'The composition of the arbitral authority or the arbitral procedure was not in accordance with the agreement of the parties, or, failing such agreement, was not in accordance with the law of the country where the arbitration took place.'

In the case under study, the Chinese party was the respondent in a shipping dispute with a foreign party. This was a relatively straightforward dispute which could have been resolved amicably by negotiation due to the low dispute value. The Chinese party was the buyer of a commodity product to be shipped to the Chinese port of destination. Pursuant to the agreement between the parties, it provided for downward price adjustment for quality deficiencies. Upon arrival at the port of destination, both parties had agreed that a neutral surveyor would take samples of the shipment for the purpose of ascertaining the quality of the commodity. In the event of dispute, the independent surveyor's report would be taken as final and binding on the parties.

Upon arrival, sample analysis had shown that the quality was substantially lower than agreed. The seller vehemently disputed the finding and proceeded to appoint a different firm of surveyors. The buyer protested that this was not in accordance with the agreement. Nevertheless, the seller's appointed surveyor was able to draw samples with the Chinese buyer duly disputing the methodology of the sample taken. The buyer maintained that the agreement between them was unambiguous that the first surveyor's report was final and binding. The second surveyor's report showed quality marginally lower than agreed.

The Chinese party acted in accordance with the agreement and applied the price downward adjustment relying on the 'official' surveyor's report. Based on the calculation applied, there was a surplus between the adjusted value and balance of payment due, therefore requiring the seller to make a refund to buyer. However, the buyer offered to cancel the differences and set-off from the entire outstanding payment, as a result settling the account. This offer was however rejected by the seller who insisted on enforcing the second report which effectively rendered the buyer's price adjustment inapplicable and only resulted in a marginal deduction under the adjusted pricing. The seller then asserted that the buyer still in fact owed them from the balance of payments. Failing a settlement following discussion, the seller commenced arbitration proceedings.

The tribunal comprised of three arbitrators of which were foreign (non-Chinese) arbitrators. This was a foreign seated ad hoc arbitration in accordance with the agreement of the parties. The Chinese party was represented by Chinese lawyers who were adequate in English if not even fairly proficient.

The entire proceedings were uneventful with lawyers for both claimant and respondent adhering to the deadlines and complying with the orders of the arbitral tribunal. It was a documents-only arbitration with each of the party arguing their case meaningfully and in accordance with most international arbitrations.

This case demonstrated the ability of a Chinese party to participate in international arbitration and comply with rules of international proceedings. Foreign arbitrators and counsels can also take comfort that Chinese parties can rise to the occasion when involved in an international dispute resolution process.

5.1.5. Case No. 5 – The globalising Chinese multinational

Parties: Chinese claimant and foreign respondent

Contract: Sales agreement

Arbitration: Foreign seated ad hoc arbitration

Nature of dispute: Product liability

The Chinese party, Digital Fuqi, is a successful privately held company in China involved in electronic parts manufacturing founded by Mr Wang, is a self-made entrepreneur. As part of its rapid expansion in China, Digital Fuqi purchased a custom designed process system from an overseas engineering specialist company, Lazer. Both parties entered into an agreement which included payment terms according to fabrication milestones of the seller. However, there was no payment retention imposed or performance guarantee required by Digital Fuqi from Lazer. Typically, however, Chinese companies would require such conditions to be in place but this was not the case in this agreement.

The system arrived on site and installations were carried out. The installed system failed to perform according to the specifications laid down by Digital Fuqi and despite numerous attempts to rectify the system, it still failed to commission successfully. Meanwhile Digital Fuqi had a strict production schedule that had to be adhered to due to their order book, so patience ran low. Lazer eventually discovered that the fault was due to software glitches attributed to their outsourced programmers which further infuriated Digital Fuqi and was also a loss of face to Mr Wang who now needed to explain the situation to his customers and board members.

Following various meetings between the two parties, Lazer eventually made an offer to compensate Digital Fuqi by way of a discount but required more time to rectify the fault. This was not accepted by Digital Fuqi because in essence they needed the system to run urgently due to their production deadlines. Furthermore, the goodwill discount was only a fraction of potential liquidated damages expected from Digital Fuqi's customers due to the delay. It was construed that Lazer was shirking its responsibility towards the whole matter. In addition to a contractual dispute, Lazer had now provoked the ire of Mr Wang and his company which further aggravated the situation.

Digital Fuqi was introduced to a foreign law firm to represent them in commencing an arbitration action against Lazer. The sales agreement provided for a foreign seated ad hoc arbitration. Despite being structured as a large corporation with formal management, Mr Wang ultimately made all the final decisions on important matters pertaining to the company including the arbitration matter. Assisting

Mr Wang with the case was Digital Fuqi's senior manager, Ms Tang, who was legally trained and used to work as a Chinese lawyer. She proved to be difficult to work with, quite likely because she considered herself a capable lawyer with vast experience in handling complex domestic legal matters including previously being involved in a foreign arbitration case before joining Digital Fuqi.

In the typical *modus operandi* of foreign lawyers, the client's approval was sought with regard to draft letters, notice of arbitration, written submissions and other documents as well as their instructions on all matters pertaining to the arbitration proceedings. Instead of being cooperative, Ms Tang would tell the foreign lawyers point blank that they should take charge not asking Digital Fuqi for every approval. The foreign lawyers patiently explained that as counsel, it was imperative to take instruction from clients and not the role of lawyers to decide for their clients. Ms Tang typically took days or sometimes weeks to reply as, partly, she needed to consult Mr Wang who had a busy schedule. When she did reply to the lawyers, instructions usually clearly suggest that they came from Mr Wang, the decision maker. However, Ms Tang would also take potshots at the lawyers by suggesting they do a better job than asking her for instructions. Sometimes, the communication could get rather unpleasant, with Ms Tang telling the lawyers 'you are paid to do the work, you should know what to do, so do not ask me'.

Unsurprisingly, such a challenging working relationship caused concern with the lawyers. Fortuitously, Mr Wang came to know about the lawyers' predicament. After clarifying that Ms Tang was a subordinate and affirming that all decisions lie with him, from that time onwards, Ms Tang's behaviour towards the lawyers took a complete reversal. Communication between Digital Fuqi and the foreign lawyers became much smoother and tended to be productive. Now everyone could focus on the arbitration proceedings instead of getting involved in bickering. Throughout the arbitration process, Mr Wang was supportive and open to all the suggestions or recommendations from the lawyers. The foreign lawyers of course had Chinese language proficient personnel who were able to communicate meaningfully with Digital Fuqi.

Some interesting observations can be seen from this case regarding the attitude of Chinese people in international arbitration. Firstly, there was still a cultural element at play whereby Digital Fuqi's senior manager applied a hierarchical approach by treating the lawyers according to a 'master-servant' relationship. Whilst sometimes this may not be intentional, it is inevitable that the attitude of 'remember who the paymaster is' mindset comes into play, a remnant of perhaps the old Chinese cultural programming and memory of the ancient Mandarin system that still stays with Chinese people. Such attitude can still be found even among overseas Chinese today whether between relatives or in business and work settings. Secondly, the relationship between the senior and subordinate, also takes precedence in that Mr Wang's 'word is decree' had to be respected by Ms Tang.

Finally, changing attitudes of modern Chinese in business can be seen in the trust developed between Mr Wang and the foreign lawyers which led to Mr Wang entrusting the dispute into their able hands. But it is also important that the communication channel must also be unencumbered as can be seen from the difficulty in discussion in the beginning, despite not having language barriers. Nevertheless, Mr Wang was receptive to international practices as he had been adequately exposed to international business through his experience from past and present dealings. Such is the changing faces of the Chinese businessperson in today's globalising economy.

5.2. Summary

The subject of international arbitration has been widely written about, researched upon and published. An academic once wrote that '[t]he subject on which I am to speak is by no means new. For that reason I suppose it ought to be regarded as very uninteresting';[203] except that this statement was made almost one hundred years ago. The importance of international commercial arbitration cannot be stressed enough, having been conclusively and widely acknowledged by so many, in the past and present. In a work written nearly a century ago, we have gained insight into what arbitration meant to those before us and now long departed, yet some of the message is still relevant and applies to us today, refreshingly reminding us why arbitration is here to stay. In referring to the advantages of arbitration, it was said:

> it avoids irritation, as there is no publicity, and no such staging of a trial as in an open court ... But it must not be supposed that arbitration is necessarily cheaper than law suits; ... although the saving of time and friendship ... are worth much.[204]

Once again, using the philosophical blind men and elephant analogy, perspectives and experiences differ from one person to the other. He who touched the tusk of the elephant viewed it differently compared to the person who touched the leg or tail of the same animal. Given the multitude of cases out there and every professional handling it differently, experiences can almost certainly be expected to be different. Some experiences may be pleasant but some could be unsurprisingly unpleasant. The case studies above highlight some of the features and experiences in relation

203 John Bassett Moore, 'International Arbitration', (1917) 7 *Proceedings of the Academy of Political Science in the City of New York* 21.

204 Samuel Rosenbaum & Herbert Harley, 'Commercial Arbitration in England', (1917) 3 *American Bar Association Journal* 26-27.

to real arbitrations involving real Chinese parties. To a certain extent, they are empirical but they also do not seek to stereotype the Chinese attitudes and perspectives rigidly or according to one mould. The 'spirit' of arbitration is one which resonates naturally with the Chinese; a closed-door confidential commercial dispute settlement method that can avoid publicity thus losing of face, a flexible process that often incorporates tolerant procedures in proceedings where court judges will have a hard time emulating arbitrators. But when it comes to the final arbitral award, it is a puissant, robust and decisive decision that strikes with deadly effectiveness at what it is supposed to; qualities that reminded us of the Chinese martial arts.

Chapter 6

Post Arbitration and Enforcing Awards

6.1. Introduction

After the conclusion of arbitration proceedings and the rendering of the awards, often little is known about the outcome of the arbitral awards, not even by arbitral institutions (in the case of administered arbitrations). The parties do not keep in touch with arbitral tribunals or arbitral institutions at the conclusion of the arbitration proceedings. If a correction or additional award is required, this will be fulfilled in accordance with the applicable rules of arbitration or laws governing the arbitration, but usually this would be resolved rather quickly. In terms of enforcement of awards overseas, with the exception of challenges to the enforcement and recognition of arbitral awards before national courts, it is unlikely that the statistics of successful enforcements will ever be known publicly.

What we certainly know is Singapore and Hong Kong are two of the most popular Asian destinations for Chinese investors and corporations as well as those from many other countries in the world, to incorporate their overseas entities. They also happen to be jurisdictions with very sound legal systems and judiciaries with exceptional integrity. In addition, both Singapore and Hong Kong are also pro-arbitration venues. As such, arbitral awards that conform to the New York Convention are likely to be sought enforcement in Singapore or Hong Kong in the first instance by winning parties. Whilst the grounds for challenging the enforcement of arbitration awards are strictly limited and restricted to the several specific grounds, when all things fail, a party may try to challenge on the grounds of public policy[205] under the New York Convention, although this is usually a futile exercise, an 'excuse' used when all arguments fail. Generally, pro-arbitration judiciaries do not easily concede public policy as a ground for refusal of enforcement of arbitral awards.

Foreign parties do regularly agree to arbitrate in China. It is observed that some medium-sized foreign enterprises, which may be new players making a foray into the Chinese market, have often agreed to China seated arbitration. When the Chinese parties obtained awards in their favour and attempted to enforce the awards in the home country of the foreign parties, it is not unheard of that they were later discovered to have been wound up or liquidated.

On the other side of the coin, foreign parties with arbitral awards rendered in their favour against Chinese parties will naturally be anxious to know they are able to enforce the awards in China. Are the Chinese courts competent and impartial when it comes to foreign and domestic parties? Is there discrimination against foreign parties seeking enforcement in China? These are no doubts some of the common questions. While there may be are reasonable concerns, it is not surprising for one to be suspicious of another foreign country's courts especially one which is not as developed as those in the UK, USA or major European countries. Not unlike others, Chinese parties with arbitral awards in their favour are equally concerned about the prospects in getting anything out of the awards. They are however less concerned about the foreign jurisdictions in which they will be seeking enforcement chiefly because they usually prudent to choose established seats (for example, Singapore, Hong Kong, London or Paris) but their real concern is if the losing, foreign parties have any assets that

---

205 Described as a 'very unruly horse, and when once you get astride it you never know where it will carry you. It may lead you from the sound law'. Burrough J in *Richardson v Mellish* (1824) 2 Bingham 229; 130 England Reports 294.

they can enforce against. Disputants sometimes get upset if they cannot be assured of the prospects of securing assets from enforcement should they go to arbitration and presumably win. Such is the risk of doing business and no dispute resolution mechanism can guarantee a perfect outcome.

6.2. Trend of foreign arbitral award enforcements in China

The question of enforcement of arbitral awards in China matters to both Chinese and foreign parties whether or not it is enforcing a foreign or Chinese award in China. If a foreign party has an award in its favour against a Chinese party, it is certain that the former will seek enforcement in China against the latter. In the reverse, if a Chinese party has an award in its favour against a WFOE, in the first instance enforcement will be sought in China. It is reasonable to expect that the WFOE would have assets in China and in theory, due to capital control, it is less likely that company funds could be repatriated too swiftly, too easily. No one likes to have arbitration awards successfully enforced against them. Therefore, with regard to this heading, any foreign or Chinese parties should be keen to know the current *status quo* regarding enforcement of arbitral awards in China.

In 1987 China acceded to the New York Convention.[206] Before China acceded to the New York Convention, it was said that Chinese 'corporations and enterprises' will 'execute foreign arbitral awards so long as they are fair and not in violation of the Chinese laws and policies'.[207] It is assumed from the plain reading of this article that Chinese corporations and enterprises will voluntarily obey the arbitral award and have it enforced against them as long as the award does not

206 See UNCITRAL website <www.uncitral.org/uncitral/en/uncitral_texts/arbitration/NYConvention_status.html>.

207 Houzhi (n 122).

violate Chinese laws and public policy. Altruistic behaviour of Chinese entities back then was certainly commendable.

In a 2008 speech made by the then Vice President (equivalent to Deputy Chief Justice) of the Supreme People's Court of China, Wang Exiang, from the beginning of 2000 till the end of 2007 a total of 12 foreign arbitral awards were refused enforcement by the SPC.[208] Grounds for the refusal of enforcement for the12 foreign awards were given as follows: four for reasons of the expiration of statute of limitations for application to enforce, five for reasons that the parties did not reach an arbitral agreement or invalid arbitration clauses, one due to the reason that the party which the award was enforced against had no assets in China, and the remaining refusal was for on the grounds that the party against which enforcement was sought had not received notice for the appointment of arbitrators or of the arbitral procedures.[209] Based on this report, foreign parties seeking to enforce foreign arbitral awards in China can take comfort in the fact that they can expect to be treated fairly. In addition, given the elucidated grounds for refusal, this certainly alleviates any concerns about lack of the transparency when seeking enforcement against losing Chinese parties by foreign parties.

More recently, Judge Song Jianli from the SPC spoke at Columbia Law School in 2013.[210] The substance of Judge Song's presentation was particularly significant not only because

---

208 Renmin University of China (RUC) International Law, Symposium Commemorating the 50th Anniversary of the New York Convention, 6 June 2008 <www.rucil.com.cn/article/default.asp?id=798>.

209 See also Henry Chen & B Ted Howes, 'Alternative Dispute Resolution: The Enforcement of Foreign Arbitration Awards in China', 2 (No 6) *Bloomberg Law Reports - Asia Pacific* 4, for English translation of the RUC International Law Symposiums speech.

210 'Supreme People's Court of China judge speaks on arbitral awards', Columbia Law School 19 Feb 2013 <www.law.columbia.edu/media_inquiries/news_events/2013/february2013/chinese-arbitral-awards>.

he was considered a rising star[211] in the Chinese judiciary who was well exposed to international arbitration but his presentation came at an opportune time in the 'golden era' of international commercial arbitration when the world was keenly looking to China for many answers regarding the conduct of arbitration in that country. Judge Song said that 'The Chinese court's efficient enforcement of foreign arbitral awards will continue into the future'[212] and that efforts to ensure effectiveness of the enforcement of foreign arbitral awards began in 2000 when the SPC was to be informed of all lower courts' refusal of enforcement. According to Judge Song, consequently the SPC had upheld only 24 out of 64 refusals reported to them. He also commented specifically on 'public policy' being one of the most common grounds used to resist enforcement which he termed as an 'escape clause'[213] which the Chinese courts tend to construe narrowly with only one award refused enforcement on grounds of public policy since 2000.

The main 'Chinese takeaway' from the above is that there is no evidence of hostility towards winning foreign parties seeking enforcement of foreign arbitral awards in China against Chinese parties. From the author's own experience, Chinese parties entering into international contracts with foreign parties have almost never demanded China seated arbitration in their contracts at the outset. They do compromise on neutral venues, most commonly Singapore and Hong Kong which are close to China. Although the decision on the choice of venue and rules of international arbitration can be attributed to the lawyers advising Chinese parties at the initial contract drafting stage, Chinese parties recognise the importance of selecting reputable jurisdictions

211 Reflecting the paradigm of the new Chinese leaders: educated in China before obtaining his postgraduate qualification overseas in the UK, then doing his academic research overseas in the UK and USA. See profile at <law.wustl.edu/m/content.aspx?id=4878>.

212 See 'SPC judge speaks' (n 212).

213 *Ibid.*

because they trust the systems in those reliable territories and can be assured of fair arbitral awards made even if the outcome was not in favour of them.

6.3. Enforcement behaviours

As already discussed in an earlier chapter, it is common for Chinese clients to think that lawyers should share part of their dispute risk and expect the lawyers to work on their cases with no fees upfront but contingent on successful recovery of funds. This seemed unethical but it is dictated by market forces, supply and demand. It worked well and will not be expected to change anytime soon. It is a tried and tested model as well as a method also prevalent in other countries including the USA. Chinese parties can get carried away with such a mindset when they attempt to enforce awards overseas. They would try their luck with foreign lawyers but are unlikely to get too far with their 'indecent' proposal.

Chinese counsel are almost certain to be paid by the Chinese parties under a contingency fee arrangement. It seems inescapable for them because if it is a case involving existing clients, their requests would have to be fulfilled for the sake of past or existing relationship. If it is a new client, given that a majority of lawyers operate on success fee basis, it is likely to be a situation of 'if you can't fight them, join them'. Therefore, it becomes crucial for the Chinese lawyer post arbitration to carry out the enforcement successfully as he/she would essentially get paid at this stage only if it is successful; and 'successful' means funds actually received. According to a Chinese lawyer:

> I worked on a case for more than two years and won. But after searching for the losing party's assets to no avail, we had to give up. I was only paid a very small, paltry expense money at the beginning. Sometimes we have to take on cases with no money paid by client.

> No, client won't pay me any goodwill fee as it can be imagined they got nothing from this case as well.

Meanwhile according to a senior Chinese lawyer who is consistently referred to by his peers as among the best in his specialisation:

> My client would pay me, say, RMB 30,000 to cover expenses. On average, each of my case would take a couple of years. Even if we lose the case, at least I get to cover some expenses including salary for my lawyers. Of course, I must add that clients would typically only advance such a generous 'expenses money' to established lawyers. It is expected that even upon successful enforcement and recovery of funds, client will renegotiate the contingency fee citing poor business or lack of money. It is expected that discounts be given or else it would be bad for the future relationship.

Often, Chinese counsel would unwillingly have 'vested interests' in the enforcement of arbitral awards. The question then becomes how enforcement of arbitral awards can be carried out overseas when the involvement of foreign lawyers becomes necessary. It has been seen how some new entrants who were keen to take on work are given seemingly impossible missions by their clients. Some of these awards are of low value and even if the foreign lawyers in the place where the enforcement is sought could and would agree to a success fee basis, the low value of the awards simply do not justify their involvement. That is if there are realisable assets belonging to the parties to which the arbitral awards are to be enforced against in the first place.

In one example, a Chinese lawyer contacted a Singapore law firm to assist with the enforcement of a China seated arbitral award. It was an *ex parte* arbitration as the Singapore respondent did not respond to the notice of arbitration nor participated in the proceedings. The arbitral award was unsurprisingly in favour of the Chinese claimant. As expected, the Chinese lawyer told the Singapore lawyers that the client has offered to pay a certain percentage basing on the successful recovery of monies under the arbitral award. Singapore lawyers are prohibited from accepting work on this basis; furthermore, there will be time costs and reimbursements associated with the enforcement process. Whilst the 'bargaining' process took place, the Singapore lawyers conducted a simple corporate search on the Singapore entity against which the enforcement was to be sought. It was discovered that the Singapore entity had been wound up even before the arbitral award was rendered. The Singapore lawyers promptly conveyed this finding to the Chinese parties and saved all the agony of bargaining over the arrangement of the matter.

In summary, enforcement is essentially a 'pay day' moment for the Chinese party and, quite commonly, the Chinese lawyers. In the agricultural parlance of a culture synonymous with the ancient Chinese, for the Chinese lawyers it is harvesting time with the hope that the yield is good.

6.4. Case study – To challenge or not to challenge?

Glorious Style, a multinational Chinese company with global offices, was embroiled in a professional fee payment dispute with Profits Now, a local consultancy firm located in South Asia. Several years into the consultancy arrangement, payment for services rendered by Profits Now was not met by Glorious Style, leading to disputes. The claimant in this case was Profits Now and the dispute was to be referred to arbitration in accordance with the rules of an international arbitration centre, seated in South East Asia. The Chinese party's representation was by a set of Chinese-foreign law firms whereas Profits Now was largely self-represented with the exception of a local counsel retained to advise and assist with matters involving legal processes.

The arbitral proceedings were not a particularly eventful, with the Chinese party applying to the court at the seat of the arbitration for injunction but this was unsuccessful and did not seem to intimidate the self-represented claimant.

The arbitration went ahead and in a rather spectacular fashion was found in favour of the claimant Profits Now, with a sum over US$ 1 million awarded. Like most losing parties, Glorious Style was not satisfied with the outcome however nothing could be done given that there is no appeal in arbitration *per se*. However, Glorious Style commenced post arbitral award investigations and made some allegations, among others that Profits Now had produced certain documents during the arbitral proceedings which Glorious Style now claimed to be questionable. Primarily, Glorious Style was hoping to succeed chiefly by invoking Article V (1) (e) of the New York Convention on grounds that the award be suspended by a competent authority of the country in which the award was made, so that enforcement could effectively be resisted elsewhere in other Convention states, including in China.

Without going into a detailed analysis of the New York Convention, it was not immediately clear if the allegation made by Glorious Style above would engage the relevant provisions under the Convention. The Chinese party should have mounted a challenge on the legitimacy of the said documents during the proceedings when their rights would have been materially or substantially harmed. To succeed on grounds of public policy would be slim.[214] The lawyers, as can be imagined, could not promise Glorious Style the chances of succeeding as would no credible professionals.

214 See Chen & Howes (n 211): comments by the Vice President of the SPC that public policy should be used with caution and that the SPC did not invoke public policy to vacate any arbitral award yet (that is, between 2000 and 2008).

Basically, the Chinese party had gone through quite an eventful experience during the entire arbitration. Having paid substantial fees to the earlier set of lawyers for the arbitration proceedings which failed, Glorious Style began to calculate as to the next steps, as they rightfully should have. If they engaged another firm of lawyers to fight the award, they would like to know their chances of winning; to spend US$ 100,000 to US$ 200,000 on legal fees to vacate the award would not seem unreasonable but if unsuccessful this would add to their burgeoning financial exposure. Glorious Style eventually chose not to do anything. It was not known if they voluntarily paid in accordance with the arbitral award. It would not have been wise on their part to await enforcement proceedings to be carried out against them; the amount awarded paled in comparison to the huge annual turnover of Glorious Style.

6.5. An overview of the laws relating to enforcement

The Chinese perspective on arbitration applies both ways, to arbitrations inside and outside of China. It is essential for foreign parties to have a basic understanding of how the enforcement process differs in a comparative analysis. As mentioned earlier, China acceded to the New York Convention in 1987. The New York Convention does not apply to arbitral awards made within China. The CAL specifies the steps for enforcement under articles 62 to 64 whereby a party may apply to the court for enforcement in accordance with the applicable provisions of China's Civil Procedure Law (CPL).[215] There are separate arbitral enforcement regimes for domestic awards, under article 237 of the CPL, and for foreign related companies under article 274 of the CPL. Juxtaposing the New York Convention with the CPL, some of the provisions under the CPL mirror those of the Convention.

215 See Appendix 3.

For a comparison of the New York Convention and the CPL, see Figure 2 on page 203.

In addition to the CPL, enforcement of New York Convention arbitral awards in China is in accordance with the SPC's Circular.[216] Article 4 of the SPC's Circular refers to conditions set out under articles V (1) and (2) of the New York Convention.

With a 'pro-arbitration' court,[217] China seated arbitral awards can be enforced under the New York Convention like foreign awards made in other contracting states in accordance with the New York Convention. As mentioned previously, Singapore is a popular arbitration venue for Chinese parties. In Singapore, nothing is heard of discrimination against Chinese arbitral awards or parties. In fact, a provision within the Singapore Arbitration Act paves the way for the enforcement of non-New York Convention awards.[218]

---

216 See Appendix 4.

217 The Chief Justice of Singapore, Sundaresh Menon, in a speech referring to Singapore's 'heavily pro-arbitration' courts, has said it is a 'near-Herculean' task when seeking the courts to set aside or refuse enforcement of an award. There is 'clear judicial support' in Singapore to promote arbitration which is consistent with the spirit of the UNCITRAL Model Law and the New York Convention, which Singapore has adopted. However, Menon CJ also qualified, rightfully so, that 'minimal curial intervention does not mean unquestioning and undiscerning deference to the decisions of arbitrators'. Sundaresh Menon, 'Judicial Attitudes towards Arbitration and Mediation in Singapore', Asean Law Association Malaysia (ALA) & Kuala Lumpur Regional Centre for Arbitration (KLRCA) Talk & Dinner 2013, Kuala Lumpur, Malaysia, 25 Oct 2013 <www.supremecourt.gov.sg/docs/default-source/default-document-library/media-room/judicial-attitudes-to-arbitration-and-mediation-in-singapore.pdf>.

218 Cap. 10, 2002 rev ed at s 46(3). Singapore wanted to make the city-state an international arbitration hub and attract international parties. '[T]his amendment ... make[s] it possible for foreign awards that cannot currently be enforced in Singapore to be enforced here. There will not be an automatic right to enforcement, as the leave of our High Court will be required.' Senior Minister of State for Law, Associate Professor Ho Peng Kee. See *Singapore Parliamentary Reports* 10th Parliament 1st session, Vol 76 No 13 (24 Apr 2003) cols 2149-51.

As for Hong Kong SAR, the mutual enforcement of arbitral awards between China and Hong Kong SAR is organised according to 'Arrangement of the Supreme People's Court on Reciprocal Enforcement of Arbitration Awards between the Mainland and the Hong Kong Special Administrative Region'.[219] Enforcement of arbitral awards in Hong Kong is covered under sections 84 and 87 of the Hong Kong Arbitration Ordinance.[220] There is no impediment to enforce ad hoc arbitral awards made in Hong Kong SAR or foreign arbitral institutions in Mainland China, according to the SPC's 'Notice of Relevant Issues on the Enforcement of Hong Kong Arbitral Awards in the Mainland' dated 30 December 2009.[221]

6.6. A case overheard in the coffee shop

A Chinese manufacturer and a Singapore company buyer entered into a contract for the purchase of goods. The Singapore party paid a small deposit but when the goods were ready to be shipped with balance of payment due, nothing was heard back from the buyer. Despite numerous attempts, the Singapore party could not be reached nor found. The Chinese manufacturer then commenced arbitration against the buyer. The arbitration clause provided for China seated arbitration in accordance with the rules of a Chinese arbitration commission and the contract was governed by Chinese law. The arbitration clause also required the dispute to be arbitrated by a tribunal of three arbitrators of which one would be a foreign arbitrator. In addition, the language of the proceedings would be English. As the Singapore party did not respond to the Chinese party's notice of arbitration, the

219 See Appendix 11: Arrangement Concerning Mutual Enforcement of Arbitral Awards between the Mainland and the Hong Kong Special Administrative Region, signed in Shenzhen on 2 June 1999.

220 Cap. 609.

221 See Appendix 12.

proceedings went ahead in their absence, *ex parte*. Firstly, an all Chinese national arbitral tribunal was constituted. Since the foreign party did not respond to the notice of arbitration and did not participate in the process of selecting the arbitrator, it was construed that the Singapore party had forfeited their rights to the proceedings. Furthermore, given the amount in dispute was low, the involvement of a non-Chinese arbitrator was thought unnecessary due to cost implications. Chinese arbitrators are typically paid very low fees and they take up arbitration cases due to the honour and prestige rather than financial motives.[222]

Secondly, since the tribunal was composed of all Chinese arbitrators and the Singapore party by its conduct had chosen not to participate in the proceedings, there was no need for the proceedings to be conducted in English. For practical reasons why incur costs and go through complications to translate the proceedings when everyone involved in the proceedings could speak Chinese anyway?

All the above arguments may appear rationally thought out except that the arbitration agreement was what it was; the contract speaks for itself. The composition of the arbitral tribunal and arbitral procedure were not in accordance with the agreement of the parties.

The arbitration proceedings concluded with the award eventually rendered in favour of the Chinese party, unsurprisingly. The story ended with the Chinese party said to be seeking to enforce the award in Singapore. What might be

---

222 Purely for general reference, according to BAC's arbitrator fees online calculator <http://arbitrator.bjac.org.cn/en/Arbitration/Fees.html>, for a dispute of US $1 million the 'arbitration fees' comprising of 'acceptance and handling fees' amount to just about RMB 35,000 or slightly over US$ 5,000. It is not clear if the fee is for a tribunal of a sole arbitrator or otherwise, and whether different fees scale would apply for arbitration with foreign elements. In comparison, an ICC dispute with the same amount would work out to about US$ 61,000 <www.iccwbo.org/products-and-services/arbitration-and-adr/arbitration/cost-and-payment/cost-calculator/>.

outcome? If the Singapore party now suddenly appeared and mounted its challenge, would they succeed? Have any of the provisions under the New York Convention been breached?

6.7. Closing summary

In reality, the risks of failing to finally obtain what is in an arbitral award through enforcement processes are clear and present risks in international commercial arbitration. Such uncertainties are no respecter of the nationalities of the parties. As discussed previously, Chinese parties would typically prefer to explore amicable settlement options before resorting to commencing arbitration. Enforcement will always be a primary concern. But, when push comes to shove, Chinese parties are not pushovers. They will not want to lose face either. Initiating legal action abroad where fees have to be paid is always a factor of paramount consideration to Chinese parties who are still accustomed to sharing risks with lawyers through contingency fee arrangements. But despite the imperfection of arbitration, it is still the best method for cross-border dispute resolution.

Chapter 7

Closing – The Beginning

7.1. Introduction – The arbitration world as it is

Statistics and data have shown that, for many years, international commercial arbitration institutions and centres all over the world have been experiencing a meteoric rise. This is evident from the volume and value of cases coming through their doors. The rise in the use of international arbitration as a method for cross-border commercial dispute settlement also corresponds with the increase in international trade volume as well as economic globalisation at least in the last two decades or so. Even the Permanent Court of Arbitration (PCA) at The Hague which is not a commercial arbitration centre in the typical sense but a 'passive' historical arbitral organisation, has not been 'spared' the boom in arbitration. Professor Philippe Sands mentioned that he first came across the PCA in 1980 as a young person during a lecture by his professor who mentioned the PCA as historical and 'not much these days', likely referring to the lack of cases and popularity.[223] In 2005, the registry of the PCA reported it had 'reached an all-time high' in terms of caseload.[224] Since then, the amount of cases at the PCA has skyrocketed.[225] Arbitration centres and institutions have been established by way of government support or encouraged initiatives or

223 'Remarks of Professor Philippe Sands QC, University College London and Matrix Chambers, on the occasion of a Celebration of the Centenary of the PCA The Hague, 18 October 2007' <https://pca-cpa.org/wp-content/uploads/sites/175/2016/01/Reflections-on-the-Current-Relevance-of-the-PCA-Presentation-by-Professor-Philippe-Sands-QC.pdf>.

224 Permanent Court of Arbitration 105th Annual Report, 2005 at 5 para 1, see <https://pca-cpa.org>.

225 See Permanent Court of Arbitration 115th Annual Report, 2015 at 13, <pca-cpa.org/wp-content/uploads/sites/175/2016/10/PCA-annual-report-2015.pdf>.

through purely private efforts by likeminded professionals. Astute governments all around the world have been quick to recognise that arbitration is a beneficial economic contributor such as benefiting professional services sector, academia, banking and tourism industries. Governments can provide neutral, convenient and conducive venue for the conduct of international arbitration proceedings, the use of its national laws (whether as contractual governing law and/or arbitration law) and undivided backing from its local courts (if necessary and required by the parties) in support of arbitration proceedings as well as at the enforcement stage.

Yet, we should not forget the original purpose of arbitration and what it was developed for. It was not designed to benefit a select few or some but it is a machinery and vehicle for people to resolve their disputes according to their choice but usually dictated by circumstances. Users of arbitration can never say that they have been coerced into using arbitration. Obviously if the arbitration agreement was proven 'wrong' or invalid, then there would be no reason to go to arbitration; there are laws to protect the weak. But the freedom to resolve one's private disputes should not be curtailed by ever increasing interferences and interventions by so-called activists and proponents said to represent the masses and acting in their best interest. To fix something which needs fixing is right but otherwise be careful not to dismantle something that works well and instead cause it to fail. A leading international arbitration practitioner, Toby Landau, described how there is an urge to make 'more rules and law' and he wittily called it 'legislitis' being a 'compulsion to make rules and protocols and laws if it moves codify it but that is not an answer'.[226] But before anyone starts telling the arbitration world to change, the following words of wisdom from a distinguished international arbitration expert Serge Lazareff should be borne

226 'The day before tomorrow: Future developments in international arbitration', Transcript of the 2009 International Arbitration Lecture by Toby Landau, QC <www.claytonutz.com/ialecture/content/previous/2009/speech_2009>.

in mind: *L'arbitrage a longtemps été un art; il est actuellement un mélange d'art et de science; il risque de devenir un exercice bureaucratique.*[227]

The development of international arbitration and the success of any initiatives lie with the users (the disputants), providers (arbitral institutions), executors (arbitrators, who play a crucial role in ad hoc arbitrations given the non-involvement of arbitral bodies) and actors (lawyers and professional service providers). The providers require the actors and users to make it work; without users of their arbitration services, nothing could happen. Yet at the same time, actors such as lawyers are involved in the promotion of the providers by way of incorporating in their contracts provisions for the use of arbitration institutions and their rules. In doing so, the many actors who also aspire to or are part of the executor 'class' are hoping to get their arbitrator career advanced by providers. Providers contribute to the advancement of the career of executors but the actors and disputants ultimately play more significant roles because they can nominate or recommend the appointment of arbitrator of their preference and choice. The interchangeable roles between actors and executors[228] at times raises concerns and is a widely debated subject today. The primary argument in support of this is that lawyers or legal experts are better positioned to handle complex legal

227 'Arbitration has long been an art; in fact it is a mixture of art and science; but it risks becoming a bureaucratic exercise.' Quoted by Michael E Schneider, 'The Essential Guidelines for the Preparation of Guidelines, Directives, Notes, Protocols and other Methods Intended to Help International Arbitration Practitioners to Avoid the Need for Independent Thinking and to Promote the Transformation of Errors into "Best Practices"', in Laurent Lévy & Yves Derain (eds), *Liber Amicorum en l'honneur de Serge Lazareff* (Editions A. Pedone 2011) 563.

228 Pia Eberhardt, Cecilia Olivet, Tyler Amos & Nick Buxton, 'Profiting from injustice: How law firms, arbitrators and financiers are fuelling an investment arbitration boom', (2012) Corporate Europe Observatory and The Transnational Institute <https://corporateeurope.org/international-trade/2012/11/profiting-injustice>. Also Emmanuel Gaillard, 'Sociology of International Arbitration', (2015) 31 *Arbitration International* 1-17.

issues now inherent in arbitrations, but the argument against it, *inter alia*, is how can professional pleaders at the same time be active judges of their own vocation. The idea of 'changing hats' may not always go well with some schools of thought. The recent trend is that some people are distancing themselves from the dual roles of counsel and arbitrator, to act only as a professional arbitrator. There is nothing wrong with dual vocations as counsel and arbitrator but from a practical standpoint it may be called into question whether one would have the time commitment and right mindset for it. Unfortunately, it is observed that some of those from among the rank of lawyers can be picky about cases when approached for potential nomination as arbitrators; they would ideally prefer large disputes so that they can expect to charge more in terms of arbitrator fees or some would only be keen in cases where they can work alongside 'seasoned' co-arbitrators under major arbitration rules. Acting as an arbitrator is less likely to be perceived by some as an honourable appointment due to the position of trust placed on them by the disputants, perhaps because there is more lucrative work awaiting them in their capacity as lawyers or professionals.

Users would be concerned about the choice of providers, executors and actors in terms of their credibility, cost, independence and flexibility. Fortunately for the providers, users do not often get to exercise their rights of arbitration centres (in the case of administered arbitrations) because it is the actors (that is the lawyers) that usually decide for the users in the contracts. Sometimes it is the users that were apathetic about the formulation of arbitration clause perhaps simply because they are less interested in disputes compared to the commercial terms in their contracts. Thus, there is also a cooperation between the providers and actors in that the actors get into the realm of the former to act as arbitrators.

Rightfully or ineptly, providers also require actors to make them succeed. Prominent actors can steer users to providers; also, providers do want prominent actors to come on board as advisory, committee or council members as endorsement. When a provider becomes popular and can attract high profiles cases, more actors want to work with them, evidently with the hope that this will increase their visibility in terms of potential appointment as arbitrators through the providers. This may unfortunately lead to an 'incestuous' relationship as commonly criticised in the arbitration world; the lawyer and arbitrator professional relationship as well as repeat appointment as arbitrators by providers. Some commentators have more harshly described the arbitration world as a 'mafia'.[229]

7.2. Discussions on China and the global growth of international arbitration

Will China be part of the global international arbitration arena? The answer is rather obvious. Arbitration is not at its infancy in China and, as it is now, Chinese corporations as well as entities are already major users of international commercial arbitration. Internally in China, the volume of domestic commercial arbitration is staggering and can be expected to increase in the future. Because China also has a pivotal role in the growth of the global economy, it is a natural progression to be part of the global development of international commercial arbitration. In discussing the above, the various possibilities basing on current trends, experience and observations will be examined below.

7.2.1. Does China want to become an international arbitration hub?

It is not a question of wanting or not wanting to but rather if there is an opportunity arises and whether China is able

229 Yves Dezalay & Bryant G. Garth, *Dealing in Virtue: International Commercial Arbitration and the Construction of a Transnational Legal Order* (University of Chicago Press 1998) 50.

to become an international arbitration player. From a factual standpoint, China has Hong Kong which is already a major international arbitration locale having a strong reputation as a major international arbitration venue as well as having vast number of highly qualified legal professionals and arbitrators to choose from. Adequate arrangements between Mainland China and Hong Kong ensure that non-China and Hong Kong parties can conduct arbitration in the Special Administrative Region with assurance.

By just looking at the statistics of cases at key Chinese arbitration commissions, the staggering numbers are evidence of very high penetration rate of domestic arbitration. This is a key element in that China is able to continuously learn about arbitration and also gain valuable experience in arbitration, giving it a strong track record. Not many countries can claim to be able to do it like China. Meanwhile, foreign users are increasingly warming up to the idea of China seated arbitration and some of the leading arbitration commissions are leading the way in making themselves diversified international arbitration bodies, not just handling domestic cases.

In reality, a country does not become an arbitration hub but its key cities do, with the exception for Singapore, which is a city state, and Hong Kong, being a Special Administrative Region of China. As it is, Beijing is already building up the reputation as an international arbitration centre with CIETAC and BAC dominant there. Shanghai is ever an important commerce hub of China and with the establishment of a Free Trade Zone (FTZ), international arbitration capabilities are building itself there. Shanghai is no doubt an attractive location for international arbitration due to its interesting history, deep rooted trade culture, infrastructure and reputation. It has the Shanghai Arbitration Commission and the Shanghai Arbitration Court of International Shipping (SACIS). Other important economic cities in China today include Shenzhen and Guangzhou; there are already active arbitration commissions there and it is a matter of time before they will emerge as important arbitration centres for international arbitration. To a large extent, a foreign disputant's level of comfort to arbitrate in China is also dependent on local level factors such as credibility, reliability or professionalism of the commissions in question.

The more appropriate answer to the question above would be that it is a matter when and not whether China will become an international arbitration hub. Even if China did not want to entertain the thought of becoming an arbitration hub, opportunities will eventually come knocking at its door. This is not a discussion about Chinese government policies but almost nearly common sense especially when Hong Kong will also contribute towards the growth of international arbitration in the Mainland from transfer of knowledge and mutually beneficial cooperation models.

7.2.2. Will China dominate the world economy through arbitration?

The above question is thought to be highly remote because arbitration is not designed for 'domination' purposes, whether politically or economically. If anything, arbitration is a partner in the global economy and trade. Typically, governments have not been too trusting too quickly as can be seen in the case of the UNCITRAL Model Law. The Model Law was intended to be a simple and widely accepted model text for states to adopt yet it took a while before it was widely adopted by countries, with some still remaining unwilling to adopt it. Conspiracists will be disappointed to learn that the arbitration world turns out to be much simpler in terms of system and 'politics'.

What may be true though is that a large part of the world's trade and commerce today involves China and Chinese parties. The Chinese government is continuing its efforts in internationalising the Renminbi currency and appears to be increasingly successful in doing so. However, there is no standard 'international arbitration currency', although the United States dollar is a popularly used currency in international contracts. However, if one day the Chinese government opened its doors to international commercial arbitration by linking trade with arbitration in China under a strategic scheme, then this could potentially pave the way for China to become the next 'go to' international arbitration venue for foreign parties. In the existing circumstances, some foreign arbitration centres have already set up presence in the Shanghai FTZ and it is a matter of time before more economic development plans will be unveiled. Perhaps some might feature a China-centric trade and arbitration package, perhaps by making it attractive for foreign parties to arbitrate Renminbi denominated disputes involving Chinese parties in China. Any such scheme could also incorporate some of the common features from the 'wish list' of arbitration, namely expedited arbitration, interim relief measures, evidentiary rules consistent with international practice and quick and effective enforcement of awards in China.

The fact is one day soon China is likely to be the single largest user of arbitration for international commercial dispute settlement. Whilst the Chinese government is likely to leave doors of opportunity open, it is not thought to be overly ambitious about international commercial arbitration. If there is already Hong Kong which is doing well in the promotion of international arbitration, why rock the boat? Also, to some extent Mainland China (as distinguished from Hong Kong SAR) recognises the fact that their standard of professional legal services still has a long way to go. Furthermore, the international arbitration community tends to use English as its *lingua franca* which is still not widely used among Chinese legal professionals.

7.2.3. Does China matter in international arbitration players' future plans?

The answer is unequivocally 'Yes!'. For instance, the ICC established an office in Mainland China in March 2016, becoming the first non-Asian headquartered arbitral institution to do so. ICC's statistics have shown that there is a more than 12% rise in the number of Chinese parties involved in ICC arbitrations, according to cases filed in 2015.[230] SIAC also established a representative office in March 2016 in the Shanghai FTZ.[231] Before ICC and SIAC, HKIAC was 'the first offshore arbitration body' to establish a representative office in Shanghai also located within the FTZ[232] Numerous other international and established arbitral institutions have also been courting China.[233] These institutions cite an increase in caseload involving Chinese parties and obviously see the future of their brand of arbitration in China. At this juncture, doing arbitration in the Shanghai FTZ is not thought to be advantageously different from doing an arbitration outside the FTZ. The CAL still applies either way. However, from a strategic point of view, these foreign arbitration institutions are acting correctly by positioning themselves in China

---

230 According to ICC Court President Alexis Mourre, 'The opening of our second regional office in Asia represents another milestone for Court expansion in Asia and will facilitate our ambitions to further leverage the growth in demand for our services not only from arbitration users in China but across the entire region.' 'New Shanghai office lays groundwork for ICC Asia developments', 24 Feb 2016. <www.iccwbo.org/News/Articles/2016/New-Shanghai-office-lays-groundwork-for-ICC-Asia-developments/>.

231 See <siac.org.sg/2014-11-03-13-33-43/about-us/siac-shanghai-office>.

232 'HKIAC opens office in Shanghai', *Asian Legal Business*, 23 Nov 2015. <www.legalbusinessonline.com/news/hkiac-opens-office-shanghai/71058>.

233 For example, ASA (Swiss Arbitration Association). 'ASA 2016 China Roadshow and Arbitration Workshops', touring Beijing, Shanghai and Shenzhen which was jointly organised with local arbitration commissions.

now and not later, so that they are well placed to be at the forefront of any liberalisation and reform plans by the Chinese government. Pursuing opportunities in China requires tenacity, determination and a long-term vision, mirroring the spirit of the Chinese people.

Foreign institutions need to have the staying power to hold out until the anticipated changes finally happen. For example, the London Court of International Arbitration (LCIA) closed its India subsidiary LCIA India after about five years citing lack of uptake and insufficient cases.[234] The strategy of LCIA India was undeniably promising with the idea of 'bringing London quality to Indian parties at Indian rates' according to its then Registrar[235] but in 2013 LCIA India was said to be handling cases in 'single digits' prompting the Registrar of LCIA India to lyrically and quite rightfully put it that: 'It is not that you open an institution and you have a flood of cases coming in. LCIA London has taken a 100 years to be in the position they are'.[236] In October 2016 the Indian Prime Minister Narendra Modi said that the government planned to promote India as an international arbitration hub.[237] This came on the back of recent reform to the Indian Arbitration and Conciliation Act; by any account, these are major developments in this second most populated country in the world.

---

234 'London Court of International Arbitration (LCIA) shuts down in India after tiny uptake' (*Legally India*, 7 Apr 2016) <www.legallyindia.com/bar-bench-litigation/london-court-of-international-arbitration-lcia-shuts-down-in-india-after-tiny-uptake>.

235 'LCIA yet to bag 10th case as high-powered Hiranandani arbitration resolved with Cherie Blair, AP Shah, Karanjawala' (*Legally India*, 8 Aug 2013) <www.legallyindia.com/201308083898/Litigation/3-year-old-lcia-still-to-get-its-10th-dispute-resolves-hiranandani-feud-with-karanjawala-pepper-hamilton>.

236 *Ibid.*

237 See generally, 'Working to make Indian an arbitration hub: PM Modi', *Times of India* (Mumbai 23 Oct 2016) <http://timesofindia.indiatimes.com/india/Working-to-make-India-an-arbitration-hub-PM-Modi/articleshow/55012833.cms>.

Foreign arbitral institutions establishing themselves in China can be expected to develop local talent capabilities which can eventually result in improving and strengthening the practice of international commercial arbitration in China at its core. Meanwhile, it is not exactly clear yet what are the strategies of foreign institutions in China given that some local Chinese arbitration commissions are already involved in international arbitrations, targeting foreign parties. No doubt the Chinese market is big and it is a generally accepted notion that competition is good, so that there can be alternatives and options. In the international dispute resolution industry, arbitration institutions are arguably in competition with each other but if it is a healthy rivalry, this should be encouraged.

7.2.4. Is China in need of major reform to its arbitration regime?

Some users and commentators have expressed their concerns about how arbitration is currently run in China. Chief among them are concerns about the professionalism of arbitration commissions, quality of local arbitrators to handle international arbitration and standards of local court judges in support of arbitration. A prominent commentator gave a long list of grievances citing examples[238] such as corruption, government influence over decisions, ethical deficiencies, conflicts of interest, bias against foreign companies, faulty methods of selecting arbitrators, lapses in confidentiality and other unfair practices, mostly from his own experiences. But to say any Chinese arbitration commission is badly run would be unfair generalisation or characterisation unless there is concrete evidence supporting such a strong allegation.

Another commentator[239] listed several 'legal obstacles' faced by arbitration in China under the CAL, without going into the

238 See Cohen (n 121) 562.

239 Fan Kun, 'Arbitration in China: Practice, Legal Obstacles and Reforms', (2008) 19 *ICC International Court of Arbitration Bulletin* 25.

details. However, there have been developments since the author's work was published in 2008, for instance the CPL was revised in 2012. According to the article, administrative intervention has led to the arbitration system becoming 'tainted'[240] in that commissions largely rely on government support for their establishment, the government retains strong control over the financial aspect of the institutions or most of the leading positions are held by government officials.

To be fair, it is not unusual for arbitration institutions to be established by or with the support of the government at the initial stage. For instance, the SIAC, which commenced operations in 1991, first operated under the aegis of the Economic Development Board and the Trade Development Board of Singapore.[241] Thereafter in 1999, the Singapore Academy of Law took over responsibility for SIAC from the two Singapore government statutory boards. Meanwhile there are arbitration institutions that were established entirely according to private initiatives. When and if interference exists,[242] it would be reasonable to ask if and how this affects the final outcome of

240 *Ibid* 35.

241 See Ang Yong Tong, 'SIAC: Arbitration in the New Millennium' <www.lawgazette.com.sg/2000-1/Jan00-23.htm>.

242 An aside, there was a widely reported case of an arbitrator from South East Asia who was said to have been led away when arriving in a European city, where he was to attend the arbitration hearing, allegedly due to interference by his government. This incident made it into quite a number of publications, and any casual search on the web will yield rather a handful of reports. In Nigel Blackaby, Constantine Partasides, Alan Redfern & Martin Hunter, *Redfern and Hunter on International Arbitration* (Oxford University Press 5th edn student version 2009) 289, paragraph 4.146 it was said that the government 'apparently exerted considerable pressure on the arbitrator it had appointed to withdraw'. Elsewhere some commentators reported it as a 'kidnap'; *inter alia*, see Pierre Lalive, 'The Transfer of Seat in International Arbitration', in James Nafziger & Symeon Symeonides (eds), *Law and Justice in a Multistate World: Essays in Honor of Arthur T. von Mehren* (Transnational Publishers 2002) 6; Peter Turner & Reza Mohtashami, *A Guide to the LCIA Arbitration Rules* (Oxford University Press 2009) para 4.139.

arbitrations and awards rendered. Are there precedence of, for example, state owned enterprises habitually winning against all other parties (both domestic and foreign) in China seated arbitration?

In the face of evidence of the various SPC directives and clarifications, it would be fairer to say that China is continuously reviewing its current arbitration law. These initiatives could demonstrate efforts of the government in keeping abreast with global developments and also given the increasing popularity of foreign and international parties arbitrating in China. It takes times for things to change in a big country like China but it is open to changes, as those who have been to China a decade ago and again now can attest.

Reform should always be on the cards. Many other countries are also constantly reviewing their positions and not sitting on their laurels. Evidently, there is always room for improvement. For instance, Hong Kong in stepping up competition has set up a sub-committee under the Law Reform Commission of Hong Kong to consider permitting third party funding for arbitration. On 12 October 2016, the Law Reform Commission released a report recommending that Hong Kong law should be amended to state that third party funding of arbitration and associated proceedings under the Arbitration Ordinance is permitted, and that appropriate financial and ethical safeguards be complied with.[243] If this recommendation becomes law, it is likely to be a game changer in Hong Kong and Asia. Chinese disputants typically want to work on contingency fee basis thus this mindset would be a perfect fit and match with third party funding opportunity.

243 See *Law Reform Commission of Hong Kong Report on Third Party Funding for Arbitration* <www.hkreform.gov.hk/en/publications/rtpf.htm>.

7.2.5. Can China contribute to the regional and global arbitration scene?

There is an unbreakable link between international trade and arbitration.[244] The importance of international commercial arbitration in trade has been long recognised by many. In an interesting article published in the *American Bar Association Journal* almost a century ago, it was stated that the importance of arbitration is realised as 'an auxiliary of orderly conduct of business between merchants residing under two or more varying jurisdiction'.[245] It is amazing how commercial arbitration had already been widely discussed such a long time ago; there is so much for us to learn from our forefathers.

Of course, it would unimaginable for a country like China which is central in the global and regional economic equations today to have no role in contributing towards the growth of arbitration. Cross-border trade and international commercial arbitration are enabler of each other. In 1952, the China Council for the Promotion of International Trade (CCPIT) was established as a national foreign trade and promotion agency. Arbitration was central in its purpose like most chambers of commerce. Consequently, the Foreign Trade Arbitration Commission was established in 1956 which was the precursor of the present day CIETAC.

China has been actively pursuing trade and economic cooperation around the world while Chinese parties have been doing cross-border trade since time immemorial. Speaking of modern and regional economic cooperation,

244 The United Nations General Assembly resolution on the Model Law on International Commercial Arbitration of the UNCITRAL states that 'the establishment of a model law on arbitration that is acceptable to States with different legal, social and economic systems contributes to the development of harmonious international economic relations', Resolution 40/72, 11 Dec 1985.

245 AJ Wolfe, 'Legal Aspects of Foreign Trade', (1922) 8 *American Bar Association Journal* 184.

more than a decade ago China and ASEAN established a partnership resulting in the Guangxi Zhuang Autonomous Region becoming China's gateway hub for China-ASEAN trade. The ASEAN-China Free Trade Area (ACFTA) was also established and the ASEAN Economic Community (AEC) which will inevitably involve China. With trade volume increasing, disputes can also be expected to rise in tandem. China has also launched an ambitious initiative called the Silk Road Economic Belt and the 21st Century Maritime Silk Road also known as the 'One Belt, One Road' (OBOR), which is the brainchild of President Xi Jinping. The concept, first unveiled in September 2013, aims to connect China with Eurasian economies through cooperation in trade, investment and infrastructure. In order to finance the OBOR initiative, President Xi announced a US$ 40 billion contribution by China to set up a Silk Road Fund.[246]

Given China's involvement in regional and global economic and trade growth, it is a natural progression for it to be involved in the resolution of cross border trade disputes. A large scale economic initiative like the OBOR would benefit from a coordinated and centralised dispute resolution system so that the integrity of the economic initiative does not fall into disrepute due to disputes. The OBOR is a cross-border and culture plan involving parties coming from vastly different legal systems and trade cultures, and therefore with a high risk of disputes. Any arbitration scheme could provide investors, stakeholders and parties a swift and systematic dispute resolution process for the sake of expediency, uniformity, fairness and cost effective settlement. There is already a precedent in the form of Dubai International Financial Centre (DIFC), a financial free zone which has its own laws different from those of the United Arab Emirates. Dubai International Arbitration Centre and the Dubai International

246 'Chronology of China's Belt and Road Initiative', *Xinhuanet* (Beijing 24 June 2016) <http://news.xinhuanet.com/english/2016-06/24/c_135464233.htm>.

Financial Centre London Court of International Arbitration joint venture are two of the arbitration centres playing pivotal roles in the promotion and conduct of arbitration in the DIFC. Parties from the Gulf and Middle East and North African are potential users of arbitration services in the DIFC.

It is thought that, in the first instance, China may be unlikely to rush into embarking on ambitious plans to become an international arbitration hub but arguably it may find itself in a situation of having to develop its own brand of international arbitration capabilities due to the many large scale international trade and economic programmes it is embarking on. However, the fact is China already has commissions that are self-motivated to be international standard institutions. They are not ostracised from the outside world and in today's age of technology and mobility, many Chinese arbitration commissions, bodies and academic are already in touch with other international arbitration and dispute resolution bodies. Another compromise could be found in developing arbitration capabilities based in Hong Kong to support Mainland China.

The Chinese brand of arbitrations is also making forays overseas. CIETAC has set up a Hong Kong office and its new arbitration rules are designed for used by international users. Under the initiative of China Law Society and the Shanghai International Economic and Trade Arbitration, the China-Africa Joint Arbitration Centre (CAJAC) was established in June 2015, in cooperation with the Arbitration Foundation of Southern Africa.[247] CAJAC has offices in Shanghai and Johannesburg and was established to cater to the increasing trade and investment relationship between China and Africa. Clearly, China is already involved in the international arbitration scene and this is set to increase over time.

---

247 See <www.shiac.org/CAJAC/aboutus_E.aspx?page=3> and <http://arbitration.co.za/pages/CAJAC.aspx>.

7.3. Looking at the crystal ball – China's future and room for improvement

Growth of arbitration is dependent on the users and the providers as well as actors. China is not short of arbitration users and arbitration commissions/institutions. In terms of lawyers and arbitration professionals, the number is increasing including among young professionals. Many young Chinese graduates today have had opportunities to go overseas for postgraduate education. They are eager, impatience and ambitious, at times leading to 'discontent' for they perceive that Chinese lawyers today are equally capable and qualified to handle any work including international arbitration cases.

Much has been discussed throughout this book about professionalism and reliability. Whilst it is not intended to be pedantic or fault-finding, a material error was spotted in an otherwise useful book on arbitration in China. The author has written that 'pursuant to art.V(1) of the NYC, "absent the parties' choice (*sic*), the law of the place of arbitration will be deemed as the parties' implied choice of applicable law"', with a footnote referring to 'Article V(1)(1) of the NYC'.[248] Article V of the 'NYC' (none other than the New York Convention) deals with the refusal of recognition and enforcement of foreign arbitral award and what was much more disappointing is the 'Article V(1)(1)' referred to does not exist. Neither did such a provision exist in the original historical text of the New York Convention signed in 1958 nor in the present official text of the same Convention. Considering that the New York Convention is an extremely important document central to the entire concept of the study and practice of international

248 See Weixia Gu, *Arbitration in China, Regulation of Arbitration Agreements and Practical Issues* (Sweet & Maxwell Thomson Reuters 2012) 178. Also compare with the historical original text with signatures <www.uncitral.org/pdf/english/texts/arbitration/NY-conv/1958NYConvention.pdf> and official text in professional publication format. <www.uncitral.org/pdf/english/texts/arbitration/NY-conv/New-York-Convention-E.pdf>.

arbitration, such an oversight is careless especially when the book is in the hands of students and new entrants to the practice of arbitration.

Any country or jurisdiction keen to become an international commercial arbitration venue will need to consider the rule of law as a paramount element that foreign disputants will be looking for. Although some countries are already popular destinations for foreign direct investments despite possible concerns about their legal systems, this is not to suggest that investors do not mind about the rule of law in the invested countries but simple because they can turn to neutral governing law and arbitral juridical seat to govern the contractual relationship. This is where international commercial arbitration steps in and explains why it is the preferred mode for cross-border commercial dispute resolution. There is no doubt that foreign investment will be boosted by legal certainty[249] but if there is doubt, then there is always the option in the worst-case scenario (which could well be the wisest decision regardless) to arbitrate in a jurisdiction with a good arbitration framework and rule of law.[250] China recognises the importance of the rule of law as demonstrated by the commitment of President Xi Jinping by telling the Politburo that 'no organisation or individual should be put above the constitution and the law'.[251]

Commercial disputes are vexatious but they cannot be prevented. Chinese parties when doing business are primarily preoccupied with making profits. Disputes require them to spend money to recover money or to defend claims against

249 K Shanmugam, 'The Rule of Law in Singapore' (Dec 2012), *Singapore Journal of Legal Studies* 357-8.

250 'Opening address by Minister for Law, K. Shanmugam, at SIAC Congress 2016', 27 May 2016 <www.mlaw.gov.sg/content/minlaw/en/news/speeches/opening-address-by-minister-for-law--k-shanmugam--at-siac-congre.html>.

251 Choi Chi-Yuk, 'Xi Jinping vows to uphold constitution and rule of law', *South China Morning Post* (Hong Kong 25 Feb 2013) <www.scmp.com/news/china/article/1157878/xi-jinping-vows-uphold-constitution-and-rule-law>.

them. As can be seen generally and not limited to Chinese parties, due to the high cost of arbitration and legal fees, arbitration can be a pyrrhic victory for some claimants. This is partly attributed to claimants typically leaving their case entirely in the hands of professional lawyers. In contrast, with third party funding for arbitration, the funder would take charge and be involved in active case management, which can include managing the lawyers (as well as their costs). Third party funding could also be provided by lawyers themselves on a contingency fee basis in which case they may only require a nominal or modest financial outlay at the outset for a claimant to start its case against another party.

It is therefore predicted that third-party funding for arbitration would be a game changer in the near future in Asia which may see it widely welcomed by Chinese parties. Hong Kong is likely to go ahead with this while Singapore is believed to be considering it as well. At this juncture, arbitration funding is already happening albeit 'under the radar', limited in terms of its scope. However, should arbitration funding be permitted and implemented in Hong Kong and Singapore, it could give rise to new impetus to a variety of arbitration third party funding products. At present, funders are conservative about who they fund and this is unsurprising due to the still limited market. But should arbitration funding be permitted, then this could spur the industry, leading to more funders emerging and perhaps taking on the 'secondary client market' which the primary funders have refused to take on. This is something financial professionals would know better and be in the position to devise innovative products.

China's international arbitration landscape will be transformed should the day arrive that the government emulates the DIFC model; the potential best candidate at present is none other than the Shanghai FTZ. Detractors may say that China's current system is opaque. However, it is a matter of determination to make it happen and China has always been able to defy its critics. The present environment already permits this, for instance, with many good foreign law firms already operating in major Chinese cities with many foreign experts and professionals ready to be involved in any internationalisation or liberalisation programme. Each of the provinces are overseen by their local government which wish to succeed, each with their own vision and ambition. The participation of China in major economic and investment plans such as the OBOR may contribute to the hastening of China's role in taking a pivotal role in the international dispute resolution world. Keeping it in the backyard tends to be Chinese culture. Whether all these will happen remains to be seen. China is a country that has sometimes defied logic or grown at astounding speed and scale.

Finally, is there room for improvement or reform with China's existing arbitration system? There is always room for improvement. After all the CAL is in force for more than two decades since its promulgation in 1994. As Lee Kuan Yew said about China, 'If it's working fine, leave it.'[252] The most common complaint about the CAL is the requirement for a China seated arbitration to be referred to a Chinese arbitration commission. This appears inflexible and lacking in terms of freedom, effectively preventing parties from conducting arbitration ad hoc and not retaining the freedom to arbitrate disputes the way they want it to be. However, arbitration commissions in China typically impose lower costs compared to other foreign arbitration institutions. Also, major and established arbitration commissions promulgate rules of arbitration which reflect international practices and adopt provisions of the UNCITRAL Model Law. Looking at Chinese arbitration commissions objectively, they are not too different from international arbitral institutions where administered arbitrations have their proponents and opponents. Typically, the more advanced and experienced arbitration users would opt for ad hoc arbitrations.

252 See Charlie Rose interview (n 62).

However, it has its fair share of inconveniences, frustrations and obstructions to the smooth conduct of arbitration proceedings.

In addition, the current CAL and directives appear less 'tolerant' of ambiguous arbitration agreements. Unclear arbitration agreements or ones that do not contain reference to an arbitration commission, failing the agreement of the parties to enter into a supplementary agreement, can render the arbitration agreement null and void. The reality is that to obtain both parties' consensus to enter into a supplementary agreement can be challenging amidst an on-going dispute. Current practice of international arbitration has it that even in the worst-case scenario of 'pathological arbitration clauses' (meaning arbitration clauses which were badly drafted) the principle of 'effective interpretation'[253] should be applied. This was inspired by Article 1157 of the French Civil Code which states that 'where a clause can be interpreted in two different ways, the interpretation enabling the clause to be effective should be adopted in preference to that which prevents the clause from being effective'. Additionally, from an international practice standpoint, it is also argued that arbitration agreements should be construed like any other form of commercial agreement therefore the 'fundamental principle of documentary interpretation is to give effect to the parties' intention'[254] as expressed in their contract.

The debate as to whether China seated ad hoc arbitrations should be allowed remains hot. What is the real advantage for foreign parties to arbitrate in China compared to Singapore, Hong Kong or London? Finally, Chinese arbitration commissions which wish to attract foreign parties to arbitrate in China using their rules need to embrace the idea of

253 John Savage & Emmanuel Gaillard (eds), *Fouchard Gaillard Goldman on International Commercial Arbitration* (Kluwer Law International 1999) 258.

254 Julian DM Lew, Loukas A Mistelis & Stefan M Kröll, *Comparative International Commercial Arbitration* (Kluwer Law International 2003) para 7-60.

including more foreign arbitrators on their panels, if they do not already do so.

7.4. Closing – It is only the beginning

It would be appropriate to ponder and reflect on some words of wisdom from Confucius that befits an auspicious ending to this book:

> The Master said, 'Grant me a few more years so that I may study at the age of fifty and I shall be free from major errors'.[255]
>
> ...
>
> The Master said, 'Even when walking in the company of two other men, I am bound to be able to learn from them. The good points of the one I copy; the bad points of the other I correct in myself'.[256]

China is a country which is learning and it will learn to be better and prosper. The People's Republic of China was founded more than six decades ago and its economic globalisation took place rapidly beginning only a few decades ago. Bertrand Russell wrote in 1922 that in China there is a 'great eagerness to acquire Western learning, not simply in order to acquire national strength and be able to resist Western aggression, but because a very large number of people consider learning a good thing in itself'. He noted that even then many Chinese students had gone to study in Europe and America and later they returned to China to modernise the Chinese outlook.[257]

The Chinese through Confucianism believe in time and the opportune moment in learning and improving. Also, as seen in the verses from Confucius above, he spoke of self-

---

255 See Confucius, *The Analects* VII:17, at 88.

256 *Ibid* VII:22, at 88.

257 Bertrand Russell, *The Basic Writings of Bertrand Russell* (Routledge Classic reprinted 2010) 531.

improvement, learning from the good in order to see the inadequacy in oneself, therefore taking on new knowledge and best practices to develop to be better. All these could well be China's recipe for success in progressing and embarking into new frontiers of the global world, now including the international dispute resolution arena.

Figure 1:
Comparison of salient points of AA 1996, IAA and CAL

Provision / Subject	AA 1996	IAA	CAL
1. Model Law	No provision, the UNICITRAL Model Law has no force of law in England & Wales or Northern Ireland yet the act is heavily based off the Model law.	s 3(1). The Model Law has force of law in Singapore subject to the Act and excepting Cap VIII of the Model Law because the part that regulates recognition and enforcement of awards is based on New York Convention which is incorporated as the Second Schedule of the IAA.	No provision and no force of law.
2. Definition of an agreement	s 6. An arbitration agreement is agreement to submit to arbitration present or future disputes (whether they are contractual or not).	s 2A. An arbitration agreement is an agreement to submit to arbitration all or certain disputes which have arisen or may arise between them in respect of a defined legal relationship, whether contractual or not. It can be in the form of an arbitration clause in a contract or in the form of a separate agreement	Cap III Art 16. An agreement shall contain an expression of intention to apply for arbitration, matters for arbitration; and a designated arbitration commission. Art 18. If any agreement is unclear or has no provisions of the above requirements then the parties are required to come to a supplementary

			agreement, else the agreement shall be null and void.
3. Formalities of an agreement	ss 5-6. An arbitration agreement shall be in writing.	s 2A (3)-(10). An arbitration agreement shall be in writing and shall be in writing it its content is recorded in any form, whether or not the arbitration agreement or contract has been concluded orally, by conduct or other means. *Inter alia*, the writing requirement is satisfied by electronic communication. (s 2A(9) provides expressly that Art 7 of UNCITRAL Model Law shall not apply as it is disapplied).	Cap III Art 16. Arbitration agreements shall be in writing.
4. Separability (or otherwise severability)	s 7. Unless otherwise stated by parties, arbitration agreements are considered separate and distinct agreements where the form part of a substantive contract.	UNCITRAL Model Law: Cap IV Art 16. An arbitration clause which forms part of a contract shall be treated as an agreement independent of the other terms of the contract.	Cap III Art 19. An arbitration agreement shall exist independently. Invalidity of a substantive contract shall not affect the validity of the arbitration agreement.

5. Competence to rule on own jurisdiction (*Competence-Competence*)	s 30. Unless otherwise agreed by the parties, a tribunal may rule on its own substantive jurisdiction.	s 10. Arbitral tribunals may rule on a plea that it has no jurisdiction. (Notwithstanding UNCITRAL Mode Law cap III Art 16(3).) (UNCITRAL Model Law cap III Art 16(1). An arbitral tribunal may rule on its own jurisdiction) The arbitral tribunal may rule at any stage of the proceedings. Parties may appeal the decision to the High Court within 30 days.	The principle is notably absent. Cap III Art 20. A party can challenge validity; the arbitration *institution* or the People's Court can be requested to rule with the People's Court taking precedent. Any challenges must be made before the tribunal's first hearing.
6. Duties of the Tribunal	s 33. Imposes a general duty upon a tribunal to be fair and impartial. Also to adopt procedures suitable and to avoid unnecessary delay or expense.	No express provision. UNCITRAL Model Law Cap V Art 18 provides for the parties to be treated with equality and each party to be given a full opportunity of presenting his case.	Cap I Art 1. The purpose of the law is to ensure impartial and prompt arbitration of disputes. Art 8. Arbitration shall be carried out independently according to law, free from interference of administrative organs, social organisation or individuals.

7. Duty of the Parties	s 40. General duty imposed on the parties for the proper and expeditious conduct of the arbitral proceedings. Includes complying without delay to determinations, procedural or evidential matters or with orders of the tribunal and where necessary obtain decisions of the court without delay.	No actual duties imposed.	No actual duties imposed.
8. Preliminary determination by courts on a point of law	s 45. A party of the proceedings may apply to the court for a determination on a point of law with notice to the other parties to the proceedings. The application will only be heard where all parties agree or made with the tribunal's permission and the court is satisfied the application is made without delay and likely to save in costs. There is no appeal to any decision given aside from	No express provisions that allow preliminary ruling on a point of law.	No express provisions that allow preliminary ruling on a point of law.

	when the court gives leave. The decision will be treated as a judgement where an award is appealed.		
9. Challenging the final award	ss 67, 68, 69. An award may be challenged by a party who gives notice to the other parties and the tribunal on grounds of an issue of substantive jurisdiction, serious irregularity or an appeal on a point of law.	UNCITRAL Model Law Cap VII Art 34. Provides a party may challenge an award already made by a tribunal. In summary, the party must show that the agreement was invalid under laws the parties agreed to subject it (or failing that, the laws of Singapore) or one party was otherwise unable to properly present his case, the composition or procedure of the arbitration was not as agreed or otherwise contrary to the laws of the state. Alternatively that the award is given on a dispute not contemplated by the parties. The application must be made within three months of the award being made.	Cap I Art 9. In the ordinary way of things, the court will not accept an application to hear a case that has already been awarded on by a tribunal. Cap V Art 58. Parties may apply for an award to be set-aside in circumstances where there is no arbitration agreement, the matter submitted is beyond the scope of the agreement or limit of authority of the arbitration commission, composition of tribunal or the proceedings was in violation of statutory procedures, forgery of

			evidence or the withholding of evidence that can impact the impartiality of the arbitration, or acceptance of bribery by the arbitrators. Otherwise the court may set aside the rule if it considers the award violates the public interest. Art 59. Such applications must be made in six months of the award received.
10. New York Convention Awards	s 100. New York Convention award is any award made outside of the United Kingdom in a territory which is a party to the New York Convention. s 101(1). New York Convention awards are recognised as binding on the parties that it relates to. It may with the leave of the court be enforced as a judgement and the award generally may be relied on in way of defence,	Directly incorporates the New York Convention into schedule II. Singapore is a signatory to the convention.	China is a signatory to the convention although it is not referred to in the Arbitration Law. It has specifically declared on the convention that it shall only enforce awards that are considered 'commercial' under national law.

	off-set or otherwise in legal proceedings. The UK is a signatory of the convention.		
11. Discharge by death of a party	s 8. Unless otherwise agreed, death does not discharge the agreement. This section does not however stop any substantive rights or obligations from being extinguished by death	No provisions within the IAA dealing with death of a party.	No provisions within the act dealing with death of a party.
12. Appointment of arbitrators	s 15(3). Number of arbitrator shall be sole arbitrator, if no agreement by the parties. s 16. Parties are free to decide on their own method of appointment however in absence, this section provides a default method of appointment. Sole arbitrators must be appointed in 28 days of service of a request. For tribunals of three arbitrators, each party will appoint one not later than 14 days of service of a request and the	s 9. Number of arbitrator shall be sole arbitrator, if no agreement by the parties. s 9A(1). For a tribunal of three arbitrators, each party shall appoint one arbitrator and the parties by agreement shall appoint the third. Where they fail to agree on such an appointment of a third arbitrator within 30 days, either party may request that the 'Appointing authority' make the appointment.	Cap IV Art 30. Arbitral tribunals may be formed of a sole arbitrator or three arbitrators with a presiding arbitrator. Art 31. Where there are three arbitrators, each party shall appoint one (or trust the chairman of the arbitration commission to make the appointment on their behalf) and jointly make or jointly entrust the chairman, the

	two appointees will appoint the third. For tribunals of two arbitrators, each party will appoint one not later than 14 days of service of a request and the two appointees will appoint the umpire. s 18. The parties are free to agree the course followed in the event of failure to appoint an arbitrator however where this is not the case any party with notice to the other may apply to the courts to exercise any of its powers to: give directions as the making of appointments or approval of current appointments, revoke appointments or to remove any necessary appointments.		appointment of the third arbitrator. Where there is one arbitrator, the parties shall jointly elect the arbitrator or jointly entrust the chairman to make the appointment. Art 32. If the parties fail to 'agree on the form of composition' or parties fail to appoint arbitrators, the chairman of the arbitration commission shall make the appointment.
13. Immunity of the tribunal	s 29(1). An arbitrator is not liable for anything done or omitted in the discharge or purported	s 25. An arbitrator is not liable for negligence in respect of anything done or omitted in the capacity as	No express provision. Cap IV Art 38. An Arbitrator will assume legal liability

	discharge of his functions as arbitrator unless the act or omission is shown to have been in bad faith. Does not apply to any agreed liability incurred by the arbitrator were he to resign under s 25.	arbitrator as well as mistake in law, face of procedure in the course of the proceedings or making of the arbitral award. s 25A. The appointing authority or arbitral institutions shall not be liable for anything done or omitted in the discharge of the duties unless it is shown to have been made in bad faith.	according to law where he has privately met with a party or agent or accepted a gift or entertainment from a party or agent (Art 34(4) or acceptance of bribe or sought personal gains (Art 58(6)).

Figure 2:
Enforcement under New York Convention, CPL for domestic awards and CPL for foreign related companies

Figure 2
Enforcement under New York Convention, CPL for domestic awards and CPL for foreign related companies

New York Convention Article V	CPL Article 237	CPL Article 274
1(a) The parties to the agreement referred to in article II were, under the law applicable to them, under some incapacity, or the said agreement is not valid under the law to which the parties have subjected it or, failing any indication thereon, under the law of the country where the award was made; or	(1) Where the parties have not stipulated an arbitration clause in the contract or have not subsequently reached a written agreement on arbitration;	(1) The parties have not stipulated any clause regarding arbitration in their contract or have not subsequently reached a written agreement on arbitration;
1(b) The party against whom the award is invoked was not given proper notice of the appointment of the arbitrator or of the arbitration proceedings or was otherwise unable to present his case; or	*No equivalent wordings*	(2) The defendant is not duly notified of the appointment of the arbitrators or the arbitration proceeding, or the defendant fails to express his defence due to the reasons for which he is not held responsible;
1(c) The award deals with a difference not contemplated by or not falling within the terms of the submission to arbitration, or it contains decisions on matters beyond the scope of the submission to arbitration, provided that, if the decisions on	(2) Where the matters being arbitrated exceed the scope of the arbitration agreement or the authority of the arbitration agency;	(4) The matters decided by arbitration exceed the scope of the arbitration agreement or the authority of the arbitration institution.

matters submitted to arbitration can be separated from those not so submitted, that part of the award which contains decisions on matters submitted to arbitration may be recognised and enforced; or		
1(d) The composition of the arbitral authority or the arbitral procedure was not in accordance with the agreement of the parties, or, failing such agreement, was not in accordance with the law of the country where the arbitration took place; or	(3) Where the formation of an arbitration tribunal or the procedure of arbitration is not in conformity with the legal procedure;	(3) The formation of the arbitration panel or the arbitration procedure is not in conformity with rules of arbitration; or
1(e) The award has not yet become binding on the parties, or has been set aside or suspended by a competent authority of the country in which, or under the law of which, that award was made.	*No equivalent wordings*	*No equivalent wordings*
2(a) The subject matter of the difference is not capable of settlement by arbitration under the law of that country; or	*No equivalent wordings*	*No equivalent wordings*
2(b) The recognition or enforcement of the award would be contrary to the public policy of that country.	If a people's court determines that the enforcement of an arbitration award would contradict the	If a people's court determines that the enforcement of an award will violate the social and public

	social and public interest, it shall make a ruling of not to enforce the award.	interest, the court shall make a ruling to disallow the enforcement of the arbitration award.
No equivalent wordings	(4) The evidence based on which the arbitral award is made is falsified;	*No equivalent wordings*
No equivalent wordings	(5) The other parties conceal the evidence from the arbitral organ and is sufficient to affect the impartiality of the arbitral award;	*No equivalent wordings*
No equivalent wordings	(6) Where the arbitrators involved in any of conducts of embezzlement, bribery, practicing favouritism for himself or relatives, twisting the law in rendering arbitration award	*No equivalent wordings*

Appendices

Appendix 1
Glossary of useful terms

Arbitration, 仲裁 (*zhòngcái*)

- Ad hoc arbitration, 临时仲裁 (*línshí zhòngcái*)
- Appointing authority, 任命机关 (*rènmìng jīguān*)
- Appointment of arbitrators, 任命仲裁员 (*rènmìng zhòngcáiyuán*)
- Arbitration law (arbitration act), 仲裁法 (*zhòngcái fǎ*)
- Arbitration commission, 仲裁委员会 (*zhòngcái wěiyuánhuì*)
- Arbitration Rules, 仲裁规则 (*zhòngcái guīzé*)
- Commercial disputes, 商业争端 (*shāngyè zhēngduān*)
- Competence-Competence, 自裁管辖 (*zìcái guǎnxiá*)
- Confidentiality, 保密性 (*bǎomìxìng*)
- Consensual process, 合意的程序 (*héyì de chéngxù*)
- Contractual, 合约性的 (*héyuēxìngde*)
- International arbitration, 国际仲裁 (*guójì zhòngcái*)
- Non-arbitrable, 不可仲裁 (*bùkě zhòngcái*)
- Parties to a dispute, 争端当事人 (*zhēngduān dāngshìrén*)
- Party autonomy, 意思自治 (*yìsi zìzhì*)

Arbitration agreement, 仲裁协议 (*zhòngcái xiéyì*)

- Arbitration clause, 仲裁条款 (*zhòngcái tiáokuǎn*)
- Governing Law, 适用的法律 (*shìyòng de fǎlǜ*)
- Intention to arbitrate, 仲裁意图 (*zhòngcái yìtú*)

Invalid arbitration agreement, 无效的仲裁协议 (*wúxiào de zhòngcái xiéyì*)

Pathological clause, 有瑕疵的条款 (*yǒuxiácī de tiáokuǎn*)

Place of arbitration, 仲裁地 (*zhòngcáidì*)

Submission agreement, 提交协议 (*tíjiāo xiéyì*)

Arbitrator, 仲裁员 (*zhòngcái yuán*)

Chairman of the Tribunal, 仲裁庭首席仲裁员 (*zhòngcáitíng shǒuxí zhòngcáiyuán*)

Challenge of arbitrators, 对仲裁员提出异议 (*duì zhòngcáiyuán tíchū yìyì*)

Fees of arbitrators, 仲裁员服务费 (*zhòngcáiyuán fúwùfèi*)

Functus officio, 已履行其职务 (*yǐ lǚxíng qí zhíwù*)

Immunity of arbitrators, 仲裁员豁免权 (*zhòngcáiyuán huòmiǎnquán*)

Impartiality, 公正性 (*gōngzhèngxìng*)

Impossibility to act, 无法履行 (*wúfǎ lǚxíng*)

Incapacity, 丧失能力 (*sàngshī nénglì*)

Independence, 独立性 (*dúlìxìng*)

Jurisdiction of the arbitral tribunal, 仲裁庭管辖权 (*zhòngcáitíng guǎnxiáquán*)

Neutrality, 中立性 (*zhōnglìxìng*)

Number of arbitrators, 仲裁员数量 (*zhòngcáiyuán shùliàng*)

Procedure for challenge, 异议程序 (*yìyì chéngxù*)

Removal of arbitrators, 移除仲裁员 (*yíchú zhòngcáiyuán*)

Replacement of arbitrators, 更换仲裁员 (*gēnghuàn zhòngcáiyuán*)

Selection of arbitrators, 甄选仲裁员 (*zhēnxuǎn zhòngcáiyuán*)

Sole arbitrator, 独任仲裁员 (*dúrèn zhòngcáiyuán*)

Arbitration Award, 仲裁裁决 (*zhòngcái cáijué*)

- correction and interpretation, 纠正和解释 (*jiūzhèng hé jiěshì*)

Additional Award, 附加裁决 (*fùjiā cáijué*)

Award on agreed terms, 依约定条款做出的裁决 (*yīyuēdìngtiáokuǎn zuòchū de cáijué*)

Clerical, typographical errors, 记录，打印错误 (*jìlù dǎyìn cuòwù*)

Dissenting Opinion, 异议意见 (*yìyì yìjiàn*)

Final and binding, 终局和有约束力 (*zhōngjú hé yǒu yuēshùlì*)

Final Award, 最终裁决 (*zuìzhōng cáijué*)

Form and Contents of Award, 裁决的形式和内容 (*cáijué de xíngshì hé nèiróng*)

Global enforceability, 全球可执行性 (*quánqiú kězhíxíngxìng*)

Grounds for challenge, 异议理由 (*yìyì lǐyóu*)

Interest, 利息 (*lìxī*)

Interim Award, 临时裁决 (*línshí cáijué*)

Reasons for Award, 裁决理由 (*cáijué lǐyóu*)

Setting aside arbitral awards, 撤销仲裁裁决 (chèxiāo zhòngcái cáijué)

Arbitration Proceedings, 仲裁程序 (*zhòngcái chéngxù*)

Breach of contract, 违反合同 (*wéifǎn hétong*)

Claim, 诉求 (*sùqiú*)

Claimant, 申请人 (*shēnqǐngrén*)

Costs of the arbitration, 仲裁费用 (*zhòngcái fèiyòng*)

Costs of the parties, 当事人费用 (*dāngshìrén fèiyòng*)

Counter-claim, 反诉 (*fǎnsù*)

Default of a party, 一方当事人缺席 (*yìfāng dāngshìrén quēxí*)

Defendant, 被申请人 (*bèishēnqǐngrén*)

Dispute Resolution, 争端解决 (*zhēngduān jiějué*)

Dispute, 争端 (*zhēngduān*)

Documents-only arbitration, 书面仲裁 (*shūmiàn zhòngcái*)

Domestic arbitration, 国内仲裁 (*guónèi zhòngcái*)

Domestic party, 国内当事人 (*guónèi dāngshìrén*)

Equal treatment of parties, 当事人平等待遇, (*dāngshìrén píngděng dàiyù*)

Ethical duties, 道德义务 (*dàodé yìwù*)

Ex parte, 单方面的 (*dānfāngmiàn de*)

Expert witness, 专家证人 (*zhuānjiā zhèngrén*)

Foreign party, 国外当事人 (*guówài dāngshìrén*)

Juridical seat, 管辖地 (*guǎnxiádì*)

Language of proceedings, 程序所用语言 (*chéngxù suǒyòng yǔyán*)

Notice of hearing, 听审通知 (*tīngshěn tōngzhī*)

Oral hearings, 口头审理 (*kǒutóu shěnlǐ*)

Pleading, 诉状 (*sùzhuàng*)

Statement of claim, 起诉状 (*qǐsùzhuàng*)

Statement of defence, 答辩状 (*dábiànzhuàng*)

Taking of evidence, 取证 (*qǔzhèng*)

Unable to present case fairly, 无法公正地呈现案件 (*wúfǎ gōngzhèng de chéngxiàn ànjiàn*)

Witness of fact, 事实证人 (*shìshí zhèngrén*)

Bilateral Investment Treaties (BITs), 双边投资条约 (*shuāngbiān tóuzī tiáoyuē*)

Chartered Institute of Arbitrators (CIArb), 特许仲裁员协会 (*tèxǔ zhòngcáiyuán xiéhuì*)

China International Economic and Trade Arbitration Commission (CIETAC), 中国国际经济贸易仲裁委员会 (*zhōngguó guójì jīngjì màoyì zhòngcái wěiyuánhuì*)

Court litigation, 法院诉讼 (*fǎyuàn sùsòng*)

Court proceeding, 法院程序 (*fǎ yuàn chéng xù*)

Judge, 法官 (*fǎguān*)

Hong Kong International Arbitration Centre, 香港国际仲裁中心 (*xiānggǎng guójì zhòngcái zhōngxīn*)

International Centre for Settlement of Investment Disputes (ICSID), 国际投资争端解决中心 (*guójì tóuzī zhēngduān jiějué zhōngxīn*)

International Chamber of Commerce (ICC), International Court of Arbitration, Paris, 国际商会，国际仲裁院，巴黎 (*guójì shānghuì, guójì zhòngcáiyuàn, bālí*)

Investment law, 投资法 (*tóuzīfǎ*)

Investor-State arbitration, 投资者-国家仲裁 (*tóuzīzhě-guójiā zhòngcái*)

London Court of International Arbitration (LCIA), 伦敦国际仲裁院 (*lúndūn guójì zhòngcáiyuàn*)

London Maritime Arbitrators Association (LMAA), 伦敦海事仲裁员协会 (*lúndūn hǎishì zhòngcáiyuán xiéhuì*)

Mediation, 调解 (*tiáojiě*)

Negotiation, 谈判 (*tánpàn*)

Permanent Court of Arbitration (PCA), 常设仲裁法院 (*chángshè zhòngcái fǎyuàn*)

Public policy [against public policy], 公共政策 [违反公共政策] (*gōnggòng zhèngcè, wéifǎn gōnggòng zhèngcè*)

Shanghai Arbitration Commission, 上海仲裁委员会 (*shànghǎi zhòngcái wěiyuánhuì*)

Shanghai Arbitration Court of International Shipping, 上海国际航运仲裁院 (*shànghǎi guójì hángyùn zhòngcáiyuàn*)

Singapore International Arbitration Centre, 新加坡国际仲裁中心 (*xīnjiāpō guójì zhòngcái zhōngxīn*)

State immunity/ sovereign immunity, 国家豁免 / 主权豁免 (*guójiā huòmiǎn / zhǔquán huòmiǎn*)

UNCITRAL Model Law on International Commercial Arbitration, 联合国国际贸易法委员会国际商事仲裁示范法 (*liánhéguó guójì màoyì fǎ wěiyuánhuì guójì shāngshì zhòngcái shìfàn fǎ*)

United Nations Commission on International Trade Law (UNCITRAL), 联合国国际贸易法委员会 (*liánhéguó guójì màoyì fǎ wěiyuánhuì*)

United Nations Convention on the Recognition and Enforcement of Foreign Arbitral Awards, New York, 1958 ('New York Convention 1958'), 联合国承认及执行外国仲裁裁决公约，1958 年，纽约 ('纽约公约') (*liánhéguó chéngrèn jí zhíxíng wàiguó zhòngcái cáijué gōngyuē, 1958 nián, niǔyuē ('niǔyuē gōngyuē'*)

United Nations, 联合国 (*liánhéguó*)

Appendix 2
China Arbitration Law[258]

(Adopted at the Ninth Meeting of the Standing Committee of the Eighth National People's Congress on 31 August 1994 and promulgated by Order No. 31 of the President of the People's Republic of China on 31 August 1994)

258 <www.npc.gov.cn/englishnpc/Law/2007-12/12/content_1383756.htm>.

Chapter I
General Provisions

Article 1

This Law is formulated in order to ensure the impartial and prompt arbitration of economic disputes, to protect the legitimate rights and interests of the parties and to safeguard the sound development of the socialist market economy.

Article 2

Contractual disputes and other disputes over rights and interests in property between citizens, legal persons and other organisations that are equal subjects may be arbitrated.

Article 3

The following disputes may not be arbitrated:

(1) marital, adoption, guardianship, support and succession disputes;

(2) administrative disputes that shall be handled by administrative organs as prescribed by law.

Article 4

The parties' submission to arbitration to resolve their dispute shall be on the basis of both parties' free will and an arbitration agreement reached between them. If a party applies for arbitration in the absence of an arbitration agreement, the arbitration commission shall not accept the case.

Article 5

If the parties have concluded an arbitration agreement and one party institutes an action in a people's court, the people's court shall not accept the case, unless the arbitration agreement is null and void.

Article 6

The arbitration commission shall be selected by the parties through agreement. In arbitration, there shall be no jurisdiction by level and no territorial jurisdiction.

Article 7

In arbitration, disputes shall be resolved on the basis of facts, in compliance with the law and in an equitable and reasonable manner.

Article 8

Arbitration shall be carried out independently according to law and shall be free from interference of administrative organs, social organisations or individuals.

Article 9

A system of a single and final award shall be practised for arbitration. If a party applies for arbitration to an arbitration commission or institutes an action in a people's court regarding the same dispute after an arbitration award has been made, the arbitration commission or the people's court shall not accept the case.

If an arbitration award is set aside or its enforcement is disallowed by the people's court in accordance with the law, a party may apply for arbitration on the basis of a new arbitration agreement reached between the parties, or institute an action in the people's court, regarding the same dispute.

Chapter II
Arbitration Commissions and the Arbitration Association

Article 10

Arbitration commissions may be established in municipalities directly under the Central Government and in cities that are the seats of the people's governments of provinces or autonomous regions. They may also be established in other cities divided into districts, according to need. Arbitration commissions shall not be established at each level of the administrative divisions.

People's governments of the cities referred to in the preceding paragraph shall arrange for the relevant departments and chambers of commerce to organise arbitration commissions in a unified manner.

The establishment of an arbitration commission shall be registered with the administrative department of justice of the relevant province, autonomous region or municipality directly under the Central Government.

Article 11

An arbitration commission shall meet the conditions set forth below:

(1) To have its own name, domicile and charter;

(2) To have the necessary property;

(3) To have the personnel that are to form the commission; and

(4) To have appointed arbitrators.

The charter of an arbitration commission shall be formulated in accordance with this Law.

Article 12

An arbitration commission shall be composed of one chairman, two to four vice chairmen and seven to eleven members.

The offices of chairman, vice chairman and members of an arbitration commission shall be held by experts in the field of law, economy and trade and persons with practical working experience. Experts in the field of law, economy and trade shall account for at least two thirds of the people forming an arbitration commission.

Article 13

An arbitration commission shall appoint its arbitrators from among righteous and upright persons.

An arbitrator shall meet one of the conditions set forth below:

(1) To have been engaged in arbitration work for at least eight years;

(2) To have worked as a lawyer for at least eight years;

(3) To have served as a judge for at least eight years;

(4) To have been engaged in legal research or legal education, possessing a senior professional title; or

(5) To have acquired the knowledge of law, engaged in the professional work in the field of economy and trade, etc., possessing a senior professional title or having an equivalent professional level.

An arbitration commission shall have a register of arbitrators in different specialisations.

Article 14

Arbitration commissions shall be independent from administrative organs and there shall be no subordinate relationships between arbitration commissions and administrative organs. There shall also be no subordinate relationships between arbitration commissions.

Article 15

China Arbitration Association is a social organisation with the status of a legal person. Arbitration commissions are members of China Arbitration Association. The charter of China Arbitration Association shall be formulated by its national congress of members.

China Arbitration Association is a self-disciplined organisation of arbitration commissions. It shall, in accordance with its charter, supervise arbitration commissions and their members and arbitrators as to whether or not they breach discipline.

China Arbitration Association shall formulate rules of arbitration in accordance with this Law and the relevant provisions of the Civil Procedure Law.

Chapter III
Arbitration Agreement

Article 16

An arbitration agreement shall include arbitration clauses stipulated in the contract and agreements of submission to arbitration that are concluded in other written forms before or after disputes arise.

An arbitration agreement shall contain the following particulars:

(1) an expression of intention to apply for arbitration;

(2) matters for arbitration; and

(3) a designated arbitration commission.

Article 17

An arbitration agreement shall be null and void under one of the following circumstances:

(1) The agreed matters for arbitration exceed the range of arbitrable matters as specified by law;

(2) One party that concluded the arbitration agreement has no capacity for civil conducts or has limited capacity for civil conducts; or

(3) One party coerced the other party into concluding the arbitration agreement.

Article 18

If an arbitration agreement contains no or unclear provisions concerning the matters for arbitration or the arbitration commission, the parties may reach a supplementary agreement. If no such supplementary agreement can be reached, the arbitration agreement shall be null and void.

Article 19

An arbitration agreement shall exist independently. The amendment, rescission, termination or invalidity of a contract shall not affect the validity of the arbitration agreement.

The arbitration tribunal shall have the power to affirm the validity of a contract.

Article 20

If a party challenges the validity of the arbitration agreement, he may request the arbitration commission to make a decision or apply to the people's court for a ruling. If one party requests the arbitration commission to make a decision and the other party applies to the people's court for a ruling, the people's court shall give a ruling.

A party's challenge of the validity of the arbitration agreement shall be raised prior to the arbitration tribunal's first hearing.

Chapter IV
Arbitration Proceedings

Section 1
Application and Acceptance

Article 21

A party's application for arbitration shall meet the following requirements:

(1) There is an arbitration agreement;

(2) There is a specific arbitration claim and there are facts and reasons therefore; and

(3) The application is within the scope of the arbitration commission's acceptability.

Article 22

To apply for arbitration, a party shall submit to the arbitration commission the written arbitration agreement and a written application for arbitration together with copies thereof.

Article 23

A written application for arbitration shall specify the following particulars:

(1) the name, sex, age, occupation, work unit and domicile of each party, or the name and domicile of legal persons or other organisations and the names and positions of their legal representatives or chief responsible persons;

(2) the arbitration claim and the facts and reasons on which it is based; and

(3) the evidence, the source of the evidence and the names and domiciles of witnesses.

Article 24

When an arbitration commission receives a written application for arbitration and considers that the application complies with the conditions for acceptance, it shall accept the application and notify the party within five days from the date of receipt. If the arbitration commission considers that the application does not comply with the conditions for acceptance, it shall inform the party in writing of its rejection of the application and explain the reasons for rejection within five days from the date of receipt.

Article 25

After an arbitration commission accepts an application for arbitration, it shall, within the time limit specified in the rules of arbitration, deliver a copy of the rules of arbitration and the register of arbitrators to the claimant, and serve one copy of the application for arbitration together with the rules of arbitration and the register of arbitrators on the respondent.

After receiving the copy of the application for arbitration, the respondent shall submit a written defence to the arbitration commission within the time limit specified in the rules of arbitration. After receiving the written defence, the arbitration commission shall serve a copy thereof on the claimant within the time limit specified in the rules of arbitration. Failure on the part of the respondent to submit a written defence shall not affect the progress of the arbitration proceedings.

Article 26

If the parties have concluded an arbitration agreement and one party has instituted an action in a people's court without declaring the existence of the arbitration agreement and, after the people's court has accepted the case, the other party submits the arbitration agreement prior to the first hearing, the people's court shall dismiss the case unless the arbitration agreement is null and void. If, prior to the first hearing, the other party has not raised an objection to the people's court's acceptance of the case, he shall be deemed to have renounced the arbitration agreement and the people's court shall continue to try the case.

Article 27

The claimant may renounce or amend its arbitration claim. The respondent may accept or refuse an arbitration claim and shall have the right to make a counter-claim.

Article 28

A party may apply for property preservation if it may become impossible or difficult for the party to implement the award due to an act of the other party or other causes.

If a party applies for property preservation, the arbitration commission shall submit the party's application to the people's court in accordance with the relevant provisions of the Civil Procedure Law.

If an application for property preservation has been wrongfully made, the applicant shall compensate the person against whom the application has been made for any loss incurred from property preservation.

Article 29

A party or statutory agent may appoint a lawyer or other agent to carry out arbitration activities. To appoint a lawyer or other agent to carry out arbitration activities, a power of attorney shall be submitted to the arbitration commission.

Section 2
Formation of Arbitration Tribunal

Article 30

An arbitration tribunal may be composed of either three arbitrators or one arbitrator. An arbitration tribunal composed of three arbitrators shall have a presiding arbitrator.

Article 31

If the parties agree that the arbitration tribunal shall be composed of three arbitrators, they shall each appoint or entrust the chairman of the arbitration commission to appoint one arbitrator. The parties shall jointly select or jointly entrust the chairman of the arbitration commission to appoint the third arbitrator who shall be the presiding arbitrator.

If the parties agree that the arbitration tribunal shall be composed of one arbitrator, they shall jointly appoint or jointly entrust the chairman of the arbitration commission to appoint the arbitrator.

Article 32

If the parties fail to agree on the method of formation of the arbitration tribunal or to select the arbitrators within the time limit specified in the rules of arbitration, the arbitrators shall be appointed by the chairman of the arbitration commission.

Article 33

After the arbitration tribunal has been formed, the arbitration commission shall notify the parties in writing of the tribunal's formation.

Article 34

In one of the following circumstances, the arbitrator must withdraw, and the parties shall also have the right to challenge the arbitrator for a withdrawal:

(1) The arbitrator is a party in the case or a close relative of a party or of an agent in the case;

(2) The arbitrator has a personal interest in the case;

(3) The arbitrator has other relationship with a party or his agent in the case which may affect the impartiality of arbitration; or

(4) The arbitrator has privately met with a party or agent or accepted an invitation to entertainment or gift from a party or agent.

Article 35

If a party challenges an arbitrator, he shall submit his challenge, with a statement of the reasons therefore, prior to the first hearing. If the matter giving rise to the challenge became known after the first hearing, the challenge may be made before the conclusion of the final hearing of the case.

Article 36

The decision as to whether or not the arbitrator should withdraw shall be made by the chairman of the arbitration commission. If the chairman of the arbitration commission serves as an arbitrator, the decision shall be made collectively by the arbitration commission.

Article 37

If an arbitrator cannot perform his duties due to his withdrawal or for other reasons, a substitute arbitrator shall be selected or appointed in accordance with this Law.

After a substitute arbitrator has been selected or appointed on account of an arbitrator's withdrawal, a party may request that the arbitration proceedings already carried out should be carried out anew. The decision as to whether to approve it or not shall be made by the arbitration tribunal. The arbitration tribunal may also make a decision of its own motion as to whether or not the arbitration proceedings already carried out should be carried out anew.

Article 38

If an arbitrator is involved in the circumstances described in item (4) of Article 34 of this Law and the circumstances are serious or involved in the circumstances described in item (6) of Article 58 of this Law, he shall assume legal liability according to law and the arbitration commission shall remove his name from the register of arbitrators.

Section 3
Hearing and Award

Article 39

Arbitration shall be conducted by means of oral hearings. If the parties agree to arbitration without oral hearings, the arbitration tribunal may render an arbitration award on the basis of the written application for arbitration, the written defence and other material.

Article 40

Arbitration shall be conducted in camera. If the parties agree to public arbitration, the arbitration may be public unless State secrets are involved.

Article 41

The arbitration commission shall notify the parties of the date of the hearing within the time limit specified in the rules of arbitration. A party may, within the time limit specified in the rules of arbitration, request a postponement of the hearing if he has justified reasons therefore. The arbitration tribunal shall decide whether or not to postpone the hearing.

Article 42

If the claimant fails to appear before the arbitration tribunal without justified reasons after having been notified in writing or leaves the hearing prior to its conclusion without the permission of the arbitration tribunal, he may be deemed to have withdrawn his application for arbitration.

If the respondent fails to appear before the arbitration tribunal without justified reasons after having been notified in writing or leaves the hearing prior to its conclusion without the permission of the arbitration tribunal, a default award may be made.

Article 43

Parties shall provide evidences in support of their own arguments.

The arbitration tribunal may, as it considers necessary, collect evidences on its own.

Article 44

If the arbitration tribunal considers that a special issue requires appraisal, it may refer the issue for appraisal to an appraisal department agreed on by the parties or to an appraisal department designated by the arbitration tribunal.

If requested by a party or required by the arbitration tribunal, the appraisal department shall send its appraiser to attend the hearing. Subject to the permission of the arbitration tribunal, the parties may question the appraiser.

Article 45

The evidence shall be presented during the hearings and may be examined by the parties.

Article 46

Under circumstances where the evidence may be destroyed or lost or difficult to obtain at a later time, a party may apply for preservation of the evidence. If a party applies for preservation of the evidence, the arbitration commission shall submit his application to the basic people's court in the place where the evidence is located.

Article 47

The parties shall have the right to carry on debate in the course of arbitration. At the end of the debate, the presiding arbitrator or the sole arbitrator shall solicit final opinions from the parties.

Article 48

The arbitration tribunal shall make records of the hearings in writing. The parties and other participants in the arbitration shall have the right to apply for supplementation or correction of the record of their own statements if they consider that such record contains omissions or errors. If no supplementation or corrections are to be made, their application therefore shall be recorded.

The record shall be signed or sealed by the arbitrators, the recordist, the parties and other participants in the arbitration.

Article 49

After an application for arbitration has been made, the parties may settle their dispute on their own. If the parties have reached a settlement agreement, they may request the arbitration tribunal to make an arbitration award in accordance with the settlement agreement; alternatively, they may withdraw their application for arbitration.

Article 50

If a party repudiates the settlement agreement after the application for arbitration has been withdrawn, he may apply for arbitration again in accordance with the arbitration agreement.

Article 51

The arbitration tribunal may carry out conciliation prior to giving an arbitration award. The arbitration tribunal shall conduct conciliation if both parties voluntarily seek conciliation. If conciliation is unsuccessful, an arbitration award shall be made promptly.

If conciliation leads to a settlement agreement, the arbitration tribunal shall make a written conciliation statement or make an arbitration award in accordance with the result of the settlement agreement. A written conciliation statement and an arbitration award shall have equal legal effect.

Article 52

A written conciliation statement shall specify the arbitration claim and the results of the settlement agreed upon between the parties. The written conciliation statement shall be signed by the arbitrators, sealed by the arbitration commission, and then served on both parties.

The written conciliation statement shall become legally effective immediately after both parties have signed for receipt thereof.

If the written conciliation statement is repudiated by a party before he signs for receipt thereof, the arbitration tribunal shall promptly make an arbitration award.

Article 53

The arbitration award shall be made in accordance with the opinion of the majority of the arbitrators. The opinion of the minority of the arbitrators may be entered in the record. If the arbitration tribunal is unable to form a majority opinion, the arbitration award shall be made in accordance with the opinion of the presiding arbitrator.

Article 54

An arbitration award shall specify the arbitration claim, the facts of the dispute, the reasons for the decision, the results of the award, the allocation of arbitration fees and the date of the award. If the parties agree that they do not wish the facts of the dispute and the reasons for the decision to be specified in the arbitration award, the same may be omitted. The arbitration award shall be signed by the arbitrators and sealed by the arbitration commission. An arbitrator with dissenting opinions as to the arbitration award may sign the award or choose not to sign it.

Article 55

In arbitration proceedings, if a part of the facts involved has already become clear, the arbitration tribunal may first make an award in respect of such part of the facts.

Article 56

If there are literal or calculation errors in the arbitration award, or if the matters which have been decided by the arbitration tribunal are omitted in the arbitration award, the arbitration tribunal shall make due corrections or supplementation. The parties may, within 30 days from the date of receipt of the award, request the arbitration tribunal to make such corrections or supplementation.

Article 57

The arbitration award shall be legally effective as of the date on which it is made.

Chapter V
Application for Setting Aside Arbitration Award

Article 58

A party may apply for setting aside an arbitration award to the intermediate people's court in the place where the arbitration commission is located if he can produce evidence which proves that the arbitration award involves one of the following circumstances:

(1) There is no arbitration agreement;

(2) The matters decided in the award exceed the scope of the arbitration agreement or are beyond the arbitral authority of the arbitration commission;

(3) The formation of the arbitration tribunal or the arbitration procedure was not in conformity with the statutory procedure;

(4) The evidence on which the award is based was forged;

(5) The other party has withheld the evidence which is sufficient to affect the impartiality of the arbitration; or

(6) The arbitrators have committed embezzlement, accepted bribes or done malpractices for personal benefits or perverted the law in the arbitration of the case.

The people's court shall rule to set aside the arbitration award if a collegial panel formed by the people's court verifies upon examination that the award involves one of the circumstances set forth in the preceding paragraph.

If the people's court determines that the arbitration award violates the public interest, it shall rule to set aside the award.

Article 59

A party that wishes to apply for setting aside the arbitration award shall submit such application within six months from the date of receipt of the award.

Article 60

The people's court shall, within two months from the date of accepting an application for setting aside an arbitration award, rule to set aside the award or to reject the application.

Article 61

If, after accepting an application for setting aside an arbitration award, the people's court considers that the case may be re-arbitrated by the arbitration tribunal, it shall notify the tribunal that it shall re-arbitrate the case within a certain time limit and shall rule to stay the setting-aside procedure. If the arbitration tribunal refuses to re-arbitrate the case, the people's court shall rule to resume the setting-aside procedure.

Chapter VI
Enforcement

Article 62

The parties shall perform the arbitration award. If a party fails to perform the arbitration award, the other party may apply to the people's court for enforcement in accordance with the relevant provisions of the Civil Procedure Law. The people's court to which the application has been made shall enforce the award.

Article 63

If the party against whom the enforcement is sought presents evidence which proves that the arbitration award involves one of the circumstances set forth in the second paragraph of Article 217 of the Civil Procedure Law, the people's court shall, after examination and verification by a collegial panel formed by the people's court, rule to disallow the award.

Article 64

If one party applies for enforcement of the arbitration award and the other party applies for setting aside the arbitration award, the people's court shall rule to suspend the procedure of enforcement.

If the people's court rules to set aside the arbitration award, it shall rule to terminate the enforcement procedure. If the people's court rules to reject the application for setting aside the arbitration award, it shall rule to resume the enforcement procedure.

Chapter VII
Special Provisions for Arbitration Involving Foreign Elements

Article 65

The provisions of this Chapter shall apply to the arbitration of disputes arising from economic, trade, transportation and maritime activities involving a foreign element. For matters not covered in this Chapter, the other relevant provisions of this Law shall apply.

Article 66

Foreign-related arbitration commissions may be organised and established by the China Chamber of International Commerce.

A foreign-related arbitration commission shall be composed of one chairman, a certain number of vice chairmen and members.

The chairman, vice chairmen and members of a foreign-related arbitration commission may be appointed by the China Chamber of International Commerce.

Article 67

A foreign-related arbitration commission may appoint arbitrators from among foreigners with special knowledge in the fields of law, economy and trade, science and technology, etc.

Article 68

If a party to a foreign-related arbitration applies for preservation of the evidence, the foreign-related arbitration commission shall submit his application to the intermediate people's court in the place where the evidence is located.

Article 69

A foreign-related arbitration tribunal may enter the details of the hearings in written records or make written minutes thereof. The written minutes may be signed or sealed by the parties and other participants in the arbitration.

Article 70

If a party presents evidence which proves that a foreign-related arbitration award involves one of the circumstances set forth in the first paragraph of Article 260 of the Civil Procedure Law, the people's court shall, after examination and verification by a collegial panel formed by the people's court, rule to set aside the award.

Article 71

If the party against whom the enforcement is sought presents evidence which proves that the foreign-related arbitration award involves one of the circumstances set forth in the first paragraph of Article 260 of the Civil Procedure Law, the people's court shall, after examination and verification by a collegial panel formed by the people's court, rule to disallow the enforcement.

Article 72

If a party applies for enforcement of a legally effective arbitration award made by a foreign-related arbitration commission and if the party against whom the enforcement is sought or such party's property is not within the territory of the People's Republic of China, he shall directly apply to a competent foreign court for recognition and enforcement of the award.

Article 73

Foreign-related arbitration rules may be formulated by the China Chamber of International Commerce in accordance with this Law and the relevant provisions of the Civil Procedure Law.

Chapter VIII
Supplementary Provisions

Article 74

If prescription for arbitration is provided by law, such provisions shall apply. In the absence of such provisions, the prescription for litigation shall apply to arbitration.

Article 75

Prior to the formulation of rules of arbitration by China Arbitration Association, arbitration commissions may formulate provisional rules of arbitration in accordance with this Law and the relevant provisions of the Civil Procedure Law.

Article 76

Parties shall pay arbitration fees according to regulations.

Measures for charging arbitration fees shall be submitted to the price control authorities for examination and approval.

Article 77

Regulations concerning arbitration of labour disputes and agricultural contractor's contract disputes arising within the agricultural collective economic organisations shall be formulated separately.

Article 78

If regulations governing arbitration promulgated prior to the implementation of this Law contravene the provisions of this Law, the provisions of this Law shall prevail.

Article 79

Arbitration institutions established prior to the implementation of this Law in the municipalities directly under the Central Government, in the cities that are the seats of the people's governments of provinces or autonomous regions and in other cities divided into districts shall be reorganised in accordance with this Law. Those of such arbitration institutions that have not been reorganised shall terminate upon the end of one year from the date of the implementation of this Law.

Other arbitration institutions established prior to the implementation of this Law that do not comply with the provisions of this Law shall terminate on the date of the implementation of this Law.

Article 80

This Law shall go into effect as of 1 September 1995.

Appendix 3
China Civil Procedure Law 2012[259]
(provisions related to arbitration)

(Adopted at the Fourth Session of the Seventh National People's Congress on 9 April 1991, and amended for the first time according to the 'Decision on Amending the 'Civil Procedure Law of the People's Republic of China'" as adopted at the 30th Session of the Standing Committee of the 10th National People's Congress on 28 October 2007, and amended for the second time according to the 'Decision on Amending the "Civil Procedure Law of the People's Republic of China"' as adopted at the 28th Session of the Standing Committee of the 11th National People's Congress on 31 August 2012.)

Chapter 6
Evidence

...

Article 81

...

Under the emergencies in which evidence is lost or it will be difficult to collect such evidence in the future, an interested party may, before the case or arbitration is filed, apply for preservation of such evidence with the people's court in the place where the evidence to be preserved is located or the place where the respondent is domiciled, or the people's court with jurisdiction over the case.

...

---

259 The English translation of the Civil Procedure Law of the People's Republic of China is from *China Law & Reference* produced by Wolters Kluwer China. With thanks to Roberto Salvi <www.inchinalaw.com>.

Chapter 8
Mediation

Article 93

In handling civil cases, the people's court may distinguish between right and wrong and mediate disputes according to the principle of parties' voluntariness and based on clear facts.

Article 94

When a people's court conducts mediation, a single judge or a collegial bench may preside in the mediation. Mediations shall be conducted locally whenever possible.

When a people's court conducts mediation, it may employ simplified methods to notify the parties and witnesses to appear in court.

Article 95

When a people's court conducts mediation, it may request assistance from relevant units or individuals. The invited units or individuals shall assist the people's court in mediation.

Article 96

A mediation agreement must be based on voluntariness of both parties, and shall not be reached through compulsion. The content of the mediation agreement may not contravene the law.

Article 97

When a mediation agreement is reached, the people's court shall draw up a written mediation agreement. A mediation agreement shall clearly set forth the claims of the action, the facts about the case, and the result of the mediation.

The mediation statement shall be signed by the judge and the court clerk, sealed by the people's court, and served on both parties. Once the mediation agreement is signed and exchanged by both parties, it shall become legally binding.

Article 98

The people's court need not draw up a mediation agreement for the following cases when an agreement is reached through mediation:

(1) Divorce cases in which both parties have become reconciled after mediation;

(2) Adoption cases in which adoptive relationship has been retained through mediation;

(3) Cases in which the claims can be immediately satisfied; and

(4) Other cases that do not require mediation statements.

Any agreement that does not require a mediation agreement shall be entered into the transcript and become legally effective after the transcript is signed or sealed by both parties, the judge, and the court clerk.

Article 99

If no agreement is reached through mediation or if one party retracts his reconciliation before the mediation agreement is served, the people's court shall render a judgment without delay.

Chapter 9
Preservation and Advance Enforcement

...

Article 101

...

Where the applicant fails to institute legal proceedings or apply for arbitration within 30 days in accordance with the law after the people's court takes preservation measures, the people's court shall rescind the said measures.

...

Chapter 10
Compulsory Measures against Obstruction of Civil Actions

...

Article 113

Where a person subject to execution colludes with other people in bad faith attempting to evade obligations specified in the legal documents through litigation, arbitration or mediation, the people's court shall, according to the seriousness of the circumstances, impose a fine on him or detain him; if a crime is constituted, his criminal responsibility shall be investigated according to the law.

...

Chapter 12
Ordinary Procedure of First Instance

Section 1
Filing and Accepting Lawsuits

...

Article 124

With respect to lawsuits described below, the people's court shall deal with them in light of their specific circumstances:

...

If, according to the law, both parties have reached a written agreement to submit their dispute to an arbitral organ for arbitration and they may not institute legal proceedings with a people's court, the people's court shall notify the plaintiff to apply to the arbitral organ for arbitration;

..

Section 5
Judgments and Rulings

...

Article 154

Rulings shall be applicable to the following:

...

(9) Cancellation of or refusal to enforce an arbitration award;

...

An appeal may be lodged against a ruling in Items (1), (2) and (3) mentioned above.

...

Chapter 20
Application and Referral of Enforcement

...

Article 237

If a party fails to comply with an award made by an arbitration institution that was established according to law, the other party may apply for enforcement to the people's court which has jurisdiction over the case. The applied people's court shall enforce the award.

If the party whom the application of enforcement is filed against provides evidence to prove that the arbitration award involves any of the following circumstances, the people's court shall, after examination and verification by a collegial bench, rule to revoke the enforcement of the arbitration award:

(1) Where the parties have not stipulated an arbitration clause in the contract or have not subsequently reached a written agreement on arbitration;

(2) Where the matters being arbitrated exceed the scope of the arbitration agreement or the authority of the arbitration agency;

(3) Where the formation of an arbitration tribunal or the procedure of arbitration is not in conformity with the legal procedure;

(4) The evidence based on which the arbitral award is made is falsified;

(5) The other parties conceal the evidence from the arbitral organ and is sufficient to affect the impartiality of the arbitral award; or

(6) Where the arbitrators involved in any of conducts of embezzlement, bribery, practicing favouritism for himself or relatives, twisting the law in rendering arbitration award.

If a people's court determines that the enforcement of an arbitration award would contradict the social and public interest, it shall make a ruling of not to enforce the award.

The above-mentioned order shall be served on both parties and the arbitration agency.

Where an arbitration award is ruled by a people's court not to be enforced, the parties may, according to the written arbitration agreement reached by them, apply to the arbitration agency for a new arbitration or bring a lawsuit to a people's court.

...

Chapter 26
Arbitration

Article 271

For disputes involving foreign economic, trade, transport, or maritime activities, if the parties have stipulated clauses on arbitration in their contracts or have subsequently reached written agreements on arbitration, they shall submit such disputes for arbitration to the foreign-affair arbitration institutions of the People's Republic of China and shall not bring lawsuits in a people's court.

If the parties have not stipulated clauses on arbitration in the contract or have not subsequently reached a written agreement on arbitration, they may file a lawsuit in a people's court.

Article 272

If a party applies for the adoption of preservation measure, the foreign-affair arbitration institution of the People's Republic of China shall submit the party's application to the intermediate people's court located in the place where the person against whom the application for the preservation is filed has his domicile or where the person's property is located.

Article 273

If one party fails to comply with the award made by a foreign-affair arbitration institution of the People's Republic of China, the other party may apply for the enforcement of the award to the intermediate people's court located in the place where the person against whom the application for the enforcement is made has his domicile or where the property of the person is located.

Article 274

If a defendant provides evidence to prove that the arbitration award made by a foreign-affair arbitration institution of the People's Republic of China involves any of the following circumstances, the people's court shall, after examination and verification by a collegial bench, rule to disallow the enforcement of the award:

(1) The parties have not stipulated any clause regarding arbitration in their contract or have not subsequently reached a written agreement on arbitration;

(2) The defendant is not duly notified of the appointment of the arbitrators or the arbitration proceeding, or the defendant fails to express his defence due to the reasons for which he is not held responsible;

(3) The formation of the arbitration panel or the arbitration procedure is not in conformity with rules of arbitration; or

(4) The matters decided by arbitration exceed the scope of the arbitration agreement or the authority of the arbitration institution.

If a people's court determines that the enforcement of an award will violate the social and public interest, the court shall make a ruling to disallow the enforcement of the arbitration award.

Article 275

If the enforcement of an arbitration award is disallowed, the parties may reach a written agreement on arbitration to re-submit their dispute for a new arbitration or file a lawsuit in a people's court.

Chapter 27
Judicial Assistance

Article 276

According to the international treaties concluded or acceded to by the People's Republic of China or the principle of reciprocity, the people's courts of China and foreign courts may request each other's assistance in the service of legal documents, the investigation and collection of evidence, or other litigation actions.

If any matter requested by a foreign court for assistance would impair the sovereignty, security, or social and public interests of the People's Republic of China, the people's court shall refuse the request.

Article 277

A request for providing of judicial assistance shall be conducted through channels stipulated in the international treaties concluded or acceded to by the People's Republic of China; if there is no treaty regarding judicial assistance between China and the foreign country, such a request may be made through diplomatic channels.

A foreign embassy or consulate to the People's Republic of China may serve legal documents to its citizens or conduct the investigation and collection of evidence on its citizens with the conditions of no laws of the People's Republic of China to be violated and no compulsory measures to be taken.

Except for the circumstances proscribed in the preceding paragraph, no foreign organ or individual may, without obtaining an approval from the relevant authorities of the People's Republic of China, serve documents or conduct any investigation and collection of evidence within the territory of the People's Republic of China.

Article 278

A letter of request for judicial assistance and its annexes submitted by a foreign court to a people's court shall be appended with Chinese translations or the texts in the language specified in the relevant international treaty.

A letter of request and its annexes submitted to a foreign court by a people's court for judicial assistance shall also be appended with the translations in the language of the country or the texts in the language specified in the relevant international treaty.

Article 279

The judicial assistance provided by the people's courts shall be carried out according to the procedure stipulated by the laws of the People's Republic of China. If a foreign court request for judicial assistance to be conducted in a special method, it may be conducted as requested as long as the special method does not violate any laws of the People's Republic of China.

Article 280

If a party applies for enforcement of a legally effective judgment or ruling made by a people's court and the party subject to the enforcement or its property is not within the territory of the People's Republic of China, the applicant may directly apply for the recognition and enforcement of the judgment or ruling to the foreign court that has jurisdiction over the case, or have the people's court request a foreign court to recognise and enforce the judgment or ruling according to the relevant provisions of the international treaties concluded or acceded to by China or on the principle of reciprocity.

If a party applies for the enforcement of a legally effective arbitration award made by a foreign-affair arbitration institution of the People's Republic of China and the party subject to the enforcement or its property is not within the territory of the People's Republic of China, the applicant may directly apply for the recognition and enforcement of the arbitration award to the foreign court that has jurisdiction over the case.

Article 281

If a legally effective judgment or ruling made by a foreign court seeks the recognition and enforcement of a people's court of the People's Republic of China, the party may directly apply to the intermediate people's court of the People's Republic of China that has the jurisdiction over the case for the recognition and enforcement, or the foreign court may, according to the provisions of the international treaties concluded or acceded to by the People's Republic of China or based on the principle of reciprocity, request the recognition and enforcement of a people's court.

Article 282

After a people's court of the People's Republic of China reviews an application or pleading for the recognition and enforcement of a legally effective judgment or ruling rendered by a foreign court according to the international treaties concluded or acceded to by the People's Republic of China or based on the principle of reciprocity, if the court considers that such a judgment or ruling does not contradict the basic principles of the laws of the People's Republic of

China nor violates the national, social, and public interest of China, the court may render a ruling to recognise its force. Where the enforcement is necessary, the court may issue an order to enforce a foreign judgment according to the relevant provisions of this Law. If a legally effective judgment or ruling rendered by a foreign court contradicts the basic principles of the law of the People's Republic of China or the national, social, and public interest of China, the people's court shall reject the application of recognition and enforcement.

Article 283

If an award made by a foreign arbitration institution needs the recognition and enforcement of a people's court of the People's Republic of China, the party shall directly apply to the intermediate people's court located in the place where the party subject to the enforcement has its domicile or where its property is located. The people's court shall deal with the matter according to the relevant provisions of the international treaties concluded or acceded to by the People's Republic of China or on the principle of reciprocity.

Article 284

This Law shall become effective as of the date of promulgation, and the Civil Procedure Law of the People's Republic of China (for Trial Implementation) shall be annulled as of the same date.

Appendix 4
Circular of Supreme People's Court on Implementing Convention on the Recognition and Enforcement of Foreign Arbitral Awards Entered by China[260]

All Higher People's Courts and Intermediate People's Courts throughout the country, all maritime courts, and railway transportation intermediate courts,

It is determined at the 18th session of the Standing Committee of the 6th National People's Congress on 2 December 1986 that China shall enter the Convention on the Recognition and Enforcement of Foreign Arbitral Awards (hereinafter referred to as the 1958 New York Convention) adopted in 1958 in New York. The Convention shall come into effect in China as of 22 April 1987. All Higher and Intermediate People's Courts shall immediately organise economic and civil judicial officers, executive personnel and other related personnel to diligently study this important Convention and to faithfully enforce the Convention. It is hereby notified several issues concerning the implementation of this Convention as follows:

Article 1

In accordance with the reciprocity reservation statement made by China when entering the Convention, this Convention shall apply to the recognition and enforcement of an arbitral award made in the territory of another Contracting State. Where there is any conflict between the provisions of this convention and the provisions of China's Civil Procedure Law (Trial Implementation), this Convention shall prevail.

Any arbitral award made within the territory of a Non-contracting State that needs to be recognised and enforced by

260 <www.cietac.org/index.php?m=Article&a=show&id=2413&l=en>.

Chinese Courts shall be handled in accordance with Article 204 of the Civil Procedure Law (Trial Implementation).

Article 2

In accordance with the commercial reservation statement made by China when entering the Convention, this Convention shall only apply to the disputes arising from contractual and non-contractual commercial legal relationship. 'Contractual and non-contractual commercial legal relationship' specifically refers to the economic rights and obligations resulted from contract, infringement or arising according to law, such as sale of goods, lease of property, project contracting, processing, technology assignment, joint adventure, joint business operation, exploration and development of natural resources, insurance, credit, labour service, surrogate, consultation service, marine/civil aviation/railway/road passenger and cargo transportation, product liability, environment pollution, marine accident, dispute over ownership, etc., and it does not include the dispute between foreign investors and the host government.

Article 3

In accordance with Article 4 of the 1958 New York Convention, the application to people's courts in China for recognition and enforcement of arbitration awards made within the territory of another contracting state shall be filed by one party of the arbitration award. The application of the party shall be accepted by the intermediate people's courts in the following places:

(1) Where the person subject to enforcement is a natural person, it shall be the place where his/her residence is registered or where his/her domicile is located;

(2) Where the person subject to enforcement is a legal person, it shall be the place where its principal executive office is located;

(3) Where the person subject to enforcement does not have residence, domicile or principal executive office in China but has property within the territory of China, it shall be the place where his//her/its property is located.

Article 4

After the people's court of China with jurisdiction receives the application of one party, it shall examine the arbitration award whose recognition and enforcement has been applied for; if the court believes that the circumstances listed in Subparagraph 1 and Subparagraph 2 of Article 5 of the 1958 New York Convention, it shall rule that the validity of award shall be recognised and that the award shall be enforced according to Civil Procedure Law (Trial Implementation); if the court holds that any of the circumstances listed in Subparagraph 2 of Article 5 exists, or the evidence provided by the person subject to enforcement proves that any of the circumstances listed in Subparagraph 1 of Article 5 exists, it shall dismiss the application and refuse to recognise and enforce the arbitration award.

Article 5

The arbitration awards whose recognition and enforcement are applied for to the people's court in China are confined to arbitration awards made by another contracting state after the 1958 New York Convention takes effect in China. The application shall be filed within the time limit for enforcement provided for in Article 169 of Civil Procedure Law (Trial Implementation).

It is hereby notified for your compliance.

Attachment I
Relevant Provisions Quoted from Convention on the Recognition and Enforcement of Foreign Arbitral Awards in this Circular

Article 4

(1) To obtain the recognition and enforcement mentioned in the preceding article, the party applying for recognition and enforcement shall, at the time of the application, supply:

A. The duly authenticated original award or a duly certified copy thereof;

B. The original agreement referred to in article II or a duly certified copy thereof.

(2) If the said award or agreement is not made in an official language of the country in which the award is relied upon, the party applying for recognition and enforcement of the award shall produce a translation of these documents into such language. The translation shall be certified by an official or sworn translator or by a diplomatic or consular agent.

Article 5

(1) Recognition and enforcement of the award may be refused, at the request of the party against whom it is invoked, only if that party furnishes to the competent authority where the recognition and enforcement is sought, proof that:

A. The parties to the agreement referred to in article II were, under the law applicable to them, under some incapacity, or the said agreement is not valid under the law to which the parties have subjected it or, failing any indication thereon, under the law of the country where the award was made; or

B. The party against whom the award is invoked was not given proper notice of the appointment of the arbitrator or of the arbitration proceedings or was otherwise unable to present his case; or

C. The award deals with a difference not contemplated by or not falling within the terms of the submission to arbitration, or it contains decisions on matters beyond the scope of the submission to arbitration, provided that, if the decisions on matters submitted to arbitration can be separated from those not so submitted, that part of the award which contains decisions on matters submitted to arbitration may be recognised and enforced; or

D. The composition of the arbitral authority or the arbitral procedure was not in accordance with the agreement of the parties, or, failing such agreement, was not in accordance with the law of the country where the arbitration took place; or

E. The award has not yet become binding on the parties, or has been set aside or suspended by a competent authority of the country in which, or under the law of which, that award was made.

(2) Recognition and enforcement of an arbitral award may also be refused if the competent authority in the country where recognition and enforcement is sought finds that:

A. The subject matter of the difference is not capable of settlement by arbitration under the law of that country; or

B. The recognition or enforcement of the award would be contrary to the public policy of that country.

Attachment II
Relevant Provisions Quoted from Civil Procedure Law of the People's Republic of China (Trial Implementation) in this Circular

Article 169

The time limit for the submission of an application for enforcement shall be one year, if both or one of the parties are individuals; it shall be six months if both parties are enterprises, institutions, government organs or other organisations.

Article 204

With regard to the determined judgment or ruling entrusted by a foreign court for enforcement, the people's court of China shall examine it in accordance with the international treaties concluded or acceded to by the People's Republic of China or in light of the principle of reciprocity; if the people's court finds that it does not contravene the basic principles of the law of the People's Republic of China nor violates State sovereignty, security and social and public interests of China, it shall recognise the validity of the judgment or ruling and enforce it in accordance with the relevant provisions of this Law. Otherwise, the judgment or ruling shall be returned to the foreign court.

Attachment III
Countries Acceded to Convention on the Recognition and Enforcement of Foreign Arbitral Awards

Denmark (1,2), France (1,2), Greece (1,2), Roman Catholic Church (1,2), the United States (1,2), Austria (1), Belgium (1), Federal Republic of Germany (1), Ireland (1), Japan (1), Luxembourg (1), Holland (1), Switzerland (1), England (1), Norway (1), Australia, Finland, New Zealand (1), San Marino, Spain, Italy, Canada, Sweden, German Democratic Republic (1,2), Hungary (1,2), Poland (1,2), Romania (1,2), Yugoslavia (1,2,3), Bulgaria (1), Czechoslovakia (1), Soviet Union, The Republic of Belarus of Soviet Union (1), Republic of Ukraine of Soviet Union (1), Botswana (1,2), Central African Republic (1,2), China (1,2), Cuba (1,2), Cyprus (1,2), Ecuador (1,2), India (1,2), Indonesia (1,2), Madagascar (1,2), Nigeria (1,2), Philippine (1,2), Trinidad and Tobago (1,2), Tunis (1,2), Guatemala (1,2), South Korea (1,2), Monaco (1,2), Kuwait (1), Morocco (1), Tanzania (1), Benin, Chile, Columbia, Democratic Kampuchea, Egypt, Ghana, Israel, Jordan, Mexico, Niger, South Africa, Sri

Lanka, Syria, Thailand, Uruguay, Djibouti, Haiti, Panama, Malaysia, Singapore

Note:

1. The country makes a statement that this Convention shall only apply to the arbitration awards made within the territory of another contracting state, that is, the country makes reciprocity reservation.

2. The country makes a statement that this Convention shall only apply to the recognised disputes arising from commercial legal relationship (contractual or non-contractual), that is, the country makes commercial reservation.

3. The country makes a statement that it shall only recognise and enforce the arbitration awards made by foreign countries after the country enters this Convention.

Appendix 5
Interpretation of the Supreme People's Court concerning Some Issues on Application of the Arbitration Law of the People's Republic of China[261]

Announcement of the Supreme People's Court

The 'Interpretation of the Supreme People's Court concerning Some Issues on Application of the Arbitration Law of the People's Republic of China', which was adopted at the 1375th meeting of the Judicial Committee of the Supreme People's Court on 26 December 2005, is hereby promulgated, and shall come into force on 8 September 2006.

23 August 2006

Interpretation of the Supreme People's Court concerning Some Issues on Application of the Arbitration Law of the People's Republic of China

(Adopted at the 1375th meeting of the Judicial Committee of the Supreme People's Court on 26 December 2005, Interpretation No. 7 [2006] of the Supreme People's Court)

In accordance with the 'Arbitration Law of the People's Republic of China', the 'Civil Litigation Law of the People's Republic of China' and other legal provisions, we hereby give our interpretation as follows concerning some issues on application of law for the people's courts to try arbitration-related cases:

261 <www.cietac.org/index.php?m=Article&a=show&id=2422&l=en>.

Article 1

The term 'agreements for arbitration in other written forms' as prescribed in Article 16 of the Arbitration Law shall include the agreements on resorting to arbitration which are reached in the forms of contracts, letters or data message (including telegraph, telefax, fax, electronic data interchange and e-mail), etc.

Article 2

Where the parties concerned synoptically agree that the matters to be arbitrated are contractual disputes, the disputes arising out of formation, effectiveness, modification, assignment, performance, liabilities for breach, interpretation, rescission, etc. of the contract may all be ascertained as matters to be arbitrated.

Article 3

Where the name of an arbitration institution as stipulated in the agreement for arbitration is inaccurate, but the specific arbitration institution can be determined, it shall be ascertained that the arbitration institution has been selected.

Article 4

Where an agreement for arbitration only stipulates the arbitration rules applicable to the dispute, it shall be deemed that the arbitration institution is not stipulated, unless the parties concerned reach a supplementary agreement or may determine the arbitration institution according to the arbitration rules agreed upon between them.

Article 5

Where an agreement for arbitration stipulates two or more arbitration institutions, the parties concerned may choose either arbitration institution upon agreement when applying for arbitration; if the parties concerned cannot agree upon the choice of the arbitration institution, the agreement for arbitration shall be ineffective.

Article 6

Where an agreement for arbitration stipulates that the disputes shall be arbitrated by the arbitration institution at a certain locality and there is only one arbitration institution in this locality, the arbitration institution shall be deemed as the stipulated arbitration institution. If there are two or more arbitration institutions, the parties concerned may choose one arbitration institution for arbitration upon agreement; if the parties concerned fail to agree upon the choice of the arbitration institution, the agreement for arbitration shall be ineffective.

Article 7

Where the parties concerned agree that they may either apply to the arbitration institution for arbitration or bring a lawsuit with people's court for settlement of dispute, the agreement for arbitration shall be ineffective, unless after one party applies to the arbitration institution for arbitration, the other party fails to propose any objection within the period prescribed in Paragraph 2 of Article 20 of the Arbitration Law.

Article 8

Where a party concerned is merged or divided after concluding an agreement for arbitration, the agreement for arbitration shall be binding upon the successor of its rights and obligations.

Where a party concerned has died after concluding an agreement for arbitration, the agreement for arbitration shall be binding upon the inheritor who inherits his rights and obligations in the matter to be arbitrated.

The circumstances prescribed in the preceding two paragraphs shall not be applicable if the parties concerned have otherwise agreed between each other when concluding the agreement for arbitration.

Article 9

Where the credits or debts are entirely or partially assigned, the agreement for arbitration shall be binding upon the assignee, unless the parties concerned have otherwise agreed, or the assignee explicitly objects to the assignment of the credits or debts or does not know there is a separate agreement for arbitration.

Article 10

Where a contract does not become effective or is cancelled after being formed, the effectiveness of the agreement for arbitration shall be ascertained under Paragraph 1 of Article 19 of the Arbitration Law.

Where the parties concerned reach an agreement for arbitration regarding a dispute when concluding the contract, the effectiveness of the agreement for arbitration shall not be impacted if the contract is not formed.

Article 11

Where a contract stipulates that an effective arbitration clause in another contract or document shall apply in order to settle the disputes, the parties concerned shall, when a contractual dispute arises, resort to arbitration according to the said arbitration clause.

Where a relevant international treaty applicable to contracts involving foreign interests contains an arbitration provision, the parties concerned shall, when a contractual dispute arises, resort to arbitration in accordance with the arbitration provision in the international treaty.

Article 12

A case in which a party concerned applies to the people's court for confirmation of the effectiveness of an agreement for arbitration shall be under the jurisdiction of the intermediate people's court at the locality of the arbitration institution agreed upon in the agreement for arbitration; if the arbitration institution in the agreement for arbitration is not clearly stipulated, the said case shall be under the jurisdiction of the intermediate people's court at the locality of conclusion of the agreement for arbitration or at the respondent's domicile.

A case on applying for confirmation of the effectiveness of an agreement for arbitration involving foreign interests shall be under the jurisdiction of the intermediate people's court at the locality of the arbitration institution agreed upon in the agreement for arbitration, at the locality of conclusion of the agreement for arbitration, or at the claimant's or respondent's domicile.

A case on the effectiveness of an agreement for arbitration of a maritime dispute shall be under the jurisdiction of the maritime court at the locality of the arbitration institution agreed upon in the agreement for arbitration, at the locality of conclusion of the agreement for arbitration, or at the claimant's or respondent's domicile; if there is no maritime court at the above-mentioned places, it shall be under the jurisdiction of the nearest maritime court.

Article 13

As required by Paragraph 2 of Article 20 of the Arbitration Law, if a party concerned fails to object to the effectiveness of the agreement for arbitration prior to the first hearing in the arbitral tribunal, and then applies to the people's court for confirming the agreement for arbitration as ineffective, the application shall not be accepted by the people's court.

Where, after an arbitration institution makes a decision on the effectiveness of an agreement for arbitration, a party concerned applies to the people's court for confirming the agreement for arbitration as effective or applies for revoking the arbitration institution's decision, the application shall not be accepted by the people's court.

Article 14

The term 'the first hearing' as mentioned in Article 26 of the Arbitration Law shall refer to the first trial in court, which is organised by the people's court after expiry of the period for defence, excluding all procedural activities prior to the trial.

Article 15

A people's court shall, when trying a case for confirmation of the effectiveness of an agreement for arbitration, form a collegial panel to make examination, and shall inquire of the parties concerned.

Article 16

The examination of the effectiveness of an agreement for arbitration which involves foreign interests shall be governed by the laws agreed upon between the parties concerned; if the parties concerned did not agree upon the applicable laws but have agreed upon the place of arbitration, the laws at the place of arbitration shall apply; if they neither agreed upon the applicable laws nor agreed upon the place of arbitration or the place of arbitration is not clearly agreed upon, the laws at the locality of the court shall apply.

Article 17

Where a party concerned applies for revocation of an arbitral award on a ground not prescribed in Article 58 of the Arbitration Law or Article 260 of the Civil Litigation Law, the application shall not be supported by the people's court.

Article 18

The term 'no agreement for arbitration' as prescribed in Item (1) of Paragraph 1 of Article 58 of the Arbitration Law shall refer to that the parties concerned did not reach an agreement for arbitration. If the agreement for arbitration is ascertained as ineffective or is revoked, it shall be deemed that there is no agreement for arbitration.

Article 19

Where a party concerned applies for revocation of an arbitral award on the ground that the matter under arbitration goes beyond the scope of the agreement for arbitration, and the application is found true from examination, the people's court shall revoke the excessive part in the arbitral award. If, however, the excessive part is inseparable from other matter under arbitration, the people's court shall revoke the arbitral award.

Article 20

The term 'violation of legal procedures' as prescribed in Article 58 of the Arbitration Law shall refer to violation of the arbitration procedures prescribed in the Arbitration Law or a circumstance under which the arbitration rules chosen by the parties concerned might affect the correct award for the case.

Article 21

Where a case regarding which a party concerned applies for revoking the domestic arbitral award is under any of the following circumstances, the people's court may, in accordance with Article 61 of the Arbitration Law, notify the arbitral tribunal to arbitrate the case for a second time within a time limit:

(1) The evidence on which the arbitral award is based is forged; or

(2) The other party concealed any evidence, which is enough to impact the impartial award.

The people's court shall state in the notice the specific ground for requiring re-arbitration.

Article 22

Where an arbitral tribunal fails to begin the re-arbitration within the time limit specified by the people's court, the people's court shall rule to terminate the revocation procedures; if the re-arbitration is not begun, the people's court shall rule to resume the revocation procedures.

Article 23

Where a party concerned is dissatisfied with a re-arbitration award, it may, within six months as of service of the re-arbitration award, apply to the people's court for revocation of the re-arbitration award in accordance with Article 58 of the Arbitration Law.

Article 24

With respect to a case regarding which a party concerned applies for revocation of the arbitral award, the people's court shall form a collegial panel to try it, and inquire of the parties concerned.

Article 25

Where, after a people's court accepts the application filed by a party concerned for revocation of the arbitral award, the other party applies for enforcement of the same arbitral award, the people's court that accepts the said enforcement application shall rule to suspend the enforcement after the acceptance.

Article 26

Where, after the application filed by a party concerned to the people's court for revocation of the arbitral award is rejected, the said party proposes its demur to no enforcement in the enforcement procedures on the same ground, such a demur shall not be supported by the people's court.

Article 27

Where a party concerned did not object to the effectiveness of an agreement for arbitration in the arbitration procedures, and requests revocation of the arbitral award or proposes demur to no enforcement on the ground of ineffectiveness of the agreement for arbitration after the arbitral award is rendered, the people's court shall not support its request or demur.

Where a party concerned objects to the effectiveness of an agreement for arbitration in the arbitration procedures, but requests revocation of the arbitral award or proposes demur to no enforcement on that ground after the arbitral award is rendered, the request or demur shall be supported by the people's court if it is found from examination to conform to Article 58 of the Arbitration Law or Article 217 or 260 of the Civil Litigation Law.

Article 28

Where a party concerned requests no enforcement of a letter of arbitral reconciliation or an arbitral award rendered on the basis of the reconciliation agreement between the parties, such a request shall not be supported by the people's court.

Article 29

A case regarding which a party concerned applies for enforcement of the arbitral award shall be under the jurisdiction of the intermediate people's court at the domicile of the party under enforcement or at the locality of the properties to be enforced.

Article 30

When actually required by the trial of a case on revocation or enforcement of an arbitral award, the people's court may ask the arbitration institution to make an explanation or may consult arbitration files from the relevant arbitration institution.

The ruling rendered by a people's court in the process of handling a case involving arbitration may be served on the relevant arbitration institution.

Article 31

The present Interpretation shall come into force as of the date of promulgation.

In case any previous judicial interpretation promulgated by the present court is inconsistent with the present Interpretation, the present Interpretation shall prevail.

Appendix 6
China International Economic and Trade Arbitration Commission (CIETAC) Arbitration Rules[262]

(Revised and adopted by the China Council for the Promotion of International Trade/China Chamber of International Commerce on 4 November 2014. Effective as of 1 January 2015)

Chapter I
General Provisions

Article 1
The Arbitration Commission

1. The China International Economic and Trade Arbitration Commission ('CIETAC'), originally named the Foreign Trade Arbitration Commission of the China Council for the Promotion of International Trade and later renamed the Foreign Economic and Trade Arbitration Commission of the China Council for the Promotion of International Trade, concurrently uses as its name the 'Arbitration Institute of the China Chamber of International Commerce'.

2. Where an arbitration agreement provides for arbitration by the China Council for the Promotion of International Trade/China Chamber of International Commerce, or by the Arbitration Commission or the Arbitration Institute of the China Council for the Promotion of International Trade/ China Chamber of International Commerce, or refers to CIETAC's previous names, it shall be deemed that the parties have agreed to arbitration by CIETAC.

262 <http://cietac.org/index.php?m=Page&a=index&id=42&l=en>.

Article 2

Structure and Duties

1. The Chairman of CIETAC shall perform the functions and duties vested in him/her by these Rules while a Vice Chairman may perform the Chairman' s functions and duties with the Chairman's authorization.

2. CIETAC has an Arbitration Court (the 'Arbitration Court'), which performs its functions in accordance with these Rules under the direction of the authorized Vice Chairman and the President of the Arbitration Court.

3. CIETAC is based in Beijing. It has sub-commissions or arbitration centres (Appendix I). The sub-commissions/ arbitration centres are CIETAC's branches, which accept arbitration applications and administer arbitration cases with CIETAC's authorization.

4. A sub-commission/arbitration centre has an arbitration court, which performs the functions of the Arbitration Court in accordance with these Rules under the direction of the president of the arbitration court of the sub-commission/ arbitration centre.

5. Where a case is administered by a sub-commission/ arbitration centre, the functions and duties vested in the President of the Arbitration Court under these Rules may, by his/her authorization, be performed by the president of the arbitration court of the relevant sub-commission/arbitration centre.

6. The parties may agree to submit their disputes to CIETAC or a sub-commission/arbitration centre of CIETAC for arbitration. Where the parties have agreed to arbitration by CIETAC, the Arbitration Court shall accept the arbitration application and administer the case. Where the parties have agreed to arbitration by a sub-commission/arbitration centre, the arbitration court of the sub-commission/arbitration centre agreed upon by the parties shall accept the arbitration application and administer the case. Where the sub-

commission/arbitration centre agreed upon by the parties does not exist or its authorization has been terminated, or where the agreement is ambiguous, the Arbitration Court shall accept the arbitration application and administer the case. In the event of any dispute, a decision shall be made by CIETAC.

Article 3
Jurisdiction

1. CIETAC accepts cases involving economic, trade and other disputes of a contractual or non-contractual nature, based on an agreement of the parties.

2. The cases referred to in the preceding paragraph include:

(a) international or foreign-related disputes;

(b) disputes related to the Hong Kong Special Administrative Region, the Macao Special Administrative Region and the Taiwan region; and

(c) domestic disputes.

Article 4
Scope of Application

1. These Rules uniformly apply to CIETAC and its sub-commissions/arbitration centres.

2. Where the parties have agreed to refer their dispute to CIETAC for arbitration, they shall be deemed to have agreed to arbitration in accordance with these Rules.

3. Where the parties agree to refer their dispute to CIETAC for arbitration but have agreed on a modification of these Rules or have agreed on the application of other arbitration rules, the parties' agreement shall prevail unless such agreement is inoperative or in conflict with a mandatory provision of the law applicable to the arbitral proceedings. Where the parties have agreed on the application of other

arbitration rules, CIETAC shall perform the relevant administrative duties.

4. Where the parties agree to refer their dispute to arbitration under these Rules without providing the name of the arbitration institution, they shall be deemed to have agreed to refer the dispute to arbitration by CIETAC.

5. Where the parties agree to refer their dispute to arbitration under CIETAC's customized arbitration rules for a specific trade or profession, the parties' agreement shall prevail. However, if the dispute falls outside the scope of the specific rules, these Rules shall apply.

Article 5
Arbitration Agreement

1. An arbitration agreement means an arbitration clause in a contract or any other form of a written agreement concluded between the parties providing for the settlement of disputes by arbitration.

2. The arbitration agreement shall be in writing. An arbitration agreement is in writing if it is contained in the tangible form of a document such as a contract, letter, telegram, telex, fax, electronic data interchange, or email. An arbitration agreement shall be deemed to exist where its existence is asserted by one party and not denied by the other during the exchange of the Request for Arbitration and the Statement of Defence.

3. Where the law applicable to an arbitration agreement has different provisions as to the form and validity of the arbitration agreement, those provisions shall prevail.

4. An arbitration clause contained in a contract shall be treated as a clause independent and separate from all other clauses of the contract, and an arbitration agreement attached to a contract shall also be treated as independent and separate from all other clauses of the contract. The validity

of an arbitration clause or an arbitration agreement shall not be affected by any modification, cancellation, termination, transfer, expiry, invalidity, ineffectiveness, rescission or non-existence of the contract.

Article 6
Objection to Arbitration Agreement and/or Jurisdiction

1. CIETAC has the power to determine the existence and validity of an arbitration agreement and its jurisdiction over an arbitration case. CIETAC may, where necessary, delegate such power to the arbitral tribunal.

2. Where CIETAC is satisfied by prima facie evidence that a valid arbitration agreement exists, it may make a decision based on such evidence that it has jurisdiction over the arbitration case, and the arbitration shall proceed. Such a decision shall not prevent CIETAC from making a new decision on jurisdiction based on facts and/or evidence found by the arbitral tribunal during the arbitral proceedings that are inconsistent with the prima facie evidence.

3. Where CIETAC has delegated the power to determine jurisdiction to the arbitral tribunal, the arbitral tribunal may either make a separate decision on jurisdiction during the arbitral proceedings or incorporate the decision in the final arbitral award.

4. Any objection to an arbitration agreement and/or the jurisdiction over an arbitration case shall be raised in writing before the first oral hearing held by the arbitral tribunal. Where a case is to be decided on the basis of documents only, such an objection shall be raised before the submission of the first substantive defence.

5. The arbitration shall proceed notwithstanding an objection to the arbitration agreement and/or jurisdiction over the arbitration case.

6. The aforesaid objections to and/or decisions on jurisdiction by CIETAC shall include objections to and/or decisions on a party's standing to participate in the arbitration.

7. CIETAC or its authorized arbitral tribunal shall decide to dismiss the case upon finding that CIETAC has no jurisdiction over an arbitration case. Where a case is to be dismissed before the formation of the arbitral tribunal, the decision shall be made by the President of the Arbitration Court. Where the case is to be dismissed after the formation of the arbitral tribunal, the decision shall be made by the arbitral tribunal.

Article 7
Place of Arbitration

1. Where the parties have agreed on the place of arbitration, the parties' agreement shall prevail.

2. Where the parties have not agreed on the place of arbitration or their agreement is ambiguous, the place of arbitration shall be the domicile of CIETAC or its sub-commission/arbitration centre administering the case. CIETAC may also determine the place of arbitration to be another location having regard to the circumstances of the case.

3. The arbitral award shall be deemed as having been made at the place of arbitration.

Article 8
Service of Documents and Periods of Time

1. All documents, notices and written materials in relation to the arbitration may be delivered in person or sent by registered mail or express mail, fax, or by any other means considered proper by the Arbitration Court or the arbitral tribunal.

2. The arbitration documents referred to in the preceding Paragraph 1 shall be sent to the address provided by the party itself or by its representative(s), or to an address agreed by the parties. Where a party or its representative(s) has not provided

an address or the parties have not agreed on an address, the arbitration documents shall be sent to such party's address as provided by the other party or its representative(s).

3. Any arbitration correspondence to a party or its representative(s) shall be deemed to have been properly served on the party if delivered to the addressee or sent to the addressee's place of business, place of registration, domicile, habitual residence or mailing address, or where, after reasonable inquiries by the other party, none of the aforesaid addresses can be found, the arbitration correspondence is sent by the Arbitration Court to the addressee's last known place of business, place of registration, domicile, habitual residence or mailing address by registered or express mail, or by any other means that can provide a record of the attempt at delivery, including but not limited to service by public notary, entrustment or retention.

4. The periods of time specified in these Rules shall begin on the day following the day when the party receives or should have received the arbitration correspondence, notices or written materials sent by the Arbitration Court.

Article 9
Good Faith

Arbitration participants shall proceed with the arbitration in good faith.

Article 10
Waiver of Right to Object

A party shall be deemed to have waived its right to object where it knows or should have known that any provision of, or requirement under, these Rules has not been complied with and yet participates in or proceeds with the arbitral proceedings without promptly and explicitly submitting its objection in writing to such non-compliance.

Chapter II
Arbitral Proceedings

Section 1
Request for Arbitration, Defence and Counterclaim

Article 11
Commencement of Arbitration

The arbitral proceedings shall commence on the day on which the Arbitration Court receives a Request for Arbitration.

Article 12
Application for Arbitration

A party applying for arbitration under these Rules shall:

1. Submit a Request for Arbitration in writing signed and/or sealed by the Claimant or its authorized representative(s), which shall, inter alia, include:

(a) the names and addresses of the Claimant and the Respondent, including the zip code, telephone, fax, email, or any other means of electronic telecommunications;

(b) a reference to the arbitration agreement that is invoked;

(c) a statement of the facts of the case and the main issues in dispute;

(d) the claim of the Claimant; and

(e) the facts and grounds on which the claim is based.

2. Attach to the Request for Arbitration the relevant documentary and other evidence on which the Claimant's claim is based.

3. Pay the arbitration fee in advance to CIETAC in accordance with its Arbitration Fee Schedule.

Article 13
Acceptance of a Case

1. Upon the written application of a party, CIETAC shall accept a case in accordance with an arbitration agreement concluded between the parties either before or after the occurrence of the dispute, in which it is provided that disputes are to be referred to arbitration by CIETAC.

2. Upon receipt of a Request for Arbitration and its attachments, where after examination the Arbitration Court finds the formalities required for arbitration application to be complete, it shall send a Notice of Arbitration to both parties together with one copy each of these Rules and CIETAC's Panel of Arbitrators. The Request for Arbitration and its attachments submitted by the Claimant shall be sent to the Respondent under the same cover.

3. Where after examination the Arbitration Court finds the formalities required for the arbitration application to be incomplete, it may request the Claimant to complete them within a specified time period. The Claimant shall be deemed not to have submitted a Request for Arbitration if it fails to complete the required formalities within the specified time period. In such a case, the Claimant's Request for Arbitration and its attachments shall not be kept on file by the Arbitration Court.

4. After CIETAC accepts a case, the Arbitration Court shall designate a case manager to assist with the procedural administration of the case.

Article 14
Multiple Contracts

The Claimant may initiate a single arbitration concerning disputes arising out of or in connection with multiple contracts, provided that:

(a) such contracts consist of a principal contract and its

ancillary contract(s), or such contracts involve the same parties as well as legal relationships of the same nature;

(b) the disputes arise out of the same transaction or the same series of transactions; and

(c) the arbitration agreements in such contracts are identical or compatible.

Article 15
Statement of Defence

1. The Respondent shall file a Statement of Defence in writing within forty-five (45) days from the date of its receipt of the Notice of Arbitration. If the Respondent has justified reasons to request an extension of the time period, the arbitral tribunal shall decide whether to grant an extension. Where the arbitral tribunal has not yet been formed, the decision on whether to grant the extension of the time period shall be made by the Arbitration Court.

2. The Statement of Defence shall be signed and/or sealed by the Respondent or its authorized representative(s), and shall, inter alia, include the following contents and attachments:

(a) the name and address of the Respondent, including the zip code, telephone, fax, email, or any other means of electronic telecommunications;

(b) the defence to the Request for Arbitration setting forth the facts and grounds on which the defence is based; and

(c) the relevant documentary and other evidence on which the defence is based.

3. The arbitral tribunal has the power to decide whether to accept a Statement of Defence submitted after the expiration of the above time period.

4. Failure by the Respondent to file a Statement of Defence shall not affect the conduct of the arbitral proceedings.

Article 16
Counterclaim

1. The Respondent shall file a counterclaim, if any, in writing within forty-five (45) days from the date of its receipt of the Notice of Arbitration. If the Respondent has justified reasons to request an extension of the time period, the arbitral tribunal shall decide whether to grant an extension. Where the arbitral tribunal has not yet been formed, the decision on whether to grant the extension of the time period shall be made by the Arbitration Court.

2. When filing the counterclaim, the Respondent shall specify the counterclaim in its Statement of Counterclaim and state the facts and grounds on which the counterclaim is based with the relevant documentary and other evidence attached thereto.

3. When filing the counterclaim, the Respondent shall pay an arbitration fee in advance in accordance with the Arbitration Fee Schedule of CIETAC within a specified time period, failing which the Respondent shall be deemed not to have filed any counterclaim.

4. Where the formalities required for filing a counterclaim are found to be complete, the Arbitration Court shall send a Notice of Acceptance of Counterclaim to the parties. The Claimant shall submit its Statement of Defence in writing within thirty (30) days from the date of its receipt of the Notice. If the Claimant has justified reasons to request an extension of the time period, the arbitral tribunal shall decide whether to grant such an extension. Where the arbitral tribunal has not yet been formed, the decision on whether to grant the extension of the time period shall be made by the Arbitration Court.

5. The arbitral tribunal has the power to decide whether to accept a counterclaim or a Statement of Defence submitted after the expiration of the above time period.

6. Failure of the Claimant to file a Statement of Defence to the Respondent's counterclaim shall not affect the conduct of the arbitral proceedings.

Article 17
Amendment to Claim or Counterclaim

The Claimant may apply to amend its claim and the Respondent may apply to amend its counterclaim. However, the arbitral tribunal may refuse any such amendment if it considers that the amendment is too late and may delay the arbitral proceedings.

Article 18
Joinder of Additional Parties

1. During the arbitral proceedings, a party wishing to join an additional party to the arbitration may file the Request for Joinder with CIETAC, based on the arbitration agreement invoked in the arbitration that prima facie binds the additional party. Where the Request for Joinder is filed after the formation of the arbitral tribunal, a decision shall be made by CIETAC after the arbitral tribunal hears from all parties including the additional party if the arbitral tribunal considers the joinder necessary.

The date on which the Arbitration Court receives the Request for Joinder shall be deemed to be the date of the commencement of arbitration against the additional party.

2. The Request for Joinder shall contain the case number of the existing arbitration; the name, address and other means of communication of each of the parties, including the additional party; the arbitration agreement invoked to join the additional party as well as the facts and grounds the request relies upon; and the claim.

The relevant documentary and other evidence on which the request is based shall be attached to the Request for Joinder.

3. Where any party objects to the arbitration agreement and/or jurisdiction over the arbitration with respect to the joinder proceedings, CIETAC has the power to decide on its jurisdiction based on the arbitration agreement and relevant evidence.

4. After the joinder proceedings commence, the conduct of the arbitral proceedings shall be decided by the Arbitration Court if the arbitral tribunal is not formed, or shall be decided by the arbitral tribunal if it has been formed.

5. Where the joinder takes place prior to the formation of the arbitral tribunal, the relevant provisions on party's nominating or entrusting of the Chairman of CIETAC to appoint arbitrator under these Rules shall apply to the additional party. The arbitral tribunal shall be formed in accordance with Article 29 of these Rules.

Where the joinder takes place after the formation of the arbitral tribunal, the arbitral tribunal shall hear from the additional party of its comments on the past arbitral proceedings including the formation of the arbitral tribunal. If the additional party requests to nominate or entrust the Chairman of CIETAC to appoint an arbitrator, both parties shall nominate or entrust the Chairman of CIETAC to appoint arbitrators again. The arbitral tribunal shall be formed in accordance with Article 29 of these Rules.

6. The relevant provisions on the submission of the Statement of Defence and the Statement of Counterclaim under these Rules shall apply to the additional party. The time period for the additional party to submit its Statement of Defence and Statement of Counterclaim shall start counting from the date of its receipt of the Notice of Joinder.

7. CIETAC shall have the power to decide not to join an additional party where the additional party is prima facie not bound by the arbitration agreement invoked in the arbitration, or where any other circumstance exists that makes the joinder inappropriate.

Article 19

Consolidation of Arbitrations

1. At the request of a party, CIETAC may consolidate two or more arbitrations pending under these Rules into a single arbitration if:

(a) all of the claims in the arbitrations are made under the same arbitration agreement;

(b) the claims in the arbitrations are made under multiple arbitration agreements that are identical or compatible and the arbitrations involve the same parties as well as legal relationships of the same nature;

(c) the claims in the arbitrations are made under multiple arbitration agreements that are identical or compatible and the multiple contracts involved consist of a principle contract and its ancillary contract(s); or

(d) all the parties to the arbitrations have agreed to consolidation.

2. In deciding whether to consolidate the arbitrations in accordance with the preceding Paragraph 1, CIETAC shall take into account the opinions of all parties and other relevant factors such as the correlation between the arbitrations concerned, including the nomination and appointment of arbitrators in the separate arbitrations.

3. Unless otherwise agreed by all the parties, the arbitrations shall be consolidated into the arbitration that was first commenced.

4. After the consolidation of arbitrations, the conduct of the arbitral proceedings shall be decided by the Arbitration Court if the arbitral tribunal is not formed, or shall be decided by the arbitral tribunal if it has been formed.

Article 20

Submission and Exchange of Arbitration Documents

1. All arbitration documents from the parties shall be submitted to the Arbitration Court.

2. All arbitration documents to be exchanged during the arbitral proceedings shall be exchanged among the arbitral tribunal and the parties by the Arbitration Court unless otherwise agreed by the parties and with the consent of the arbitral tribunal or otherwise decided by the arbitral tribunal.

Article 21

Copies of Arbitration Documents

When submitting the Request for Arbitration, the Statement of Defence, the Statement of Counterclaim, evidence, and other arbitration documents, the parties shall make their submissions in quintuplicate. Where there are multiple parties, additional copies shall be provided accordingly. Where the party applies for preservation of property or protection of evidence, it shall also provide additional copies accordingly. Where the arbitral tribunal is composed of a sole arbitrator, the number of copies submitted may be reduced by two.

Article 22

Representation

A party may be represented by its authorized Chinese and/ or foreign representative(s) in handling matters relating to the arbitration. In such a case, a Power of Attorney shall be forwarded to the Arbitration Court by the party or its authorized representative(s).

Article 23

Conservatory and Interim Measures

1. Where a party applies for conservatory measures pursuant to the laws of the People's Republic of China, CIETAC shall forward the party's application to the competent court designated by that party in accordance with the law.

2. In accordance with the applicable law or the agreement of the parties, a party may apply to the Arbitration Court for emergency relief pursuant to the CIETAC Emergency Arbitrator Procedures (Appendix III). The emergency arbitrator may decide to order or award necessary or appropriate emergency measures. The decision of the emergency arbitrator shall be binding upon both parties.

3. At the request of a party, the arbitral tribunal may decide to order or award any interim measure it deems necessary or proper in accordance with the applicable law or the agreement of the parties and may require the requesting party to provide appropriate security in connection with the measure.

Section 2

Arbitrators and the Arbitral Tribunal

Article 24

Duties of Arbitrator

An arbitrator shall not represent either party, and shall be and remain independent of the parties and treat them equally.

Article 25

Number of Arbitrators

1. The arbitral tribunal shall be composed of one or three arbitrators.

2. Unless otherwise agreed by the parties or provided by these Rules, the arbitral tribunal shall be composed of three arbitrators.

Article 26
Nomination or Appointment of Arbitrator

1. CIETAC maintains a Panel of Arbitrators which uniformly applies to itself and all its sub-commissions/arbitration centres. The parties shall nominate arbitrators from the Panel of Arbitrators provided by CIETAC.

2. Where the parties have agreed to nominate arbitrators from outside CIETAC' s Panel of Arbitrators, an arbitrator so nominated by the parties or nominated according to the agreement of the parties may act as arbitrator subject to the confirmation by the Chairman of CIETAC.

Article 27
Three-Arbitrator Tribunal

1. Within fifteen (15) days from the date of receipt of the Notice of Arbitration, the Claimant and the Respondent shall each nominate, or entrust the Chairman of CIETAC to appoint, an arbitrator, failing which the arbitrator shall be appointed by the Chairman of CIETAC.

2. Within fifteen (15) days from the date of the Respondent's receipt of the Notice of Arbitration, the parties shall jointly nominate, or entrust the Chairman of CIETAC to appoint, the third arbitrator, who shall act as the presiding arbitrator.

3. The parties may each recommend one to five arbitrators as candidates for the presiding arbitrator and shall each submit a list of recommended candidates within the time period specified in the preceding Paragraph 2. Where there is only one common candidate on the lists, such candidate shall be the presiding arbitrator jointly nominated by the parties. Where there is more than one common candidate on

the lists, the Chairman of CIETAC shall choose the presiding arbitrator from among the common candidates having regard to the circumstances of the case, and he/she shall act as the presiding arbitrator jointly nominated by the parties. Where there is no common candidate on the lists, the presiding arbitrator shall be appointed by the Chairman of CIETAC.

4. Where the parties have failed to jointly nominate the presiding arbitrator according to the above provisions, the presiding arbitrator shall be appointed by the Chairman of CIETAC.

Article 28

Sole-Arbitrator Tribunal

Where the arbitral tribunal is composed of one arbitrator, the sole arbitrator shall be nominated pursuant to the procedures stipulated in Paragraphs 2, 3 and 4 of Article 27 of these Rules.

Article 29

Multiple-Party Tribunal

1. Where there are two or more Claimants and/or Respondents in an arbitration case, the Claimant side and/or the Respondent side, following discussion, shall each jointly nominate or jointly entrust the Chairman of CIETAC to appoint one arbitrator.

2. The presiding arbitrator or the sole arbitrator shall be nominated in accordance with the procedures stipulated in Paragraphs 2, 3 and 4 of Article 27 of these Rules. When making such nomination pursuant to Paragraph 3 of Article 27 of these Rules, the Claimant side and/or the Respondent side, following discussion, shall each submit a list of their jointly agreed candidates.

3. Where either the Claimant side or the Respondent side fails to jointly nominate or jointly entrust the Chairman of

CIETAC to appoint one arbitrator within fifteen (15) days from the date of its receipt of the Notice of Arbitration, the Chairman of CIETAC shall appoint all three members of the arbitral tribunal and designate one of them to act as the presiding arbitrator.

Article 30
Considerations in Appointing Arbitrators

When appointing arbitrators pursuant to these Rules, the Chairman of CIETAC shall take into consideration the law applicable to the dispute, the place of arbitration, the language of arbitration, the nationalities of the parties, and any other factor(s) the Chairman considers relevant.

Article 31
Disclosure

1. An arbitrator nominated by the parties or appointed by the Chairman of CIETAC shall sign a Declaration and disclose any facts or circumstances likely to give rise to justifiable doubts as to his/her impartiality or independence.

2. If circumstances that need to be disclosed arise during the arbitral proceedings, the arbitrator shall promptly disclose such circumstances in writing.

3. The Declaration and/or the disclosure of the arbitrator shall be submitted to the Arbitration Court to be forwarded to the parties.

Article 32
Challenge to Arbitrator

1. Upon receipt of the Declaration and/or the written disclosure of an arbitrator, a party wishing to challenge the arbitrator on the grounds of the disclosed facts or circumstances shall forward the challenge in writing within ten (10) days from the date of such receipt. If a party fails

to file a challenge within the above time period, it may not subsequently challenge the arbitrator on the basis of the matters disclosed by the arbitrator.

2. A party having justifiable doubts as to the impartiality or independence of an arbitrator may challenge that arbitrator in writing and shall state the facts and reasons on which the challenge is based with supporting evidence.

3. A party may challenge an arbitrator in writing within fifteen (15) days from the date it receives the Notice of Formation of the Arbitral Tribunal. Where a party becomes aware of a reason for a challenge after such receipt, the party may challenge the arbitrator in writing within fifteen (15) days after such reason has become known to it, but no later than the conclusion of the last oral hearing.

4. The challenge by one party shall be promptly communicated to the other party, the arbitrator being challenged and the other members of the arbitral tribunal.

5. Where an arbitrator is challenged by one party and the other party agrees to the challenge, or the arbitrator being challenged voluntarily withdraws from his/her office, such arbitrator shall no longer be a member of the arbitral tribunal. However, in neither case shall it be implied that the reasons for the challenge are sustained.

6. In circumstances other than those specified in the preceding Paragraph 5, the Chairman of CIETAC shall make a final decision on the challenge with or without stating the reasons.

7. An arbitrator who has been challenged shall continue to serve on the arbitral tribunal until a final decision on the challenge has been made by the Chairman of CIETAC.

Article 33
Replacement of Arbitrator

1. In the event that an arbitrator is prevented de jure or de facto from fulfilling his/her functions, or fails to fulfil his/her functions in accordance with the requirements of these Rules or within the time period specified in these Rules, the Chairman of CIETAC shall have the power to replace the arbitrator. Such arbitrator may also voluntarily withdraw from his/her office.

2. The Chairman of CIETAC shall make a final decision on whether or not an arbitrator should be replaced with or without stating the reasons.

3. In the event that an arbitrator is unable to fulfil his/her functions due to challenge or replacement, a substitute arbitrator shall be nominated or appointed within the time period specified by the Arbitration Court according to the same procedure that applied to the nomination or appointment of the arbitrator being challenged or replaced. If a party fails to nominate or appoint a substitute arbitrator accordingly, the substitute arbitrator shall be appointed by the Chairman of CIETAC.

4. After the replacement of an arbitrator, the arbitral tribunal shall decide whether and to what extent the previous proceedings in the case shall be repeated.

Article 34
Continuation of Arbitration by Majority

After the conclusion of the last oral hearing, if an arbitrator on a three-member tribunal is unable to participate in the deliberations and/or to render the award owing to his/her demise or to his/her removal from CIETAC's Panel of Arbitrators, or for any other reason, the other two arbitrators may request the Chairman of CIETAC to replace that arbitrator pursuant to Article 33 of these Rules. After consulting with the parties and upon the approval of the Chairman of CIETAC, the other two arbitrators may also continue the arbitral proceedings and make decisions, rulings, or render the award. The Arbitration Court shall notify the parties of the above circumstances.

Section 3
Hearing

Article 35
Conduct of Hearing

1. The arbitral tribunal shall examine the case in any way it deems appropriate unless otherwise agreed by the parties. Under all circumstances, the arbitral tribunal shall act impartially and fairly and shall afford a reasonable opportunity to both parties to present their case.

2. The arbitral tribunal shall hold oral hearings when examining the case. However, the arbitral tribunal may examine the case on the basis of documents only if the parties so agree and the arbitral tribunal consents or the arbitral tribunal deems that oral hearings are unnecessary and the parties so agree.

3. Unless otherwise agreed by the parties, the arbitral tribunal may adopt an inquisitorial or adversarial approach in hearing the case having regard to the circumstances of the case.

4. The arbitral tribunal may hold deliberations at any place or in any manner that it considers appropriate.

5. Unless otherwise agreed by the parties, the arbitral tribunal may, if it considers it necessary, issue procedural orders or question lists, produce terms of reference, or hold pre-hearing conferences, etc. With the authorization of the other members of the arbitral tribunal, the presiding arbitrator may decide on the procedural arrangements for the arbitral proceedings at his/her own discretion.

Article 36
Place of Oral Hearing

1. Where the parties have agreed on the place of an oral hearing, the case shall be heard at that agreed place except in the circumstances stipulated in Paragraph 3 of Article 82 of these Rules.

2. Unless otherwise agreed by the parties, the place of oral hearings shall be in Beijing for a case administered by the Arbitration Court or at the domicile of the sub-commission/ arbitration centre administering the case, or if the arbitral tribunal considers it necessary and with the approval of the President of the Arbitration Court, at another location.

Article 37
Notice of Oral Hearing

1. Where a case is to be examined by way of an oral hearing, the parties shall be notified of the date of the first oral hearing at least twenty (20) days in advance of the oral hearing. A party having justified reasons may request a postponement of the oral hearing. However, the party shall communicate such request in writing to the arbitral tribunal within five (5) days of its receipt of the notice of the oral hearing. The arbitral tribunal shall decide whether or not to postpone the oral hearing.

2. Where a party has justified reasons for its failure to submit a request for a postponement of the oral hearing in accordance with the preceding Paragraph 1, the arbitral tribunal shall decide whether or not to accept the request.

3. A notice of a subsequent oral hearing, a notice of a postponed oral hearing, as well as a request for postponement of such an oral hearing, shall not be subject to the time periods specified in the preceding Paragraph 1.

Article 38
Confidentiality

1. Hearings shall be held in camera. Where both parties request an open hearing, the arbitral tribunal shall make a decision.

2. For cases heard in camera, the parties and their representatives, the arbitrators, the witnesses, the interpreters, the experts consulted by the arbitral tribunal, the appraisers appointed by the arbitral tribunal and other relevant persons shall not disclose to any outsider any substantive or procedural matters relating to the case.

Article 39
Default

1. If the Claimant fails to appear at an oral hearing without showing sufficient cause, or withdraws from an on-going oral hearing without the permission of the arbitral tribunal, the Claimant may be deemed to have withdrawn its application for arbitration. In such a case, if the Respondent has filed a counterclaim, the arbitral tribunal shall proceed with the hearing of the counterclaim and make a default award.

2. If the Respondent fails to appear at an oral hearing without showing sufficient cause, or withdraws from an on-going oral hearing without the permission of the arbitral tribunal, the arbitral tribunal may proceed with the arbitration and make a default award. In such a case, if the Respondent has filed a counterclaim, the Respondent may be deemed to have withdrawn its counterclaim.

Article 40
Record of Oral Hearing

1. The arbitral tribunal may arrange for a written and/or an audio-visual record to be made of an oral hearing.

The arbitral tribunal may, if it considers it necessary, take minutes of the oral hearing and request the parties and/or their representatives, witnesses and/or other persons involved to sign and/or affix their seals to the written record or the minutes.

2. The written record, the minutes and the audio-visual record of an oral hearing shall be available for use and reference by the arbitral tribunal.

3. At the request of a party, the Arbitration Court may, having regard to the specific circumstances of the arbitration, decide to engage a stenographer to make a stenographic record of an oral hearing, the cost of which shall be advanced by the parties.

Article 41

Evidence

1. Each party shall bear the burden of proving the facts on which it relies to support its claim, defence or counterclaim and provide the basis for its opinions, arguments and counter-arguments.

2. The arbitral tribunal may specify a time period for the parties to produce evidence and the parties shall produce evidence within the specified time period. The arbitral tribunal may refuse to admit any evidence produced after that time period. If a party experiences difficulties in producing evidence within the specified time period, it may apply for an extension before the end of the period. The arbitral tribunal shall decide whether or not to extend the time period.

3. If a party bearing the burden of proof fails to produce evidence within the specified time period, or if the produced evidence is not sufficient to support its claim or counterclaim, it shall bear the consequences thereof.

Article 42
Examination of Evidence

1. Where a case is examined by way of an oral hearing, the evidence shall be produced at the oral hearing and may be examined by the parties.

2. Where a case is to be decided on the basis of documents only, or where the evidence is submitted after the hearing and both parties have agreed to examine the evidence by means of writing, the parties may examine the evidence in writing. In such circumstances, the parties shall submit their written opinions on the evidence within the time period specified by the arbitral tribunal.

Article 43
Investigation and Evidence Collection by the Arbitral Tribunal

1. The arbitral tribunal may undertake investigation and collect evidence as it considers necessary.

2. When investigating and collecting evidence, the arbitral tribunal may notify the parties to be present. In the event that one or both parties fail to be present after being notified, the investigation and collection of evidence shall proceed without being affected.

3. Evidence collected by the arbitral tribunal through its investigation shall be forwarded to the parties for their comments.

Article 44
Expert's Report and Appraiser's Report

1. The arbitral tribunal may consult experts or appoint appraisers for clarification on specific issues of the case. Such an expert or appraiser may be a Chinese or foreign institution or natural person.

2. The arbitral tribunal has the power to request the parties, and the parties are also obliged, to deliver or produce to the expert or appraiser any relevant materials, documents, property, or physical objects for examination, inspection or appraisal by the expert or appraiser.

3. Copies of the expert's report and the appraiser's report shall be forwarded to the parties for their comments. At the request of either party and with the approval of the arbitral tribunal, the expert or appraiser shall participate in an oral hearing and give explanations on the report when the arbitral tribunal considers it necessary.

Article 45
Suspension of the Arbitral Proceedings

1. Where the parties jointly or separately request a suspension of the arbitral proceedings, or under circumstances where such suspension is necessary, the arbitral proceedings may be suspended.

2. The arbitral proceedings shall resume as soon as the reason for the suspension disappears or the suspension period ends.

3. The arbitral tribunal shall decide whether to suspend or resume the arbitral proceedings. Where the arbitral tribunal has not yet been formed, the decision shall be made by the President of the Arbitration Court.

Article 46
Withdrawal and Dismissal

1. A party may withdraw its claim or counterclaim in its entirety. In the event that the Claimant withdraws its claim in its entirety, the arbitral tribunal may proceed with its examination of the counterclaim and render an arbitral award thereon. In the event that the Respondent withdraws its counterclaim in its entirety, the arbitral tribunal may proceed

with the examination of the claim and render an arbitral award thereon.

2. A party may be deemed to have withdrawn its claim or counterclaim if the arbitral proceedings cannot proceed for reasons attributable to that party.

3. A case may be dismissed if the claim and counterclaim have been withdrawn in their entirety. Where a case is to be dismissed prior to the formation of the arbitral tribunal, the President of the Arbitration Court shall make a decision on the dismissal. Where a case is to be dismissed after the formation of the arbitral tribunal, the arbitral tribunal shall make the decision.

4. The seal of CIETAC shall be affixed to the Dismissal Decision referred to in the preceding Paragraph 3 and Paragraph 7 of Article 6 of these Rules.

Article 47
Combination of Conciliation with Arbitration

1. Where both parties wish to conciliate, or where one party wishes to conciliate and the other party's consent has been obtained by the arbitral tribunal, the arbitral tribunal may conciliate the dispute during the arbitral proceedings. The parties may also settle their dispute by themselves.

2. With the consents of both parties, the arbitral tribunal may conciliate the case in a manner it considers appropriate.

3. During the process of conciliation, the arbitral tribunal shall terminate the conciliation proceedings if either party so requests or if the arbitral tribunal considers that further conciliation efforts will be futile.

4. The parties shall sign a settlement agreement where they have reached settlement through conciliation by the arbitral tribunal or by themselves.

5. Where the parties have reached a settlement agreement through conciliation by the arbitral tribunal or by themselves,

they may withdraw their claim or counterclaim, or request the arbitral tribunal to render an arbitral award or a conciliation statement in accordance with the terms of the settlement agreement.

6. Where the parties request for a conciliation statement, the conciliation statement shall clearly set forth the claims of the parties and the terms of the settlement agreement. It shall be signed by the arbitrators, sealed by CIETAC, and served upon both parties.

7. Where conciliation is not successful, the arbitral tribunal shall resume the arbitral proceedings and render an arbitral award.

8. Where the parties wish to conciliate their dispute but do not wish to have conciliation conducted by the arbitral tribunal, CIETAC may, with the consents of both parties, assist the parties to conciliate the dispute in a manner and procedure it considers appropriate.

9. Where conciliation is not successful, neither party may invoke any opinion, view or statement, and any proposal or proposition expressing acceptance or opposition by either party or by the arbitral tribunal in the process of conciliation as grounds for any claim, defence or counterclaim in the subsequent arbitral proceedings, judicial proceedings, or any other proceedings.

10. Where the parties have reached a settlement agreement by themselves through negotiation or conciliation before the commencement of an arbitration, either party may, based on an arbitration agreement concluded between them that provides for arbitration by CIETAC and the settlement agreement, request CIETAC to constitute an arbitral tribunal to render an arbitral award in accordance with the terms of the settlement agreement. Unless otherwise agreed by the parties, the Chairman of CIETAC shall appoint a sole arbitrator to form such an arbitral tribunal, which shall examine the case

in a procedure it considers appropriate and render an award in due course. The specific procedure and time period for rendering the award shall not be subject to other provisions of these Rules.

Chapter III
Arbitral Award

Article 48
Time Period for Rendering Award

1. The arbitral tribunal shall render an arbitral award within six (6) months from the date on which the arbitral tribunal is formed.

2. Upon the request of the arbitral tribunal, the President of the Arbitration Court may extend the time period if he/she considers it truly necessary and the reasons for the extension truly justified.

3. Any suspension period shall be excluded when calculating the time period in the preceding Paragraph 1.

Article 49
Making of Award

1. The arbitral tribunal shall independently and impartially render a fair and reasonable arbitral award based on the facts of the case and the terms of the contract, in accordance with the law, and with reference to international practices.

2. Where the parties have agreed on the law applicable to the merits of their dispute, the parties' agreement shall prevail. In the absence of such an agreement or where such agreement is in conflict with a mandatory provision of the law, the arbitral tribunal shall determine the law applicable to the merits of the dispute.

3. The arbitral tribunal shall state in the award the claims, the facts of the dispute, the reasons on which the award is based, the result of the award, the allocation of the arbitration costs, and the date on which and the place at which the award is made. The facts of the dispute and the reasons on which the award is based may not be stated in the award if the parties have so agreed, or if the award is made in accordance with the terms of a settlement agreement between the parties. The arbitral tribunal has the power to fix in the award the specific time period for the parties to perform the award and the liabilities for failure to do so within the specified time period.

4. The seal of CIETAC shall be affixed to the arbitral award.

5. Where a case is examined by an arbitral tribunal composed of three arbitrators, the award shall be rendered by all three arbitrators or a majority of the arbitrators. A written dissenting opinion shall be kept with the file and may be appended to the award. Such dissenting opinion shall not form a part of the award.

6. Where the arbitral tribunal cannot reach a majority opinion, the arbitral award shall be rendered in accordance with the presiding arbitrator's opinion. The written opinions of the other arbitrators shall be kept with the file and may be appended to the award. Such written opinions shall not form a part of the award.

7. Unless the arbitral award is made in accordance with the opinion of the presiding arbitrator or the sole arbitrator and signed by the same, the arbitral award shall be signed by a majority of the arbitrators. An arbitrator who has a dissenting opinion may or may not sign his/her name on the award.

8. The date on which the award is made shall be the date on which the award comes into legal effect.

9. The arbitral award is final and binding upon both parties. Neither party may bring a lawsuit before a court or make a request to any other organization for revision of the award.

Article 50

Partial Award

1. Where the arbitral tribunal considers it necessary, or where a party so requests and the arbitral tribunal agrees, the arbitral tribunal may first render a partial award on any part of the claim before rendering the final award. A partial award is final and binding upon both parties.

2. Failure of either party to perform a partial award shall neither affect the arbitral proceedings nor prevent the arbitral tribunal from making the final award.

Article 51

Scrutiny of Draft Award

The arbitral tribunal shall submit its draft award to CIETAC for scrutiny before signing the award. CIETAC may bring to the attention of the arbitral tribunal issues addressed in the award on the condition that the arbitral tribunal's independence in rendering the award is not affected.

Article 52

Allocation of Fees

1. The arbitral tribunal has the power to determine in the arbitral award the arbitration fees and other expenses to be paid by the parties to CIETAC.

2. The arbitral tribunal has the power to decide in the arbitral award, having regard to the circumstances of the case, that the losing party shall compensate the winning party for the expenses reasonably incurred by it in pursuing the case. In deciding whether or not the winning party's expenses incurred in pursuing the case are reasonable, the arbitral tribunal shall take into consideration various factors such as the outcome and complexity of the case, the workload of the winning party and/or its representative(s), the amount in dispute, etc.

Article 53
Correction of Award

1. Within a reasonable time after the award is made, the arbitral tribunal may, on its own initiative, make corrections in writing of any clerical, typographical or calculation errors, or any errors of a similar nature contained in the award.

2. Within thirty (30) days from its receipt of the arbitral award, either party may request the arbitral tribunal in writing for a correction of any clerical, typographical or calculation errors, or any errors of a similar nature contained in the award. If such an error does exist in the award, the arbitral tribunal shall make the correction in writing within thirty (30) days of its receipt of the written request for the correction.

3. The above written correction shall form a part of the arbitral award and shall be subject to the provisions in Paragraphs 4 to 9 of Article 49 of these Rules.

Article 54
Additional Award

1. Where any matter which should have been decided by the arbitral tribunal was omitted from the arbitral award, the arbitral tribunal may, on its own initiative, make an additional award within a reasonable time after the award is made.

2. Either party may, within thirty (30) days from its receipt of the arbitral award, request the arbitral tribunal in writing for an additional award on any claim or counterclaim which was advanced in the arbitral proceedings but was omitted from the award. If such an omission does exist, the arbitral tribunal shall make an additional award within thirty (30) days of its receipt of the written request.

3. Such additional award shall form a part of the arbitral award and shall be subject to the provisions in Paragraphs 4 to 9 of Article 49 of these Rules.

Article 55

Performance of Award

1. The parties shall perform the arbitral award within the time period specified in the award. If no time period is specified in the award, the parties shall perform the award immediately.

2. Where one party fails to perform the award, the other party may apply to a competent court for enforcement of the award in accordance with the law.

Chapter IV

Summary Procedure

Article 56

Application

1. The Summary Procedure shall apply to any case where the amount in dispute does not exceed RMB 5,000,000 unless otherwise agreed by the parties; or where the amount in dispute exceeds RMB 5,000,000, yet one party applies for arbitration under the Summary Procedure and the other party agrees in writing; or where both parties have agreed to apply the Summary Procedure.

2. Where there is no monetary claim or the amount in dispute is not clear, CIETAC shall determine whether or not to apply the Summary Procedure after full consideration of relevant factors, including but not limited to the complexity of the case and the interests involved.

Article 57
Notice of Arbitration

Where after examination the Claimant's arbitration application is accepted for arbitration under the Summary Procedure, the Arbitration Court shall send a Notice of Arbitration to both parties.

Article 58
Formation of the Arbitral Tribunal

Unless otherwise agreed by the parties, a sole-arbitrator tribunal shall be formed in accordance with Article 28 of these Rules to hear a case under the Summary Procedure.

Article 59
Defence and Counterclaim

1. The Respondent shall submit its Statement of Defence, evidence and other supporting documents within twenty (20) days of its receipt of the Notice of Arbitration. Counterclaim, if any, shall also be filed with evidence and supporting documents within such time period.

2. The Claimant shall file its Statement of Defence to the Respondent's counterclaim within twenty (20) days of its receipt of the counterclaim and its attachments.

3. If a party has justified reasons to request an extension of the time period, the arbitral tribunal shall decide whether to grant such extension. Where the arbitral tribunal has not yet been formed, such decision shall be made by the Arbitration Court.

Article 60

Conduct of Hearing

The arbitral tribunal may examine the case in the manner it considers appropriate. The arbitral tribunal may decide whether to examine the case solely on the basis of the written materials and evidence submitted by the parties or to hold an oral hearing after hearing from the parties of their opinions.

Article 61

Notice of Oral Hearing

1. For a case examined by way of an oral hearing, after the arbitral tribunal has fixed a date for the first oral hearing, the parties shall be notified of the date at least fifteen (15) days in advance of the oral hearing. A party having justified reasons may request a postponement of the oral hearing. However, the party shall communicate such request in writing to the arbitral tribunal within three (3) days of its receipt of the notice of the oral hearing. The arbitral tribunal shall decide whether or not to postpone the oral hearing.

2. If a party has justified reasons for failure to submit a request for a postponement of the oral hearing in accordance with the preceding Paragraph 1, the arbitral tribunal shall decide whether to accept such a request.

3. A notice of a subsequent oral hearing, a notice of a postponed oral hearing, as well as a request for postponement of such oral hearing, shall not be subject to the time periods specified in the preceding Paragraph 1.

Article 62

Time Period for Rendering Award

1. The arbitral tribunal shall render an arbitral award within three (3) months from the date on which the arbitral tribunal is formed.

2. Upon the request of the arbitral tribunal, the President of the Arbitration Court may extend the time period if he/she considers it truly necessary and the reasons for the extension truly justified.

3. Any suspension period shall be excluded when calculating the time period in the preceding Paragraph 1.

Article 63
Change of Procedure

The Summary Procedure shall not be affected by any amendment to the claim or by the filing of a counterclaim. Where the amount in dispute of the amended claim or that of the counterclaim exceeds RMB 5,000,000, the Summary Procedure shall continue to apply unless the parties agree or the arbitral tribunal decides that a change to the general procedure is necessary.

Article 64
Context Reference

The relevant provisions in the other Chapters of these Rules shall apply to matters not covered in this Chapter.

Chapter V
Special Provisions for Domestic Arbitration

Article 65
Application

1. The provisions of this Chapter shall apply to domestic arbitration cases.

2. The provisions of the Summary Procedure in Chapter IV shall apply if a domestic arbitration case falls within the scope of Article 56 of these Rules.

Article 66

Acceptance of a Case

1. Upon receipt of a Request for Arbitration, where the Arbitration Court finds the Request to meet the requirements specified in Article 12 of these Rules, the Arbitration Court shall notify the parties accordingly within five (5) days from its receipt of the Request. Where a Request for Arbitration is found not to be in conformity with the requirements, the Arbitration Court shall notify the party in writing of its refusal of acceptance with reasons stated.

2. Upon receipt of a Request for Arbitration, where after examination, the Arbitration Court finds the Request not to be in conformity with the formality requirements specified in Article 12 of these Rules, it may request the Claimant to comply with the requirements within a specified time period.

Article 67

Formation of the Arbitral Tribunal

The arbitral tribunal shall be formed in accordance with the provisions of Articles 25, 26, 27, 28, 29 and 30 of these Rules.

Article 68

Defence and Counterclaim

1. Within twenty (20) days from the date of its receipt of the Notice of Arbitration, the Respondent shall submit its Statement of Defence, evidence and other supporting documents. Counterclaim, if any, shall also be filed with evidence and other supporting documents within the time period.

2. The Claimant shall file its Statement of Defence to the Respondent's counterclaim within twenty (20) days from the date of its receipt of the counterclaim and its attachments.

3. If a party has justified reasons to request an extension of the time period, the arbitral tribunal shall decide whether to grant such extension. Where the arbitral tribunal has not yet been formed, such decision shall be made by the Arbitration Court.

Article 69
Notice of Oral Hearing

1. For a case examined by way of an oral hearing, after the arbitral tribunal has fixed a date for the first oral hearing, the parties shall be notified of the date at least fifteen (15) days in advance of the oral hearing. A party having justified reason may request a postponement of the oral hearing. However, the party shall communicate such request in writing to the arbitral tribunal within three (3) days of its receipt of the notice of the oral hearing. The arbitral tribunal shall decide whether or not to postpone the oral hearing.

2. If a party has justified reasons for failure to submit a request for a postponement of the oral hearing in accordance with the preceding Paragraph 1, the arbitral tribunal shall decide whether to accept such a request.

3. A notice of a subsequent oral hearing, a notice of a postponed oral hearing, as well as a request for postponement of such oral hearing, shall not be subject to the time periods specified in the preceding Paragraph 1.

Article 70
Record of Oral Hearing

1. The arbitral tribunal shall make a written record of the oral hearing. Any party or participant in the arbitration may

apply for a correction upon finding any omission or mistake in the record regarding its own statements. If the application is refused by the arbitral tribunal, it shall nevertheless be recorded and kept with the file.

2. The written record shall be signed or sealed by the arbitrator(s), the recorder, the parties, and any other participant in the arbitration.

Article 71
Time Period for Rendering Award

1. The arbitral tribunal shall render an arbitral award within four (4) months from the date on which the arbitral tribunal is formed.

2. Upon the request of the arbitral tribunal, the President of the Arbitration Court may extend the time period if he/she considers it truly necessary and the reasons for the extension truly justified.

3. Any suspension period shall be excluded when calculating the time period in the preceding Paragraph 1.

Article 72
Context Reference

The relevant provisions in the other Chapters of these Rules, with the exception of Chapter VI, shall apply to matters not covered in this Chapter.

Chapter VI
Special Provisions for Hong Kong Arbitration

Article 73
Application

1. CIETAC has established the CIETAC Hong Kong Arbitration Centre in the Hong Kong Special Administrative

Region. The provisions of this Chapter shall apply to arbitration cases accepted and administered by the CIETAC Hong Kong Arbitration Centre.

2. Where the parties have agreed to submit their disputes to the CIETAC Hong Kong Arbitration Centre for arbitration or to CIETAC for arbitration in Hong Kong, the CIETAC Hong Kong Arbitration Centre shall accept the arbitration application and administer the case.

Article 74
Place of Arbitration and Law Applicable to the Arbitral Proceedings

Unless otherwise agreed by the parties, for an arbitration administered by the CIETAC Hong Kong Arbitration Centre, the place of arbitration shall be Hong Kong, the law applicable to the arbitral proceedings shall be the arbitration law of Hong Kong, and the arbitral award shall be a Hong Kong award.

Article 75
Decision on Jurisdiction

Any objection to an arbitration agreement and/or the jurisdiction over an arbitration case shall be raised in writing no later than the submission of the first substantive defence. The arbitral tribunal shall have the power to determine the existence and validity of the arbitration agreement and its jurisdiction over the arbitration case.

Article 76
Nomination or Appointment of Arbitrator

The CIETAC Panel of Arbitrators in effect shall be recommended in arbitration cases administered by the

CIETAC Hong Kong Arbitration Centre. The parties may nominate arbitrators from outside the CIETAC's Panel of Arbitrators. An arbitrator so nominated shall be subject to the confirmation of the Chairman of CIETAC.

Article 77

Interim Measures and Emergency Relief

1. Unless otherwise agreed by the parties, the arbitral tribunal has the power to order appropriate interim measures at the request of a party.

2. Where the arbitral tribunal has not yet been formed, a party may apply for emergency relief pursuant to the CIETAC Emergency Arbitrator Procedures (Appendix III).

Article 78

Seal on Award

The seal of the CIETAC Hong Kong Arbitration Centre shall be affixed to the arbitral award.

Article 79

Arbitration Fees

The CIETAC Arbitration Fee Schedule III (Appendix II) shall apply to the arbitration cases accepted and administered in accordance with this Chapter.

Article 80

Context Reference

The relevant provisions in the other Chapters of these Rules, with the exception of Chapter V, shall apply to matters not covered in this Chapter.

Chapter VII
Supplementary Provisions

Article 81
Language

1. Where the parties have agreed on the language of arbitration, their agreement shall prevail. In the absence of such agreement, the language of arbitration to be used in the proceedings shall be Chinese. CIETAC may also designate another language as the language of arbitration having regard to the circumstances of the case.

2. If a party or its representative(s) or witness(es) requires interpretation at an oral hearing, an interpreter may be provided either by the Arbitration Court or by the party.

3. The arbitral tribunal or the Arbitration Court may, if it considers it necessary, require the parties to submit a corresponding translation of their documents and evidence into Chinese or other languages.

Article 82
Arbitration Fees and Costs

1. Apart from the arbitration fees charged in accordance with its Arbitration Fee Schedule, CIETAC may charge the parties for any other additional and reasonable actual costs, including but not limited to arbitrators' special remuneration, their travel and accommodation expenses incurred in dealing with the case, engagement fees of stenographers, as well as the costs and expenses of experts, appraisers or interpreters appointed by the arbitral tribunal. The Arbitration Court shall, after hearing from the arbitrator and the party concerned, determine the arbitrator's special remuneration with reference to the standards of arbitrators' fees and expenses set forth in the CIETAC Arbitration Fee Schedule III (Appendix II).

2. Where a party has nominated an arbitrator but fails to advance a deposit for such actual costs as the special remuneration, travel and accommodation expenses of the nominated arbitrator within the time period specified by CIETAC, the party shall be deemed not to have nominated the arbitrator.

3. Where the parties have agreed to hold an oral hearing at a place other than the domicile of CIETAC or its relevant sub-commission/arbitration centre, they shall advance a deposit for the actual costs such as travel and accommodation expenses incurred thereby. In the event that the parties fail to do so within the time period specified by CIETAC, the oral hearing shall be held at the domicile of CIETAC or its relevant sub-commission/arbitration centre.

4. Where the parties have agreed to use two or more than two languages as the languages of arbitration, or where the parties have agreed on a three-arbitrator tribunal in a case where the Summary Procedure shall apply in accordance with Article 56 of these Rules, CIETAC may charge the parties for any additional and reasonable costs.

Article 83
Interpretation

1. The headings of the articles in these Rules shall not be construed as interpretations of the contents of the provisions contained therein.

2. These Rules shall be interpreted by CIETAC.

Article 84
Coming into Force

These Rules shall be effective as of 1 January 2015. For cases administered by CIETAC or its sub-commissions/arbitration centres before these Rules come into force, the Arbitration Rules effective at the time of acceptance shall apply, or where both parties agree, these Rules shall apply.

Appendix 7
China International Economic and Trade Arbitration Commission (CIETAC)
Financial Disputes Arbitration Rules[263]

(Revised and Adopted by the China Council for the Promotion of International Trade/China Chamber of International Commerce on November 4, 2014. Effective as from 1 January 2015)

Chapter I
General Provisions

Article 1

These Rules are formulated for the purpose of impartial and prompt resolution of disputes arising from financial transactions between the parties.

Article 2

The China International Economic and Trade Arbitration Commission (hereinafter referred to as the 'CIETAC' and also known as the Arbitration Institute of the China Chamber of International Commerce') independently and impartially resolves, by means of arbitration, disputes arising from, or in connection with, financial transactions between the parties.

The term 'financial transactions' shall refer to transactions arising between financial institutions inter se, or arising between financial institutions and other natural or legal persons in the currency, capital, foreign exchange, gold and insurance markets that relate to financing in both domestic and foreign currencies, and the assignment and sale of financial instruments and documents denominated in both

263 <www.cietac.org/index.php?m=Page&a=index&id=108&l=en>.

domestic and foreign currencies, including but not limited to:

1. Loans;
2. Deposit certificates;
3. Guarantees
4. Letters of credit;
5. Negotiable instruments;
6. Fund transactions and fund trusts;
7. Bonds;
8. Collection and remittance of foreign currencies;
9. Factoring;
10. Reimbursement agreements between banks; and
11. Securities and futures.

Article 3

These Rules shall apply to any financial dispute accepted by the CIETAC for arbitration where the parties have agreed upon the application thereof. Failing such agreement, the Arbitration Rules of the CIETAC shall apply.

The CIETAC shall make a ruling on objections with regard to whether the dispute between the parties arises from, or is in connection with, a financial transaction, or whether these Rules should be applied to the dispute between the parties.

Article 4

Where the parties have agreed on any modification of these Rules, the parties' agreement shall prevail except where such agreement is inoperative or in conflict with a mandatory provision of the law of the place of arbitration.

Where the parties agree to refer their disputes to arbitration under these Rules without providing the name of an arbitration institution, they shall be deemed to have agreed to refer the dispute to arbitration by the CIETAC.

Article 5

The CIETAC shall have the power to determine the existence and validity of an arbitration agreement and its jurisdiction over an arbitration case. The CIETAC may, if necessary, delegate such power to the arbitral tribunal. Where the validity of the arbitration agreement is challenged and one party requests the CIETAC to make a decision thereon while the other party applies to the People's Court for a ruling, such a ruling shall be made by the People's Court.

The arbitration shall proceed notwithstanding an objection to the arbitration agreement and/or jurisdiction over the arbitration case.

Article 6

The parties may appoint arbitrators from the Panel of Arbitrators provided by CIETAC.

Where the parties have agreed to appoint arbitrators from outside of the CIETAC's Panel of Arbitrators, the arbitrators so appointed by the parties or nominated according to the agreement of the parties may act as arbitrator if the appointment is confirmed by the Chairman of CIETAC in accordance with the law. Such confirmation shall be made, or not made, without stating the reasons therefor.

Where the appointment of an arbitrator is to be made by the Chairman of CIETAC, the Chairman may, unless otherwise agreed by the parties, appoint such arbitrator from the Panel of Arbitrators provided by CIETAC.

Article 7

An arbitrator appointed by the parties or by the Chairman of the CIETAC shall sign a Declaration and disclose to the CIETAC in writing any facts or circumstances likely to give rise to justifiable doubts as to his/her impartiality or independence.

Chapter II
Arbitration Proceedings

Article 8

The arbitration proceedings shall commence on the date on which the Arbitration Court of the CIETAC receives a Request for Arbitration.

Article 9

A party applying for arbitration shall:

1. Submit a Request for Arbitration in writing signed by and/or affixed with the seal of the Claimant and/or its authorized representative(s), which shall, inter alia, include:

(a) the names, addresses and methods for communications of the Claimant and the Respondent, including the zip code, telephone, telex, fax and telegraph numbers, Email addresses or any other means of electronic telecommunications;

(b) a reference to the arbitration agreement that is invoked;

(c) a statement of the facts of the case and the main issues in dispute;

(d) the claim of the Claimant; and

(e) the facts and grounds on which the claim is based.

2. Attach to the Request for Arbitration the relevant evidence supporting the facts on which the Claimant's claim is based.

3. Make payment of the arbitration fee in advance to the CIETAC according to its Financial Arbitration Fee Schedule.

Article 10

Where the Arbitration Court of the CIETAC finds that a Request for Arbitration satisfies the requirements for arbitration, it shall notify the parties in writing of its acceptance of the Request for Arbitration within five (5) days from the date of receipt of the Request. Should the Arbitration Court of the CIETAC find that the Request for Arbitration does not satisfy the requirements for arbitration, it shall notify the parties in writing of its rejection of the request for arbitration and the reasons therefor.

Article 11

Together with the Notice of Arbitration for the acceptance of the Request for Arbitration, the Arbitration Court of CIETAC shall furnish to the Claimant these Rules, the Arbitration Rules of CIETAC, and the Panel of Arbitrators of CIETAC.

Together with the Notice of Arbitration for the acceptance of the Request for Arbitration, the Arbitration Court of CIETAC shall furnish to the Respondent a copy of the Claimant's Request for Arbitration and the documents annexed thereto, these Rules, the Arbitration Rules of CIETAC and the Panel of Arbitrators of CIETAC.

Article 12

The arbitral tribunal shall be composed of one or three arbitrators. Where the parties have not agreed upon the number of arbitrators, the Chairman of the CIETAC shall decide whether the arbitral tribunal shall be composed of one or three arbitrators.

Unless otherwise agreed by the parties, where the arbitral tribunal is composed of one arbitrator, the Claimant and the Respondent shall, within ten (10) working days from the date of receipt of the Notice of Arbitration by the party who last receives it, jointly appoint a sole arbitrator or entrust the Chairman of the CIETAC to affect such appointment.

Unless otherwise agreed by the parties, where the arbitral tribunal is composed of three arbitrators, the Claimant and the Respondent shall, within ten (10) working days from the date of receipt of the Notice of Arbitration, respectively appoint an arbitrator or entrust the Chairman of the CIETAC to effect such appointment, and shall, within ten (10) working days from the date of receipt of the Notice of Arbitration by the party who last receives it, jointly appoint a third arbitrator, or alternatively, shall entrust the Chairman of the CIETAC to effect such appointment. The third arbitrator shall be the presiding arbitrator.

Where there are two or more Claimants and/or Respondents in an arbitration case, the Claimant's side and/or the Respondent' side each shall, through consultation, jointly appoint an arbitrator, or alternatively, jointly entrust the Chairman of the CIETAC to affect such appointment.

Unless otherwise agreed by the parties, where a party fails to appoint an arbitrator or fails to entrust the Chairman of the CIETAC to affect such appointment in due course, such arbitrator shall be appointed by the Chairman of the CIETAC.

Article 13

Unless otherwise agreed by the parties, the Respondent shall, within fifteen (15) working days from the date of receipt of the Notice of Arbitration, submit its written Statement of Defence and the relevant evidence to the Arbitration Court of the CIETAC.

Unless otherwise agreed by the parties, the Respondent shall, within the foregoing time period, file its counterclaim in writing, if any, with the Arbitration Court of the CIETAC.

Article 14

Unless otherwise agreed by the parties, the Claimant shall, within fifteen (15) working days from the date of receipt of the Statement of Counterclaim and the attachment of the Respondent, file its written Statement of Defence to the Respondent's counterclaim with the Arbitration Court of the CIETAC.

Article 15

The arbitral tribunal may conduct the arbitration in such way as it deems appropriate. The arbitral tribunal shall treat the parties with equality and afford each party reasonable opportunities for presentations.

Unless otherwise agreed by the parties, the arbitral tribunal may adopt an inquisitorial or adversarial approach when examining the case, having regard to the circumstances of the case.

Article 16

During the arbitral proceedings, the arbitral tribunal may issue procedural directions and lists of questions, and hold pre-hearing meetings and preliminary hearings, etc.

Article 17

Where a time period for producing evidence has been agreed upon by the parties or has been set by the arbitral tribunal, the parties shall produce their evidence to the arbitral tribunal within the specified time period.

Where no such time period for producing evidence is agreed upon by the parties or set by the arbitral tribunal, the parties shall file all written statements and relevant evidence with the Arbitration Court of the CIETAC not less than three (3) working days prior to the date of the first oral hearing.

Unless otherwise agreed by the parties or decided by the arbitral tribunal, the arbitral tribunal may refuse to admit any written statement or evidence submitted by any party beyond the time period for producing evidence.

Article 18

The arbitral tribunal shall hold an oral hearing when examining the case. However, the oral hearing may be omitted and the case shall be examined on the basis of documents only if the parties so request or agree and the arbitral tribunal also deems that the oral hearing is unnecessary. If the oral hearing is to be held, the Arbitration Court of the CIETAC shall serve a Notice of Oral Hearing on each party at least ten (10) working days in advance of the oral hearing date.

Article 19

With the consent of the President of the Arbitration Court of the CIETAC, the time period specified in Article 12 may be extended.

With the consent of the arbitral tribunal, the time periods respectively specified in Articles 13, 14 and 18 may be extended.

Article 20

Where the parties have agreed on the place of arbitration in writing, their agreement shall prevail. Failing such agreement, the place of arbitration shall be the domicile of the CIETAC or its sub-commission/arbitration centres. The arbitral award shall be deemed as being made at the place of arbitration.

Unless otherwise agreed by the parties, the arbitral tribunal may conduct oral hearings or other activities at any place it deems appropriate.

Chapter III
Award

Article 21

Subject to mandatory provisions of law, the parties to any case involving a foreign-related element may agree upon the law to be applied to the merits of the dispute. Failing such agreement, the arbitral tribunal shall apply the law that it determines to be appropriate. In all cases, the arbitral tribunal shall take into account the terms of the contract, the general usages and standard practices of specific business sectors, and abide by the principles of fairness and reasonableness.

Article 22

Unless otherwise agreed by the parties, the arbitral tribunal shall render an arbitral award within forty-five (45) working days from the date on which the arbitral tribunal is formed.

At the request of the arbitral tribunal, the President of the Arbitration Court of the CIETAC may extend the said time period if he/she considers it truly necessary and the reasons for the extension truly justified. Each such extension may not exceed twenty (20) working days.

Article 23

Before signing an award, the arbitral tribunal shall submit its draft award to the CIETAC. Without affecting the independence of the arbitrators in rendering the award, the CIETAC may draw the arbitrators' attention to matters pertaining to the award.

Chapter IV
Miscellaneous

Article 24

All documents, notices and written materials in relation to the arbitration may be sent to the parties and/or their authorized representative(s) in person, or by registered mail or express mail, facsimile, telex, cable, Email or by any other proper means.

Article 25

Unless otherwise agreed by the parties or decided by the arbitral tribunal, for the purposes of these Rules, the term 'working day' shall mean a working day at the domicile of the CIETAC.

Article 26

In the event of any inconsistency between these Rules and the Arbitration Rules of the CIETAC, these Rules shall prevail.

For matters not covered in these Rules, the Arbitration Rules of the CIETAC shall apply.

Article 27

These Rules uniformly apply to the CIETAC and its Sub-Commissions/Centres. Where arbitration proceedings are administered by a Sub-Commission/Centre, the functions and duties under these Rules allocated to the Chairman, the Arbitration Court and the President of the Arbitration Court of the CIETAC shall be performed, respectively, by a Vice-Chairman authorized by the Chairman, the Arbitration Court and the President of the Arbitration Court of the relevant Sub-Commission.

Article 28

These Rules shall be interpreted by the CIETAC.

Appendix 8
Beijing Arbitration Commission Arbitration Rules[264]

(Revised and adopted at the First Meeting of the Fifth Session of the Beijing Arbitration Commission on 9 July 2014. Effective as from 1 April 2015)

Chapter I
General Provisions

Article 1
The Beijing Arbitration Commission

(1) The Beijing Arbitration Commission (the 'BAC') is an arbitral institution, registered in Beijing, China, to resolve contractual disputes and other disputes over property rights and interests between natural persons, legal persons and other organisations.

(2) The BAC is also known as the Beijing International Arbitration Centre (the 'BIAC'). Where the parties designate the BIAC as the arbitral institution in their arbitration agreement [Article 4(1)], the arbitration shall be administered by the BAC.

(3) The Chairman of the BAC (the 'Chairman') or, with the authorisation of the Chairman, one of the Vice-Chairmen or the Secretary-General of the BAC, shall perform the functions and duties vested in the Chairman by the BAC Arbitration Rules (the 'Rules').

(4) The Secretariat of the BAC (the 'Secretariat') shall handle the day-to-day affairs of the BAC. For each case, the Secretariat shall designate a member of its staff as the case manager (the 'Case Manager'), who shall attend to the

264 <http://arbitrator.bjac.org.cn/en/Arbitration/index.html>.

procedural administration and the provision of services relating to the case.

Article 2
Scope of Application

(1) The Rules shall apply where the parties have agreed to submit their dispute to the BAC for arbitration. Where the parties have agreed on certain procedural matters or the application of a different set of arbitration rules, their agreement shall prevail, unless the agreement is unenforceable or in conflict with the mandatory rules of law of the seat of arbitration. Where the parties have agreed on the application of a different set of arbitration rules, the BAC shall perform the corresponding administrative functions and duties.

(2) Where the parties have agreed to apply the Rules, but have not designated an arbitral institution, they shall be deemed to have agreed to submit their disputes to the BAC for arbitration.

(3) In respect of any matters not expressly provided for in the Rules, the BAC may administer and the Arbitral Tribunal may conduct the arbitration in such manner as it considers appropriate, to ensure the efficient and fair resolution of disputes between the parties.

(4) When applying the Rules, the BAC, the Arbitral Tribunal, the parties and their representatives shall act in accordance with the principles of good faith, collaboration, and appropriate resolution of the dispute.

Article 3
Waiver of Right to Object

A party who knows or ought reasonably to know of a failure to comply with any provision of the Rules or any term of the arbitration agreement, but nevertheless takes part in or continues to take part in the arbitral proceedings without promptly raising its objection to such non-compliance in writing to the BAC or the Arbitral Tribunal, shall be deemed to have waived its right to object to such non-compliance.

Chapter II
Arbitration Agreement

Article 4
Definition and Form of Arbitration Agreements

(1) An arbitration agreement is an agreement by the parties to submit any dispute which has arisen or which may arise from or in connection with an arbitrable legal relationship between the parties to arbitration [Article 1(1)]. An arbitration agreement may take the form of an arbitration clause included in a contract or any other written arbitration agreement.

(2) An arbitration agreement shall be in written form. 'Written form' includes, but is not limited to, contractual instruments, letters and electronic data messages (including telexes, facsimiles, electronic data interchange, and e-mails), and any other form where the contents are retrievable.

(3) Where, during exchange of the Application for Arbitration [Article 7(1)(b)] and the Statement of Defence [Article 10(1)(a)], one party asserts the existence of an arbitration agreement but the other party does not deny this, a written arbitration agreement between the parties shall be deemed to exist.

Article 5
Separability of Arbitration Agreements

An arbitration agreement shall be independent of the contract in which it is contained. The validity of the arbitration agreement shall be determined separately, and shall not be affected by the fact that the contract has been concluded, modified, terminated, rescinded or avoided, or is null and void, no longer effective or not yet in force.

Article 6

Objection to Jurisdiction

(1) If a party objects to the existence or validity of an arbitration agreement [Article 4 and 5] or to jurisdiction, it may raise an objection to jurisdiction with the BAC. Any objection shall be raised in writing before the first hearing. Where the parties have agreed to a documents-only arbitration [Article 24(2)], any written objection shall be raised within the time limit for the submission of the defence [Article 10(1)].

(2) If a party fails to raise any objection to jurisdiction pursuant to Article 6(1), it shall be deemed to have accepted that the BAC has jurisdiction.

(3) The raising of any objection to jurisdiction by any party with the BAC shall not affect the progress of arbitral proceedings.

(4) The BAC, or the Arbitral Tribunal as authorised by the BAC, may determine an objection as to jurisdiction. The Arbitral Tribunal may make its decision on jurisdiction either during the arbitral proceedings or in the arbitral award.

(5) Where the BAC, or the Arbitral Tribunal as authorised by the BAC, determines that it has no jurisdiction, an order for dismissal of the case shall be made by the Arbitral Tribunal, or if no Arbitral Tribunal has been constituted, by the BAC.

Chapter III
Application for Arbitration, Defence and Counterclaim

Article 7
Application for Arbitration

(1) A party applying for arbitration (the 'Claimant') shall submit:

(a) the arbitration agreement;

(b) its application for arbitration (the 'Application for Arbitration'), containing the following information:

(i) the names, addresses, postcodes, telephone numbers, facsimile numbers, email addresses and details of any other effective means of communication with the Claimant and the Respondent; where a party concerned is a legal person or other organisation, the name, position, address, postcode, telephone number, facsimile number, email address and details of any other effective means of communication with the legal representative or the person in charge;

(ii) its claim for relief (the 'Claim'), and the facts and grounds on which the Claim is based;

(c) the evidence and/or other supporting documents on which the Application for Arbitration is based; and

(d) proof of the Claimant's identity.

(2) The Claimant shall deposit an advance on the arbitration fees in accordance with the provisions of the Case Acceptance Fee Schedule of the Beijing Arbitration Commission and the Case Handling Fee Schedule of the Beijing Arbitration Commission [Annex 1]. Where the amount in dispute is not specified in the Application for Arbitration, the BAC shall determine the amount in dispute or the amount of the arbitration fees that shall be deposited in advance.

(3) If a party experiences difficulties with depositing the required advance on the arbitration fees, it may apply to the BAC for an extension of time, and the BAC shall determine such application. If a party has neither deposited the required advance nor applied for an extension of time, or has failed to deposit the full amount of the advance on arbitration fees within an extended time limit granted by the BAC, it shall be deemed not to have submitted or to have withdrawn its Application for Arbitration, as the case may be.

Article 8

Acceptance

(1) After receiving the Application for Arbitration [Article 7], the BAC shall, if it finds that the requirements for acceptance have been met, accept the Application for Arbitration within 5 days from the date of deposit by the Claimant of its advance on the arbitration fees.

(2) Where the Application for Arbitration does not comply with the requirements of Article 7(1), the Claimant shall rectify it within the time limit specified by the BAC, failing which the Claimant shall be deemed not to have submitted an Application for Arbitration.

(3) The arbitral proceedings shall be deemed to commence on the date of acceptance of the Application for Arbitration by the BAC.

Article 9

Notice of Arbitration

Within 10 days of the acceptance of the Application for Arbitration, the BAC shall send to the Claimant a notice of acceptance (the 'Notice of Acceptance'), a copy of the Rules, and a list of the BAC's Panel of Arbitrators [Article 18] (the 'Panel of Arbitrators'). The BAC shall send to the Respondent a request for submission of the defence (the 'Request for

Submission of Defence'), as well as a copy of the Application for Arbitration, together with its attachments, a copy of the Rules and a list of the Panel of Arbitrators.

Article 10
Defence

(1) Within 15 days of receiving the Request for Submission of Defence, the Respondent shall submit:

(a) its statement of defence (the 'Statement of Defence'), containing the following information:

(i) the name, address, postcode, telephone number, facsimile number, email address and details of any other effective means of communication with the Respondent; where a party concerned is a legal person or other organisation, the name, position, address, postcode, telephone number, facsimile number, email address and details of any other effective means of communication with the legal representative or the person in charge;

(ii) its defence to the Claim, and the facts and grounds on which the defence is based;

(b) the evidence and/or other supporting documents on which the defence is based; and

(c) proof of the Respondent's identity.

(2) Within 10 days of receiving the Statement of Defence, the BAC shall send to the Claimant a copy of the Statement of Defence, together with its attachments.

(3) Failure by the Respondent to submit its Statement of Defence shall not affect the progress of the arbitral proceedings.

Article 11

Counterclaim

(1) The Respondent shall file its counterclaim (the 'Counterclaim'), if any, by submitting a written application for counterclaim (the 'Application for Counterclaim') within 15 days from the date of receiving the Request for Submission of Defence. If the Counterclaim is raised after the expiration of the time limit (a 'late Counterclaim'), the decision on whether or not to accept a late Counterclaim shall be made by the Arbitral Tribunal, or if no Arbitral Tribunal has been constituted, by the BAC.

(2) When determining whether or not to accept a late Counterclaim, the BAC or the Arbitral Tribunal, as the case may be, shall take into account the necessity to hear the late Counterclaim and the Claim at the same time in a single arbitration, the extent of the delay in lodging the Application for Counterclaim, unnecessary delay that will be caused to the arbitral proceedings and any other relevant factors.

(3) The provisions of Articles 7 and 8 of the Rules shall apply *mutatis mutandis* to the submission and acceptance of the Counterclaim.

(4) Within 10 days of accepting the Counterclaim, the BAC shall send to the Claimant a request for submission of its defence to the Respondent's Counterclaim (the 'Request for Submission of Defence to Counterclaim'), as well as the Application for Counterclaim together with its attachments.

(5) The provisions of Article 10 shall apply to submission by the Claimant of its statement of defence to the Counterclaim (the 'Statement of Defence to Counterclaim').

(6) Any other matters concerning the Counterclaim which are not expressly provided for in these Rules shall be dealt with by reference to provisions concerning the Application for Arbitration [Article 7], insofar as they are relevant.

Article 12
Amendments to Claim or Counterclaim

(1) A party may apply to amend its Claim or Counterclaim. The application to amend (the 'Application to Amend') shall be in writing and will be determined by the Arbitral Tribunal or, if no Arbitral Tribunal has been constituted, by the BAC.

(2) Where an Application to Amend is unreasonably delayed and may adversely affect the ordinary course of the arbitral proceedings, the BAC or the Arbitral Tribunal may refuse such amendment.

(3) The provisions of Articles 7 to 10 of the Rules shall apply *mutatis mutandis* to the submission of, acceptance of and response to an Application to Amend.

Article 13
Joinder of Additional Parties

(1) Before the Arbitral Tribunal is constituted, the parties may apply to join an additional party to the arbitration under the same arbitration agreement, subject to approval by the BAC.

(2) A party applying to join an additional party to the arbitration shall submit an application for arbitration against the additional party (the 'Application for Joinder'). The provisions of Articles 7 to 10 of the Rules shall apply *mutatis mutandis* in respect of the content of such application, its acceptance and the submission of a defence.

(3) No Application for Joinder will be accepted after the Arbitral Tribunal has been constituted, unless the Claimant, the Respondent and the party to be joined otherwise agree.

Article 14
Claims between Multiple Parties

(1) Where there are two or more Claimants or Respondents in a single arbitration, or any additional party is joined to the arbitration [Article 13], any party may raise claims against any other party under the same arbitration agreement. The decision on whether or not to accept such claims shall be made by the Arbitral Tribunal, or if no Arbitral Tribunal has been constituted, by the BAC.

(2) The provisions of Articles 7 to 10 and Article 12 shall apply *mutatis mutandis* to the submission and acceptance of, defence(s) to and amendment of, claims raised under this Article.

Article 15
Submission of Documents and Number of Copies

(1) Unless otherwise agreed by the parties, the parties shall submit to the BAC documents in the arbitration, which the BAC shall forward to the Arbitral Tribunal and to the other parties. If the parties agree to submit documents in the arbitration directly to the Arbitral Tribunal, copies of such documents shall be filed with the BAC.

(2) The Application for Arbitration [Article 7], the Statement of Defence [Article 10], the Application for Counterclaim [Article 11], evidence and any other written documents shall be submitted in quintuplicate. Where there are more than two parties, additional copies shall be provided accordingly. If the Arbitral Tribunal comprises a sole arbitrator, the number of copies shall be reduced by two.

Article 16
Preservation Measures

(1) In the event that enforcement of any award is likely to become difficult or if any other detriment is likely to be

caused to one party as a result of the conduct of the other party or of the existence of any other relevant factors, a party may apply for an order to preserve property or assets of the other party's, or to require that party to take or to refrain from taking certain actions.

(2) A party may apply for an order to preserve evidence if there is a risk that such evidence might be lost, destroyed or might subsequently become difficult to obtain.

(3) Where a party submits an application to the BAC under Article 16(1) or (2), the BAC shall forward the application to the competent court for determination.

(4) In urgent circumstances, such as where a party's lawful rights and interests would be irreparably damaged, or evidence might be lost, destroyed or subsequently become difficult to obtain if no preservation measure is applied for immediately, a party may file an application for preservation measures before submitting its Application for Arbitration under Article 7.

Article 17
Representation

Where a party engages one or more representatives for the arbitration, it shall submit to the BAC a power of attorney setting out the matters specifically entrusted to each representative and the scope of each representative's authority.

Chapter IV
The Arbitral Tribunal

Article 18
Panel of Arbitrators

The BAC shall establish a Panel of Arbitrators. The parties shall choose arbitrators from the Panel of Arbitrators maintained by the BAC.

Article 19
Composition of the Arbitral Tribunal

(1) Unless otherwise agreed by the parties or provided for in the Rules, the Arbitral Tribunal shall comprise 3 arbitrators.

(2) Within 15 days of receiving the Notice of Arbitration [Article 9], each party shall nominate or request the Chairman to appoint an arbitrator from the Panel of Arbitrators [Article 18]. If a party fails to nominate an arbitrator or fails to request the Chairman to appoint an arbitrator within the time limit, the arbitrator shall be appointed by the Chairman.

(3) Within 15 days of receiving by the Respondent of the Notice of Arbitration, the parties shall jointly nominate or jointly request the Chairman to appoint the presiding arbitrator. The parties may each nominate between 1 and 3 arbitrator(s) as candidate(s) for the role of presiding arbitrator within the time limit. Where the parties agree or make an application to the BAC, the BAC may also provide a list of between 5 and 7 candidates from which the parties may each select between 1 and 4 candidates within the time limit fixed by Article 19(2) as the presiding arbitrator. Where there is only one common candidate on both parties' lists for nomination or selection, that candidate shall be deemed to have been jointly nominated by both parties as presiding arbitrator. If there are two or more common candidates, the Chairman shall, taking into consideration the particular

circumstances of the case, appoint one of those candidates as the presiding arbitrator, who shall be deemed to have been jointly nominated by the parties. If there are no common candidates, the Chairman shall appoint an arbitrator who is not on the list of nomination or the list of selection as the presiding arbitrator, as the case may be.

(4) If the parties fail to nominate the presiding arbitrator jointly, in accordance with Article 19(2) and (3), the presiding arbitrator shall be appointed by the Chairman.

(5) Where there are two or more Claimants or Respondents, each set of Claimants or Respondents shall, by agreement, jointly nominate or jointly request the Chairman to appoint an arbitrator. If no joint nomination or joint request has been made within 15 days of receiving the Notice of Arbitration by the last party, the Chairman shall then appoint the arbitrator.

(6) In the event of a joinder [Article 13], the joined party shall nominate the arbitrator jointly with either the Claimant or the Respondent, as the case may be. If no such a nomination has been made, all members of the Arbitral Tribunal shall be appointed by the Chairman.

(7) Where a party nominates an arbitrator who resides outside Beijing, that party shall bear the necessary travel and accommodation expenses incurred by that arbitrator for hearing the case. If that party has not deposited the advance on such expenses within the period specified by the BAC [Article 7(2)], it shall be deemed not to have nominated that arbitrator. In this event, the Chairman may appoint another arbitrator for that party in accordance with this Article.

(8) Where an arbitrator declines to accept a party's nomination or is unable to participate in the arbitration, due to illness or any other relevant factors that may prevent him or her from performing an arbitrator's usual functions and duties, that party shall nominate another arbitrator within 5 days of receipt of notice of re-nomination (the 'Notice of Re-

nomination'). If that party fails to nominate another arbitrator within the time limit, the arbitrator shall be appointed by the Chairman.

Article 20

Notice of Constitution of the Arbitral Tribunal

Within 5 days of the constitution of the Arbitral Tribunal, the BAC shall notify the parties accordingly. The Case Manager [Article 1(4)] shall forward the case file to the Arbitral Tribunal promptly thereafter.

Article 21

Disclosure by Arbitrators

(1) Upon accepting appointment, each arbitrator shall sign a statement of independence and impartiality, a copy of which shall be forwarded to each party by the Case Manager.

(2) If, at any time, an arbitrator becomes aware of circumstances relating to either party or its authorised representatives, that are likely to lead any party to have reasonable doubts about his or her independence or impartiality, the arbitrator shall disclose such circumstances in writing.

(3) Within 10 days of receiving a written disclosure under Article 21(2), either party shall state in writing whether it intends to challenge the arbitrator.

(4) The provisions of Article 22(1), (2), (4), (5) and (6) shall apply to the challenge to an arbitrator on the basis of circumstances disclosed by the arbitrator under Article 21(2).

(5) A party who fails to challenge an arbitrator within the period of time specified in Article 22(3) shall not be permitted to challenge the arbitrator at a later time during the arbitral proceedings on the basis of the circumstances already disclosed by the arbitrator.

Article 22
Challenge to the Arbitrator

(1) A party may challenge any arbitrator on the basis of its reasonable doubts as to the independence or impartiality of the arbitrator.

(2) A challenge shall be made in writing and accompanied by the grounds of the challenge and supporting evidence.

(3) A challenge shall be raised before the first oral hearing. A challenge based on circumstances that become known after the first oral hearing may be raised prior to the closure of the final oral hearing. Without prejudice to Article 21(3), where no further oral hearing will be conducted, or in a documents-only arbitration, a challenge shall be raised within 10 days after the challenging party becomes aware of the circumstances giving rise to a challenge.

(4) The Case Manager shall promptly forward the application for challenge (the 'Application for Challenge') to the other party and to each member of the Arbitral Tribunal.

(5) Where a party challenges an arbitrator and the other party concurs with the challenge, or the challenged arbitrator withdraws voluntarily upon being informed of the challenge, that arbitrator shall no longer participate in the arbitration. Neither of these circumstances shall imply that the grounds on which the challenge is based are established.

(6) Unless Article 22(5) applies, the Chairman shall decide on the challenge. The decision of the Chairman shall be final. The Chairman may decide, according to the particular circumstances of the case and as a matter of discretion, whether or not to provide reasons for the decision.

(7) A party who, after becoming aware of the composition of the Arbitral Tribunal, appoints authorised representatives [Article 17] whose appointment may give rise to grounds for the challenge of any arbitrator, shall be deemed to have waived its right to challenge the arbitrator on those grounds; the right of the other party to challenge the arbitrator shall not, however,

be affected. Additional costs resulting from any delay caused to the arbitral proceedings in these circumstances shall be borne by the party responsible for giving rise to the grounds for challenge.

Article 23
Replacement of the Arbitrator

(1) An arbitrator shall be removed if he or she becomes unable to conduct the arbitration as a result of death, or illness, or withdraws from the arbitration, or the Chairman decides that he or she is to withdraw from the arbitration [Article 22(6)], or is requested by all the parties to withdraw from the arbitration [Article 22(5)].

(2) An arbitrator may also be removed on the initiative of the Chairman if the Chairman decides that the arbitrator is prevented de jure or de facto from fulfilling his or her functions and duties as an arbitrator, or is not fulfilling his or her functions and duties as required by the Rules.

(3) Before making any decision pursuant to the provisions of Article 23(2), the Chairman shall provide the parties and all members of the Arbitral Tribunal with an opportunity to comment thereon in writing.

(4) If the arbitrator to be removed was nominated by a party, that party shall nominate a substitute arbitrator within 5 days of its receipt of the notice of removal. If the arbitrator to be removed was appointed by the Chairman, the Chairman shall appoint a substitute arbitrator. Within 5 days of such nomination or appointment of the substitute arbitrator, the BAC shall send a notice of reconstitution of the Arbitral Tribunal to the parties. After the reconstitution of the Arbitral Tribunal, either party may request the previous arbitral proceedings to be repeated and the Arbitral Tribunal shall determine whether such repetition is necessary. The Arbitral Tribunal may also, on its own initiative, decide whether and to what extent the previous arbitral proceedings

shall be repeated. If the Arbitral Tribunal decides to repeat the arbitral proceedings in their entirety, the time limit provided for in Articles 47, 58 and 68 shall be recalculated from the date of the reconstitution of the Arbitral Tribunal.

Chapter V
The Arbitral Proceedings

Article 24
Mode of Proceeding

(1) The Arbitral Tribunal shall hold an oral hearing.

(2) If the parties agree on a documents-only arbitration, or if the Arbitral Tribunal considers an oral hearing unnecessary and the parties so agree, the Arbitral Tribunal may decide the arbitration on the basis of the documents submitted by the parties.

(3) Regardless of the mode of proceeding adopted, the Arbitral Tribunal shall treat the parties fairly and impartially and give each party a reasonable opportunity to make submissions and arguments.

Article 25
Confidentiality

(1) All arbitration hearings shall be conducted in private. If the parties agree on a public hearing, the arbitration hearing may proceed in public, except where the case involves state secrets, any third party's commercial secrets, or any relevant circumstances in which the Arbitral Tribunal considers that a public hearing is inappropriate.

(2) Where an arbitration is conducted in private, neither the parties, nor their authorised representatives, nor any witnesses, arbitrators, experts consulted by the Arbitral Tribunal and appraisers appointed by the Arbitral Tribunal,

nor the staff of the BAC shall disclose to third parties any information concerning the arbitration, whether substantive or procedural.

Article 26

Seat of Arbitration

(1) Unless otherwise agreed by the parties, the seat of arbitration shall be the location of the BAC. The BAC may also determine the seat of arbitration according to the particular circumstances of the case.

(2) The arbitral award shall be deemed to have been rendered at the seat of the arbitration.

Article 27

Place of Hearing

(1) Unless the parties otherwise agree, hearings shall be held at the BAC's premises.

(2) If the parties agree upon a hearing at any other location, the resulting additional costs shall be borne by the parties. The parties shall deposit an advance on such additional costs in accordance with the proportion agreed by them or decided upon by the Arbitral Tribunal within a period specified by the BAC. If such deposit is not made, the hearing shall be held at the BAC's premises.

Article 28

Concurrent Hearings

(1) The Arbitral Tribunal may, upon meeting all of the following conditions, order concurrent hearings:

(a) the arbitrations concerned involve the same or related subject-matter;

(b) a party applies for concurrent hearings with the consent of all other parties concerned; and

(c) the composition of the Arbitral Tribunals in the arbitrations concerned is identical.

(2) The Arbitral Tribunal may, according to the particular circumstances of the case, decide on the detailed procedure for the arbitral proceedings as a result of its order.

Article 29
Consolidation of Arbitrations

(1) Where the parties so agree, or where one party applies and the BAC, in its discretion, considers it necessary, the BAC may decide to consolidate two or more arbitrations pending under the Rules into a single arbitration. Where an order for consolidation is made, arbitrations shall be consolidated into the arbitration that commenced first, unless otherwise agreed by the parties.

(2) In deciding whether or not to order consolidation, the BAC shall take into account the specific circumstances of arbitration agreements on which the relevant arbitrations are based, the nexus between those arbitrations, the stage that each set of arbitration proceedings has reached, the arbitrators already nominated or appointed in the relevant arbitrations and any other relevant factors.

Article 30
Notice of Hearing

(1) Where an arbitration is to be conducted by way of an oral hearing, the Arbitral Tribunal shall notify the parties of the date of the first hearing at least 10 days in advance. The first hearing may be rescheduled to an earlier date by the Arbitral Tribunal with the agreement of the parties. A party may, no less than 5 days in advance of the hearing, request a postponement of the first hearing, provided that there are grounds justifying the postponement. The Arbitral Tribunal shall, in its discretion, decide whether

or not to postpone the first hearing, having regard to all relevant circumstances.

(2) A notification of the date of any subsequent hearing, or of the date of a postponed hearing, shall not be subject to the 10-day time limit in Article 30(1).

Article 31

Default

(1) Having been duly notified in writing of the hearing under Article 30, if the Claimant fails to appear at the hearing without any justification, or withdraws from an ongoing hearing without the permission of the Arbitral Tribunal, the Claimant may be deemed to have withdrawn its Application for Arbitration. Where the Respondent has raised a Counterclaim, the Claimant's default shall not affect the hearing of the Counterclaim by the Arbitral Tribunal.

(2) Having been duly notified in writing of the hearing, if the Respondent fails to appear at the hearing without any justification, or withdraws from an ongoing hearing without the permission of the Arbitral Tribunal, the Arbitral Tribunal may proceed with the arbitration. Where the Respondent has raised a Counterclaim, such Counterclaim shall be deemed to have been withdrawn.

Article 32

Production of Evidence

(1) Each party shall bear the burden of proving the facts relied upon to support its claim or defence.

(2) The Arbitral Tribunal may require the parties to produce their evidence within a specified period of time and the parties shall comply with any such order. The Arbitral Tribunal may reject any evidence not produced within the specified period of time, unless the parties agree otherwise or the Arbitral Tribunal considers it necessary to accept the evidence.

(3) If a party having the burden of proof fails to produce evidence within the specified period of time, or if the evidence produced is insufficient to discharge its burden of proof, it shall bear the adverse consequences of such failure.

(4) Each party shall properly bind, number, and paginate the evidence it produces. The file of evidence shall be accompanied by a list stating briefly the title of each piece of evidence and the purpose of producing it. The evidence list shall be signed, sealed and dated.

(5) Any reproduction, photograph, duplicate, or abridged version of any document or any item produced by one party to another party shall be deemed to be identical to the original copy, unless the other party challenges its authenticity.

(6) Unless otherwise agreed by the parties or otherwise provided for in the Rules, evidence and written documents submitted in a foreign language shall be accompanied by a Chinese translation. The Arbitral Tribunal may, if necessary, require the parties to provide a translation of the evidence and of any written documents in another language or languages.

Article 33
Investigation and Collection of Evidence by Arbitral Tribunal

(1) If a party makes an application and the Arbitral Tribunal considers it necessary, or there is no such application but the Arbitral Tribunal considers it necessary according to the particular circumstances of the case, the Arbitral Tribunal may undertake investigations and/or collect evidence on its own initiative. If the Arbitral Tribunal considers it necessary to require the parties to be present when it undertakes investigations or collects evidence, it shall notify the parties in a timely fashion. Provided that the parties have been duly notified, the Arbitral Tribunal may proceed with the investigations or the collection of evidence even if they fail to appear.

(2) Evidence collected by the Arbitral Tribunal on its own initiative shall be forwarded to both parties for their comments in a timely fashion before an award is made.

Article 34
Appraisal

(1) If a party requests an appraisal and the Arbitral Tribunal agrees with the request, or neither party makes an application but the Arbitral Tribunal considers it necessary to conduct an appraisal, the Arbitral Tribunal may notify the parties to nominate an appraiser jointly within a period of time specified by the Arbitral Tribunal. If the parties fail to do so, the appraiser shall be appointed by the Arbitral Tribunal.

(2) The parties shall deposit an advance on the appraisal costs in accordance with a proportion agreed by them or decided upon by the Arbitral Tribunal. The Arbitral Tribunal may decide not to conduct the appraisal if the parties do not deposit an advance.

(3) The Arbitral Tribunal may require the parties, and the parties shall be under an obligation, to provide or present to the appraiser any relevant document, data, property or any other goods required for the appraisal. The Arbitral Tribunal shall decide upon any disagreement between any party and the appraiser as to whether a document, data, property or any other goods required for the appraisal is relevant to the case.

(4) The appraiser shall provide an appraisal report in writing. A copy of the appraisal report shall be sent to each party. Each party may express opinions on the appraisal report.

(5) If the Arbitral Tribunal considers it necessary or if any party so requests, the Arbitral Tribunal may notify the appraiser to attend the hearing. The parties may, with the permission of the Arbitral Tribunal, question the appraiser on relevant aspects of the appraisal report.

(6) Any period of time taken to conduct an appraisal shall not be taken into account for the purposes of calculating the

time limits provided for in Articles 47, 58 and 68 of these Rules.

Article 35
Procedural Orders

The Arbitral Tribunal may, according to the particular circumstances of the case, make procedural orders, including but not limited to the preparation of the procedural timetable for the hearing, issuing lists of questions, holding pre-hearing conferences, and producing terms of reference. The Arbitral Tribunal may authorise the presiding arbitrator to make any of these procedural orders.

Article 36
Examination of Evidence

(1) The Arbitral Tribunal may, according to the particular circumstances of the case, require the parties to take appropriate steps to verify the authenticity of the copies of the evidence. The Arbitral Tribunal may delegate the Case Manager to coordinate this process.

(2) Where an oral hearing is to be held, evidence exchanged between the parties prior to the hearing shall be presented by them for examination during the hearing. Evidence produced by a party may be admitted and accepted as the basis of fact finding without being presented at the hearing for examination if the other party has acknowledged its admissibility and the Arbitral Tribunal has, during the hearing, confirmed the other party's acknowledgement of this.

(3) Where evidence is produced by any party during or after the hearing and the Arbitral Tribunal decides to admit the evidence without holding any further hearings, the Arbitral Tribunal may require the other party to comment on such evidence in writing within a specified period of time.

Article 37

Assessment of Evidence

(1) The Arbitral Tribunal shall have the authority to assess the evidence. It shall also decide on whether or not to adopt an appraiser's opinion.

(2) When assessing any evidence, the Arbitral Tribunal may, in addition to referring to relevant laws, regulations and judicial interpretations, conduct its assessment by taking into consideration factors such as industry practices and trade usages, and shall consider the case in its totality.

Article 38

Presentation of Arguments

Each party may present oral arguments during the hearing [Article 24(1)]. The Arbitral Tribunal may also require the parties to submit written arguments on particular issues according to the circumstances of the case.

Article 39

Closing Statements

At the closing of the hearing, the Arbitral Tribunal shall invite closing statements from the parties, which may be presented either orally during the hearing or in writing within a period of time specified by the Arbitral Tribunal.

Article 40

Record of Hearing

(1) The Arbitral Tribunal shall make a written record of the hearing, except in the case of conciliation proceedings [Article 42 and 67].

(2) The Arbitral Tribunal may make an audio or video record of the hearing.

(3) A party or any other participant in the arbitration may request the rectification of any omission or error in the written record of their oral statement. The request shall be recorded if the Arbitral Tribunal does not allow the rectification.

(4) The Arbitral Tribunal, person who makes the recording, the parties and other participants in the arbitration shall sign or affix their seals on the written record.

(5) Upon a joint request by both parties, or a request by one party that has been approved by the BAC, the BAC may appoint one or more stenographers to record the hearing. The resulting additional costs shall be borne by the parties or the requesting party, as the case may be.

Article 41
Withdrawal of an Application for Arbitration and Dismissal of a Case

(1) The Claimant may withdraw the Application for Arbitration [Article 7]. Where the Respondent has raised a Counterclaim [Article 11], withdrawal of the Application for Arbitration shall not affect the hearing and determination of such counterclaim by the Arbitral Tribunal. The Respondent may withdraw its counterclaim. Withdrawal of the Counterclaim shall not affect the hearing and determination of the Claimant's claim by the Arbitral Tribunal.

(2) Where all claims and counterclaims (if any) have been withdrawn, the case can be dismissed. Dismissal of the case shall be decided by the Arbitral Tribunal, or if no Arbitral Tribunal has been constituted, by the BAC.

(3) Where it becomes unnecessary or impossible to continue the arbitral proceedings for any reason, the BAC or the Arbitral Tribunal, as the case may be, may dismiss the case.

(4) Where the case has been dismissed, the BAC may decide whether to refund the advance on the arbitration fees or any

other fees paid in advance, as well as the specific amount of such refund, according to the circumstances of the case.

Article 42
Conciliation by the Tribunal

(1) The Arbitral Tribunal may, at the request or with the consent of the parties, conduct a conciliation of the case in such manner as it considers appropriate.

(2) If the conciliation leads to a settlement, the parties may withdraw their claims and counterclaims (if any), or may request the Arbitral Tribunal either to issue a Statement of Conciliation [Article 42(3)] or to render an award in accordance with the terms of the settlement agreement.

(3) The Statement of Conciliation shall state the claims and the terms of the resulting settlement agreement reached by the parties. It shall be signed by the arbitrators, sealed by the BAC, and served on all the parties. The Statement of Conciliation shall be legally binding after all the parties have acknowledged receipt of it in writing.

(4) The Arbitral Tribunal shall rectify any clerical and computational errors or similar errors in the Statement of Conciliation. The parties may request such rectification within 30 days from the date on which the parties sign the receipt of the Statement of Conciliation. Any such rectification shall become part of the Statement of Conciliation and shall take effect immediately after being served on the parties.

(5) If the conciliation fails to lead to a settlement, neither party shall be permitted to adduce evidence of or to refer to or use any statements, opinions, views or proposals expressed by the other party or by the Arbitral Tribunal during the conciliation as in support of any claim, defence, or counterclaim in the subsequent arbitral proceedings, or as grounds in any judicial or other proceedings.

Article 43
Independent Conciliation

(1) During the arbitral proceedings, the parties may enter into a voluntary settlement agreement or may apply to the Mediation Centre of the BAC (the 'Mediation Centre') for mediation by the mediators of the Mediation Centre in accordance with the Mediation Rules of the Mediation Centre of the BAC.

(2) Where a settlement agreement is concluded through an independent conciliation under this Article, the parties may jointly request the constitution of an Arbitral Tribunal either to issue a Statement of Conciliation or to render an award in accordance with the terms of the settlement agreement. The parties shall bear the resulting additional costs.

Article 44
Suspension and Resumption of Arbitral Proceedings

(1) If the parties jointly request, or if one party requests and the other parties do not object, the arbitral proceedings may be suspended. The arbitral proceedings may be resumed if one party so requests or the BAC or the Arbitral Tribunal deems this necessary.

(2) The arbitral proceedings may be suspended if any exceptional circumstances occur that necessitate suspension. The arbitral proceedings shall be resumed once such circumstances cease to exist. (3) The suspension and resumption of the arbitral proceedings shall be decided by the Arbitral Tribunal, or if no Arbitral Tribunal has been constituted, by the BAC. Any period of time during which the arbitral proceedings were suspended shall not be taken into account for the calculation of the time limits provided for in Articles 47, 58 and 68.

Article 45
Continuation of the Arbitral Proceedings with Majority of the Arbitral Tribunal

In the event that, after the conclusion of the last hearing, an arbitrator on a three-member Arbitral Tribunal is unable to participate in the deliberations and render an award as a result of his or her death or for other reasons, the Chairman may replace that arbitrator with a substitute arbitrator, pursuant to Article 23 of the Rules. Alternatively, provided that the parties consent and with the approval of the Chairman, the two remaining arbitrators may continue with the arbitral proceedings and make decisions, or an award.

Chapter VI
Decisions and Awards

Article 44
Suspension and Resumption of Arbitral Proceedings

(1) If the parties jointly request, or if one party requests and the other parties do not object, the arbitral proceedings may be suspended. The arbitral proceedings may be resumed if one party so requests or the BAC or the Arbitral Tribunal deems this necessary.

(2) The arbitral proceedings may be suspended if any exceptional circumstances occur that necessitate suspension. The arbitral proceedings shall be resumed once such circumstances cease to exist.

(3) The suspension and resumption of the arbitral proceedings shall be decided by the Arbitral Tribunal, or if no Arbitral Tribunal has been constituted, by the BAC. Any period of time during which the arbitral proceedings were suspended shall not be taken into account for the calculation of the time limits provided for in Articles 47, 58 and 68.

Article 45
Continuation of the Arbitral Proceedings with Majority of the Arbitral Tribunal

In the event that, after the conclusion of the last hearing, an arbitrator on a three-member Arbitral Tribunal is unable to participate in the deliberations and render an award as a result of his or her death or for other reasons, the Chairman may replace that arbitrator with a substitute arbitrator, pursuant to Article 23 of the Rules. Alternatively, provided that the parties consent and with the approval of the Chairman, the two remaining arbitrators may continue with the arbitral proceedings and make decisions, or an award.

Article 46
Decisions on Procedural Matters

(1) The Arbitral Tribunal may decide upon procedural matters during the arbitral proceedings.

(2) Any decision of an Arbitral Tribunal comprising 3 arbitrators shall be made by a majority of the arbitrators. If the Arbitral Tribunal fails to reach a majority decision, the decision of the presiding arbitrator shall prevail.

(3) The presiding arbitrator may, with the consent of the parties or with the authorisation of the Arbitral Tribunal, decide upon procedural matters.

Article 47
Time Limit for Rendering the Award

The Arbitral Tribunal shall render its award within 4 months of its constitution [Articles 19 and 20]. If there are special circumstances justifying an extension of this period, the Secretary-General may approve an appropriate extension of time at the request of the presiding arbitrator.

Article 48

Rendering the Award

(1) The award of an Arbitral Tribunal comprising 3 arbitrators shall be made by a majority of the arbitrators. The minority dissenting opinion may be recorded in writing. If the Arbitral Tribunal fails to reach a majority decision, the award shall be made in accordance with the opinion of the presiding arbitrator.

(2) The award shall state the claims, the facts associated with the dispute, the reasons upon which the award is based, operative directions disposing of the dispute, the allocation of arbitration fees [Article 51], the date of the award, and the seat of the arbitration. The Arbitral Tribunal shall not be required to state the facts associated with the dispute or the reasons upon which the award is based if the parties so agree, or if the award is made in accordance with the terms of a settlement agreement between the parties [Articles 42 and 43].

(3) The award shall be signed by each member of the Arbitral Tribunal. A dissenting arbitrator may elect not to sign the award. An arbitrator who elects not to sign the award shall issue a dissenting opinion in writing, which shall be sent by the BAC to the parties together with the award. A dissenting opinion shall not form part of the award.

(4) After an award has been signed by the arbitrator(s), the BAC's seal shall be affixed to it.

Article 49

Partial Award and Interim Award

(1) Where the Arbitral Tribunal considers it necessary, or where a party so requests and the Arbitral Tribunal approves, the Arbitral Tribunal may render a partial award disposing of particular claims before proceeding to render the final award.

(2) Where the Arbitral Tribunal considers it necessary, or

where a party so requests and the Arbitral Tribunal approves, the Arbitral Tribunal may render an interim award on disputed procedural or substantive issues.

(3) The parties concerned shall perform any partial award and interim award. Failure by any party to perform a partial award or an interim award shall neither affect the subsequent arbitral proceedings nor prevent the Arbitral Tribunal from rendering the final award.

Article 50
Validity and Performance of the Award

(1) An award shall be legally binding from the date on which it is made.

(2) After an award has been made, the parties concerned shall perform the award in accordance with the time limit for performance specified in the award. Where an award does not specify the time limit for performance, it shall be performed immediately. Where any party fails to perform the award, the other party may apply to the competent court for enforcement.

Article 51
Allocation of Costs

(1) The Arbitral Tribunal may determine in its award how the arbitration fees and any expenses actually incurred shall be borne by the parties, including but not limited to appraisal fees, evaluation fees and audit fees.

(2) Unless otherwise agreed by the parties, the costs of the arbitration shall in principle be borne by the losing party. If either party is only partially successful, the Arbitral Tribunal shall determine the proportion of each party's share of the costs on the basis of the extent of liability of each party. If the parties reach a settlement either independently or as a result

of conciliation by the Arbitral Tribunal [Article 42], they may agree upon the proportion of their respective shares.

(3) Where the circumstances described in Article 22(7) of the Rules apply, or there exist any other breaches of the Rules that cause delay in the arbitral proceedings, the allocation of arbitration costs to the party at fault shall not be limited by the provisions in Article 51(2). Where other costs are incurred or increased due to such delay in the arbitral proceedings, the party causing the delay shall also bear the costs so incurred or increased.

(4) The Arbitral Tribunal may, pursuant to a party's request, order that the losing party shall bear the winning party's reasonable costs and expenses for the conduct of the arbitration, including but not limited to attorney's fees, the costs of preservation measures, travel and accommodation expenses, and notarial fees. Where the Arbitral Tribunal determines the amount of these costs and expenses, it shall take into consideration the outcome of the case, its complexity, the actual workload of the parties or their attorneys, the amount in dispute and any other relevant factors.

Article 52
Correction of the Award and Supplementary Award

(1) The Arbitral Tribunal shall correct any clerical error or computational error, and address any omission of issues that have been raised by a party in its claim and decided upon by the Arbitral Tribunal but omitted in the operative directions disposing of the dispute. In the event that any claim is omitted entirely from the award, the Arbitral Tribunal shall render a supplementary award thereon.

(2) Upon discovering the existence of any of the circumstances described in Article 52(1), a party may, within

30 days of the date of receiving the award, request in writing that the Arbitral Tribunal rectify the award or render a supplementary award.

(3) Any rectification by or supplementary award of the Arbitral Tribunal shall form part of the original arbitral award.

Chapter VII
Expedited Procedure

Article 53
Scope of the Application of Expedited Procedure

(1) Unless otherwise agreed by the parties, the expedited procedure set out in this Chapter (the 'Expedited Procedure') shall apply if the amount in dispute does not exceed RMB 1,000,000.

(2) The parties may also agree to apply the Expedited Procedure where the amount in dispute exceeds RMB 1,000,000. In such a case, the arbitration fees shall be reduced accordingly.

(3) If the parties agree to apply the ordinary procedure (the 'Ordinary Procedure') when the amount in dispute does not exceed RMB 1,000,000, they shall bear any resulting additional arbitration fees.

(4) Where Chapter VIII of the Rules makes special provisions for the Expedited Procedure, such provisions shall apply.

Article 54
Composition of the Arbitral Tribunal

(1) Arbitrations conducted in accordance with the Expedited Procedure shall be heard by a sole arbitrator.

(2) Within 10 days of receipt of the Notice of Arbitration [Article 9] by all parties, the parties shall jointly nominate a

sole arbitrator or jointly request the Chairman to appoint a sole arbitrator from the Panel of Arbitrators. The sole arbitrator may be selected in the manner prescribed by Article 19(3). If the parties fail jointly to nominate a sole arbitrator or request the Chairman to appoint a sole arbitrator within the specified period, the Chairman will appoint the sole arbitrator.

Article 55
Time Limit for Defence and Counterclaim

Within 10 days of receipt of the Request for Submission of Defence [Article 9], the Respondent shall submit to the BAC its Statement of Defence [Article 10], together with any relevant supporting documents. A Counterclaim [Article 11], if any, shall also be submitted within 10 days of receipt of the Request for Submission of Defence, together with any relevant supporting documents.

Article 56
Notice of Hearing

(1) Where an oral hearing [Article 24(1)] is to be held, the Arbitral Tribunal shall notify the parties of the date of the hearing at least 3 days in advance.

(2) If the Arbitral Tribunal decides to hear the case by way of oral hearing, it shall hold one hearing only. Where necessary, however, the Arbitral Tribunal may on its own initiative decide to hold further hearings. Notification of the date of any further hearing shall not, however, be subject to the 3-day time limit under Article 56(1).

Article 57
Expedited Procedure Converted into Ordinary Procedure

(1) Proceedings under the Expedited Procedure may be converted into proceedings under the Ordinary Procedure

upon the joint request of the parties or upon the request of one party with the approval of the other parties.

(2) Proceedings under the Expedited Procedure shall not be affected by reason of any amendment to the Claim, the submission of a Counterclaim or any amendment causing the amount in dispute to exceed RMB 1,000,000. If a party is of the opinion that the proceedings under the Expedited Procedure may be so affected, it may request the Chairman to convert the proceedings into proceedings under the Ordinary Procedure. The Chairman shall decide whether or not to approve such application.

(3) The parties shall agree upon their respective proportions of the advance on the additional arbitration fees arising from the conversion of proceedings from the Expedited Procedure into the Ordinary Procedure. Where the parties fail so to agree, such proportions shall be determined by the BAC. Where the parties fail to deposit an advance on the resulting additional costs in accordance with the requirements of the BAC, no conversion of procedure shall be ordered.

(4) In the event of conversion of proceedings from the Expedited Procedure into the Ordinary Procedure after the constitution of the Arbitral Tribunal, the parties shall, within 5 days of receipt of a notice of the conversion of the procedure ('Notice of Conversion of Procedure'), respectively nominate or respectively request the Chairman to appoint their arbitrators in accordance with Article 19 of the Rules. Unless otherwise agreed by the parties, the sole arbitrator originally appointed shall become the presiding arbitrator. The reconstituted Arbitral Tribunal shall decide whether and to what extent the arbitral proceedings conducted prior to the reconstitution shall be repeated. Where the reconstituted Arbitral Tribunal decides to repeat the arbitral proceedings in their entirety, the time limit provided for in Articles 47 and 68 of the Rules shall be recalculated from the date of the reconstitution of the Arbitral Tribunal.

(5) The Expedited Procedure shall cease to apply to the arbitral proceedings from the date of conversion.

Article 58

Time Limit for Rendering the Award

The Arbitral Tribunal shall render its award within 75 days from the date of its constitution. If there are special circumstances justifying an extension of this period, the Secretary-General may approve an appropriate extension of time at the request of the sole arbitrator.

Article 59

Reference to other Provisions of the Rules

In respect of matters not provided for in this Chapter, other relevant provisions of the Rules shall apply.

Chapter VIII

Special Provisions for International Commercial Arbitration

Article 60

Scope of Application of this Chapter

(1) Unless otherwise agreed by the parties, the provisions of this Chapter shall apply to international commercial arbitrations. In respect of matters not provided for in this Chapter, the other relevant provisions of the Rules shall apply.

(2) Arbitrations relating to the Hong Kong Special Administrative Region ('SAR'), the Macao SAR and the Taiwan region may be conducted by reference to the provisions of this Chapter.

(3) Any dispute between the parties as to the existence of international elements shall be referred to the Arbitral Tribunal for a decision. The decision of the Arbitral Tribunal

shall not affect arbitral proceedings already conducted. This Chapter shall apply if the Arbitral Tribunal decides that international elements exist in the case.

Article 61

Arbitration Fees

In respect of an international commercial arbitration case, the parties may agree to pay arbitration fees in accordance with the Arbitration Fee Schedule for International Commercial Arbitration set out in Annex 2 to these Rules.

Article 62

Interim Measures

(1) At the request of the parties, the Arbitral Tribunal may order any interim measures it deems appropriate in accordance with the applicable law. An order for interim measures may take the form of a decision of the Arbitral Tribunal, an interim award [Article 49], or any other form permitted by the applicable law. Where necessary, the Arbitral Tribunal may require the requesting parties to provide appropriate security.

(2) The parties may also directly apply for interim measures to the competent court in accordance with the applicable law.

Article 63

Emergency Arbitrator

(1) After the acceptance of the case by the BAC [Articles 8 and 9] and before the constitution of the Arbitral Tribunal [Article 19 or Article 64], any party that wishes to apply for interim measures may submit a written application to the BAC for the appointment of an emergency arbitrator in accordance with the applicable law. The BAC shall decide whether or not to approve such application.

(2) Where the BAC approves the appointment of an emergency arbitrator, it shall appoint an emergency arbitrator from the Panel of Arbitrators within 2 days after the parties concerned pay the corresponding fees in accordance with the Schedule set out in Annex 3 to these Rules, and shall notify the parties of such appointment.

(3) The provisions of Articles 21 and 22 shall apply *mutatis mutandis* to disclosure by and challenge to an emergency arbitrator and the procedures applicable to these matters.

(4) An emergency arbitrator shall consider the application for interim measures in such manner as he or she deems appropriate, and shall ensure that the parties have a reasonable opportunity to present their cases.

(5) The emergency arbitrator shall issue a decision, order or award, stating the grounds on which the interim measures are based, within 15 days after his or her appointment. Such decision, order or award shall be sent to the parties after being signed by the emergency arbitrator and affixed with the seal of the BAC.

(6) Where a party objects to a decision, order or award made by the emergency arbitrator, it may apply to the emergency arbitrator for an amendment to or the suspension or revocation of such decision, order or award within 3 days of receipt of such decision, order or award. The emergency arbitrator will decide whether or not to approve such application.

(7) Unless otherwise agreed by the parties, the emergency arbitrator shall not subsequently act as an arbitrator in the proceedings to which the application for interim measures relates.

(8) Any decision, order or award made by an emergency arbitrator [Article 63(5)] will not be binding upon the Arbitral Tribunal. The Arbitral Tribunal may amend, suspend or revoke such a decision, order or award.

Article 64
Composition of the Arbitral Tribunal

(1) Arbitrators may be selected by the parties from the Panel of Arbitrators maintained by the BAC [Article 18] or from amongst arbitrators who are not on the Panel of Arbitrators.

(2) Parties who wish to select arbitrators who are not on the Panel of Arbitrators shall submit their candidates' resumes and contact details to the BAC. A candidate selected from amongst arbitrators who are not on the Panel of Arbitrators may act as an arbitrator with the approval of the BAC.

(3) Within 20 days of receipt of the Notice of Acceptance [Article 9], the parties shall, pursuant to the provisions of Article 19, nominate or request the Chairman to appoint their arbitrators and jointly nominate or jointly request the Chairman to appoint the presiding arbitrator. If the parties fail to nominate or request the Chairman to appoint their arbitrators or the presiding arbitrator in accordance with those provisions, the arbitrators or the presiding arbitrator shall be appointed by the Chairman.

(4) Where a party agrees to an increased fee for a foreign arbitrator, that party shall deposit a corresponding advance on costs within the period specified by the BAC. If a party fails to deposit such advance on costs within the period specified, it shall be deemed not to have nominated the arbitrator. The Chairman may then appoint an arbitrator for that party in accordance with the Rules.

(5) Where Article 53 applies, the Arbitral Tribunal shall be constituted in accordance with Article 54 of the Rules.

Article 65
Defence and Counterclaim

Within 45 days (or 30 days where Article 53 applies) of receipt of the Request for Submission of Defence [Article 9], the Respondent shall submit to the BAC its Statement of

Defence [Article 10], together with any relevant supporting documents. The Respondent shall also submit in writing the Application for Counterclaim [Article 11], if any, within the time limit.

Article 66
Notice of Hearing

(1) Where an oral hearing is to be held, the Arbitral Tribunal shall notify the parties of the date of the hearing at least 30 days (or 10 days where Article 53 applies) in advance of the hearing. The date of the first hearing may be brought forward by the Arbitral Tribunal with the agreement of the parties. A party may request in writing a postponement of the first hearing, no less than 12 days (or 5 days where Article 53 applies) in advance, provided that there are grounds justifying the postponement. The Arbitral Tribunal shall decide whether or not to order postponement.

(2) A notification of the date of any further hearing or postponed hearing shall not be subject to the 30-day or 10-day requirement under Article 66(1).

Article 67
Conciliation by the Tribunal

(1) The Arbitral Tribunal may, with the consent of the parties, conduct a conciliation of the case in such manner as it considers appropriate.

(2) If, upon the termination of unsuccessful conciliation proceedings, all parties request the replacement of an arbitrator on the ground that the outcome of the award may be affected by the conciliation proceedings, the Chairman may approve such request. The resulting additional costs shall be borne by all the parties.

Article 68

Time Limit for Rendering the Award

The Arbitral Tribunal shall render its award within 6 months (or 90 days where Article 53 applies) of the date of its constitution. If there are special circumstances justifying an extension of this period, the Secretary-General may approve an appropriate extension of time at the request of the presiding arbitrator or the sole arbitrator, as the case may be.

Article 69

Applicable Law

(1) The Arbitral Tribunal shall apply the law agreed upon by the parties to decide the dispute. Unless otherwise agreed by the parties, the agreed applicable law refers to the substantive rules of law but not to the rules of conflict of laws.

(2) In the absence of an agreed choice of law, the Arbitral Tribunal may determine the applicable law according to all the relevant circumstances of the case.

(3) By agreement of the parties, whether before or during the arbitral proceedings, the Arbitral Tribunal may render its award as *amiable compositeur* or *ex aequo et bono*. Such award shall not, however, violate the mandatory provisions of the applicable law and the public interest.

(4) In all cases, the Arbitral Tribunal shall render its award in accordance with the valid terms of the parties' agreement and take into account the relevant industry practices and trade usages.

Chapter IX
Supplementary Provisions

Article 70
Calculation of Time Limits

(1) Any period of time specified or determined in accordance with the Rules shall start to run on the day following the date on which such period commences. The day on which such period commences does not form part of the period of time.

(2) If the day following the date on which the period of time commences is an official holiday or a non-business day at the place of the service, the period of time shall begin to run on the first following business day. Official holidays or non-business days occurring within such period are included in the calculation of the period of time. If the last day of the relevant period of time falls on an official holiday or a non-business day, the period of time shall expire on the first following business day.

(3) Time for delivery shall not be included in the period of time. Any arbitral document, notice, or material that has been mailed or dispatched within the time limit shall be deemed to have been delivered in time.

(4) If a party exceeds a time limit because of force majeure events or other legitimate reasons, it may apply for an extension of that time limit within 10 days of the events or other reasons ceasing to have effect. The BAC or the Arbitral Tribunal, as the case may be, shall decide upon the application.

Article 71
Service

(1) Arbitral documents, notices and other materials may be served on the parties or their authorised representatives in person or by mail, courier, facsimile, email, or any other

means that the BAC or the Arbitral Tribunal, as the case may be, considers appropriate.

(2) Arbitral documents, notices and materials shall be deemed to have been served if they have been delivered to the parties or their authorised representatives in person or by mail to the addressee's place of business, place of registration, place of residence, address indicated on ID card, *Hukou* address, address for service agreed by the parties or any other correspondence address provided by the addressee or the counterparty.

(3) If, despite reasonable inquiries, the addressee's place of business, place of registration, place of residence, address indicated on ID card, *Hukou* address, address for service agreed by the parties, or other correspondence address cannot be found, service shall be deemed to have been effected if the document, notice or material is delivered to the addressee's last known place of business, place of registration, place of residence, address indicated on ID card, *Hukou* address, address for service agreed by the parties or other correspondence address, whether by mail, courier or by any other means of delivery which allows for a record of delivery.

Article 72
Language

(1) The parties may agree upon the language(s) to be used in the arbitral proceedings. Where the parties make no such agreement, the BAC or the Arbitral Tribunal, as the case may be, may determine that Chinese and/or any other language(s) shall be used in the arbitral proceedings according to the particular circumstances of the case.

(2) Where the parties have agreed upon the use of two or more languages in the arbitral proceedings, the Arbitral Tribunal may, upon obtaining consent from the parties, decide to adopt one language. If the parties fail to reach a unanimous agreement thereon, the arbitral proceedings

may be conducted in multiple languages, in which case the resulting additional costs shall be borne by the parties.

(3) The BAC or the Arbitral Tribunal, as the case may be, may determine, in accordance with the particular circumstances of the case, whether or not written documents in international commercial arbitral proceedings shall be accompanied by a translation into Chinese or other language(s).

(4) If translation services are required by the parties or their authorised representatives or witnesses, translators may be provided either by the BAC or by the parties themselves. The parties shall bear the costs of translation.

Article 73
Interpretation of the Rules

(1) The Rules shall be interpreted by the BAC.

(2) Other documents issued by the BAC shall not constitute part of the Rules, unless the BAC states otherwise.

Article 74
Official Versions of the Rules

Each of the Chinese, English and other language versions of the Rules published by the BAC is an official version. In the event of any conflict between the different versions, the Chinese version shall prevail.

Article 75
Implementation of the Rules

The Rules shall take effect on April 1, 2015 and apply to all cases accepted by the BAC on or after that date. For cases accepted by the BAC before the Rules came into effect, the edition of the

Arbitration Rules effective at the time of such acceptance shall apply. These Rules may, however, apply in such a case if the parties so agree and with the approval of the BAC.

Appendix 9
Shanghai Arbitration Commission Arbitration Rules[265]

(Revised by the 1st Meeting of the 5th Committee of Shanghai Arbitration Commission on October 19, 2012. Effective as of January 1, 2013)

Chapter I
General Provisions

Article 1
Basis of Formulation

The rule is formulated with a view to ensure fair and timely arbitration of civil and commercial disputes, reliable protection to legitimate rights and interests of parties concerned, pursuant to the *Arbitration Law of the People's Republic of China* (referred to as 'Arbitration Law' hereinafter) and other relevant laws.

Article 2
Jurisdiction

Shanghai Arbitration Commission (SHAC) and its sub-commissions (collectively hereinafter referred to as 'SHAC') shall accept contractual disputes and other disputes arising from property rights between natural persons, legal persons or other economic organisations if parties or either party concerned are (or is) Chinese or foreign equal subject(s).

The following disputes cannot be put to arbitration:

1. Disputes arising from marriage, adoption, guardianship, bringing up of children and inheritance.

---

265 <www.accsh.org/index.php?m=content&c=index&a=lists&catid=73&pdfurl=http://www.accsh.org/uploadfile/2015/1230/20151230031858260.pdf>.

2. Labour disputes.

3. Disputes that have been stipulated by administrative organs.

4. Disputes over contracts for undertaking agricultural projects within agricultural collective economic organisations.

Article 3

Arbitration Agreement

SHAC accepts arbitral cases based on the Request for Arbitration of the Claimant and the Arbitration Agreement between parties.

An arbitration agreement includes arbitration clauses in a contract, and any other forms of written agreement concluded between the parties either before or after the occurrence of the dispute.

An arbitration agreement shall be treated as independent. The validity of arbitration agreement shall not be affected by any modification, transfer, cancellation, termination, or ineffectiveness, invalidity, expiry, or non-existence of the contract.

Article 4

Resolution of Dispute

SHAC shall have the power to determine the existence and validity of an arbitration agreement and its jurisdiction over an arbitration case based on application of parties.

Article 5

Basis of Award

The arbitral tribunal shall independently, impartially and timely render a fair and reasonable arbitral award based on the facts of the case, in accordance with the law, and with reference to international practices.

Article 6
Finality of Award

The arbitral award is final. After the award is given, the arbitration commission shall not accept the re-application of the suit concerning the same dispute by any of the parties concerned.

Article 7
Service of Documents

Documents, notices and other materials in relation to the arbitration may be delivered in person or sent by registered mail or express mail, fax, or by any other means considered proper by SHAC or the arbitral tribunal.

The arbitration documents referred to in the preceding paragraph shall be sent to the address provided by the party itself or by its representative(s), or to an address agreed by the parties. Where a party or its representative(s) has not provided an address or the parties have not agreed on an address, the arbitration documents shall be sent to such party's address as provided by the other party or its representative(s).

Any arbitration correspondence to a party or its representative(s) shall be deemed to have been properly served on the party if delivered to the addressee or sent to the addressee's place of business, registration, domicile, habitual residence or mailing address, or where, after reasonable inquiries by the other party, none of aforesaid addresses can be found, the arbitration correspondence is sent by SHAC to the addressee's last known place of business, registration, domicile, habitual residence or mailing address by registered or express mail, or by any other means that can provide a record of the attempt at delivery.

Parties concerned shall issue written Confirmation of Service Address. Therefore the legal consequences arising from failure of service shall be borne by the party that made the confirmation.

Article 8
Scope of Application

The parties shall be deemed to have agreed to arbitration in accordance with these Rules if they have agreed to arbitration by SHAC. But where the parties have agreed on other arbitration proceedings or application rules, the parties' agreement shall prevail with the approval of SHAC.

Where the parties agree to refer their dispute to arbitration under these Rules without providing the name of the arbitration institution, they shall be deemed to have agreed to refer the dispute to arbitration by SHAC.

Chapter II
Request for Application, Defence and Counterclaim

Article 9
Conditions for Arbitration Application

The parties concerned should meet the following requirements in applying for arbitration:

1. The Claimant is a natural person, legal person or other organisation with direct interests in the case.

2. There is a specific Respondent.

3. There is an agreement for arbitration.

4. There are specific requests for arbitration and facts and reasons.

5. The matters to be put to arbitration shall fall into the limits of the authority of SHAC.

Article 10

Application Documents Submission

A Claimant applying for arbitration shall submit a Request for Arbitration and the following documents:

1. Certifications of parties' standing to participate in the arbitration.

2. Arbitration agreement, text of contract and its attachments.

3. Relevant evidences and supporting documents.

The Claimant shall submit copies of Request for Arbitration, materials and documents listed in the preceding paragraph according to the number of members of arbitration tribunal and the Respondent(s) agreed by parties or pursuant to the provision of the Rules.

Where the claimant is represented by representative(s) in submitting the Request for Arbitration, a Power of Attorney and the representative(s)' identification documents shall be submitted.

Article 11

The Application for Arbitration

The application for arbitration shall specify the following matters:

1. Basic information of the Claimant and Respondent: name, sex, age, profession, work unit, residence, zip code, telecommunication numbers and etc. of parties concerned as natural persons; the name, residence, zip code, telecommunication numbers of parties concerned as legal persons or other organisations and the name, position and contact information of the legal representatives or principal leading members.

2. The basis of the arbitration.

3. The claimants' claim and the facts and evidence on which the claim is based.

4. Evidence and sources of evidence, name, residence and zip code, telecommunication numbers of witnesses.

The Claimant shall sign the application for arbitration. Where the Claimant is legal person or other organisations, legal representatives or principal leading members should sign the application, or the seal of work unit shall be affixed.

Article 12
Acceptance

The SHAC shall notify the Claimant to pay the arbitration fee in advance if it deems the application for arbitration conforming to requirements. After the arbitration fee is prepaid, SHAC shall accept the application within five days and deliver the Notice of Acceptance and its attachments, these Rules and SHAC's Panel of arbitrators to the Claimant.

If SHAC deems the application unconformable to requirements, it shall notify the parties concerned in writing and state the reasons.

If SHAC deems the materials submitted by the Claimant to be incomplete, it may request the Claimant to complete them within a specified time period. If the Claimant completes the materials within the specified time period, the application is deemed conforming to requirements. If the Claimant fails to complete the materials within the specified time period, the application is deemed invalid.

Article 13
Notice of Arbitration

After SHAC has delivered the Notice of Acceptance, it shall deliver the Notice of Arbitration and its attachment, these Rules and SHAC's Panel of arbitrators, as well as the copies of the arbitration application and its attachment to the Respondent within five days.

Article 14
Case Manager

After SHAC accepts an arbitration application, it shall designate 1 or 2 Case Manager.

Case Managers are designated to assist with the procedural administration of the arbitration.

Article 15
Raising Objections

An objection to an arbitration agreement or the acceptance of a case shall be raised in writing before the first oral hearing is held by the arbitral tribunal. Where a case is to be decided on the basis of documents only, such an objection shall be raised in writing before the end of the specified time period for defence.

Article 16
Waiver of Right to Object

The party concerned shall be deemed to admit the validity of the arbitration agreement where it fails to raise an objection within the time period specified in Article 15.

The party concerned shall be deemed to recognise the jurisdiction of SHAC over the case where if fails to raise an objection to the acceptance of the case within the time period specified in Article 15.

Article 17
Handling Objections

Where SHAC is satisfied by prima facie evidence that an arbitration agreement providing for arbitration by SHAC exists, it may make a decision based on such evidence that it has jurisdiction over the arbitration case, and the arbitration shall proceed.

Such a decision shall not prevent SHAC from making a new decision on jurisdiction based on facts and/or evidence found by the arbitral tribunal during the arbitration proceedings that are inconsistent with the prima facie evidence.

Article 18

Statement of Defence

The Respondent shall submit a Statement of Defence and relevant materials as well as the documents proving a party's standing to participate in the arbitration to SHAC within fifteen (15) days from the date of receipt of the Notice of Arbitration.

After SHAC receives the Statement of Defence and the relevant documentary and other evidence from the Respondent, it shall deliver the copy of the Statement of Defence and its attachment to the Claimant.

Failure by the Respondent to submit a Statement of Defence shall not affect the conduct of the arbitration proceedings.

Article 19

Counterclaim

The Respondent is entitled to raise a counterclaim.

When filing its counterclaim, the Respondent shall specify its counterclaim in its Statement of Counterclaim and state the facts and grounds on which its counterclaim is based with the relevant documentary and other evidence attached thereto.

The Respondent shall submit the Statement of Counterclaim to SHAC within fifteen (15) days from the date of receipt of the Notice of Arbitration. Where a Statement of Counterclaim is submitted after the expiration of the above time limit, it shall not be accepted with exception to approval of the Claimant.

The counterclaim raised by the Respondent shall be within the scope of Arbitration Agreement. The subject of the counterclaim shall be the Claimant in the arbitration claim.

The SHAC shall notify the counterclaimant to pay the arbitration fee in advance if it deems the counterclaim conforming to requirements. After the arbitration fee is prepaid, SHAC shall accept the counterclaim and send a Notice of Acceptance of Counterclaim to the Respondent, and deliver the Notice of Counterclaim Arbitration, copy of Statement of Counterclaim and its attachment to the Claimant within five (5) days.

The Claimant shall submit its Statement of Defence to SHAC within ten (10) days from the date of receipt of the Notice. If Claimant fails to submit a Statement of Defence shall not affect the conduct of the arbitration proceedings.

The claim and counterclaim should be consolidated into a single arbitration.

Article 20
Amendment to the Claim

The party concerned may apply to amend its claim before the conclusion of the first oral hearing. However, the arbitral tribunal may not permit any such amendment if it considers that the amendment is too late and may delay the arbitration proceedings.

Where the legal relation or the validity of the civil act claimed by the party concerned is inconsistent with what is recognised by the arbitral tribunal based on the fact of the case, the arbitral tribunal may notify the party concerned to amend its claim or counterclaim. Failure of any such amendment by the party concerned shall not affect the conduct of arbitration proceedings.

Article 21

Custody of Property

Whereas due to the acts of the other party or other reasons, the arbitration award cannot be or is hard to be executed, the parties concerned may apply to have the property put under custody. Whereas a party concerned has applied for custody of the property, SHAC shall submit the party's application to the competent court in accordance with relevant law.

Article 22

Appointment of Attorney

The party concerned may entrust attorneys to handle matters relating to arbitration. In the case in which attorneys are entrusted with the handling of arbitration matters, the attorneys shall produce a Power of Attorney and its proof of identity to SHAC.

Matters of authorisation and limits of power shall be specified in Power of Attorney.

Article 23

Prepayment of Arbitration Fee

When filing an application for arbitration or counterclaim, the Claimant or Respondent shall pay an arbitration fee in advance according to the provisions of SHAC.

The arbitration fee includes both the acceptance fee and arbitration fee.

If the party concerned fails to prepay the arbitration fee within a specified time period, it shall be deemed to have withdrawn its Request for Arbitration or counterclaim.

Article 24
Allocation of Fees

The arbitration fee is determined by the arbitral tribunal. Where settlement is reached through conciliation by the arbitral tribunal or by the parties themselves, the amount or proportion of arbitration fee allocated to each party shall be determined by consultation. Where consultation fails, the arbitration fee shall be determined by the arbitral tribunal.

Article 25
Withdrawal of Application for Arbitration or Counterclaim

After SHAC accepts an application for arbitration or counterclaim, a party may apply to withdraw its claim or counterclaim. Where an application for withdrawal prior to the formation of the arbitral tribunal, SHAC shall make a decision on the withdrawal. Where an application for withdrawal after the formation of the arbitral tribunal, the arbitral tribunal shall make the decision.

If application for withdrawal is approved, the prepaid arbitration fee shall not be refunded. The prepaid registration fee shall be handled in the following ways: if the arbitral tribunal has not been established, the fee of registration can be refunded in entirety; if the arbitral tribunal has been established, the fee of registration can be refunded according to certain conditions.

Chapter III
Formation of Arbitral Tribunal

Article 26
Panel of Arbitrators

SHAC establishes a Panel of Arbitrators, and a Professional Panel of Arbitrators according to specific requirements.

The parties shall nominate arbitrators from the Panel of Arbitrators or Professional Panel of Arbitrators provided by SHAC.

Article 27
Composition of Arbitral Tribunal

An arbitral tribunal may be composed of one arbitrator or three arbitrators. In the case of three arbitrators, there should be a chief arbitrator.

Article 28
Nomination of Arbitrator

Where the amount in dispute exceeds RMB 1,000,000 or where the amount in dispute does not exceed RMB 1,000,000 but the parties agree to have an arbitral tribunal composed of three arbitrators, all parties shall each nominate one arbitrator from the Panel of Arbitrators to compose the arbitral tribunal within the periods of time specified in the Notice of Acceptance and the Notice of Arbitration. All parties concerned shall jointly nominate one presiding arbitrator.

The parties may each nominate one to three arbitrators as candidates for presiding arbitrator from the Panel of Presiding Arbitrators recommended by SHAC. Where there is one common candidate nominated by all parties, such candidate shall be the presiding arbitrator jointly nominated by the parties. Where there are two or more common candidates nominated by all parties, the Chairman of SHAC shall choose a presiding arbitrator from among the common candidates. Where there is no common candidate or the parties fail to nominate arbitrators, it shall be deemed as the parties have failed to jointly nominate the presiding arbitrator.

Where one party is composed of two or more people, they shall jointly nominate one arbitrator or presiding arbitrator for the arbitral tribunal.

Where all parties agree to or under these Rules that the arbitral tribunal is composed of one arbitrator, all parties shall jointly nominate one arbitrator from the Panel of Arbitrators or the list of recommended candidates of SHAC within the specified periods of time

Article 29
Prepayment of Special Arbitration Fee

Where the parties have nominated an arbitrator who resides or works outside of the Shanghai Administrative Area, they shall pay reasonable costs such as travel and accommodation expenses incurred in dealing with the case according to the notice of SHAC. But where parties fail to pay in advance, they shall be deemed not to have nominated the arbitrator.

Article 30
Appointment of Arbitrator

In one of the following cases, the Chairman of SHAC appoints members of arbitral tribunal:

1. Where all parties jointly entrust the Chairman of SHAC to appoint the arbitrators.

2. Where one party is composed of two or more people who fail to jointly nominate arbitrators.

3. Where parties concerned fail to nominate arbitrators or fail to nominate arbitrators within the above time period.

4. Where parties shall jointly nominate arbitrators but have failed to do so.

5. In circumstances stipulated in Article 29 of these Rules.

Article 31
Notice of the Formation of Arbitral Tribunal

After the formation of an arbitral tribunal, SHAC shall deliver the Notice of the Formation of Arbitral tribunal to all parties and members of the arbitral tribunal.

Article 32
Arbitrator Withdrawal Application

After receipt of Notice of the Formation of Arbitral Tribunal, an arbitrator shall report to SHAC and request withdrawal whereas one of the cases provided for in Article 34 of the Arbitration Law is found.

Article 33
Challenge to the Arbitrator

Where a party considers an arbitrator shall be withdrawn, it has the right to challenge that arbitrator. The challenged shall be stated in writing before the first hearing.

If the reasons are known only after the first hearing, they may be stated in writing before the end of the last hearing. Where a party fails to state the challenge in writing before the end of the last hearing, it shall be deemed as no challenge to the arbitrator.

In requesting for withdrawal, parties concerned shall state reasons and relevant materials.

Article 34
Withdrawal and Replacement of Arbitrator

The withdrawal of an arbitrator shall be decided upon by the chairman of the arbitration commission. Whereas the chairman of SHAC serves as an arbitrator, the withdrawal shall be decided upon collectively by SHAC.

After the formation of arbitral tribunal and before the render of award, where an arbitrator requests withdrawal voluntarily or the chairman of SHAC considers the arbitrator is prevented de jure or de facto from fulfilling his/her functions according these Rules, the arbitrator can be replaced.

Article 35
Re-nomination or Reappointment of Arbitrator

Where an arbitrator withdraws from a arbitral tribunal for reasons in Article 34 of this Rules, an arbitrator shall be re-nominated by party concerned or reappointed by Chairman of SHAC according to these Rules. If a party fails to nominate a substitute arbitrator accordingly, the substitute arbitrator shall be appointed by the Chairman of SHAC.

After re-nomination or reappointment of arbitrator, arbitration proceedings shall be restarted, except that parties have asserted jointly that the current arbitration proceeding shall not be restarted.

Chapter IV
Evidence

Article 36
Burden of Proof

Each party shall bear the burden of proving the facts on which it relies to support its claim, counterclaim or defence.

If a party bearing the burden of proof fails to produce

evidence that is sufficient t support its claim, it shall bear the consequences thereof.

Article 37
Time Limitations on Evidence Submission

Parties concerned shall produce evidence to SHAC within the time period specified by SHAC or the arbitral tribunal. Where a party fails to produce evidence with the specified time period, it shall be deemed to have waived its right to proof.

If a party experiences difficulties in producing evidence within the specified time period, it shall apply for an extension in writing to SHAC or the arbitral tribunal within the time period. SHAC or the arbitral tribunal shall decide whether or not to extend the time period.

Where the evidence is produced after that time period, the arbitral tribunal may decide whether or not to accept and examine the evidence.

Article 38
Forms of Evidence

Evidence produced by parties concerned includes documentary evidence, material evidence, audio and video evidence, depositions, appraisals, records of onsite investigation and other statutory evidence.

Documentary evidence and material evidence shall be original. If it is too difficult to produce originals, then copies, excerpts, photos, etc. thereof can instead be produced with description of sources.

If documentary evidence produced is in a foreign language, the arbitral tribunal can require party concerned to present translations in Chinese and/or other languages directly at the discretion of the arbitral tribunal.

Article 39
Collection of Evidence

The arbitral tribunal may undertake investigations and collect evidence on its own initiative as it considers necessary.

When investigating and collecting evidence on its own initiative, the arbitral tribunal may notify the parties to be present. In the event that one or both parties fail to be present after being notified, the investigation and collection of evidence shall proceed without being affected.

Article 40
Protection of Evidence

Where evidence may be lost or is difficult to be recollected later, a party can apply for protection of evidence.

Where a party applies for protection of evidence, SHAC shall forward the application to the court with jurisdiction according to the laws.

Article 41
Appraisal

Where a party applies for appraisal and the arbitral tribunal approves the application, or where the parties concerned didn't apply for appraisal but the arbitral tribunal considers necessary, then evidence shall be forwarded to relevant legal institution for appraisal. Where there's no specified legal institution, the arbitral tribunal shall notify parties concerned to jointly nominate an institution or appraiser within specified time period. Where parties concerned cannot reach an agreement, the arbitral tribunal shall designate the institution or appraiser. Parties concerned shall pay the appraisal fee in advance with the time period specified by the arbitral tribunal. The arbitral tribunal shall decide the allocation of appraisal fee in the award.

The appraisal institution can be Chinese institution or foreign institution. The appraiser can be Chinese expert or foreign expert.

Copies of appraisal report shall be serviced to all parties before the oral hearing. Parties concerned can raise a written dissenting opinion on the appraisal report.

After application of Party Concerned and approval of Arbitral tribunal, Appraiser shall appear in the Tribunal to be cross-examined by Party Concerned. Appraiser can reply to Party Concerned in writing if Appraiser cannot appear in the Tribunal due to special circumstances. The applicant shall prepay fee of appraiser.

If a party bearing the burden of proof fails to prepay the fee within the specified time period or fails to provide relevant documents, materials and other items, which make it impossible to carry on the appraisal, the party shall bear the consequences thereof.

Article 42
Evidence and Examination of Evidence

Evidence shall be produced during the course of hearing and may be examined by the parties under the arrangement of the arbitral tribunal.

Where evidence is produced during the course of hearing, the arbitral tribunal shall decide whether or not to accept it. Where accepted by the arbitral tribunal and agreed by the other party, the evidence can be examined during the course of hearing. Where the other party objects to examine the evidence during the course of hearing, the arbitral tribunal shall afford reasonable preparation time to the other party to examine evidence and allow it to submit counter-evidence. The arbitral tribunal can hold another oral hearing to examine the evidence or request the party to submit its written opinions on the evidence within the specified time period. Where a party applies for witnesses to testify in court, it shall be agreed by the arbitral tribunal. The applicant shall pay the reasonable costs incurred by witnesses in attending the court.

Article 43
Additional Evidence

The arbitral tribunal can request a party to submit additional evidence after the oral hearing if it considers necessary. Where a party fails to submit evidence within the specified time period shall be deemed as incapable of producing additional evidence. If the additional evidence is produced after the specified time period, the arbitral tribunal shall decide whether or not to examine it unless agreed by the other party.

Article 44
Recognition of Evidence

The arbitral tribunal shall recognise the evidence examined by all parties.

Where a party has neither confirmed nor denied facts stated by the other party, and still fails to state its opinion after being inquired of by the arbitral tribunal, it shall be deemed to have confirmed the facts.

Where a party confirms unfavourable facts and evidence in the arbitration application, claims and counter-claims and in other written statements, the arbitral tribunal shall confirm the unfavourable facts and evidence unless the party has gone back on its word with sufficient counter-evidence.

Where testimony indicates that a party has unfavourable evidence in their possession and refuses to produce that evidence, corresponding claims can be deduced as established.

Chapter V
Hearing

Article 45
Conduct of Hearing

The arbitral tribunal shall hold oral hearings to hear a case. Whereas the parties concerned agree not to hold oral hearings, the arbitral tribunal may give the award based on the arbitration application, claims and counter-claims and other documents.

The oral hearing may not be held in open sessions. The parties and their representatives, the witnesses, the arbitrators, the experts consulted by the arbitral tribunal, the appraisers appointed by the arbitral tribunal and other relevant persons shall bear the burden of confidentiality, and shall not disclose to any outsider any substantive or procedural matters relating to the case unless otherwise stipulated by law.

Whereas parties concerned agree to have the case heard in open sessions, they shall submit a written agreement to SHAC five (5) days before the first oral hearing, except cases that involve State secrets.

The place of oral hearings shall be decided by SHAC. Where parties have otherwise agreed on or jointly requested alternative locations with the approval of SHAC, the case can be heard at other locations. Additional fees wherefrom shall be borne by requesting parties.

Article 46
Consolidation of Arbitrations

Where cases involve the same parties and objects of arbitration that belong to the same category, or that belong to different but relevant categories, the arbitral tribunal can decide, with the consent of the parties involved, to consolidate two or more cases.

Where cases involving different arbitral tribunal members cannot be consolidated for hearing.

Article 47
Notice of Hearing

Notice of the first hearing shall be serviced to all parties ten (10) days before the hearing.

The date of the first hearing can be advanced by negotiation of Parties and approval of arbitral tribunal. Time for service of Notice of Hearing is unrestricted by the preceding article. Where a party having justified reasons may request a postponement of the oral hearing in writing five (5) days in advance of the oral hearing. The arbitral tribunal shall decide whether or not to postpone the oral hearing.

Article 48
Default

Whereas a claimant or counter-claimant is absent from the hearing without justifiable reasons after receiving the written notice or withdraws from hearing half way without the prior permission by the arbitral tribunal, it may be deemed as a withdrawal of claims or counter-claims.

Whereas a respondent is absent from the hearing without justifiable reasons after receiving the written notice or withdraws from hearing half way without prior permission by the arbitration tribunal, it may give the award by default.

Article 49
Hearing Procedure

The arbitral tribunal shall announce the formation of the arbitral tribunal in the first hearing and inquire of parties whether they will challenge any of the arbitrators.

Members of the arbitral tribunal shall promise to comply

with the Arbitration Law and the Rules in the first hearing, and perform their duties independently, fairly and timely.

In the course of the hearing, parties are entitled to make statements, produce evidence, examine evidence and debate. After the debate, the arbitral tribunal shall inquire of the parties to make a closing statement.

Article 50
Record of Hearing

The arbitral tribunal shall record the hearing in writing, and may arrange for an audio record at the same time. Whereas the parties concerned or other people involved in the arbitration find something in their statements left out in the recording or misrecorded, they have the right to apply for correction. The arbitral tribunal shall decide whether or not to approve it. Whereas corrections are not made, the application shall be recorded. The written records of the hearing shall be signed or affixed with seals by the arbitrators, minute keepers, the parties concerned and other people participating in the arbitration. Whereas parties concerned refuse to sign or affix with seals shall be enclosed in attachment.

Article 51
Reconciliation

After the parties have applied for arbitration, they may reach reconciliation on their own initiative. Whereas a reconciliation agreement has been reached, a request may be made to the arbitration tribunal for an award based on the reconciliation agreement or the application for arbitration may be withdrawn.

Whereas the parties concerned have gone back on their word after they have reached a reconciliation agreement, they may apply for arbitration according to the arbitration agreement.

Chapter VI
Conciliation

Article 52
Principle of Conciliation

The arbitral tribunal organises intermediation in the principle of voluntariness.

Where the terms of the settlement agreement are not included in the claims, it shall be permitted.

The terms of the settlement agreement shall not impair the interests of the state, collective and a third party.

Article 53
Time and Location of Intermediation

Arbitral tribunal can organise intermediation during or after a hearing.

The arbitral tribunal can organise intermediation before hearing if parties agree to intermediation voluntarily or if facts of the case are explicit.

Time and location of intermediation shall be agreed upon by parties and approved by the arbitral tribunal; the arbitral tribunal can also designate time and location.

Article 54
Involvement of Third Party

If one of the parties applies for a third party intermediary and the other party and the third party approve the application, the arbitral tribunal shall notify the third party with the details of participation. If the third party agrees to undertake civil liabilities, the arbitral tribunal shall respect its intentions.

Article 55

Invocation of Terms of Conciliation

The conciliation proceedings shall not be recorded.

Any statement, opinion, view or proposal stated by either party or by arbitrators in the process of conciliation, shall not be invoked by either party in the subsequent arbitration proceedings, judicial proceedings, or any other proceedings.

The arbitral tribunal shall not take the opinions stated by either party in the conciliation proceedings as grounds to render an award.

Article 56

Results of Conciliation

Whereas an agreement is reached through conciliation, the arbitral tribunal shall compile the conciliation document or make an award based on the results of the agreement. Where the settlement can be fulfilled immediately or the parties concerned do not need to make an conciliation document or the settlement agreement of an award shall be written down in the record, the record becomes legally binding immediately after being signed or affixed with seals by all parties, arbitrators and the case manager.

If the conciliation cannot reach an agreement or any party concerned has gone back on his word before receiving the document of conciliation, the arbitral tribunal shall make a timely ruling.

Article 57

Document of Conciliation

The document of conciliation shall specify the condition of the parties concerned, the arbitration claims and the result of the agreement between the parties.

The document of conciliation shall be signed by the arbitrator and affixed with the seal of SHAC before being delivered to the parties concerned. The document of conciliation becomes legally binding immediately upon received by parties concerned.

The document of conciliation and the arbitral award are equally binding legally.

Article 58
Correction of Conciliation Document

The arbitral tribunal shall correct typographical or typographical errors in the document of conciliation; parties concerned can apply to arbitral tribunal for correction within thirty (30) days after receiving the document of conciliation.

Decision on correction made by the arbitral tribunal and the document of conciliation are equally binding legally.

Chapter VII
Arbitral Award

Article 59
Making of Award

Where the arbitral tribunal is composed of three arbitrators, the case shall be deliberated before issuance of an award. The case manager shall write down the deliberation in record. An arbitral award shall be decided by the majority of the arbitrators and the views of the minority can be written down in the record. Whereas a majority vote cannot be reached, the award shall be decided based on the opinion of the chief arbitrator.

Where the arbitral tribunal is composed of one arbitrator, the award shall be decided by the arbitrator directly.

Article 60
Partial Award

In the hearing of a case, the arbitral tribunal may pass the ruling on part of the facts that have already been made clear.

Article 61
Compensation of Reasonable Expenses

The arbitral tribunal has the power to decide that the default party to compensate the observant party for the expenses reasonably incurred by it in pursuing the case.

Article 62
Time Limit for Hearing

The arbitral tribunal shall render an arbitral award within four (4) months from the date on which the arbitral tribunal is formed. If the time limit for hearing shall be extended due to special circumstances, the arbitral tribunal shall apply to the Chairman of SHAC for approval. Any suspension period and the time for audition, appraisal, review, checking, evaluation and inspection of special issues, and the time period required in writing by parties concerned for settling the case by themselves outside the tribunal, shall be excluded when calculating the time limit in the preceding Paragraph 1.

Article 63
Making of Award

The arbitral award shall specify the basic information of the parties concerned, arbitration claims, facts in disputes, reasons for award, result of the award, arbitration expenses and date of the award given. Whereas parties concerned object to the specification of the facts in dispute and reasons for the ruling, such specification and reasons may be omitted.

The arbitral award shall be signed by arbitrators and affixed with the seals of SHAC. An arbitrator holding differences of views may sign or may not sign the award.

Article 64
Correction of Award

An arbitral tribunal shall correct the errors involving context or computation and add things that have been omitted in the rulings in the arbitral award. The parties concerned may apply for correction with the arbitral tribunal within 30 days after the receipt of the award.

The correction of the arbitral award shall be corrected or supplemented in the form of decision on correction.

The decision on correction is an integral part of arbitral award and is equally binding legally. The correction and supplement in the decision takes legal effect upon its issuing.

Article 65
Effectiveness of Arbitral Award

The arbitral award takes legal effect upon its issuing.

Article 66
Carrying out of Award and Enforcement

The parties shall automatically carry out the arbitral award within the time period specified in the award. If no time limit is specified in the award, the parties shall carry out the award immediately.

Where one party fails to carry out the award, the other party may apply to a competent court for enforcement of the award in accordance with the Chinese law. Where a case shall be carried out in a foreign country, the party may apply to a competent court for enforcement of the award in accordance with the Convention on the Recognition and Enforcement of Foreign Arbitral Awards approved by the United Nations Conference on International Commercial Arbitration on 10 June 1958, or other international treaties and bilateral treaties concluded or joined by China.

Chapter VIII
Summary Procedure

Article 67
Standard of Summary Procedure

Unless otherwise agreed by the parties that the case is examined by an arbitral tribunal composed of three arbitrators, Summary Procedure shall apply to any case where the amount in dispute does not exceed RMB 1,000,000; or to any case where the amount in dispute exceeds RMB 1,000,000, yet all parties concerned decide to examine the case under the Summary Procedure.

If the amount in dispute exceeds RMB 1,000,000 after modification of claims by parties concerned or the sum of amount in dispute and amount of counterclaim exceeds RMB 1,000,000, the summary procedure is also applicable, unless parties concerned jointly decide not to apply this Rule or SHAC considers it to be not applicable.

Article 68
Formation and Notice of Arbitral Tribunal

For arbitral case applicable to the Chapter, the arbitral tribunal shall be formed of a sole-arbitrator.

After the formation of the arbitral tribunal, SHAC shall send a Notice of the Formation of the Arbitral Tribunal to the arbitrators and parties concerned.

Article 69

Notice of Hearing

For a case examined by way of a hearing, the Notice of Hearing shall be delivered to parties concerned seven (7) days for the first hearing.

Where a party have justified reason to postpone the hearing shall raise the application three (3) days before the hearing. The arbitral tribunal shall decide whether or not to postpone the hearing.

A notice of a subsequent hearing shall not be subject to the time periods specified in the preceding Paragraph 1.

Article 70

Time Limit for Hearing

For a case applicable to the rules of this Chapter, the arbitral award shall render an arbitral award within two (2) months from the date on which the arbitral tribunal is formed. In special circumstance, the arbitral tribunal shall apply to SHAC for approval on extension of the time limit.

Article 71

Context Reference

The relevant provisions in the other Chapters of these Rules shall apply to matters not covered in this Chapter.

Chapter IX

Special Provisions for International Commercial and Foreign-related Arbitrations

Article 72

Condition of Application

Where parties concerned submit international or foreign-related civil and commercial disputes to SHAC, the provisions of this Chapter shall apply.

The provisions of this Chapter shall apply to cases related to Hong Kong, Macao and Taiwan.

Article 73

Submission of Statement of Defence and other Documents

The respondent shall file a Statement of Defence in writing within forty-five (45) days from the date of receipt of the Notice of Arbitration, and shall, inter alia, submit the following documents:

1. Certifications of Respondent's standing to participate in the arbitration;

2. Relevant evidence on which the defence is based;

3. Documentary that supports its opinion.

Failure of the Respondent to file a Statement of Defence shall not affect the arbitration proceedings.

Article 74

Counterclaim

The Respondent shall file a counterclaim, if any, in writing within forty-five (45) days from the date of receipt of the Notice of Arbitration.

The Claimant shall file a Statement of Defence to the

Respondent's counterclaim within forty-five (45) days from the date of receipt of the Notice of Counterclaim Arbitration; where the Claimant fails to file a Statement of Defence shall not affect the conduct of the arbitration proceedings.

Article 75
Formation of Arbitral Tribunal

Where the amount in dispute does not exceed RMB 1,000,000, the arbitral tribunal is composed of one arbitrator, unless agreed by parties otherwise. Where the amount in dispute exceeds RMB 1,000,000, the arbitral tribunal is composed of three arbitrators, unless agreed by parties otherwise.

All parties shall nominate arbitrators within the periods of time specified in the Notice of Acceptance or Notice of Arbitration, and submit a list of nominated arbitrators to SHAC.

Article 76
Notice of Hearing

If a case is heard for the first time, the Notice of Hearing shall be delivered to parties concerned thirty (30) days in advance of the hearing.

A party having justified reasons to postpone the hearing shall submit an application of postponement to SHAC twelve (12) days in advance of the hearing. The arbitral tribunal shall decide whether or not to postpone the hearing.

Article 77
Advancing the Time of Oral Hearing

If parties concerned apply for an earlier oral hearing, the arbitral tribunal shall decide whether or not to accept the application. Where the arbitral tribunal decides to advance the time of oral hearing, the period of time to deliver the

Notice of Hearing shall not be subject to the time periods specified in the preceding Paragraph 1.

Article 78

Time Limit for Award

The arbitral award shall be rendered within six (6) months from the date on which the arbitral tribunal is formed. If the time limit needs to be extended, the arbitral tribunal shall apply to the Chairman of SHAC for approval.

Article 79

Laws Governing Objections to Validity of Arbitration Agreement

Where concerned parties involved in international and foreign-related civil and commercial disputes object to the validity of the arbitration agreement, SHAC shall decide the validity of the arbitration agreement according to the law selected and agreed upon by the parties concerned; where parties have agreed on the location of arbitration but not on the applicable laws, that location's arbitration laws shall apply; where parties concerned have neither agreed on the applicable laws nor the location of arbitration or if the agreement on the location of arbitration is not clear, the laws of the country where SHAC is located shall apply.

Article 80

Context Reference

The relevant provisions in the other Chapters of these Rules shall be applied to matters not covered in this Chapter.

Chapter X
Supplementary Provisions

Article 81
Oral and Written Language

Cases arbitrated by SHAC shall be done so in the oral and written language of the People's Republic of China. Where the parties have agreed on an alternative language of arbitration, their agreement shall prevail.

If a party concerned requires interpretation, the interpreter will be chosen in a collective effort of all concerned parties. Where the interpreter is provided by SHAC, fees shall be borne by the parties.

Article 82
Limitations on Effective Period for Arbitration

Where there is a limit on the effective period for the arbitration stipulated in the law, the limit shall apply. Where there is not a limit on the effective period for the arbitration stipulated by the law, the provisions about limits for proceedings shall apply.

Article 83
Calculation of Time Period

The expression 'within (time period)' or 'no more than (time period)' herein means that the time period is inclusive. The expression 'more than (time period)', 'over (time period)' or 'before (time period)' herein means that the time period is exclusive.

If the time period is calculated by day or month herein, the first day is exclusive. Calculation begins from the next day.

If the last day of the time period is a statutory holiday, the time period will extend to the next business day after the holiday. On the last day of the time period, the deadline is the closing of business that day.

If the time period is extended, the new time period shall be calculated from the date after the expiration of the original period.

Article 84

Affiliated Arbitral Institutions

The arbitral institutions set up by SHAC in fields of finance, intellectual property rights and international shipping can accept and hear the disputes where parties concerned have agreed to arbitration by SHAC or the affiliated institutions.

Other affiliated institutions set up by SHAC can accept cases under the entrustment of SHAC.

Article 85

Customisation of Special Rules

SHAC can customise some other affiliated arbitral institutions or arbitration rules of some special field if necessary.

Article 86

Context Reference

The relevant rules of the *Civil Procedural Law of People's Republic of China* shall apply to matters not covered in these Rules.

Article 87

Text of Rules

The Chinese text of these Rules issued by SHAC shall prevail.

Article 88

Interpretation

These Rules shall be interpreted by SHAC.

Article 89

Coming to Force

These Rules shall be effective from 1 January 2013.

For the cases accepted before these Rules come into force, the Arbitration Rules effective at the time of acceptance shall apply, or where both parties agree, these Rules shall apply.

Appendix 10
Hong Kong International Arbitration Centre (HKIAC)
Administered Arbitration Rules[266]

Introduction

These Rules have been adopted by the Council of the Hong Kong International Arbitration Centre (HKIAC) for use by parties who seek the formality and convenience of an administered arbitration.

Application

These Rules may be adopted in an arbitration agreement or by an agreement in writing at any time before or after a dispute has arisen. These Rules may be adopted for use in both domestic and international arbitral proceedings. Provisions regarding the scope of application of these Rules are set out in Article 1.

Effectiveness

These Rules have been adopted to take effect from 1 November 2013, in accordance with the provisions of Article 1 of the Rules.

Suggested Clauses

1. The following model clause may be adopted by the parties to a contract who wish to refer any future disputes to arbitration in accordance with these Rules:

'Any dispute, controversy, difference or claim arising out of or relating to this contract, including the existence, validity, interpretation, performance, breach or termination thereof

266 <http://hkiac.org/arbitration/rules-practice-notes/administered-arbitration-rules#1>.

or any dispute regarding noncontractual obligations arising out of or relating to it shall be referred to and finally resolved by arbitration administered by the Hong Kong International Arbitration Centre (HKIAC) under the HKIAC Administered Arbitration Rules in force when the Notice of Arbitration is submitted.

* The law of this arbitration clause shall be ... (*Hong Kong law*).

The seat of arbitration shall be ... (*Hong Kong*).

** The number of arbitrators shall be ... (*one* or *three*).

** The arbitration proceedings shall be conducted in ... (*insert language*).'

**The law of the arbitration clause generally governs the existence, scope, validity, interpretation, performance, breach, termination and enforceability of the arbitration clause. It does not replace the law governing the substantive contract.*

***Optional*

2. Parties to an existing dispute in which neither an arbitration clause nor a previous agreement with respect to arbitration exists, who wish to refer such dispute to arbitration under the HKIAC Administered Arbitration Rules, may agree to do so in the following terms:

'We, the undersigned, agree to refer to arbitration administered by the Hong Kong International Arbitration Centre (HKIAC) under the HKIAC Administered Arbitration Rules any dispute, controversy, difference or claim (including any dispute regarding non-contractual obligations) arising out of or relating to: (Brief description of contract under which disputes, controversies, differences or claims have arisen or may arise.)

* The law of this arbitration agreement shall be ... (*Hong Kong law*).

The seat of arbitration shall be ... (*Hong Kong*).

** The number of arbitrators shall be ... (*one* or *three*).

** The arbitration proceedings shall be conducted in ... (*insert language*).

Signed: __________ (Claimant)

Signed: __________ (Respondent)

Date: __________'

**The law of the arbitration agreement generally governs the existence, scope, validity, interpretation, performance, breach, termination and enforceability of the arbitration agreement. It does not replace the law governing the substantive contract.*

***Optional*

Section I
General Rules

Article 1
Scope of Application

1.1. These Rules shall govern arbitrations where an arbitration agreement (whether entered into before or after a dispute has arisen) either: (a) provides for these Rules to apply; or (b) subject to Articles 1.2 and 1.3 below, provides for arbitration 'administered by HKIAC' or words to similar effect.

1.2. Nothing in these Rules shall prevent parties to a dispute or arbitration agreement from naming HKIAC as appointing authority, or from requesting certain administrative services from HKIAC, without subjecting the arbitration to the provisions contained in these Rules. For the avoidance of doubt, these Rules shall not govern arbitrations where an arbitration agreement provides for arbitration under other rules, including other rules adopted by HKIAC from time to time.

1.3. Subject to Article 1.4, these Rules shall come into force on 1 November 2013 and, unless the parties have agreed otherwise, shall apply to all arbitrations falling within Article

1.1 in which the Notice of Arbitration is submitted on or after that date.

1.4. The provisions contained in Articles 23.1, 28, 29 and Schedule 4 shall not apply if the arbitration agreement was concluded before the date on which these Rules came into force, unless otherwise agreed by the parties.

Article 2

Notices and Calculation of Periods of Time

2.1. Any notice or other written communication pursuant to these Rules shall be deemed to be received by a party or arbitrator or by HKIAC if:

a. delivered by hand, registered post or courier service to (i) the address of the addressee or its representative as notified in writing in the arbitration; or (ii) in the absence of (i), to the address specified in any applicable agreement between the relevant parties; or (iii) in the absence of (i) or (ii), to any address which the addressee holds out to the world at the time of such delivery; or (iv) in the absence of (i), (ii) or (iii), to any last known address of the addressee; or

b. transmitted by facsimile, e-mail or any other means of telecommunication that provides a record of its transmission, including the time and date, to: (i) the facsimile number or email address (or equivalent) of that person or its representative as notified in the arbitration; or (ii) in the absence of (i), to the facsimile number or email address (or equivalent) specified in any applicable agreement between the relevant parties; or (iii) in the absence of (i) and (ii), to any facsimile number or email address (or equivalent) which the addressee holds out to the world at the time of such transmission.

2.2. Any such notice or written communication shall be deemed to be received on the earliest day when it is delivered pursuant to paragraph (a) above or transmitted pursuant to paragraph (b) above. For this purpose, the date shall be determined according to the local time at the place of receipt.

Where such notice or written communication is being delivered or transmitted to more than one party, or more than one arbitrator, such notice or written communication shall be deemed to be received when it is delivered or transmitted pursuant to paragraph (a) or (b) above to the last intended recipient.

2.3. For the purposes of calculating a period of time under these Rules, such period shall begin to run on the day following the day when a notice, notification, communication or proposal is received or deemed to be received. If the last day of such period is an official holiday or a non-business day at the place of receipt, the period shall be extended until the first business day which follows. Official holidays or non-business days occurring during the running of the period of time shall be included in calculating the period.

2.4. If the circumstances of the case so justify, HKIAC may amend the time limits provided for in these Rules, as well as any time limits that it has set. HKIAC shall not amend any time limits set by the arbitral tribunal unless it directs otherwise.

Article 3
Interpretation of Rules

3.1. HKIAC shall have the power to interpret all provisions of these Rules. The arbitral tribunal shall interpret the Rules insofar as they relate to its powers and duties hereunder. In the event of any inconsistency between such interpretation and any interpretation by HKIAC, the arbitral tribunal's interpretation shall prevail.

3.2. HKIAC has no obligation to give reasons for any decision it makes in respect of any arbitration commenced under these Rules. All decisions made by HKIAC under these Rules are final and, to the extent permitted by any applicable law, not subject to appeal.

3.3. References in the Rules to 'HKIAC' are to the Council of HKIAC or any committee, sub-committee or other body or person specifically designated by it to perform the functions referred to herein, or, where applicable, to the Secretary General of HKIAC for the time being and other staff members of the Secretariat of HKIAC.

3.4. References in the Rules to 'Claimant' include one or more claimants and references to 'Respondent' include one or more respondents.

3.5. References to 'additional party' include one or more additional parties and references to 'party' or 'parties' include claimants, respondents or additional parties.

3.6. References in the Rules to the 'arbitral tribunal' include one or more arbitrators. Such references do not include an Emergency Arbitrator as defined at paragraph 1 of Schedule 4.

3.7. References in the Rules to 'witness' include one or more witnesses and references to 'expert' include one or more experts.

3.8. References in the Rules to 'claim' or 'counterclaim' include any claim or claims by any party against any other party. References to 'defence' include any defence or defences by any party to any claim or counterclaim submitted by any other party, including any defence for the purpose of a set-off.

3.9. References in the Rules to 'award' include, inter alia, an interim, interlocutory, partial or final award, save for any award made by an Emergency Arbitrator as referred to in Schedule 4.

3.10. References in the Rules to the 'seat' of arbitration shall mean the place of arbitration as referred to in Article 20.1 of the UNCITRAL Model Law on International Commercial Arbitration as adopted on 21 June 1985 and as amended on 7 July 2006.

3.11. These Rules include all Schedules attached thereto as

amended from time to time by HKIAC, in force on the date the Notice of Arbitration is submitted.

3.12. HKIAC may from time to time issue practice notes to supplement, regulate and implement these Rules for the purpose of facilitating the administration of arbitrations governed by these Rules.

3.13. English is the original language of these Rules. In the event of any discrepancy or inconsistency between the English version and the version in any other language, the English version shall prevail.

Section II
Commencement of the Arbitration

Article 4
Notice of Arbitration

4.1. The party initiating recourse to arbitration (hereinafter called the 'Claimant') shall submit a Notice of Arbitration in writing to HKIAC at its address, facsimile number or email address.

4.2. An arbitration shall be deemed to commence on the date on which a copy of the Notice of Arbitration is received by HKIAC. For the avoidance of doubt, this date shall be determined in accordance with the provisions of Articles 2.1 and 2.2.

4.3. The Notice of Arbitration shall include the following:

a. a demand that the dispute be referred to arbitration;

b. the names and (in so far as known) the addresses, telephone and fax numbers, and email addresses of the parties and of their counsel;

c. a copy of the arbitration agreement(s) invoked;

d. a reference to the contract(s) or other legal instrument(s) out of or in relation to which the dispute arises;

e. a description of the general nature of the claim and an indication of the amount involved, if any;

f. the relief or remedy sought;

g. a proposal as to the number of arbitrators (i.e. one or three), if the parties have not previously agreed thereon;

h. the Claimant's proposal regarding the designation of a sole arbitrator under Article 7, or the Claimant's designation of an arbitrator under Article 8; and

i. confirmation that copies of the Notice of Arbitration and any exhibits included therewith have been or are being served simultaneously on all other parties (hereinafter called the 'Respondent') by one or more means of service to be identified in such confirmation.

4.4. The Notice of Arbitration shall be accompanied by payment, by cheque or transfer to the account of HKIAC, of the Registration Fee as required by Schedule 1.

4.5. The Notice of Arbitration shall be submitted in the language of the arbitration as agreed by the parties. If no agreement has been reached between the parties, the Notice of Arbitration shall be submitted in either English or Chinese.

4.6. The Notice of Arbitration may also include the Statement of Claim referred to in Article 16.

4.7. If the Notice of Arbitration is incomplete or if the Registration Fee is not paid, HKIAC may request the Claimant to remedy the defect within an appropriate period of time. If the Claimant complies with such directions within the applicable time limit, the arbitration shall be deemed to have commenced under Article 4.2 on the date the initial version was received by HKIAC. If the Claimant fails to comply, the Notice of Arbitration shall be deemed not to have been validly submitted and the arbitration shall be deemed not to have commenced under Article 4.2 without prejudice to the Claimant's right to submit the same claim at a later date in a subsequent Notice of Arbitration.

4.8. The Claimant shall notify and lodge documentary verification with HKIAC of the date of receipt by Respondent of the Notice of Arbitration and any exhibits included therewith.

Article 5
Answer to the Notice of Arbitration

5.1. Within 30 days from receipt of the Notice of Arbitration, the Respondent shall submit to HKIAC an Answer to the Notice of Arbitration. This Answer to the Notice of Arbitration shall include the following: (a) the name, address, telephone and fax numbers, and email address of the Respondent and of its counsel (if different from the description contained in the Notice of Arbitration); (b) any plea that an arbitral tribunal constituted under these Rules lacks jurisdiction; (c) the Respondent's comments on the particulars set forth in the Notice of Arbitration, pursuant to Article 4.3(e); (d) the Respondent's answer to the relief or remedy sought in the Notice of Arbitration, pursuant to Article 4.3(f); (e) the Respondent's proposal as to the number of arbitrators (i.e. one or three), if the parties have not previously agreed thereon; (f) the parties' joint designation of a sole arbitrator under Article 7 or the Respondent's designation of an arbitrator under Article 8; and (g) confirmation that copies of the Answer to the Notice of Arbitration and any exhibits included therewith have been or are being served simultaneously on all other parties to the arbitration by one or more means of service to be identified in such confirmation.

5.2. The Answer to the Notice of Arbitration shall be submitted in the language of the arbitration as agreed by the parties. If no agreement has been reached between the parties, the Answer to the Notice of Arbitration shall be submitted in either English or Chinese.

5.3. The Answer to the Notice of Arbitration may also include the Statement of Defence referred to in Article 17, if the Notice of Arbitration contained the Statement of Claim referred to in Article 16.

5.4. Any counterclaim or set-off defence shall to the extent possible be raised with the Respondent's Answer to the Notice of Arbitration, which should include in relation to any such counterclaim or set-off defence:

a. a reference to the contract(s) or other legal instrument(s) out of or in relation to which it arises;

b. a description of the general nature of the counterclaim and/or set-off defence and an indication of the amount involved, if any;

c. the relief or remedy sought.

5.5. If no counterclaim or set-off defence is raised with the Respondent's Answer to the Notice of Arbitration, or if there is no indication of the amount of the counterclaim or set-off, HKIAC shall rely upon the information provided by the Claimant pursuant to Article 4.3(e) for its determination of: (a) HKIAC's Administrative Fees referred to in Article 33.1(f) and Schedule 1; (b) the arbitral tribunal's fees (where Article 10.1(b) and Schedule 3 applies); and (c) whether the provisions of Article 41 (the 'Expedited Procedure') may be applicable.

5.6. Once the Registration Fee has been paid and the arbitral tribunal has been confirmed, HKIAC shall transmit the file to the arbitral tribunal.

Section III
The Arbitral Tribunal

Article 6
Number of Arbitrators

6.1. If the parties have not agreed upon the number of arbitrators, HKIAC shall decide whether the case shall be referred to a sole arbitrator or to three arbitrators, taking into account the circumstances of the case.

6.2. Where a case is handled under an Expedited Procedure in accordance with Article 41, the provisions of Article 41.2(a) and (b) shall apply.

Article 7
Appointment of a Sole Arbitrator

7.1. Unless the parties have agreed otherwise and subject to Articles 9, 10, 11.1 to 11.4: (a) where the parties have agreed that the dispute shall be referred to a sole arbitrator, they shall jointly designate the sole arbitrator within 30 days from the date when the Notice of Arbitration was received by the Respondent; (b) where the parties have not agreed upon the number of arbitrators and HKIAC has decided that the dispute shall be referred to a sole arbitrator, the parties shall jointly designate the sole arbitrator within 30 days from the date when HKIAC's decision was received by the last of them.

7.2. If the parties fail to designate the sole arbitrator within the applicable time limit, HKIAC shall appoint the sole arbitrator.

Article 8
Appointment of Three Arbitrators

8.1. Where a dispute between two parties is referred to three arbitrators, the arbitral tribunal shall be constituted as follows unless the parties have agreed otherwise:

a. where the parties have agreed that the dispute shall be referred to three arbitrators, each party shall designate, in the Notice of Arbitration and the Answer to the Notice of Arbitration, respectively, one arbitrator. If either party fails to designate an arbitrator, HKIAC shall appoint the arbitrator;

b. where the parties have not agreed upon the number of arbitrators and HKIAC has decided that the dispute shall be referred to three arbitrators, the Claimant shall designate an arbitrator within 15 days from receipt of HKIAC's decision, and the Respondent shall designate an arbitrator within 15 days from receipt of notification of the Claimant's designation. If a party fails to designate an arbitrator, HKIAC shall appoint the arbitrator;

c. the two arbitrators so appointed shall designate a third arbitrator who shall act as the presiding arbitrator of the arbitral tribunal. Failing such designation within 30 days from the confirmation of the second arbitrator, HKIAC shall appoint the presiding arbitrator.

8.2. Where there are more than two parties to the arbitration and the dispute is to be referred to three arbitrators, the arbitral tribunal shall be constituted as follows unless the parties have agreed otherwise:

a. the Claimant or group of Claimants shall designate an arbitrator and the Respondent or group of Respondents shall designate an arbitrator in accordance with the procedure in Article 8.1(a) or (b), as applicable;

b. if the parties have designated arbitrators in accordance with Article 8.2(a), the procedure in Article 8.1(c) shall apply to the designation of the presiding arbitrator;

c. In the event of any failure to designate arbitrators under Article 8.2(a) or if the parties do not all agree in writing that they represent two separate sides (as Claimant(s) and Respondent(s) respectively) for the purposes of designating arbitrators, HKIAC may appoint all members of the arbitral tribunal without regard to any party's designation.

8.3. Appointment of the arbitral tribunal pursuant to Article 8.1 or 8.2 shall be subject to Articles 9, 10 and 11.1 to 11.4.

Article 9

Confirmation of the Arbitral Tribunal

9.1. All designations of any arbitrator, whether made by the parties or the arbitrators, are subject to confirmation by HKIAC, upon which the appointments shall become effective.

9.2. The designation of an arbitrator shall be confirmed on the terms of: (a) Schedule 2; or (b) Schedule 3; as applicable, in accordance with Article 10 and subject to any variations agreed by all parties and any changes HKIAC considers appropriate.

Article 10
Fees and Expenses of the Arbitral Tribunal

10.1. The fees and expenses of the arbitral tribunal shall be determined according to either:

a. an hourly rate in accordance with Schedule 2, including the terms and conditions contained therein; or

b. the schedule of fees based on the sum in dispute referred to in Schedule 3, including the terms and conditions contained therein. The parties shall agree the method for determining the fees and expenses of the arbitral tribunal, and shall inform HKIAC of the applicable method within 30 days of the date on which the Respondent receives the Notice of Arbitration. If the parties fail to agree on the applicable method, the arbitral tribunal's fees and expenses shall be determined in accordance with the terms of Schedule 2.

10.2. Where the fees of the arbitral tribunal are to be determined in accordance with Schedule 2,

a. the applicable rate for each co-arbitrator shall be the rate agreed between that co-arbitrator and the designating party;

b. the applicable rate for a sole or presiding arbitrator shall be the rate agreed between that arbitrator and the parties, subject to paragraphs 9.3 and 9.5 of Schedule 2. Where the parties fail to agree the rate of an arbitrator, HKIAC may determine the rate.

10.3. Where the fees of the arbitral tribunal are determined in conformity with Schedule 3, such fees shall be fixed by HKIAC in accordance with that Schedule and the following rules:

a. the fees of the arbitral tribunal shall be reasonable in amount, taking into account the amount in dispute, the complexity of the subject-matter, the time spent by the arbitral tribunal and any secretary appointed under Article 13.4, and any other circumstances of the case, including, but not limited to, the discontinuation of the arbitration in case of settlement or for any other reason; b. where a case is referred to three arbitrators, HKIAC, at its discretion, shall have the right to increase the total fees up to a maximum which shall normally not exceed three times the fees of a sole arbitrator;

c. the arbitral tribunal's fees may exceed the amounts calculated in accordance with Schedule 3 where in the opinion of HKIAC there are exceptional circumstances, which shall include but shall not be limited to the parties conducting the arbitration in a manner not reasonably contemplated by the arbitral tribunal at the time of appointment.

Article 11

Qualifications and Challenge of Arbitral Tribunal

11.1. An arbitral tribunal confirmed under these Rules shall be and remain at all times impartial and independent of the parties.

11.2. Subject to Article 11.3, as a general rule, where the parties to an arbitration under these Rules are of different nationalities, a sole arbitrator or the presiding arbitrator of an arbitral tribunal shall not have the same nationality as any party unless specifically agreed otherwise by all parties in writing.

11.3 Notwithstanding the general rule in Article 11.2, in appropriate circumstances and provided that none of the parties objects within a time limit set by HKIAC, the sole arbitrator or the presiding arbitrator of the arbitral tribunal may be of the same nationality as any of the parties.

11.4. Before confirmation, a prospective arbitrator shall (a) sign a statement confirming his or her availability to decide the dispute and his or her impartiality and independence; and (b) disclose any circumstances likely to give rise to justifiable doubts as to his or her impartiality or independence. An arbitrator, once confirmed and throughout the arbitration, shall disclose without delay any such circumstances to the parties unless they have already been informed by him or her of these circumstances.

11.5. No party or its representatives shall have any *ex parte* communication relating to the arbitration with any arbitrator, or with any candidate to be designated as arbitrator by a party, except to advise the candidate of the general nature of the dispute, to discuss the candidate's qualifications, availability or independence, or to discuss the suitability of candidates for the designation of a third arbitrator, where the parties or party-designated arbitrators are to designate that arbitrator. No party or its representatives shall have any *ex parte* communication relating to the arbitration with any candidate for the presiding arbitrator.

11.6. Any arbitrator may be challenged if circumstances exist that give rise to justifiable doubts as to the arbitrator's impartiality or independence, or if the arbitrator does not possess qualifications agreed by the parties, or if the arbitrator becomes de jure or de facto unable to perform his or her functions or for other reasons fails to act without undue delay. A party may challenge the arbitrator designated by it or in whose appointment it has participated only for reasons of which it becomes aware after the designation has been made.

11.7. A party who intends to challenge an arbitrator shall send notice of its challenge within 15 days after the confirmation of that arbitrator has been notified to the challenging party or within 15 days after that party became aware or ought reasonably to have become aware of the circumstances mentioned in Article 11.6.

11.8. The challenge shall be notified to HKIAC, all other parties, the arbitrator who is challenged and the other members of the arbitral tribunal. The notification shall be in writing and shall state the reasons for the challenge.

11.9. Unless the arbitrator being challenged withdraws or the non-challenging party agrees to the challenge within 15 days from receipt of the notice of challenge, HKIAC shall decide on the challenge. Pending the determination of the challenge, the arbitral tribunal (including the challenged arbitrator) may continue the arbitration.

11.10. If an arbitrator withdraws or a party agrees to a challenge under Article 11.9, no acceptance of the validity of any ground referred to in Article 11.6 shall be implied.

Article 12
Replacement of an Arbitrator

12.1. Subject to Articles 12.2, 27.11 and 28.5, where an arbitrator dies, has been successfully challenged, has been otherwise removed or has resigned a substitute arbitrator shall be appointed pursuant to the rules that were applicable to the appointment of the arbitrator being replaced. These rules shall apply even if during the process of appointing the arbitrator being replaced, a party had failed to exercise its right to designate or to participate in the appointment.

12.2. If, at the request of a party, HKIAC determines that, in view of the exceptional circumstances of the case, it would be justified for a party to be deprived of its right to designate a substitute arbitrator, HKIAC may, after giving an opportunity to the parties and the remaining arbitrators to express their views:

a. appoint the substitute arbitrator; or

b. after the proceedings are declared closed under Article 30.1, authorise the other arbitrators to proceed with the arbitration and make any decision or award.

12.3. If an arbitrator is replaced, the arbitration shall resume at the stage where the arbitrator was replaced or ceased to perform his or her functions, unless the arbitral tribunal decides otherwise.

Section IV
Conduct of Arbitration

Article 13
General Provisions

13.1. Subject to these Rules, the arbitral tribunal shall adopt suitable procedures for the conduct of the arbitration in order to avoid unnecessary delay or expense, having regard to the complexity of the issues and the amount in dispute, and provided that such procedures ensure equal treatment of the parties and afford the parties a reasonable opportunity to present their case.

13.2. At an early stage of the arbitration and in consultation with the parties, the arbitral tribunal shall prepare a provisional timetable for the arbitration, which shall be provided to the parties and HKIAC.

13.3. Subject to Article 11.5, all documents or information supplied to the arbitral tribunal by one party shall at the same time be communicated by that party to the other parties and HKIAC.

13.4. The arbitral tribunal may, after consulting with the parties, appoint a secretary. The secretary shall remain at all times impartial and independent of the parties, and shall disclose any circumstances likely to give rise to justifiable doubts as to his or her impartiality or independence prior to his or her appointment. A secretary, once appointed and throughout the arbitration, shall disclose without delay any such circumstances to the parties unless they have already been informed by him or her of these circumstances.

13.5. The arbitral tribunal and the parties shall do everything necessary to ensure the fair and efficient conduct of the arbitration.

13.6. The parties may be represented by persons of their choice, subject to Article 13.5. The names, addresses, telephone and fax numbers, and email addresses of party representatives shall be communicated in writing to the other parties and HKIAC. The arbitral tribunal or HKIAC may require proof of authority of any party representatives.

13.7. In all matters not expressly provided for in these Rules, HKIAC, the arbitral tribunal and the parties shall act in the spirit of these Rules.

13.8. The arbitral tribunal shall make every reasonable effort to ensure that an award is valid.

Article 14

Seat and Venue of the Arbitration

14.1. The parties may agree on the seat of arbitration. Where there is no agreement as to seat the seat of arbitration shall be Hong Kong, unless the arbitral tribunal determines, having regard to the circumstances of the case, that another seat is more appropriate.

14.2. Unless the parties have agreed otherwise, the arbitral tribunal may meet at any location outside of the seat of arbitration which it considers appropriate for consultation among its members, hearing witnesses, experts or the parties, or the inspection of goods, other property or documents. The arbitration shall nonetheless be treated for all purposes as an arbitration conducted at the seat.

Article 15
Language

15.1. Subject to agreement by the parties, the arbitral tribunal shall, promptly after its appointment, determine the language or languages of the arbitration. This determination shall apply to the Statement of Claim, the Statement of Defence, any further written statements, any award, and, if oral hearings take place, to the language or languages to be used in such hearings.

15.2. The arbitral tribunal may order that any documents annexed to the Statement of Claim or Statement of Defence, and any supplementary documents or exhibits submitted in the course of the arbitration, delivered in their original language, shall be accompanied by a translation into the language or languages of the arbitration agreed upon by the parties or determined by the arbitral tribunal.

Article 16
Statement of Claim

16.1. Unless the Statement of Claim was contained in the Notice of Arbitration (or the Claimant elects to treat the Notice of Arbitration as the Statement of Claim), the Claimant shall communicate its Statement of Claim in writing to all other parties and to each member of the arbitral tribunal within a period of time to be determined by the arbitral tribunal.

16.2. The Statement of Claim shall include the following particulars: (a) the names, addresses, telephone numbers and email addresses of the parties; (b) a statement of the facts supporting the claim; (c) the points at issue; (d) the legal arguments supporting the claim; and (e) the relief or remedy sought.

16.3. The Claimant shall annex to its Statement of Claim all documents on which it relies.

16.4. The arbitral tribunal may vary any of the requirements referred to in Article 16 as it considers fit.

Article 17

Statement of Defence

17.1. Unless the Statement of Defence was contained in the Answer to the Notice of Arbitration (or the Respondent elects to treat the Answer to the Notice of Arbitration as the Statement of Defence), the Respondent shall communicate its Statement of Defence in writing to all other parties and to each member of the arbitral tribunal within a period of time to be determined by the arbitral tribunal.

17.2. The Statement of Defence shall reply to the particulars of the Statement of Claim (set out in Article 16.2(b), (c) and (d)). If the Respondent has raised an objection to the jurisdiction or to the proper constitution of the arbitral tribunal, the Statement of Defence shall contain the factual and legal basis of such objection.

17.3. Where there is a counterclaim or a set-off defence, the Statement of Defence shall also include the following particulars:

a. a statement of the facts supporting the counterclaim or set-off defence;

b. the points at issue;

c. the legal arguments supporting the counterclaim or set-off defence; and

d. the relief or remedy sought.

17.4. The Respondent shall annex to its Statement of Defence all documents on which it relies.

17.5. The arbitral tribunal may vary any of the requirements referred to in Article 17 as it considers fit.

Article 18

Amendments to the Claim or Defence

18.1. During the course of the arbitration a party may amend or supplement its claim or defence unless the arbitral tribunal considers it inappropriate to allow such amendment having regard to the circumstances of the case. However, a claim or defence may not be amended in such a manner that the amended claim or defence falls outside the jurisdiction of the arbitral tribunal.

18.2. HKIAC may adjust its Administrative Fees and the arbitral tribunal's fees (where appropriate) if a party amends its claim or defence.

Article 19
Jurisdiction of the Arbitral Tribunal

19.1. The arbitral tribunal may rule on its own jurisdiction under these Rules, including any objections with respect to the existence, validity or scope of the arbitration agreement(s).

19.2. The arbitral tribunal shall have the power to determine the existence or the validity of the contract of which an arbitration clause forms a part. For the purposes of Article 19, an arbitration clause which forms part of a contract and which provides for arbitration under these Rules shall be treated as an agreement independent of the other terms of the contract. A decision by the arbitral tribunal that the contract is null and void shall not necessarily entail the invalidity of the arbitration clause.

19.3. A plea that the arbitral tribunal does not have jurisdiction shall be raised if possible in the Answer to the Notice of Arbitration, and shall be raised no later than in the Statement of Defence referred to in Article 17, or, with respect to a counterclaim, in the Reply to the Counterclaim. A party is not precluded from raising such a plea by the fact that it has designated, or participated in the designation of, an arbitrator. A plea that the arbitral tribunal is exceeding the scope of its authority shall be raised as soon as the matter alleged to be beyond the scope of its authority is raised during the arbitration. The arbitral tribunal may, in either case, admit a later plea if it considers the delay justified.

19.4. If a question arises as to the existence, validity or scope of the arbitration agreement(s) or to the competence of HKIAC to administer an arbitration before the constitution of the arbitral tribunal, HKIAC may decide whether and to what extent the arbitration shall proceed. The arbitration shall proceed if and to the extent that HKIAC is satisfied, prima facie, that an arbitration agreement under the Rules may exist. Any question as to the jurisdiction of the arbitral tribunal shall be decided by the arbitral tribunal once confirmed pursuant to Article 19.1.

19.5. HKIAC's decision pursuant to Article 19.4 is without prejudice to the admissibility or merits of any party's pleas.

Article 20
Further Written Statements

The arbitral tribunal shall decide which further written statements, if any, in addition to the Statement of Claim and the Statement of Defence, shall be required from the parties or may be presented by them and shall set the periods of time for communicating such statements.

Article 21
Periods of Time

The periods of time set by the arbitral tribunal for the communication of written statements (including the Statement of Claim and Statement of Defence) should not exceed 45 days. However, the arbitral tribunal may, even in circumstances where the relevant period has already expired, extend time limits if it concludes that an extension is justified.

Article 22
Evidence and Hearings

22.1. Each party shall have the burden of proving the facts relied on to support its claim or defence.

22.2. The arbitral tribunal shall determine the admissibility, relevance, materiality and weight of the evidence, including whether to apply strict rules of evidence.

22.3. At any time during the arbitration the arbitral tribunal may allow or require a party to produce documents, exhibits or other evidence that the arbitral tribunal determines to be relevant to the case and material to its outcome. The arbitral tribunal shall have the power to admit or exclude any documents, exhibits or other evidence.

22.4. The arbitral tribunal shall decide whether to hold oral hearings for the presentation of evidence or for oral arguments, or whether the arbitration shall be conducted on the basis of documents and other materials. The arbitral tribunal shall hold such hearings at an appropriate stage of the arbitration, if so requested by a party or if it considers fit. In the event of an oral hearing, the arbitral tribunal shall give the parties adequate advance notice of the relevant date, time and place.

22.5. Any person may be a witness or an expert. If a witness or expert is to be heard, each party shall communicate to the arbitral tribunal and to the other party the name and address of the witness or expert it intends to present, and the subject upon and the language in which such witness or expert will give his or her testimony, within such time as shall be agreed or as shall be specified by the arbitral tribunal.

22.6. The arbitral tribunal may make directions for the translation of oral statements made at a hearing and for a record of the hearing if it deems that either is necessary in the circumstances of the case. 22.7 Hearings shall be held in private unless the parties agree otherwise. The arbitral tribunal may require any witness or expert to leave the hearing room at any time during the hearing. The arbitral tribunal is free to determine the manner in which a witness or expert is examined.

22.7. Hearings shall be held in private unless the parties agree otherwise. The arbitral tribunal may require any witness or expert to leave the hearing room at any time during the hearing. The arbitral tribunal is free to determine the manner in which a witness or expert is examined.

Article 23

Interim Measures of Protection and Emergency Relief

23.1. A party may apply for urgent interim or conservatory relief (the 'Emergency Relief') prior to the constitution of the arbitral tribunal pursuant to the procedures set out in Schedule 4 (the 'Emergency Arbitrator Procedures').

23.2. At the request of either party, the arbitral tribunal may order any interim measures it deems necessary or appropriate.

23.3. An interim measure, whether in the form of an order or award or in another form, is any temporary measure ordered by the arbitral tribunal at any time prior to the issuance of the award by which the dispute is finally decided, that a party, for example and without limitation:

a. maintain or restore the status quo pending determination of the dispute;

b. take action that would prevent, or refrain from taking action that is likely to cause, current or imminent harm or prejudice to the arbitral process itself;

c. provide a means of preserving assets out of which a subsequent award may be satisfied; or

d. preserve evidence that may be relevant and material to the resolution of the dispute.

23.4. When deciding a party's request for an interim measure under Article 23.2, the arbitral tribunal shall take into account the circumstances of the case. Relevant factors may include, but are not limited to:

a. harm not adequately reparable by an award of damages is likely to result if the measure is not ordered, and such harm substantially outweighs the harm that is likely to result to the party against whom the measure is directed if the measure is granted; and

b. there is a reasonable possibility that the requesting party will succeed on the merits of the claim. The determination on this possibility shall not affect the discretion of the arbitral tribunal in making any subsequent determination.

23.5. The arbitral tribunal may modify, suspend or terminate an interim measure it has granted, upon application of any party or, in exceptional circumstances and upon prior notice to the parties, on the arbitral tribunal's own initiative.

23.6. The arbitral tribunal may require the party requesting an interim measure to provide appropriate security in connection with the measure.

23.7. The arbitral tribunal may require any party promptly to disclose any material change in the circumstances on the basis of which an interim measure was requested or granted.

23.8. The party requesting an interim measure may be liable for any costs and damages caused by the measure to any party if the arbitral tribunal later determines that, in the circumstances then prevailing, the measure should not have been granted. The arbitral tribunal may award such costs and damages at any point during the arbitration.

23.9. A request for interim measures addressed by any party to a competent judicial authority shall not be deemed incompatible with the arbitration agreement(s), or as a waiver thereof.

Article 24
Security for Costs

The arbitral tribunal may make an order requiring a party to provide security for the costs of the arbitration.

Article 25
Tribunal-Appointed Experts

25.1. To assist it in the assessment of evidence, the arbitral tribunal, after consulting with the parties, may appoint one or more experts. The arbitral tribunal may meet privately with any tribunal-appointed expert. Such expert shall report to the arbitral tribunal, in writing, on specific issues to be determined by the arbitral tribunal. The arbitral tribunal shall establish terms of reference for the expert, and shall communicate a copy of the expert's terms of reference to the parties and HKIAC.

25.2. The parties shall give the expert any relevant information or produce for his or her inspection any relevant documents or goods that he or she may require of them. Any dispute between a party and such expert as to the relevance of the required information or production shall be referred to the arbitral tribunal for decision.

25.3. Upon receipt of the expert's report, the arbitral tribunal shall send a copy of the report to the parties who shall be given the opportunity to express, in writing, their opinions on the report. The parties shall be entitled to examine any document on which the expert has relied in his or her report.

25.4. At the request of either party the expert, after delivery of the report, shall attend a hearing at which the parties shall have the opportunity to be present and to examine the expert. At this hearing either party may present experts in order to testify on the points at issue. The provisions of Articles 22.2 to 22.7 shall be applicable to such proceedings.

25.5. The provisions of Article 11 shall apply by analogy to any expert appointed by the arbitral tribunal.

Article 26
Default

26.1. If, within the period of time set by the arbitral tribunal, the Claimant has failed to communicate its Statement of Claim without showing sufficient cause for such failure, the arbitral tribunal shall issue an order for the termination of the arbitration unless the Respondent has brought a counterclaim and wishes the arbitration to continue, in which case the tribunal may proceed with the arbitration in respect of the counterclaim.

26.2. If, within the period of time set by the arbitral tribunal, the Respondent has failed to communicate its Statement of Defence without showing sufficient cause for such failure, the arbitral tribunal may proceed with the arbitration.

26.3. If one of the parties, duly notified under these Rules, fails to present its case in accordance with these Rules including as directed by the arbitral tribunal, without showing sufficient cause for such failure, the arbitral tribunal may proceed with the arbitration and make an award on the basis of the evidence before it.

Article 27
Joinder of Additional Parties

27.1. The arbitral tribunal shall have the power to allow an additional party to be joined to the arbitration provided that, prima facie, the additional party is bound by an arbitration agreement under these Rules giving rise to the arbitration, including any arbitration under Article 28 or 29.

27.2. The arbitral tribunal's decision pursuant to Article 27.1 is without prejudice to its power to subsequently decide any question as to its jurisdiction arising from such decision.

27.3. A party wishing to join an additional party to the arbitration shall submit a Request for Joinder to HKIAC. HKIAC may fix a time limit for the submission of a Request for Joinder.

27.4. The Request for Joinder shall include the following:

a. the case reference of the existing arbitration;

b. the names and addresses, telephone numbers, and email addresses of each of the parties, including the additional party;

c. a request that the additional party be joined to the arbitration;

d. a reference to the contract(s) or other legal instrument(s) out of or in relation to which the request arises;

e. a statement of the facts supporting the request;

f. the points at issue;

g. the legal arguments supporting the request;

h. the relief or remedy sought; and

i. confirmation that copies of the Request for Joinder and any exhibits included therewith have been or are being served simultaneously on all other parties and the arbitral tribunal, where applicable, by one or more means of service to be identified in such confirmation. A copy of the contract(s), and of the arbitration agreement(s) if not contained in the contract(s), shall be annexed to the Request for Joinder.

27.5 Within 15 days of receiving the Request for Joinder, the additional party shall submit to HKIAC an Answer to the Request for Joinder. The Answer to the Request for Joinder shall include the following:

a. the name, address, telephone and fax numbers, and email address of the additional party and its counsel (if different from the description contained in the Request for Joinder);

b. any plea that the arbitral tribunal has been improperly constituted and/or lacks jurisdiction over the additional party;

c. the additional party's comments on the particulars set forth in the Request for Joinder, pursuant to Article 27.4(a) to (g);

d. the additional party's answer to the relief or remedy sought in the Request for Joinder, pursuant to Article 27.4(h);

e. details of any claims by the additional party against any other party to the arbitration; and

f. confirmation that copies of the Answer to the Request for Joinder and any exhibits included therewith have been or are being served simultaneously on all other parties and the arbitral tribunal, where applicable, by one or more means of service to be identified in such confirmation.

27.6. A third party wishing to be joined as an additional party to the arbitration shall submit a Request for Joinder to HKIAC. The provisions of Article 27.4 shall apply to such Request for Joinder.

27.7. Within 15 days of receiving a Request for Joinder pursuant to Article 27.3 or 27.6, the parties shall submit their comments on the Request for Joinder to HKIAC. Such comments may include (without limitation) the following particulars:

a. any plea that the arbitral tribunal lacks jurisdiction over the additional party;

b. comments on the particulars set forth in the Request for Joinder, pursuant to Article 27.4(a) to (g);

c. answer to the relief or remedy sought in the Request for Joinder, pursuant to Article 27.4(h);

d. details of any claims against the additional party; and

e. confirmation that copies of the comments have been or are being served simultaneously on all other parties and the arbitral tribunal, where applicable, by one or more means of service to be identified in such confirmation.

27.8. Where HKIAC receives a Request for Joinder before the date on which the arbitral tribunal is confirmed, HKIAC may decide whether, prima facie, the additional party is bound by an arbitration agreement under these Rules giving rise to the arbitration, including any arbitration under Article 28 or 29. If so, HKIAC may join the additional party to the arbitration. Any question as to the jurisdiction of the arbitral tribunal arising from HKIAC's decision under this Article 27.8 shall be decided by the arbitral tribunal once confirmed, pursuant to Article 19.1.

27.9. HKIAC's decision pursuant to Article 27.8 is without prejudice to the admissibility or merits of any party's pleas.

27.10. Where an additional party is joined to the arbitration, the date on which the Request for Joinder is received by HKIAC shall be deemed to be the date on which the arbitration in respect of the additional party commences.

27.11. Where an additional party is joined to the arbitration before the date on which the arbitral tribunal is confirmed, all parties to the arbitration shall be deemed to have waived their right to designate an arbitrator, and HKIAC may revoke the appointment of any arbitrators already designated or confirmed. In these circumstances, HKIAC shall appoint the arbitral tribunal.

27.12. The revocation of the appointment of an arbitrator under Article 27.11 is without prejudice to:

a. the validity of any act done or order made by that arbitrator before his or her appointment was revoked; and

b. his or her entitlement to be paid his or her fees and expenses subject to Schedule 2 or 3 as applicable.

27.13. The parties waive any objection, on the basis of any decision to join an additional party to the arbitration, to the validity and/or enforcement of any award made by the arbitral tribunal in the arbitration, in so far as such waiver can validly be made.

27.14. HKIAC may adjust its Administrative Fees and the arbitral tribunal's fees (where appropriate) after a Request for Joinder has been submitted.

Article 28

Consolidation of Arbitrations

28.1. HKIAC shall have the power, at the request of a party (the 'Request for Consolidation') and after consulting with the parties and any confirmed arbitrators, to consolidate two or more arbitrations pending under these Rules where:

a. the parties agree to consolidate; or

b. all of the claims in the arbitrations are made under the same arbitration agreement; or

c. the claims are made under more than one arbitration agreement, a common question of law or fact arises in both or all of the arbitrations, the rights to relief claimed are in respect of, or arise out of, the same transaction or series of transactions, and HKIAC finds the arbitration agreements to be compatible.

28.2. The party making the request shall provide copies of the Request for Consolidation to all other parties and to any confirmed arbitrators.

28.3. In deciding whether to consolidate, HKIAC shall take into account the circumstances of the case. Relevant factors may include, but are not limited to, whether one or more arbitrators have been designated or confirmed in more than one of the arbitrations, and if so, whether the same or different arbitrators have been confirmed.

28.4. Where HKIAC decides to consolidate two or more arbitrations, the arbitrations shall be consolidated into the arbitration that commenced first, unless all parties agree or HKIAC decides otherwise taking into account the circumstances of the case. HKIAC shall provide copies of such decision to all parties and to any confirmed arbitrators in all arbitrations.

28.5. The consolidation of two or more arbitrations is without prejudice to the validity of any act done or order made by a court in support of the relevant arbitration before it was consolidated.

28.6. Where HKIAC decides to consolidate two or more arbitrations, the parties to all such arbitrations shall be deemed to have waived their right to designate an arbitrator, and HKIAC may revoke the appointment of any arbitrators already designated or confirmed. In these circumstances, HKIAC shall appoint the arbitral tribunal in respect of the consolidated proceedings.

28.7. The revocation of the appointment of an arbitrator under Article 28.6 is without prejudice to:

a. the validity of any act done or order made by that arbitrator before his or her appointment was revoked;

b. his or her entitlement to be paid his or her fees and expenses subject to Schedule 2 or 3 as applicable; and

c. the date when any claim or defence was raised for the purpose of applying any limitation bar or any similar rule or provision.

28.8. The parties waive any objection, on the basis of HKIAC's decision to consolidate, to the validity and/or enforcement of any award made by the arbitral tribunal in the consolidated proceedings, in so far as such waiver can validly be made.

28.9. HKIAC may adjust its Administrative Fees and the arbitral tribunal's fees (where appropriate) after a Request for Consolidation has been submitted.

Article 29
Single Arbitration under Multiple Contracts

29.1. Claims arising out of or in connection with more than one contract may be made in a single arbitration, provided that:

a. all parties to the arbitration are bound by each arbitration agreement giving rise to the arbitration;

b. a common question of law or fact arises under each arbitration agreement giving rise to the arbitration;

c. the rights to relief claimed are in respect of, or arise out of, the same transaction or series of transactions; and

d. the arbitration agreements under which those claims are made are compatible.

29.2. The parties waive any objection, on the basis of the commencement of a single arbitration under Article 29, to the validity and/or enforcement of any award made by the arbitral tribunal in the arbitration, in so far as such waiver can validly be made.

Article 30
Closure of Proceedings

30.1. When it is satisfied that the parties have had a reasonable opportunity to present their case, the arbitral tribunal shall declare the proceedings closed. Thereafter, no further submission or argument may be made, or evidence produced, unless the tribunal reopens the proceedings in accordance with Article 30.2.

30.2. The arbitral tribunal may, if it considers it necessary owing to exceptional circumstances, decide, on its own initiative or upon application of a party, to reopen the proceedings at any time before the award is made.

Article 31
Waiver

A party who knows or ought reasonably to know that any provision of, or requirement arising under, these Rules (including the arbitration agreement(s)) has not been complied with and yet proceeds with the arbitration without promptly stating its objection to such non-compliance, shall be deemed to have waived its right to object.

Section V
Awards, Decisions and Orders of the Arbitral Tribunal

Article 32
Decisions

32.1. When there is more than one arbitrator, any award or other decision of the arbitral tribunal shall be made by a majority of the arbitrators. If there is no majority, the award shall be made by the presiding arbitrator alone.

32.2. With the prior agreement of all members of the arbitral tribunal, the presiding arbitrator may make procedural rulings alone.

Article 33
Costs of the Arbitration

33.1. The arbitral tribunal shall determine the costs of the arbitration in its award. The term 'costs of the arbitration' includes only:

a. the fees of the arbitral tribunal, as determined in accordance with Article 10;

b. the reasonable travel and other expenses incurred by the arbitral tribunal;

c. the reasonable costs of expert advice and of other assistance required by the arbitral tribunal;

d. the reasonable travel and other expenses of witnesses and experts;

e. the reasonable costs for legal representation and assistance if such costs were claimed during the arbitration;

f. the Registration Fee and Administrative Fees payable to HKIAC in accordance with Schedule 1.

33.2. The arbitral tribunal may apportion all or part of the costs of the arbitration referred to in Article 33.1 between the parties if it determines that apportionment is reasonable, taking into account the circumstances of the case.

33.3. With respect to the costs of legal representation and assistance referred to in Article 33.1(e), the arbitral tribunal, taking into account the circumstances of the case, may direct that the recoverable costs of the arbitration, or any part of the arbitration, shall be limited to a specified amount.

33.4. Where arbitrations are consolidated pursuant to Article 28, the arbitral tribunal in the consolidated arbitration shall allocate the costs of the arbitration in accordance with Article 33.2 and 33.3. Such costs shall include, but shall not be limited to, the fees of any arbitral tribunal designated or confirmed and any other costs incurred in an arbitration that was subsequently consolidated into another arbitration.

33.5. When the arbitral tribunal issues an order for the termination of the arbitration or makes an award on agreed terms, it or HKIAC shall determine the costs of the arbitration referred to in Article 33.1, in the text of that order or award.

Article 34
Form and Effect of the Award

34.1. The arbitral tribunal may make a single award or separate awards regarding different issues at different times and in respect of all parties involved in the arbitration in the form of interim, interlocutory, partial or final awards. If appropriate, the arbitral tribunal may also issue interim awards on costs.

34.2. Awards shall be made in writing and shall be final and binding on the parties and any person claiming through or under any of the parties. The parties and any such person shall be deemed to have waived their rights to any form of recourse or defence in respect of enforcement and execution of any award, in so far as such waiver can validly be made.

34.3. The parties undertake to comply without delay with any award or order made by the arbitral tribunal, including any award or order made in any consolidated proceedings under Article 28 or any arbitration under Article 29.

34.4. An award shall state the reasons upon which it is based unless the parties have agreed that no reasons are to be given.

34.5. An award shall be signed by the arbitral tribunal. It shall state the date on which it was made and the seat of arbitration as determined under Article 14 and shall be deemed to have been made at the seat of the arbitration. Where there are three arbitrators and any of them fails to sign, the award shall state the reason for the absence of the signature(s).

34.6. Subject to any lien, originals of the award signed by the arbitrators and affixed with the seal of HKIAC shall be communicated to the parties and HKIAC by the arbitral tribunal. HKIAC shall be supplied with an original copy of the award.

Article 35

Applicable Law, *Amiable Compositeur*

35.1. The arbitral tribunal shall decide the substance of the dispute in accordance with the rules of law agreed upon by the parties. Any designation of the law or legal system of a given jurisdiction shall be construed, unless otherwise expressed, as directly referring to the substantive law of that jurisdiction and not to its conflict of laws rules. Failing such designation by the parties, the arbitral tribunal shall apply the rules of law which it determines to be appropriate.

35.2. The arbitral tribunal shall decide as *amiable compositeur* or *ex aequo et bono* only if the parties have expressly agreed that the arbitral tribunal should do so.

35.3. In all cases, the arbitral tribunal shall decide the case in accordance with the terms of the relevant contract(s) and may take into account the usages of the trade applicable to the transaction(s).

Article 36
Settlement or Other Grounds for Termination

36.1. If, before the award is made, the parties agree on a settlement of the dispute, the arbitral tribunal shall either issue an order for the termination of the arbitration or, if requested by both parties and accepted by the arbitral tribunal, record the settlement in the form of an arbitral award on agreed terms. The arbitral tribunal is not obliged to give reasons for such an award.

36.2. If, before the award is made, the continuation of the arbitration becomes unnecessary or impossible for any reason not mentioned in Article 36.1, the arbitral tribunal shall issue an order for the termination of the arbitration. The arbitral tribunal shall issue such an order unless a party raises a justifiable objection, having been given a reasonable opportunity to comment upon the proposed course of action.

36.3. Copies of the order for termination of the arbitration or of the arbitral award on agreed terms, signed by the arbitral tribunal, shall be communicated by the arbitral tribunal to the parties and HKIAC. Where an arbitral award on agreed terms is made, the provisions of Articles 34.2, 34.3, 34.5 and 34.6 shall apply.

Article 37
Correction of the Award

37.1. Within 30 days after receipt of the award, either party, with notice to the other party, may request the arbitral tribunal to correct in the award any errors in computation, any clerical or typographical errors, or any errors of similar nature. The arbitral tribunal may set a time limit, normally not exceeding

15 days, for the other party to comment on such request.

37.2. The arbitral tribunal shall make any corrections it considers appropriate within 30 days after receipt of the request but may extend such period of time if necessary.

37.3. The arbitral tribunal may within 30 days after the date of the award make such corrections on its own initiative.

37.4. The arbitral tribunal has the power to make any further correction to the award which is necessitated by or consequential on (a) the interpretation of any point or part of the award under Article 38; or (b) the issue of any additional award under Article 39.

37.5. Such corrections shall be in writing, and the provisions of Articles 34.2 to 34.6 shall apply.

Article 38

Interpretation of the Award

38.1. Within 30 days after receipt of the award, either party, with notice to the other party, may request that the arbitral tribunal give an interpretation of the award. The arbitral tribunal may set a time limit, normally not exceeding 15 days, for the other party to comment on such request.

38.2. Any interpretation considered appropriate by the arbitral tribunal shall be given in writing within 30 days after receipt of the request but the tribunal may extend such period of time if necessary.

38.3. The arbitral tribunal has the power to give any further interpretation of the award which is necessitated by or consequential on

a. the correction of any error in the award under Article 37; or

b. the issue of any additional award under Article 39.

38.4. Any interpretation given under Article 38 shall form part of the award and the provisions of Articles 34.2 to 34.6 shall apply.

Article 39

Additional Award

39.1. Within 30 days after receipt of the award, either party, with notice to the other party, may request the arbitral tribunal to make an additional award as to claims presented in the arbitration but omitted from the award. The arbitral tribunal may set a time limit, normally not exceeding 30 days, for the other party to comment on such request.

39.2. If the arbitral tribunal considers the request for an additional award to be justified, it shall make the additional award within 60 days after receipt of the request but may extend such period of time if necessary.

39.3. The arbitral tribunal has the power to make an additional award which is necessitated by or consequential on

a. the correction of any error in the award under Article 37; or

b. the interpretation of any point or part of the award under Article 38.

39.4. When an additional award is made, the provisions of Articles 34.2 to 34.6 shall apply.

Article 40

Deposits for Costs

40.1. As soon as practicable after receipt of the Notice of Arbitration by the Respondent, HKIAC shall, in principle, request the Claimant and the Respondent each to deposit with HKIAC an equal amount as an advance for the costs referred to in Article 33.1, paragraphs (a), (b), (c) and (f). HKIAC shall provide a copy of such request to the arbitral tribunal.

40.2. Where a Respondent submits a counterclaim, or it otherwise appears appropriate in the circumstances, HKIAC may request separate deposits.

40.3. During the course of the arbitration HKIAC may request the parties to make supplementary deposits with HKIAC. HKIAC shall provide a copy of such request(s) to the arbitral tribunal.

40.4. If the required deposits are not paid in full to HKIAC within 30 days after receipt of the request, HKIAC shall so inform the parties in order that one or another of them may make the required payment. If such payment is not made, the arbitral tribunal may order the suspension or termination of the arbitration or continue with the arbitration on such basis and in respect of such claim or counterclaim as the tribunal considers fit.

40.5. In its final award, the arbitral tribunal shall render an account to the parties of the deposits received by HKIAC. Any unexpended balance shall be returned to the parties by HKIAC.

40.6. HKIAC shall place the deposit(s) made by the parties in interest bearing deposit account(s) at a reputable licensed Hong Kong deposit-taking institution. In selecting the account(s), HKIAC shall have due regard to the possible need to make the deposited funds available immediately.

Section VI
Other Provisions

Article 41
Expedited Procedure

41.1. Prior to the constitution of the arbitral tribunal, a party may apply to HKIAC in writing for the arbitration to be conducted in accordance with Article 41.2 where:

a. the amount in dispute representing the aggregate of any claim and counterclaim (or any set-off defence) does not exceed HKD 25,000,000 (twenty-five million Hong Kong Dollars); or

b. the parties so agree; or 3. in cases of exceptional urgency.

41.2. When HKIAC, after considering the views of the parties, grants an application made pursuant to Article 41.1, the arbitral proceedings shall be conducted in accordance with an Expedited Procedure based upon the foregoing provisions of these Rules, subject to the following changes:

a. the case shall be referred to a sole arbitrator, unless the arbitration agreement provides for three arbitrators;

b. if the arbitration agreement provides for three arbitrators, HKIAC shall invite the parties to agree to refer the case to a sole arbitrator. If the parties do not agree, the case shall be referred to three arbitrators;

c. HKIAC may shorten the time limits provided for in the Rules, as well as any time limits that it has set;

d. after the submission of the Answer to the Notice of Arbitration, the parties shall in principle be entitled to submit one Statement of Claim and one Statement of Defence (and Counterclaim) and, where applicable, one Statement of Defence in reply to the Counterclaim;

e. the arbitral tribunal shall decide the dispute on the basis of documentary evidence only, unless it decides that it is appropriate to hold one or more hearings;

f. the award shall be made within six months from the date when HKIAC transmitted the file to the arbitral tribunal. In exceptional circumstances, HKIAC may extend this time limit;

g. the arbitral tribunal shall state the reasons upon which the award is based in summary form, unless the parties have agreed that no reasons are to be given.

41.3. Unless the parties agree otherwise, the Expedited Procedure contained in Article 41 shall not apply to any consolidated proceedings under Article 28 or to any arbitration commenced under Article 29.

Article 42
Confidentiality

42.1. Unless otherwise agreed by the parties, no party may publish, disclose or communicate any information relating to: (a) the arbitration under the arbitration agreement(s); or (b) an award made in the arbitration.

42.2. The provisions of Article 42.1 also apply to the arbitral tribunal, any Emergency Arbitrator appointed in accordance with Schedule 4, expert, witness, secretary of the arbitral tribunal and HKIAC.

42.3. The provisions in Article 42.1 do not prevent the publication, disclosure or communication of information referred to in Article 42.1 by a party:

a. (i) to protect or pursue a legal right or interest of the party; or

(ii) to enforce or challenge the award referred to in Article 42.1;

in legal proceedings before a court or other judicial authority;

b. to any government body, regulatory body, court or tribunal where the party is obliged by law to make the publication, disclosure or communication; or

c. to a professional or any other adviser of any of the parties, including any actual or potential witness or expert.

42.4. The deliberations of the arbitral tribunal are confidential.

42.5. An award may be published, whether in its entirety or in the form of excerpts or a summary, only under the following conditions:

a. a request for publication is addressed to HKIAC;

b. all references to the parties' names are deleted; and

c. no party objects to such publication within the time limit fixed for that purpose by HKIAC. In the case of an objection, the award shall not be published.

Article 43
Exclusion of Liability

43.1. None of the Council of HKIAC nor any committee, sub-commitee or other body or person specifically designated by it to perform the functions referred to in these Rules, nor the Secretary General of HKIAC or other staff members of the Secretariat of HKIAC, the arbitral tribunal, any Emergency Arbitrator, tribunal-appointed expert or secretary of the arbitral tribunal shall be liable for any act or omission in connection with an arbitration conducted under these Rules, save where such act was done or omitted to be done dishonestly.

43.2. After the award has been made and the possibilities of correction, interpretation and additional awards referred to in Articles 37 to 39 have lapsed or been exhausted, neither HKIAC nor the arbitral tribunal, any Emergency Arbitrator, tribunal-appointed expert or secretary of the arbitral tribunal shall be under an obligation to make statements to any person about any matter concerning the arbitration, nor shall a party seek to make any of these persons a witness in any legal or other proceedings arising out of the arbitration.

Schedule 1

Registration and Administrative Fees

(All amounts are in Hong Kong Dollars, hereinafter 'HKD')

Effective 1 February 2015

1. Registration Fee

1.1. When submitting a Notice of Arbitration, the Claimant shall pay a Registration Fee in the amount set by HKIAC, as stated on HKIAC's website on the date the Notice of Arbitration is submitted.

1.2. If the Claimant fails to pay the Registration Fee, HKIAC shall not proceed with the arbitration subject to Article 4.7 of the Rules.

1.3. The Registration Fee is not refundable.

2. HKIAC's Administrative Fees

2.1. HKIAC's Administrative Fee shall be determined in accordance with the following table:

Administrative Fee

[omitted]

2.2. Claims and counterclaims are aggregated for the determination of the amount in dispute. The same rule applies to any set-off defence, unless the arbitral tribunal, after consulting with the parties, concludes that such set-off defence will not require significant additional work.

2.3. An interest claim shall not be taken into account for the calculation of the amount in dispute. However, when the interest claim exceeds the amounts claimed in principal, the interest claim alone shall be considered in calculating the amount in dispute.

2.4. Pursuant to Articles 18.2, 27.14 or 28.8 or where in the opinion of HKIAC there are exceptional circumstances,

HKIAC's Administrative Fees may exceed the amounts calculated in accordance with paragraph 2.1.

2.5. If the amount in dispute is not quantified, HKIAC's Administrative Fees shall be fixed by HKIAC, taking into account the circumstances of the case.

2.6. Amounts in currencies other than Hong Kong Dollars shall be converted into Hong Kong Dollars at the rate of exchange published by HSBC Bank on the date the Notice of Arbitration is submitted or at the time any new claim, set-off defence or amendment to a claim or defence is filed.

Schedule 2

Arbitral Tribunal's Fees, Expenses, Terms and Conditions

Based on Hourly Rates

Effective 1 November 2013

1. Scope of Application and Interpretation

1.1. Subject to Article 9.2 of the Rules, this Schedule shall apply to arbitrations in which the arbitral tribunal's fees and expenses are to be determined in accordance with Article 10.1(a) of the Rules and to the appointment of an Emergency Arbitrator under Schedule 4.

1.2. HKIAC may interpret the terms of this Schedule as well as the scope of application of the Schedule as it considers appropriate.

1.3. This Schedule is supplemented by the Practice Note on Arbitral Tribunal's Fees, Expenses, Terms and Conditions Based on Schedule 2 and Hourly Rates in force on the date the Notice of Arbitration is submitted.

2. Payments to Arbitral Tribunal

2.1. Payments to the arbitral tribunal shall generally be made by HKIAC from funds deposited by the parties in accordance with Article 40 of the Rules. HKIAC may direct the parties, in such proportions as it considers appropriate, to make one or more interim or final payments to the arbitral tribunal.

2.2. If insufficient funds are held at the time a payment is required, the invoice for the payment may be submitted to the parties for settlement by them direct.

2.3. Payments to the arbitral tribunal shall be made in Hong Kong Dollars unless the tribunal directs otherwise.

2.4. The parties are jointly and severally liable for the fees and expenses of an arbitrator, irrespective of which party appointed the arbitrator.

3. Arbitral Tribunal's Expenses

3.1. The arbitral tribunal shall be reimbursed for its reasonable expenses in accordance with the Practice Note referred to at paragraph 1.3.

3.2. The expenses of the arbitral tribunal shall not be included in the arbitral tribunal's fees charged by reference to hourly rates under paragraph 9 of this Schedule.

4. Administrative Expenses

The parties shall be responsible for expenses reasonably incurred and relating to administrative and support services engaged for the purposes of the arbitration, including, but not limited to, the cost of hearing rooms, interpreters and transcription services. Such expenses may be paid directly from the deposits referred to in Article 40 of the Rules as and when they are incurred.

5. Fees and Expenses Payable to Replaced Arbitrators

Where an arbitrator is replaced pursuant to Article 12, 27 or 28 of the Rules, HKIAC shall decide the amount of fees and expenses to be paid for the replaced arbitrator's services (if any), having taken into account the circumstances of the case, including, but not limited to, the applicable method for determining the arbitrator's fees, work done by the arbitrator in connection with the arbitration, and the complexity of the subject-matter.

6. Fees and Expenses of Secretary to Arbitral Tribunal

Where the arbitral tribunal appoints a secretary in accordance with Article 13.4 of the Rules, such secretary shall be remunerated at a rate which shall not exceed the rate set by HKIAC, as stated on HKIAC's website on the date the Notice of Arbitration is submitted. The secretary's fees and expenses shall be charged separately. The arbitral tribunal shall determine the total fees and expenses of a secretary under Article 33.1(c) of the Rules.

7. Lien on Award

HKIAC and the arbitral tribunal shall have a lien over any awards issued by the tribunal to secure the payment of their outstanding fees and expenses, and may accordingly refuse to release any such awards to the parties until all such fees and expenses have been paid in full, whether jointly or by one or other of the parties.

8. Governing law

The terms of this Schedule and any non-contractual obligation arising out of or in connection with them shall be governed by and construed in accordance with Hong Kong law.

9. Arbitral Tribunal's Fee Rates

9.1. An arbitrator shall be remunerated at an hourly rate for all work reasonably carried out in connection with the arbitration.

9.2. Subject to paragraphs 9.3 and 9.4 of this Schedule, the rate referred to in paragraph 9.1 is to be agreed in accordance with Article 10.2 of the Rules. An arbitrator shall agree in writing upon fee rates in accordance with paragraph 9 of this Schedule prior to the confirmation of his or her appointment by HKIAC in accordance with Article 9 of the Rules.

9.3. An arbitrator's agreed hourly rate shall not exceed a rate set by HKIAC, as stated on HKIAC's website on the date the Notice of Arbitration is submitted.

9.4. Subject to paragraph 9.3, an arbitrator may review and increase his or her agreed hourly rate by no more than 10% on each anniversary of the confirmation of his or her appointment by HKIAC.

9.5. Higher rates may be charged if expressly agreed in writing by all parties to the arbitration or if HKIAC so determines in exceptional circumstances.

9.6. If an arbitrator is required to travel for the purposes of fulfilling obligations as an arbitrator, the arbitrator shall be entitled to charge and to be reimbursed for:

a. time spent travelling but not working at a rate of 50% of the agreed hourly rate; and

b. time spent working whilst travelling at the full agreed hourly rate.

10. Cancellation Fees

10.1. All hearings booked shall be paid for, subject to the following conditions:

a. if a booking is cancelled at the request of the arbitral tribunal, it will not be charged;

b. if a booking is cancelled at the request of a party less than 30 days before the day booked it shall be paid at a daily rate of 75% of eight times the applicable hourly rate;

c. if a booking is cancelled at the request of a party less than 60 days but more than 30 days before the day booked, it shall be paid at a daily rate of 50% of eight times the applicable hourly rate;

d. if a booking is cancelled at the request of a party more than 60 days before the day booked it will not be charged; and

e. in all cases referred to above, credit will be given against all time spent on the case during the day(s) booked.

10.2. Where hearing days are cancelled or postponed other than by agreement of all parties, this may be taken into account when considering any subsequent allocation of costs.

Schedule 3
Arbitral Tribunal's Fees, Expenses, Terms and Conditions
Based on Sum in Dispute

(All amounts are in Hong Kong Dollars, hereinafter 'HKD')

Effective 1 November 2013

1. Scope of Application and Interpretation

1.1. Subject to paragraph 1.2 below and Article 9.2 of the Rules, this Schedule applies to arbitrations in which the arbitral tribunal's fees and expenses are to be determined in accordance with Article 10.1(b) of the Rules.

1.2. This Schedule shall not apply to the appointment of an Emergency Arbitrator under Schedule 4.

1.3. HKIAC may interpret the terms of this Schedule as well as the scope of application of the Schedule as it considers appropriate.

1.4. This Schedule is supplemented by the Practice Note on Arbitral Tribunal's Fees, Expenses, Terms and Conditions Based on Schedule 3 and the Sum in Dispute in force on the date the Notice of Arbitration is submitted.

2. Payments to Arbitral Tribunal

2.1. Payments to the arbitral tribunal shall generally be made by HKIAC from funds deposited by the parties in accordance with Article 40 of the Rules. HKIAC may direct the parties, in such proportions as it considers appropriate, to make one or more interim or final payments to the arbitral tribunal.

2.2. If insufficient funds are held at the time a payment is required, the invoice for the payment may be submitted to the parties for settlement by them direct.

2.3. Payments to the arbitral tribunal shall be made in Hong Kong Dollars unless the tribunal directs otherwise.

2.4. The parties are jointly and severally liable for the fees and expenses of an arbitrator, irrespective of which party appointed the arbitrator.

3. Arbitral Tribunal's Expenses

3.1. The arbitral tribunal shall be reimbursed for its reasonable expenses in accordance with the Practice Note referred to at paragraph 1.4.

3.2. The expenses of the arbitral tribunal shall not be included in the determination of fees charged in accordance with paragraph 6 of this Schedule.

4. Administrative Expenses

The parties shall be responsible for expenses reasonably incurred and relating to administrative and support services engaged for the purposes of the arbitration, including, but not limited to, the cost of hearing rooms, interpreters and transcription services. Such expenses may be paid directly from the deposits referred to in Article 40 of the Rules as and when they are incurred.

5. Fees and Expenses Payable to Replaced Arbitrators

Where an arbitrator is replaced pursuant to Article 12, 27 or 28 of the Rules, HKIAC shall decide the amount of fees and expenses to be paid for the replaced arbitrator's services (if any), having taken into account the circumstances of the case, including, but not limited to, the applicable method for determining the arbitrator's fees, work done by the arbitrator in connection with the arbitration, and the complexity of the subject-matter.

6. Determination of Arbitral Tribunal's Fees

6.1. The arbitral tribunal's fees shall be calculated in accordance with the following table. The fees calculated in accordance with the table represent the maximum amount payable to one arbitrator.

Arbitral Tribunal Fee

[omitted]

6.2. The arbitral tribunal's fees shall cover the activities of the arbitral tribunal from the time the file is transmitted to it until the last award.

6.3. Claims and counterclaims are added for the determination of the amount in dispute. The same rule applies to any set-off defence, unless the arbitral tribunal, after consulting with the parties, concludes that such set-off defence will not require significant additional work.

6.4. An interest claim shall not be taken into account for the calculation of the amount in dispute. However, when the interest claim exceeds the amounts claimed in principal, the interest claim alone shall be considered in calculating the amount in dispute.

6.5. Pursuant to Articles 10.3(c), 18.2, 27.14 or 28.8 or in other exceptional circumstances, the arbitral tribunal's fees may exceed the amounts calculated in accordance with paragraph 6.1.

6.6. If the amount in dispute is not quantified, the arbitral tribunal's fees shall be fixed by HKIAC, taking into account the circumstances of the case.

7. Lien on Award

HKIAC and the arbitral tribunal shall have a lien over any awards issued by the tribunal to secure the payment of their outstanding fees and expenses, and may accordingly refuse to release any such awards to the parties until all such fees and expenses have been paid in full, whether jointly or by one or other of the parties.

8. Governing law

The terms of this Schedule and any non-contractual obligation arising out of or in connection with it shall be governed by and construed in accordance with Hong Kong law.

Schedule 4
Emergency Arbitrator Procedures

Effective 1 November 2013

1.

A party requiring Emergency Relief may, concurrent with or following the filing of a Notice of Arbitration but prior to the constitution of the arbitral tribunal, submit an application (the 'Application') for the appointment of an emergency arbitrator (the 'Emergency Arbitrator') to HKIAC.

2.

The Application shall be submitted in accordance with any of the means specified in Article 2.1 of the Rules. The Application shall include the following information:

a. the names and (in so far as known) the addresses, telephone and fax numbers, and email addresses of the parties to the Application and of their counsel;

b. a description of the circumstances giving rise to the Application and of the underlying dispute referred to arbitration;

c. a statement of the Emergency Relief sought;

d. the reasons why the applicant needs the Emergency Relief on an urgent basis that cannot await the constitution of an arbitral tribunal;

e. the reasons why the applicant is entitled to such Emergency Relief;

f. any relevant agreement(s) and, in particular, the arbitration agreement(s);

g. comments on the language, the seat of the Emergency Relief proceedings, and the applicable law;

h. confirmation of payment, by cheque or transfer to the account of HKIAC, of the amount referred to in paragraph 6 of this Schedule (the 'Application Deposit'); and

i. confirmation that copies of the Application and any exhibits included therewith have been or are being served simultaneously on all other parties to the arbitration by one or more means of service to be identified in such confirmation.

3.

The Application may contain such other documents or information as the applicant considers appropriate or as may contribute to the efficient examination of the Application.

4.

Two copies of the Application shall be provided, one copy for the Emergency Arbitrator and one copy for HKIAC.

5.

If HKIAC determines that it should accept the Application, HKIAC shall seek to appoint an Emergency Arbitrator within two days after receipt of both the Application and the Application Deposit.

6.

The Application Deposit is the amount set by HKIAC, as stated on HKIAC's website on the date the Application is submitted. The Application Deposit consists of HKIAC's administrative expenses and the Emergency Arbitrator's fees and expenses. The Emergency Arbitrator's fees shall be determined by HKIAC by reference to his or her hourly rate subject to the terms set out in Schedule 2. HKIAC may, at any time during the Emergency Relief proceedings, decide to increase the Emergency Arbitrator's fees or HKIAC's administrative expenses, taking into account, inter alia, the nature of the case and the nature and amount of work performed by the Emergency Arbitrator and HKIAC. If the party which submitted the Application fails to pay the increased fees and/or expenses within the time limit fixed by HKIAC, the Application shall be dismissed.

7.

Once the Emergency Arbitrator has been appointed, HKIAC shall so notify the parties to the Application and shall transmit the file to the Emergency Arbitrator. Thereafter, all written communications from the parties shall be submitted directly to the Emergency Arbitrator with a copy to the other party to the Application and HKIAC. A copy of any written communications from the Emergency Arbitrator to the parties shall also be copied to HKIAC.

8.

Article 11 of the Rules shall apply to the Emergency Arbitrator, except that the time limits set out in Articles 11.7 and 11.9 are shortened to three days.

9.

Where an Emergency Arbitrator dies, has been successfully challenged, has been otherwise removed, or has resigned, HKIAC shall seek to appoint a substitute Emergency Arbitrator within two days. If an Emergency Arbitrator withdraws or a party agrees to terminate an Emergency Arbitrator's appointment under paragraph 8 of this Schedule, no acceptance of the validity of any ground referred to in Article 11.6 of the Rules shall be implied. If the Emergency Arbitrator is replaced, the Emergency Relief proceedings shall resume at the stage where the Emergency Arbitrator was replaced or ceased to perform his or her functions, unless the substitute Emergency Arbitrator decides otherwise.

10.

If the parties have agreed on the seat of arbitration, such seat shall be the seat of the Emergency Relief proceedings. Where the parties have not agreed on the seat of arbitration, and without prejudice to the arbitral tribunal's determination of the seat of arbitration pursuant to Article 14.1 of the Rules, the seat of the Emergency Relief proceedings shall be Hong Kong.

11.

Taking into account the urgency inherent in the Emergency Relief proceedings and ensuring that each party has a reasonable opportunity to be heard on the Application, the Emergency Arbitrator may conduct such proceedings in such a manner as the Emergency Arbitrator considers appropriate.

The Emergency Arbitrator shall have the power to rule on objections that the Emergency Arbitrator has no jurisdiction, including any objections with respect to the existence, validity or scope of the arbitration clause(s) or of the separate arbitration agreement(s), and shall resolve any disputes over the applicability of this Schedule.

12.

Any decision, order or award of the Emergency Arbitrator on the Application (the 'Emergency Decision') shall be made within fifteen days from the date on which HKIAC transmitted the file to the Emergency Arbitrator. This period of time may be extended by agreement of the parties or, in appropriate circumstances, by HKIAC.

13.

The Emergency Decision may be made even if in the meantime the file has been transmitted to the arbitral tribunal.

14.

Any Emergency Decision shall:

a. be made in writing;

b. state the date when it was made and summary reasons upon which the Emergency Decision is based (including a determination on whether the Application is admissible under Article 23.1 of the Rules and whether the Emergency Arbitrator has jurisdiction to grant the Emergency Relief); and

c. be signed by the Emergency Arbitrator.

15.

Any Emergency Decision shall fix the costs of the Emergency Relief proceedings and decide which of the parties shall bear them or in what proportion they shall be borne by the parties, subject always to the power of the arbitral tribunal to determine finally the apportionment of such costs in accordance with Article 33 of the Rules. The costs of the Emergency Relief proceedings include HKIAC's administrative expenses, the Emergency Arbitrator's fees and expenses and the reasonable and other legal costs incurred by the parties for the Emergency Relief proceedings.

16.

Any Emergency Decision shall have the same effect as an interim measure granted pursuant to Article 23 of the Rules and shall be binding on the parties when rendered. By agreeing to arbitration under these Rules, the parties undertake to comply with any Emergency Decision without delay.

17.

The Emergency Arbitrator shall be entitled to order the provision of appropriate security by the party seeking Emergency Relief.

18.

Any Emergency Decision may, upon a reasoned request by a party, be modified, suspended or terminated by the Emergency Arbitrator or the arbitral tribunal (once constituted).

19.

Any Emergency Decision ceases to be binding:

a. if the Emergency Arbitrator or the arbitral tribunal so decides;

b. upon the arbitral tribunal rendering a final award, unless the arbitral tribunal expressly decides otherwise;

c. upon the withdrawal of all claims or the termination of the arbitration before the rendering of a final award; or

d. if the arbitral tribunal is not constituted within 90 days from the date of the Emergency Decision. This period of time may be extended by agreement of the parties or, in appropriate circumstances, by HKIAC.

20.

Subject to paragraph 13 of this Schedule, the Emergency Arbitrator shall have no further power to act once the arbitral tribunal is constituted.

21.

The Emergency Arbitrator may not act as arbitrator in any arbitration relating to the dispute that gave rise to the Application and in respect of which the Emergency Arbitrator has acted, unless otherwise agreed by the parties to the arbitration.

22.

The Emergency Arbitrator Procedures are not intended to prevent any party from seeking urgent interim or conservatory measures from a competent judicial authority at any time.

23.

In all matters not expressly provided for in this Schedule, the Emergency Arbitrator shall act in the spirit of the Rules.

24.

The Emergency Arbitrator shall make every reasonable effort to ensure that an Emergency Decision is valid.

Appendix 11
Agreement Concerning Mutual Enforcement of Arbitral Awards Between the Mainland and the Hong Kong Special Administrative Region[267]

In accordance with the provision of Article 95 of the Basic Law of the Hong Kong Special Administrative Region of the People's Republic of China and through mutual consultations between the Supreme People's Court and the Government of the Hong Kong Special Administrative Region (HKSAR), the Courts of the HKSAR agree to enforce the awards made pursuant to the Arbitration Law of the People's Republic of China by the arbitral authorities in the Mainland (the list to be supplied by the Legislative Affairs Office of the State Council through the Hong Kong and Macao Affairs Office of the State Council) and the People's Courts of the Mainland agree to enforce the awards made in the HKSAR pursuant to the Arbitration Ordinance of the HKSAR. The following arrangement is made in respect of mutual enforcement of arbitral awards by the Mainland and the HKSAR:

1. Where a party fails to comply with an arbitral award, whether made in the Mainland or in the HKSAR, the other party may apply to the relevant court in the place where the party against whom the application is filed is domiciled or in the place where the property of the said party is situated to enforce the award.

2. For the purpose of Article 1 above, 'relevant court', in the case of the Mainland, means the Intermediate People's Court of the place where the party against whom the application is filed is domiciled or the place in which the property of the

267 <www.doj.gov.hk/eng/topical/pdf/mainlandmutual2e.pdf>.

said party is situated and, in the case of the HKSAR, means the High Court of the HKSAR.

If the place where the party against whom the application is filed is domiciled or the place where the property of the said party is situated falls within the jurisdiction of different Intermediate People's Courts of the Mainland the applicant may apply to any one of the People's Courts to enforce the award. The applicant shall not file his application with two or more People's Courts.

If the place where the party against whom the application is filed is domiciled or the place where the property of the said party is situated is in the Mainland as well as in the HKSAR, the applicant shall not file applications with relevant courts of the two places at the same time. Only when the result of the enforcement of the award by the court of one place is insufficient to satisfy the liabilities may the applicant apply to the court of another place for enforcement of the outstanding liabilities. The total amount recovered from enforcing the award in the courts of the two places one after the other shall in no case exceed the amount awarded.

3. The applicant shall submit the following documents in applying to the relevant court for enforcement of an award, made either in the Mainland or in the HKSAR:

i) An application for enforcement;

ii) The arbitral award;

iii) The arbitration agreement.

4. An application for enforcement shall contain the following:

(1) Where the applicant is a natural person, his name and address; where the applicant is a legal entity or any other organisation, its name and address and the name of its legally authorised representative;

(2) Where the party against whom the application is filed is a natural person, his name and address; where the party against whom the application is filed is a legal entity or any other organisation, its name and address and the name of its legally authorized representative;

(3) Where the applicant is a legal entity or any other organisation, a copy of the enterprise registration record shall be submitted. Where the applicant is a foreign legal entity or any other foreign organisation, the corresponding notarisation and authentication material shall be submitted;

(4) The grounds for and the particulars of the application for enforcement; the place where the property of the party against whom the application is filed is situated and the status of the property.

Application for enforcement made in the Mainland shall be in the Chinese language. If the arbitral award or arbitration agreement is not in the Chinese language, the applicant shall submit a duly certified Chinese translation of it.

5. The time limit for an applicant to apply to the relevant court for enforcement of the arbitral award, whether made in the Mainland or in the HKSAR, shall be governed by the law on limitation period of the place of enforcement.

6. Upon receipt of an application for enforcement from an applicant, the relevant court shall handle the application and enforce the award according to the legal procedure of the place of enforcement.

7. The party against whom an application is filed may, after receiving notice of an arbitral award, whether made in the Mainland or in the HKSAR, adduce evidence to show any of the situations set out below. Upon such evidence being examined and any of the said situations being found proved,

the relevant court may refuse to enforce the arbitral award:

(1) A party to the arbitration agreement was, under the law applicable to him, under some incapacity, or the arbitration agreement was not valid under the law to which the parties subjected it, or, failing any indication thereon, under the law of the place in which the arbitral award was made;

(2) The party against whom the application is filed was not given proper notice of the appointment of the arbitrator or was otherwise unable to present his case;

(3) The award deals with a difference not contemplated by or not falling within the terms of the submission to arbitration, or the award contains decisions on matters beyond the scope of the submission to arbitration. However, if the award contains decisions on matters submitted to arbitration that can be separated from those not so submitted, that part of the award which contains decisions on matters submitted to arbitration shall be enforced;

(4) The composition of the arbitral authority or the arbitral procedure was not in accordance with agreement of the parties or, failing such agreement, with the law of the place where the arbitration took place;

(5) The award has not yet become binding on the parties, or has been set aside or suspended by the court or in accordance with the law of the place where the arbitration took place;

If the relevant court finds that under the law of the place of enforcement, the dispute is incapable of being settled by arbitration, then the court may refuse to enforce the award

The enforcement of the award may be refused if the court of the Mainland holds that the enforcement of the arbitral award in the Mainland would be contrary to the public interests of the Mainland, or if the court of the HKSAR decides that the enforcement of the arbitral award in Hong Kong would be contrary to the public policy of the HKSAR.

8. The applicant, in applying to the relevant court to enforce an arbitral award, whether made in the Mainland or in the

HKSAR, shall pay the enforcement fees prescribed by the court of enforcement.

9. Applications made after 1st July, 1997 for enforcement of arbitral awards, whether made in the Mainland or in the HKSAR, shall be enforced according to this Arrangement.

10. In respect of applications for enforcement made between 1st July, 1997 and the coming into force of this Arrangement, both parties agree that:

Where the applications for enforcement cannot, for some reasons, be made to the court of the Mainland or the court of the HKSAR between 1st July, 1997 and the coming into force of this Arrangement, then, in the case of the applicant being a legal entity or any other organization, the application for enforcement may be made within six months after this Arrangement comes into force and, in the case of the applicant being a natural person, the application for enforcement may be made within one year after this Arrangement comes into force.

Parties to cases which the court of the Mainland or the HKSAR had, between 1st July, 1997 and the coming into force of this Arrangement, refused to handle or to enforce the award, shall be allowed to make fresh application for enforcement.

11. Any problem arising in the course of implementing this Arrangement and any amendment to this Arrangement shall be resolved through consultations between the Supreme People's Court and the Government of the HKSAR.

Appendix 12
Supreme People's Court Notice of Relevant Issues on the Enforcement of Hong Kong Arbitral Awards in the Mainland[268]

Fa [2009] No. 415

The Higher People's Courts of all provinces, autonomous regions and municipalities directly under the Central Government, the Production and Construction Corps Branch Court of the Higher People's Court of Xinjiang Uygur Autonomous Region,

Recently, the People's Courts or parties concerned have asked this Court whether the parties concerned can apply for enforcement in the Mainland of ad hoc arbitral awards made in the Hong Kong Special Administrative Region and the arbitral awards made in Hong Kong by the International Court of Arbitration of the International Chamber of Commerce pursuant to the 'Arrangement Concerning Mutual Enforcement of Arbitral Awards between the Mainland and the Hong Kong Special Administrative Region' (hereinafter referred to as 'the Arrangement'). In order to ensure the proper application and uniform enforcement of the Arrangement by the People's Courts in dealing with such cases, notice of the relevant issues is hereby given as follows:

Where an application has been made by a party to the People's Court for enforcement of an ad hoc arbitral award made in the Hong Kong Special Administrative Region or an arbitral award made in the Hong Kong Special Administrative Region by the International Court of Arbitration of the

268 <www.doj.gov.hk/eng/topical/pdf/notice_enforcement_HK_arbitral_awards_e.pdf>.

International Chamber of Commerce or other foreign arbitration institutions, the People's Court should examine it in accordance with the provisions of the Arrangement. In the absence of any situations set out in Article 7 of the Arrangement, the arbitral award shall be enforced in the Mainland.

(Official Seal of the

Supreme People's Court of the People's Republic of China affixed)

30 December 2009

Appendix 13
Singapore International Arbitration Centre (SIAC)
Arbitration Rules[269]

6th Edition, 1 August 2016

Rule 1

Scope of Application and Interpretation

1.1. Where the parties have agreed to refer their disputes to SIAC for arbitration or to arbitration in accordance with the SIAC Rules, the parties shall be deemed to have agreed that the arbitration shall be conducted pursuant to and administered by SIAC in accordance with these Rules.

1.2. These Rules shall come into force on 1 August 2016 and, unless otherwise agreed by the parties, shall apply to any arbitration which is commenced on or after that date.

1.3. In these Rules:

'Award' includes a partial, interim or final award and an award of an Emergency Arbitrator;

'Committee of the Court' means a committee consisting of not less than two members of the Court appointed by the President (which may include the President);

'Court' means the Court of Arbitration of SIAC and includes a Committee of the Court;

'Emergency Arbitrator' means an arbitrator appointed in accordance with paragraph 3 of Schedule 1;

'Practice Notes' mean the guidelines published by the Registrar from time to time to supplement, regulate and implement these Rules;

'President' means the President of the Court and includes any Vice President and the Registrar;

---

269 Arbitration Rules of the Singapore International Arbitration Centre SIAC Rules (6th Edition, 1 August 2016)

'Registrar' means the Registrar of the Court and includes any Deputy Registrar;

'Rules' means the Arbitration Rules of the Singapore International Arbitration Centre (6th Edition, 1 August 2016);

'SIAC' means the Singapore International Arbitration Centre; and

'Tribunal' includes a sole arbitrator or all the arbitrators where more than one arbitrator is appointed.

Any pronoun in these Rules shall be understood to be gender-neutral. Any singular noun shall be understood to refer to the plural in the appropriate circumstances.

Rule 2

Notice and Calculation of Periods of Time

2.1. For the purposes of these Rules, any notice, communication or proposal shall be in writing. Any such notice, communication or proposal may be delivered by hand, registered post or courier service, or transmitted by any form of electronic communication (including electronic mail and facsimile), or delivered by any other appropriate means that provides a record of its delivery. Any notice, communication or proposal shall be deemed to have been received if it is delivered: (i) to the addressee personally or to its authorised representative; (ii) to the addressee's habitual residence, place of business or designated address; (iii) to any address agreed by the parties; (iv) according to the practice of the parties in prior dealings; or (v) if, after reasonable efforts, none of these can be found, then at the addressee's last-known residence or place of business.

2.2. Any notice, communication or proposal shall be deemed to have been received on the day it is delivered in accordance with Rule 2.1.

2.3. For the purpose of calculating any period of time under these Rules, such period shall begin to run on the day following the day when a notice, communication or proposal is deemed to have been received. Unless the Registrar or the Tribunal determines otherwise, any period of time under these Rules is to be calculated in accordance with Singapore Standard Time (GMT +8).

2.4. Any non-business days at the place of receipt shall be included in calculating any period of time under these Rules. If the last day of any period of time under these Rules is not a business day at the place of receipt in accordance with Rule 2.1, the period is extended until the first business day which follows.

2.5. The parties shall file with the Registrar a copy of any notice, communication or proposal concerning the arbitral proceedings.

2.6. Except as provided in these Rules, the Registrar may at any time extend or abbreviate any time limits prescribed under these Rules.

Rule 3

Notice of Arbitration

3.1. A party wishing to commence an arbitration under these Rules (the 'Claimant') shall file with the Registrar a Notice of Arbitration which shall include:

a. a demand that the dispute be referred to arbitration;

b. the names, addresses, telephone numbers, facsimile numbers and electronic mail addresses, if known, of the parties to the arbitration and their representatives, if any;

c. a reference to the arbitration agreement invoked and a copy of the arbitration agreement;

d. a reference to the contract or other instrument (e.g. investment treaty) out of or in relation to which the dispute arises and, where possible, a copy of the contract or other instrument;

e. a brief statement describing the nature and circumstances of the dispute, specifying the relief claimed and, where possible, an initial quantification of the claim amount;

f. a statement of any matters which the parties have previously agreed as to the conduct of the arbitration or with respect to which the Claimant wishes to make a proposal;

g. a proposal for the number of arbitrators if not specified in the arbitration agreement;

h. unless otherwise agreed by the parties, the nomination of an arbitrator if the arbitration agreement provides for three arbitrators, or a proposal for a sole arbitrator if the arbitration agreement provides for a sole arbitrator;

i. any comment as to the applicable rules of law;

j. any comment as to the language of the arbitration; and

k. payment of the requisite filing fee under these Rules.

3.2. The Notice of Arbitration may also include the Statement of Claim referred to in Rule 20.2.

3.3. The date of receipt of the complete Notice of Arbitration by the Registrar shall be deemed to be the date of commencement of the arbitration. For the avoidance of doubt, the Notice of Arbitration is deemed to be complete when all the requirements of Rule 3.1 and Rule 6.1(b) (if applicable) are fulfilled or when the Registrar determines that there has been substantial compliance with such requirements. SIAC shall notify the parties of the commencement of the arbitration.

3.4. The Claimant shall, at the same time as it files the Notice of Arbitration with the Registrar, send a copy of the Notice of Arbitration to the Respondent, and shall notify the Registrar that it has done so, specifying the mode of service employed and the date of service.

Rule 4

Response to the Notice of Arbitration

4.1. The Respondent shall file a Response with the Registrar within 14 days of receipt of the Notice of Arbitration. The Response shall include:

a. a confirmation or denial of all or part of the claims, including, where possible, any plea that the Tribunal lacks jurisdiction;

b. a brief statement describing the nature and circumstances of any counterclaim, specifying the relief claimed and, where possible, an initial quantification of the counterclaim amount;

c. any comment in response to any statements contained in the Notice of Arbitration under Rule 3.1 or any comment with respect to the matters covered in such Rule;

d. unless otherwise agreed by the parties, the nomination of an arbitrator if the arbitration agreement provides for three arbitrators or, if the arbitration agreement provides for a sole arbitrator, comments on the Claimant's proposal for a sole arbitrator or a counter-proposal; and

e. payment of the requisite filing fee under these Rules for any counterclaim.

4.2. The Response may also include the Statement of Defence and a Statement of Counterclaim, as referred to in Rule 20.3 and Rule 20.4.

4.3. The Respondent shall, at the same time as it files the Response with the Registrar, send a copy of the Response to the Claimant, and shall notify the Registrar that it has done so, specifying the mode of service employed and the date of service.

Rule 5

Expedited Procedure

5.1. Prior to the constitution of the Tribunal, a party may file an application with the Registrar for the arbitral proceedings to be conducted in accordance with the Expedited Procedure under this Rule, provided that any of the following criteria is satisfied:

a. the amount in dispute does not exceed the equivalent amount of S$6,000,000, representing the aggregate of the claim, counterclaim and any defence of set-off;

b. the parties so agree; or

c. in cases of exceptional urgency.

The party applying for the arbitral proceedings to be conducted in accordance with the Expedited Procedure under this Rule 5.1 shall, at the same time as it files an application for the proceedings to be conducted in accordance with the Expedited Procedure with the Registrar, send a copy of the application to the other party and shall notify the Registrar that it has done so, specifying the mode of service employed and the date of service.

5.2. Where a party has filed an application with the Registrar under Rule 5.1, and where the President determines, after considering the views of the parties, and having regard to the circumstances of the case, that the arbitral proceedings shall be conducted in accordance with the Expedited Procedure, the following procedure shall apply:

a. the Registrar may abbreviate any time limits under these Rules;

b. the case shall be referred to a sole arbitrator, unless the President determines otherwise;

c. the Tribunal may, in consultation with the parties, decide if the dispute is to be decided on the basis of documentary evidence only, or if a hearing is required for the examination of any witness and expert witness as well as for any oral argument;

d. the final Award shall be made within six months from the date when the Tribunal is constituted unless, in exceptional circumstances, the Registrar extends the time for making such final Award; and

e. the Tribunal may state the reasons upon which the final Award is based in summary form, unless the parties have agreed that no reasons are to be given.

5.3. By agreeing to arbitration under these Rules, the parties agree that, where arbitral proceedings are conducted in accordance with the Expedited Procedure under this Rule 5, the rules and procedures set forth in Rule 5.2 shall apply even in cases where the arbitration agreement contains contrary terms.

5.4. Upon application by a party, and after giving the parties the opportunity to be heard, the Tribunal may, having regard to any further information as may subsequently become available, and in consultation with the Registrar, order that the arbitral proceedings shall no longer be conducted in accordance with the Expedited Procedure. Where the Tribunal decides to grant an application under this Rule 5.4, the arbitration shall continue to be conducted by the same Tribunal that was constituted to conduct the arbitration in accordance with the Expedited Procedure.

Rule 6

Multiple Contracts

6.1. Where there are disputes arising out of or in connection with more than one contract, the Claimant may:

a. file a Notice of Arbitration in respect of each arbitration agreement invoked and concurrently submit an application to consolidate the arbitrations pursuant to Rule 8.1; or

b. file a single Notice of Arbitration in respect of all the arbitration agreements invoked which shall include a statement identifying each contract and arbitration agreement invoked and a description of how the applicable criteria under Rule 8.1 are satisfied. The Claimant shall be deemed to have commenced multiple arbitrations, one in respect of each arbitration agreement invoked, and the Notice of Arbitration under this Rule 6.1(b) shall be deemed to be an application to consolidate all such arbitrations pursuant to Rule 8.1.

6.2. Where the Claimant has filed two or more Notices of Arbitration pursuant to Rule 6.1(a), the Registrar shall accept payment of a single filing fee under these Rules for all the arbitrations sought to be consolidated. Where the Court rejects the application for consolidation, in whole or in part, the Claimant shall be required to make payment of the requisite filing fee under these Rules in respect of each arbitration that has not been consolidated.

6.3. Where the Claimant has filed a single Notice of Arbitration pursuant to Rule 6.1(b) and the Court rejects the application for consolidation, in whole or in part, it shall file a Notice of Arbitration in respect of each arbitration that has not been consolidated, and the Claimant shall be required to make payment of the requisite filing fee under these Rules in respect of each arbitration that has not been consolidated.

Rule 7

Joinder of Additional Parties

7.1. Prior to the constitution of the Tribunal, a party or non-party to the arbitration may file an application with the Registrar for one or more additional parties to be joined in an arbitration pending under these Rules as a Claimant or a Respondent, provided that any of the following criteria is satisfied:

a. the additional party to be joined is prima facie bound by the arbitration agreement; or

b. all parties, including the additional party to be joined, have consented to the joinder of the additional party.

7.2. An application for joinder under Rule 7.1 shall include:

a. the case reference number of the pending arbitration;

b. the names, addresses, telephone numbers, facsimile numbers and electronic mail addresses, if known, of all parties, including the additional party to be joined, and their representatives, if any, and any arbitrators who have been nominated or appointed in the pending arbitration;

c. whether the additional party is to be joined as a Claimant or a Respondent;

d. the information specified in Rule 3.1(c) and Rule 3.1(d);

e. if the application is being made under Rule 7.1(b), identification of the relevant agreement and, where possible, a copy of such agreement; and

f. a brief statement of the facts and legal basis supporting the application.

The application for joinder is deemed to be complete when all the requirements of this Rule 7.2 are fulfilled or when the Registrar determines that there has been substantial compliance with such requirements. SIAC shall notify all parties, including the additional party to be joined, when the application for joinder is complete.

7.3. The party or non-party applying for joinder under Rule 7.1 shall, at the same time as it files an application for joinder with the Registrar, send a copy of the application to all parties, including the additional party to be joined, and shall notify the Registrar that it has done so, specifying the mode of service employed and the date of service.

7.4. The Court shall, after considering the views of all parties, including the additional party to be joined, and having regard to the circumstances of the case, decide whether to grant, in whole or in part, any application for joinder under Rule 7.1. The Court's decision to grant an application for joinder under this Rule 7.4 is without prejudice to the Tribunal's power to subsequently decide any question as to its jurisdiction arising from such decision. The Court's decision to reject an application for joinder under this Rule 7.4, in whole or in part, is without prejudice to any party's or non-party's right to apply to the Tribunal for joinder pursuant to Rule 7.8.

7.5. Where an application for joinder is granted under Rule 7.4, the date of receipt of the complete application for joinder shall be deemed to be the date of commencement of the arbitration in respect of the additional party.

7.6. Where an application for joinder is granted under Rule 7.4, the Court may revoke the appointment of any arbitrators appointed prior to the decision on joinder. Unless otherwise agreed by all parties, including the additional party joined, Rule 9 to Rule 12 shall apply as appropriate, and the respective timelines thereunder shall run from the date of receipt of the Court's decision under Rule 7.4.

7.7. The Court's decision to revoke the appointment of any arbitrator under Rule 7.6 is without prejudice to the validity of any act done or order or Award made by the arbitrator before his appointment was revoked.

7.8. After the constitution of the Tribunal, a party or non-party to the arbitration may apply to the Tribunal for one or more additional parties to be joined in an arbitration pending under these Rules as a Claimant or a Respondent, provided that any of the following criteria is satisfied:

a. the additional party to be joined is prima facie bound by the arbitration agreement; or

b. all parties, including the additional party to be joined, have consented to the joinder of the additional party.

Where appropriate, an application to the Tribunal under this Rule 7.8 may be filed with the Registrar.

7.9. Subject to any specific directions of the Tribunal, the provisions of Rule 7.2 shall apply, *mutatis mutandis*, to an application for joinder under Rule 7.8.

7.10. The Tribunal shall, after giving all parties, including the additional party to be joined, the opportunity to be heard, and having regard to the circumstances of the case, decide whether to grant, in whole or in part, any application for joinder under Rule 7.8. The Tribunal's decision to grant an application for joinder under this Rule 7.10 is without prejudice to its power to subsequently decide any question as to its jurisdiction arising from such decision.

7.11. Where an application for joinder is granted under Rule 7.10, the date of receipt by the Tribunal or the Registrar, as the case may be, of the complete application for joinder shall be deemed to be the date of commencement of the arbitration in respect of the additional party.

7.12. Where an application for joinder is granted under Rule 7.4 or Rule 7.10, any party who has not nominated an arbitrator or otherwise participated in the constitution of the Tribunal shall be deemed to have waived its right to nominate an arbitrator or otherwise participate in the constitution of the Tribunal, without prejudice to the right of such party to challenge an arbitrator pursuant to Rule 14.

7.13. Where an application for joinder is granted under Rule 7.4 or Rule 7.10, the requisite filing fee under these Rules shall be payable for any additional claims or counterclaims.

Rule 8

Consolidation

8.1. Prior to the constitution of any Tribunal in the arbitrations sought to be consolidated, a party may file an application with the Registrar to consolidate two or more arbitrations pending under these Rules into a single arbitration, provided that any of the following criteria is satisfied in respect of the arbitrations to be consolidated:

a. all parties have agreed to the consolidation;

b. all the claims in the arbitrations are made under the same arbitration agreement; or

c. the arbitration agreements are compatible, and: (i) the disputes arise out of the same legal relationship(s); (ii) the disputes arise out of contracts consisting of a principal contract and its ancillary contract(s); or (iii) the disputes arise out of the same transaction or series of transactions.

8.2. An application for consolidation under Rule 8.1 shall include:

a. the case reference numbers of the arbitrations sought to be consolidated;

b. the names, addresses, telephone numbers, facsimile numbers and electronic mail addresses, if known, of all parties and their representatives, if any, and any arbitrators who have been nominated or appointed in the arbitrations sought to be consolidated;

c. the information specified in Rule 3.1(c) and Rule 3.1(d);

d. if the application is being made under Rule 8.1(a), identification of the relevant agreement and, where possible, a copy of such agreement; and

e. a brief statement of the facts and legal basis supporting the application.

8.3. The party applying for consolidation under Rule 8.1 shall, at the same time as it files an application for consolidation with the Registrar, send a copy of the application to all parties and shall notify the Registrar that it has done so, specifying the mode of service employed and the date of service.

8.4. The Court shall, after considering the views of all parties, and having regard to the circumstances of the case, decide whether to grant, in whole or in part, any application for consolidation under Rule 8.1. The Court's decision to grant an application for consolidation under this Rule 8.4 is without prejudice to the Tribunal's power to subsequently decide any question as to its jurisdiction arising from such decision. The Court's decision to reject an application for consolidation under this Rule 8.4, in whole or in part, is without prejudice to any party's right to apply to the Tribunal for consolidation pursuant to Rule 8.7. Any arbitrations that are not consolidated shall continue as separate arbitrations under these Rules.

8.5. Where the Court decides to consolidate two or more arbitrations under Rule 8.4, the arbitrations shall be consolidated into the arbitration that is deemed by the Registrar to have commenced first, unless otherwise agreed by all parties or the Court decides otherwise having regard to the circumstances of the case.

8.6. Where an application for consolidation is granted under Rule 8.4, the Court may revoke the appointment of any arbitrators appointed prior to the decision on consolidation. Unless otherwise agreed by all parties, Rule 9 to Rule 12 shall apply as appropriate, and the respective timelines thereunder shall run from the date of receipt of the Court's decision under Rule 8.4.

8.7. After the constitution of any Tribunal in the arbitrations sought to be consolidated, a party may apply to the Tribunal to consolidate two or more arbitrations pending under these Rules into a single arbitration, provided that any of the following criteria is satisfied in respect of the arbitrations to be consolidated:

a. all parties have agreed to the consolidation;

b. all the claims in the arbitrations are made under the same arbitration agreement, and the same Tribunal has been constituted in each of the arbitrations or no Tribunal has been constituted in the other arbitration(s); or

c. the arbitration agreements are compatible, the same Tribunal has been constituted in each of the arbitrations or no Tribunal has been constituted in the other arbitration(s), and: (i) the disputes arise out of the same legal relationship(s); (ii) the disputes arise out of contracts consisting of a principal contract and its ancillary contract(s); or (iii) the disputes arise out of the same transaction or series of transactions.

8.8. Subject to any specific directions of the Tribunal, the provisions of Rule 8.2 shall apply, *mutatis mutandis,* to an application for consolidation under Rule 8.7.

8.9. The Tribunal shall, after giving all parties the opportunity to be heard, and having regard to the circumstances of the case, decide whether to grant, in whole or in part, any application for consolidation under Rule 8.7. The Tribunal's decision to grant an application for consolidation under this Rule 8.9 is without prejudice to its power to subsequently decide any question as to its jurisdiction arising from such decision. Any arbitrations that are not consolidated shall continue as separate arbitrations under these Rules.

8.10. Where an application for consolidation is granted under Rule 8.9, the Court may revoke the appointment of any arbitrators appointed prior to the decision on consolidation.

8.11. The Court's decision to revoke the appointment of any arbitrator under Rule 8.6 or Rule 8.10 is without prejudice to the validity of any act done or order or Award made by the arbitrator before his appointment was revoked.

8.12. Where an application for consolidation is granted under Rule 8.4 or Rule 8.9, any party who has not nominated an arbitrator or otherwise participated in the constitution of the Tribunal shall be deemed to have waived its right to nominate an arbitrator or otherwise participate in the constitution of the Tribunal, without prejudice to the right of such party to challenge an arbitrator pursuant to Rule

Rule 9

Number and Appointment of Arbitrators

9.1. A sole arbitrator shall be appointed in any arbitration under these Rules unless the parties have otherwise agreed; or it appears to the Registrar, giving due regard to any proposals by the parties, that the complexity, the quantum involved or other relevant circumstances of the dispute, warrants the appointment of three arbitrators.

9.2. If the parties have agreed that any arbitrator is to be appointed by one or more of the parties, or by any third person including by the arbitrators already appointed, that agreement shall be deemed an agreement to nominate an arbitrator under these Rules.

9.3. In all cases, the arbitrators nominated by the parties, or by any third person including by the arbitrators already appointed, shall be subject to appointment by the President in his discretion.

9.4. The President shall appoint an arbitrator as soon as practicable. Any decision by the President to appoint an arbitrator under these Rules shall be final and not subject to appeal.

9.5. The President may appoint any nominee whose appointment has already been suggested or proposed by any party.

9.6. The terms of appointment of each arbitrator shall be fixed by the Registrar in accordance with these Rules and any Practice Notes for the time being in force, or in accordance with the agreement of the parties.

Rule 10

Sole Arbitrator

10.1. If a sole arbitrator is to be appointed, either party may propose to the other party the names of one or more persons to serve as the sole arbitrator. Where the parties have reached an agreement on the nomination of a sole arbitrator, Rule 9.3 shall apply.

10.2. If within 21 days after the date of commencement of the arbitration, or within the period otherwise agreed by the parties or set by the Registrar, the parties have not reached an agreement on the nomination of a sole arbitrator, or if at any time either party so requests, the President shall appoint the sole arbitrator.

Rule 11

Three Arbitrators

11.1. If three arbitrators are to be appointed, each party shall nominate one arbitrator.

11.2. If a party fails to make a nomination of an arbitrator within 14 days after receipt of a party's nomination of an arbitrator, or within the period otherwise agreed by the parties or set by the Registrar, the President shall proceed to appoint an arbitrator on its behalf.

11.3. Unless the parties have agreed upon another procedure for appointing the third arbitrator, or if such agreed procedure does not result in a nomination within the period agreed by the parties or set by the Registrar, the President shall appoint the third arbitrator, who shall be the presiding arbitrator.

Rule 12

Multi-party Appointment of Arbitrator(s)

12.1. Where there are more than two parties to the arbitration, and a sole arbitrator is to be appointed, the parties may agree to jointly nominate the sole arbitrator. In the absence of such joint nomination having been made within 28 days of the date of commencement of the arbitration or within the period otherwise agreed by the parties or set by the Registrar, the President shall appoint the sole arbitrator.

12.2. Where there are more than two parties to the arbitration, and three arbitrators are to be appointed, the Claimant(s) shall jointly nominate one arbitrator and the Respondent(s) shall jointly nominate one arbitrator. The third arbitrator, who shall be the presiding arbitrator, shall be appointed in accordance with Rule 11.3. In the absence of both such joint nominations having been made within 28 days of the date of commencement of the arbitration or within the period otherwise agreed by the parties or set by the Registrar, the President shall appoint all three arbitrators and shall designate one of them to be the presiding arbitrator.

Rule 13
Qualifications of Arbitrators

13.1. Any arbitrator appointed in an arbitration under these Rules, whether or not nominated by the parties, shall be and remain at all times independent and impartial.

13.2. In appointing an arbitrator under these Rules, the President shall have due regard to any qualifications required of the arbitrator by the agreement of the parties and to such considerations that are relevant to the impartiality or independence of the arbitrator.

13.3. The President shall also consider whether the arbitrator has sufficient availability to determine the case in a prompt and efficient manner that is appropriate given the nature of the arbitration.

13.4. A nominated arbitrator shall disclose to the parties and to the Registrar any circumstances that may give rise to justifiable doubts as to his impartiality or independence as soon as reasonably practicable and in any event before his appointment.

13.5. An arbitrator shall immediately disclose to the parties, to the other arbitrators and to the Registrar any circumstances that may give rise to justifiable doubts as to his impartiality or independence that may be discovered or arise during the arbitration.

13.6. No party or person acting on behalf of a party shall have any *ex parte* communication relating to the case with any arbitrator or with any candidate for appointment as party-nominated arbitrator, except to advise the candidate of the general nature of the controversy and of the anticipated proceedings; to discuss the candidate's qualifications, availability or independence in relation to the parties; or to discuss the suitability of candidates for selection as the presiding arbitrator where the parties or party-nominated arbitrators are to participate in that selection. No party or person acting on behalf of a party shall have any *ex parte* communication relating to the case with any candidate for presiding arbitrator.

Rule 14

Challenge of Arbitrators

14.1. Any arbitrator may be challenged if circumstances exist that give rise to justifiable doubts as to the arbitrator's impartiality or independence or if the arbitrator does not possess any requisite qualification on which the parties have agreed.

14.2. A party may challenge the arbitrator nominated by it only for reasons of which it becomes aware after the appointment has been made.

Rule 15

Notice of Challenge

15.1. A party that intends to challenge an arbitrator shall file a notice of challenge with the Registrar in accordance with the requirements of Rule 15.2 within 14 days after receipt of the notice of appointment of the arbitrator who is being challenged or within 14 days after the circumstances specified in Rule 14.1 or Rule 14.2 became known or should have reasonably been known to that party.

15.2. The notice of challenge shall state the reasons for the challenge. The date of receipt of the notice of challenge by the Registrar shall be deemed to be the date the notice of challenge is filed. The party challenging an arbitrator shall, at the same time as it files a notice of challenge with the Registrar, send the notice of challenge to the other party, the arbitrator who is being challenged and the other members of the Tribunal (or if the Tribunal has not yet been constituted, any appointed arbitrator), and shall notify the Registrar that it has done so, specifying the mode of service employed and the date of service.

15.3. The party making the challenge shall pay the requisite challenge fee under these Rules in accordance with the applicable Schedule of Fees. If the party making the challenge fails to pay the challenge fee within the time limit set by the Registrar, the challenge shall be considered as withdrawn.

15.4. After receipt of a notice of challenge under Rule 15.2, the Registrar may order a suspension of the arbitral proceedings until the challenge is resolved. Unless the Registrar orders the suspension of the arbitral proceedings pursuant to this Rule 15.4, the challenged arbitrator shall be entitled to continue to participate in the arbitration pending the determination of the challenge by the Court in accordance with Rule 16.

15.5. Where an arbitrator is challenged by a party, the other party may agree to the challenge, and the Court shall remove the arbitrator if all parties agree to the challenge. The challenged arbitrator may also voluntarily withdraw from office. In neither case does this imply acceptance of the validity of the grounds for the challenge.

15.5. Where an arbitrator is challenged by a party, the other party may agree to the challenge, and the Court shall remove the arbitrator if all parties agree to the challenge. The challenged arbitrator may also voluntarily withdraw from office. In neither case does this imply acceptance of the validity of the grounds for the challenge.

15.6. If an arbitrator is removed or withdraws from office in accordance with Rule 15.5, a substitute arbitrator shall be appointed in accordance with the procedure applicable to the nomination and appointment of the arbitrator being replaced. This procedure shall apply even if, during the process of appointing the challenged arbitrator, a party failed to exercise its right to nominate an arbitrator. The time limits applicable to the nomination and appointment of the substitute arbitrator shall commence from the date of receipt of the agreement of the other party to the challenge or the challenged arbitrator's withdrawal from office.

Rule 16

Decision on Challenge

16.1. If, within seven days of receipt of the notice of challenge under Rule 15, the other party does not agree to the challenge and the arbitrator who is being challenged does not withdraw voluntarily from office, the Court shall decide the challenge. The Court may request comments on the challenge from the parties, the challenged arbitrator and the other members of the Tribunal (or if the Tribunal has not yet been constituted, any appointed arbitrator), and set a schedule for such comments to be made.

16.2. If the Court accepts the challenge to an arbitrator, the Court shall remove the arbitrator, and a substitute arbitrator shall be appointed in accordance with the procedure applicable to the nomination and appointment of the arbitrator being replaced. The time limits applicable to the nomination and appointment of the substitute arbitrator shall commence from the date of the Registrar's notification to the parties of the decision by the Court.

16.3. If the Court rejects the challenge to an arbitrator, the challenged arbitrator shall continue with the arbitration.

16.4. The Court's decision on any challenge to an arbitrator under this Rule 16 shall be reasoned, unless otherwise agreed by the parties, and shall be issued to the parties by the Registrar. Any such decision on any challenge by the Court shall be final and not subject to appeal.

Rule 17

Replacement of an Arbitrator

17.1. Except as otherwise provided in these Rules, in the event of the death, resignation, withdrawal or removal of an arbitrator during the course of the arbitral proceedings, a substitute arbitrator shall be appointed in accordance with the procedure applicable to the nomination and appointment of the arbitrator being replaced.

17.2. In the event that an arbitrator refuses or fails to act or perform his functions in accordance with the Rules or within prescribed time limits, or in the event of any de jure or de facto impossibility by an arbitrator to act or perform his functions, the procedure for challenge and replacement of an arbitrator provided in Rule 14 to Rule 16 and Rule 17.1 shall apply.

17.3. The President may, at his own initiative and in his discretion, remove an arbitrator who refuses or fails to act or to perform his functions in accordance with the Rules or within prescribed time limits, or in the event of a de jure or de facto impossibility of an arbitrator to act or perform his functions, or if the arbitrator does not conduct or participate in the arbitration with due diligence and/or in a manner that ensures the fair, expeditious, economical and final resolution of the dispute. The President shall consult the parties and the members of the Tribunal, including the arbitrator to be removed (or if the Tribunal has not yet been constituted, any appointed arbitrator) prior to the removal of an arbitrator under this Rule.

Rule 18

Repetition of Hearings in the Event of Replacement of an Arbitrator

If the sole or presiding arbitrator is replaced in accordance with the procedure in Rule 15 to Rule 17, any hearings held previously shall be repeated unless otherwise agreed by the parties. If any other arbitrator is replaced, any hearings held previously may be repeated at the discretion of the Tribunal after consulting with the parties. If the Tribunal has issued an interim or partial Award, any hearings relating solely to that Award shall not be repeated, and the Award shall remain in effect.

Rule 19
Conduct of the Proceedings

19.1. The Tribunal shall conduct the arbitration in such manner as it considers appropriate, after consulting with the parties, to ensure the fair, expeditious, economical and final resolution of the dispute.

19.2. The Tribunal shall determine the relevance, materiality and admissibility of all evidence. The Tribunal is not required to apply the rules of evidence of any applicable law in making such determination.

19.3. As soon as practicable after the constitution of the Tribunal, the Tribunal shall conduct a preliminary meeting with the parties, in person or by any other means, to discuss the procedures that will be most appropriate and efficient for the case.

19.4. The Tribunal may, in its discretion, direct the order of proceedings, bifurcate proceedings, exclude cumulative or irrelevant testimony or other evidence and direct the parties to focus their presentations on issues the decision of which could dispose of all or part of the case.

19.5. Unless otherwise agreed by the parties, the presiding arbitrator may make procedural rulings alone, subject to revision by the Tribunal.

19.6. All statements, documents or other information supplied to the Tribunal and/or the Registrar by a party shall simultaneously be communicated to the other party.

19.7. The President may, at any stage of the proceedings, request the parties and the Tribunal to convene a meeting to discuss the procedures that will be most appropriate and efficient for the case. Such meeting may be conducted in person or by any other means.

Rule 20

Submissions by the Parties

20.1. Unless the Tribunal determines otherwise, the submission of written statements shall proceed as set out in this Rule.

20.2. Unless already submitted pursuant to Rule 3.2, the Claimant shall, within a period of time to be determined by the Tribunal, send to the Respondent and the Tribunal a Statement of Claim setting out in full detail:

a. a statement of facts supporting the claim;

b. the legal grounds or arguments supporting the claim; and

c. the relief claimed together with the amount of all quantifiable claims.

20.3. Unless already submitted pursuant to Rule 4.2, the Respondent shall, within a period of time to be determined by the Tribunal, send to the Claimant and the Tribunal a Statement of Defence setting out in full detail:

a. a statement of facts supporting its defence to the Statement of Claim;

b. the legal grounds or arguments supporting such defence; and

c. the relief claimed.

20.4. If a Statement of Counterclaim is made, the Claimant shall, within a period of time to be determined by the Tribunal, send to the Respondent and the Tribunal a Statement of Defence to Counterclaim setting out in full detail:

a. a statement of facts supporting its defence to the Statement of Counterclaim;

b. the legal grounds or arguments supporting such defence; and

c. the relief claimed.

20.5. A party may amend its claim, counterclaim or other submissions unless the Tribunal considers it inappropriate to allow such amendment having regard to the delay in making it or prejudice to the other party or any other circumstances. However, a claim or counterclaim may not be amended in such a manner that the amended claim or counterclaim falls outside the scope of the arbitration agreement.

20.6. The Tribunal shall decide which further submissions shall be required from the parties or may be presented by them. The Tribunal shall fix the periods of time for communicating such submissions.

20.7. All submissions referred to in this Rule shall be accompanied by copies of all supporting documents which have not previously been submitted by any party.

20.8. If the Claimant fails within the time specified to submit its Statement of Claim, the Tribunal may issue an order for the termination of the arbitral proceedings or give such other directions as may be appropriate.

20.9. If the Respondent fails to submit its Statement of Defence, or if at any point any party fails to avail itself of the opportunity to present its case in the manner directed by the Tribunal, the Tribunal may proceed with the arbitration.

Rule 21

Seat of the Arbitration

21.1. The parties may agree on the seat of the arbitration. Failing such an agreement, the seat of the arbitration shall be determined by the Tribunal, having regard to all the circumstances of the case.

21.2. The Tribunal may hold hearings and meetings by any means it considers expedient or appropriate and at any location it considers convenient or appropriate.

Rule 22

Language of the Arbitration

22.1. Unless otherwise agreed by the parties, the Tribunal shall determine the language to be used in the arbitration.

22.2. If a party submits a document written in a language other than the language(s) of the arbitration, the Tribunal, or if the Tribunal has not been constituted, the Registrar, may order that party to submit a translation in a form to be determined by the Tribunal or the Registrar.

Rule 23

Party Representatives

23.1. Any party may be represented by legal practitioners or any other authorised representatives. The Registrar and/ or the Tribunal may require proof of authority of any party representatives.

23.2. After the constitution of the Tribunal, any change or addition by a party to its representatives shall be promptly communicated in writing to the parties, the Tribunal and the Registrar.

Rule 24

Hearings

24.1. Unless the parties have agreed on a documents-only arbitration or as otherwise provided in these Rules, the Tribunal shall, if either party so requests or the Tribunal so decides, hold a hearing for the presentation of evidence and/ or for oral submissions on the merits of the dispute, including any issue as to jurisdiction.

24.2. The Tribunal shall, after consultation with the parties, set the date, time and place of any meeting or hearing and shall give the parties reasonable notice.

24.3. If any party fails to appear at a meeting or hearing without showing sufficient cause for such failure, the Tribunal may proceed with the arbitration and may make the Award based on the submissions and evidence before it.

24.4. Unless otherwise agreed by the parties, all meetings and hearings shall be in private, and any recordings, transcripts, or documents used in relation to the arbitral proceedings shall remain confidential.

Rule 25

Witnesses

25.1. Before any hearing, the Tribunal may require the parties to give notice of the identity of witnesses, including expert witnesses, whom the parties intend to produce, the subject matter of their testimony and its relevance to the issues.

25.2. The Tribunal may allow, refuse or limit the appearance of witnesses to give oral evidence at any hearing.

25.3. Any witness who gives oral evidence may be questioned by each of the parties, their representatives and the Tribunal in such manner as the Tribunal may determine.

25.4. The Tribunal may direct the testimony of witnesses to be presented in written form, either as signed statements or sworn affidavits or any other form of recording. Subject to Rule 25.2, any party may request that such a witness should attend for oral examination. If the witness fails to attend for oral examination, the Tribunal may place such weight on the written testimony as it thinks fit, disregard such written testimony, or exclude such written testimony altogether.

25.5. It shall be permissible for any party or its

representatives to interview any witness or potential witness (that may be presented by that party) prior to his appearance to give oral evidence at any hearing.

Rule 26

Tribunal-Appointed Experts

26.1. Unless otherwise agreed by the parties, the Tribunal may:

a. following consultation with the parties, appoint an expert to report on specific issues; and

b. require a party to give any expert appointed under Rule 26.1(a) any relevant information, or to produce or provide access to any relevant documents, goods or property for inspection.

26.2. Any expert appointed under Rule 26.1(a) shall submit a report in writing to the Tribunal. Upon receipt of such written report, the Tribunal shall deliver a copy of the report to the parties and invite the parties to submit written comments on the report.

26.3. Unless otherwise agreed by the parties, if the Tribunal considers it necessary or at the request of any party, an expert appointed under Rule 26.1(a) shall, after delivery of his written report, participate in a hearing. At the hearing, the parties shall have the opportunity to examine such expert.

Rule 27

Additional Powers of the Tribunal

Unless otherwise agreed by the parties, in addition to the other powers specified in these Rules, and except as prohibited by the mandatory rules of law applicable to the arbitration, the Tribunal shall have the power to:

a. order the correction or rectification of any contract, subject to the law governing such contract;

b. except as provided in these Rules, extend or abbreviate any time limits prescribed under these Rules or by its directions;

c. conduct such enquiries as may appear to the Tribunal to be necessary or expedient;

d. order the parties to make any property or item in their possession or control available for inspection;

e. order the preservation, storage, sale or disposal of any property or item which is or forms part of the subject matter of the dispute;

f. order any party to produce to the Tribunal and to the other parties for inspection, and to supply copies of, any document in their possession or control which the Tribunal considers relevant to the case and material to its outcome;

g. issue an order or Award for the reimbursement of unpaid deposits towards the costs of the arbitration;

h. direct any party or person to give evidence by affidavit or in any other form;

i. direct any party to take or refrain from taking actions to ensure that any Award which may be made in the arbitration is not rendered ineffectual by the dissipation of assets by a party or otherwise;

j. order any party to provide security for legal or other costs in any manner the Tribunal thinks fit;

k. order any party to provide security for all or part of any amount in dispute in the arbitration;

l. proceed with the arbitration notwithstanding the failure or refusal of any party to comply with these Rules or with the Tribunal's orders or directions or any partial Award or to attend any meeting or hearing, and to impose such sanctions as the Tribunal deems appropriate in relation to such failure or refusal;

m. decide, where appropriate, any issue not expressly or impliedly raised in the submissions of a party provided such issue has been clearly brought to the notice of the other party and that other party has been given adequate opportunity to respond;

n. determine the law applicable to the arbitral proceedings; and

o. determine any claim of legal or other privilege.

Rule 28

Jurisdiction of the Tribunal

28.1. If any party objects to the existence or validity of the arbitration agreement or to the competence of SIAC to administer an arbitration, before the Tribunal is constituted, the Registrar shall determine if such objection shall be referred to the Court. If the Registrar so determines, the Court shall decide if it is prima facie satisfied that the arbitration shall proceed. The arbitration shall be terminated if the Court is not so satisfied. Any decision by the Registrar or the Court that the arbitration shall proceed is without prejudice to the power of the Tribunal to rule on its own jurisdiction.

28.2. The Tribunal shall have the power to rule on its own jurisdiction, including any objections with respect to the existence, validity or scope of the arbitration agreement. An arbitration agreement which forms part of a contract shall be treated as an agreement independent of the other terms of the contract. A decision by the Tribunal that the contract is null and void shall not entail ipso jure the invalidity of the arbitration agreement, and the Tribunal shall not cease to have jurisdiction by reason of any allegation that the contract is non-existent or null and void.

28.3. Any objection that the Tribunal:

a. does not have jurisdiction shall be raised no later than in a Statement of Defence or in a Statement of Defence to a Counterclaim; or

b. is exceeding the scope of its jurisdiction shall be raised within 14 days after the matter alleged to be beyond the scope of the Tribunal's jurisdiction arises during the arbitral proceedings.

The Tribunal may admit an objection raised by a party outside the time limits under this Rule 28.3 if it considers the delay justified. A party is not precluded from raising an objection under this Rule 28.3 by the fact that it has nominated, or participated in the nomination of, an arbitrator.

28.4. The Tribunal may rule on an objection referred to in Rule 28.3 either as a preliminary question or in an Award on the merits.

28.5. A party may rely on a claim or defence for the purpose of a set-off to the extent permitted by these Rules and the applicable law.

Rule 29

Early Dismissal of Claims and Defences

29.1. A party may apply to the Tribunal for the early dismissal of a claim or defence on the basis that:

a. a claim or defence is manifestly without legal merit; or

b. a claim or defence is manifestly outside the jurisdiction of the Tribunal.

29.2. An application for the early dismissal of a claim or defence under Rule 29.1 shall state in detail the facts and legal basis supporting the application. The party applying for early dismissal shall, at the same time as it files the application with the Tribunal, send a copy of the application to the other party, and shall notify the Tribunal that it has done so, specifying the mode of service employed and the date of service.

29.3. The Tribunal may, in its discretion, allow the application for the early dismissal of a claim or defence under Rule 29.1 to proceed. If the application is allowed to proceed, the Tribunal shall, after giving the parties the opportunity to be heard, decide whether to grant, in whole or in part, the application for early dismissal under Rule 29.1.

29.4. If the application is allowed to proceed, the Tribunal shall make an order or Award on the application, with reasons, which may be in summary form. The order or Award shall be made within 60 days of the date of filing of the application, unless, in exceptional circumstances, the Registrar extends the time.

Rule 30

Interim and Emergency Relief

30.1. The Tribunal may, at the request of a party, issue an order or an Award granting an injunction or any other interim relief it deems appropriate. The Tribunal may order the party requesting interim relief to provide appropriate security in connection with the relief sought.

30.2. A party that wishes to seek emergency interim relief prior to the constitution of the Tribunal may apply for such relief pursuant to the procedures set forth in Schedule 1.

30.3. A request for interim relief made by a party to a judicial authority prior to the constitution of the Tribunal, or in exceptional circumstances thereafter, is not incompatible with these Rules.

Rule 31

Applicable Law, *Amiable Compositeur* and *Ex Aequo et Bono*

31.1. The Tribunal shall apply the law or rules of law designated by the parties as applicable to the substance of the dispute. Failing such designation by the parties, the Tribunal shall apply the law or rules of law which it determines to be appropriate.

31.2. The Tribunal shall decide as *amiable compositeur* or *ex aequo et bono* only if the parties have expressly authorised it to do so.

31.3. In all cases, the Tribunal shall decide in accordance with the terms of the contract, if any, and shall take into account any applicable usage of trade.

Rule 32

The Award

32.1. The Tribunal shall, as promptly as possible, after consulting with the parties and upon being satisfied that the parties have no further relevant and material evidence to produce or submission to make with respect to the matters to be decided in the Award, declare the proceedings closed. The Tribunal's declaration that the proceedings are closed shall be communicated to the parties and to the Registrar.

32.2. The Tribunal may, on its own motion or upon application of a party but before any Award is made, re-open the proceedings. The Tribunal's decision that the proceedings are to be re-opened shall be communicated to the parties and to the Registrar. The Tribunal shall close any re-opened proceedings in accordance with Rule 32.1.

32.3. Before making any Award, the Tribunal shall submit such Award in draft form to the Registrar. Unless the Registrar extends the period of time or unless otherwise agreed by the parties, the Tribunal shall submit the draft Award to the Registrar not later than 45 days from the date on which the Tribunal declares the proceedings closed. The Registrar may, as soon as practicable, suggest modifications as to the form of the Award and, without affecting the Tribunal's liberty to decide the dispute, draw the Tribunal's attention to points of substance. No Award shall be made by the Tribunal until it has been approved by the Registrar as to its form.

32.4. The Award shall be in writing and shall state the reasons upon which it is based unless the parties have agreed that no reasons are to be given.

32.5. Unless otherwise agreed by the parties, the Tribunal may make separate Awards on different issues at different times.

32.6. If any arbitrator fails to cooperate in the making of the Award, having been given a reasonable opportunity to do so, the remaining arbitrators may proceed. The remaining arbitrators shall provide written notice of such refusal or failure to the Registrar, the parties and the absent arbitrator. In deciding whether to proceed with the arbitration in the absence of an arbitrator, the remaining arbitrators may take into account, among other things, the stage of the arbitration, any explanation provided by the absent arbitrator for his refusal to participate and the effect, if any, upon the enforceability of the Award should the remaining arbitrators proceed without the absent arbitrator. The remaining arbitrators shall explain in any Award made the reasons for proceeding without the absent arbitrator.

32.7. Where there is more than one arbitrator, the Tribunal shall decide by a majority. Failing a majority decision, the presiding arbitrator alone shall make the Award for the Tribunal.

32.8. The Award shall be delivered to the Registrar, who shall transmit certified copies to the parties upon full settlement of the costs of the arbitration.

32.9. The Tribunal may award simple or compound interest on any sum which is the subject of the arbitration at such rates as the parties may have agreed or, in the absence of such agreement, as the Tribunal determines to be appropriate, in respect of any period which the Tribunal determines to be appropriate.

32.10. In the event of a settlement, and if the parties so request, the Tribunal may make a consent Award recording the settlement. If the parties do not require a consent Award, the parties shall confirm to the Registrar that a settlement has been reached, following which the Tribunal shall be discharged and the arbitration concluded upon full settlement of the costs of the arbitration.

32.11. Subject to Rule 33 and Schedule 1, by agreeing to arbitration under these Rules, the parties agree that any Award shall be final and binding on the parties from the date it is made, and undertake to carry out the Award immediately and without delay. The parties also irrevocably waive their rights to any form of appeal, review or recourse to any State court or other judicial authority with respect to such Award insofar as such waiver may be validly made.

32.12. SIAC may, with the consent of the parties and the Tribunal, publish any Award with the names of the parties and other identifying information redacted.

Rule 33

Correction of Awards, Interpretation of Awards and Additional Awards

33.1. Within 30 days of receipt of an Award, a party may, by written notice to the Registrar and the other party, request the Tribunal to correct in the Award any error in computation, any clerical or typographical error or any error of a similar nature. If the Tribunal considers the request to be justified, it shall make the correction within 30 days of receipt of the request. Any correction, made in the original Award or in a separate memorandum, shall constitute part of the Award.

33.2. The Tribunal may correct any error of the type referred to in Rule 33.1 on its own initiative within 30 days of the date of the Award.

33.3. Within 30 days of receipt of an Award, a party may, by written notice to the Registrar and the other party, request the Tribunal to make an additional Award as to claims presented in the arbitration but not dealt with in the Award. If the Tribunal considers the request to be justified, it shall make the additional Award within 45 days of receipt of the request.

33.4. Within 30 days of receipt of an Award, a party may, by written notice to the Registrar and the other party, request that the Tribunal give an interpretation of the Award. If the Tribunal considers the request to be justified, it shall provide the interpretation in writing within 45 days after receipt of the request. The interpretation shall form part of the Award.

33.5. The Registrar may, if necessary, extend the period of time within which the Tribunal shall make a correction of an Award, interpretation of an Award or an additional Award under this Rule.

33.6. The provisions of Rule 32 shall apply in the same manner with the necessary or appropriate changes in relation to a correction of an Award, interpretation of an Award and to any additional Award made.

Rule 34

Fees and Deposits

34.1. The Tribunal's fees and SIAC's fees shall be ascertained in accordance with the Schedule of Fees in force at the time of commencement of the arbitration. The parties may agree to alternative methods of determining the Tribunal's fees prior to the constitution of the Tribunal.

34.2. The Registrar shall fix the amount of deposits payable towards the costs of the arbitration. Unless the Registrar directs otherwise, 50% of such deposits shall be payable by the Claimant and the remaining 50% of such deposits shall be payable by the Respondent. The Registrar may fix separate deposits on costs for claims and counterclaims, respectively.

34.3. Where the amount of the claim or the counterclaim is not quantifiable at the time payment is due, a provisional estimate of the costs of the arbitration shall be made by the Registrar. Such estimate may be based on the nature of the controversy and the circumstances of the case. This estimate may be adjusted in light of such information as may subsequently become available.

34.4. The Registrar may from time to time direct parties to make further deposits towards the costs of the arbitration.

34.5. Parties are jointly and severally liable for the costs of the arbitration. Any party is free to pay the whole of the deposits towards the costs of the arbitration should the other party fail to pay its share.

34.6. If a party fails to pay the deposits directed by the Registrar either wholly or in part:

a. the Tribunal may suspend its work and the Registrar may suspend SIAC's administration of the arbitration, in whole or in part; and

b. the Registrar may, after consultation with the Tribunal (if constituted) and after informing the parties, set a time limit on the expiry of which the relevant claims or counterclaims shall be considered as withdrawn without prejudice to the party reintroducing the same claims or counterclaims in another proceeding.

34.7. In all cases, the costs of the arbitration shall be finally determined by the Registrar at the conclusion of the proceedings. If the claim and/or counterclaim is not quantified, the Registrar shall finally determine the costs of the arbitration, as set out in Rule 35, in his discretion. The Registrar shall have regard to all the circumstances of the case, including the stage of proceedings at which the arbitration concluded. In the event that the costs of the arbitration determined are less than the deposits made, there shall be a refund in such proportions as the parties may agree, or failing an agreement, in the same proportions as the deposits were made.

34.8. All deposits towards the costs of the arbitration shall be made to and held by SIAC. Any interest which may accrue on such deposits shall be retained by SIAC.

34.9. In exceptional circumstances, the Registrar may direct the parties to pay an additional fee, in addition to that prescribed in the applicable Schedule of Fees, as part of SIAC's administration fees.

Rule 35

Costs of the Arbitration

35.1. Unless otherwise agreed by the parties, the Tribunal shall specify in the Award the total amount of the costs of the arbitration. Unless otherwise agreed by the parties, the Tribunal shall determine in the Award the apportionment of the costs of the arbitration among the parties.

35.2. The term 'costs of the arbitration' includes:

a. the Tribunal's fees and expenses and the Emergency Arbitrator's fees and expenses, where applicable;

b. SIAC's administration fees and expenses; and

c. the costs of any expert appointed by the Tribunal and of any other assistance reasonably required by the Tribunal.

Rule 36

Tribunal's Fees and Expenses

36.1. The fees of the Tribunal shall be fixed by the Registrar in accordance with the applicable Schedule of Fees or, if applicable, with the method agreed by the parties pursuant to Rule 34.1, and the stage of the proceedings at which the arbitration concluded. In exceptional circumstances, the Registrar may determine that an additional fee over that prescribed in the applicable Schedule of Fees shall be paid.

36.2. The Tribunal's reasonable out-of-pocket expenses necessarily incurred and other allowances shall be reimbursed in accordance with the applicable Practice Note.

Rule 37

Party's Legal and Other Costs

The Tribunal shall have the authority to order in its Award that all or a part of the legal or other costs of a party be paid by another party.

Rule 38

Exclusion of Liability

38.1. Any arbitrator, including any Emergency Arbitrator, any person appointed by the Tribunal, including any administrative secretary and any expert, the President, members of the Court, and any directors, officers and employees of SIAC, shall not be liable to any person for any negligence, act or omission in connection with any arbitration administered by SIAC in accordance with these Rules.

38.2. SIAC, including the President, members of the Court, directors, officers, employees or any arbitrator, including any Emergency Arbitrator, and any person appointed by the Tribunal, including any administrative secretary and any expert, shall not be under any obligation to make any statement in connection with any arbitration administered by SIAC in accordance with these Rules. No party shall seek to make the President, any member of the Court, director, officer, employee of SIAC, or any arbitrator, including any Emergency Arbitrator, and any person appointed by the Tribunal, including any administrative secretary and any expert, act as a witness in any legal proceedings in connection with any arbitration administered by SIAC in accordance with these Rules.

Rule 39

Confidentiality

39.1. Unless otherwise agreed by the parties, a party and any arbitrator, including any Emergency Arbitrator, and any person appointed by the Tribunal, including any administrative secretary and any expert, shall at all times treat all matters relating to the proceedings and the Award as confidential. The discussions and deliberations of the Tribunal shall be confidential.

39.2. Unless otherwise agreed by the parties, a party or any arbitrator, including any Emergency Arbitrator, and any person appointed by the Tribunal, including any administrative secretary and any expert, shall not, without the prior written consent of the parties, disclose to a third party any such matter except:

a. for the purpose of making an application to any competent court of any State to enforce or challenge the Award;

b. pursuant to the order of or a subpoena issued by a court of competent jurisdiction;

c. for the purpose of pursuing or enforcing a legal right or claim;

d. in compliance with the provisions of the laws of any State which are binding on the party making the disclosure or the request or requirement of any regulatory body or other authority;

e. pursuant to an order by the Tribunal on application by a party with proper notice to the other parties; or

f. for the purpose of any application under Rule 7 or Rule 8 of these Rules.

39.3. In Rule 39.1, 'matters relating to the proceedings' includes the existence of the proceedings, and the pleadings, evidence and other materials in the arbitral proceedings and all other documents produced by another party in the proceedings or the Award arising from the proceedings, but excludes any matter that is otherwise in the public domain.

39.4. The Tribunal has the power to take appropriate measures, including issuing an order or Award for sanctions or costs, if a party breaches the provisions of this Rule.

Rule 40

Decisions of the President, the Court and the Registrar

40.1. Except as provided in these Rules, the decisions of the President, the Court and the Registrar with respect to all matters relating to an arbitration shall be conclusive and binding upon the parties and the Tribunal. The President, the Court and the Registrar shall not be required to provide reasons for such decisions, unless the Court determines otherwise or as may be provided in these Rules. The parties agree that the discussions and deliberations of the Court are confidential.

40.2. Save in respect of Rule 16.1 and Rule 28.1, the parties waive any right of appeal or review in respect of any decisions of the President, the Court and the Registrar to any State court or other judicial authority.

Rule 41

General Provisions

41.1. Any party that proceeds with the arbitration without promptly raising any objection to a failure to comply with any provision of these Rules, or of any other rules applicable to the proceedings, any direction given by the Tribunal, or any requirement under the arbitration agreement relating to the constitution of the Tribunal or the conduct of the proceedings, shall be deemed to have waived its right to object.

41.2. In all matters not expressly provided for in these Rules, the President, the Court, the Registrar and the Tribunal shall act in the spirit of these Rules and shall make every reasonable effort to ensure the fair, expeditious and economical conclusion of the arbitration and the enforceability of any Award.

41.3. In the event of any discrepancy or inconsistency between the English version of these Rules and any other languages in which these Rules are published, the English version shall prevail.

Schedule 1
Emergency Arbitrator

1. A party that wishes to seek emergency interim relief may, concurrent with or following the filing of a Notice of Arbitration but prior to the constitution of the Tribunal, file an application for emergency interim relief with the Registrar. The party shall, at the same time as it files the application for emergency interim relief, send a copy of the application to all other parties. The application for emergency interim relief shall include:

a. the nature of the relief sought;

b. the reasons why the party is entitled to such relief; and

c. a statement certifying that all other parties have been provided with a copy of the application or, if not, an explanation of the steps taken in good faith to provide a copy or notification to all other parties.

2. Any application for emergency interim relief shall be accompanied by payment of the non-refundable administration fee and the requisite deposits under these Rules towards the Emergency Arbitrator's fees and expenses for proceedings pursuant to this Schedule 1. In appropriate cases, the Registrar may increase the amount of the deposits requested from the party making the application. If the additional deposits are not paid within the time limit set by the Registrar, the application shall be considered as withdrawn.

3. The President shall, if he determines that SIAC should accept the application for emergency interim relief, seek to appoint an Emergency Arbitrator within one day of receipt

by the Registrar of such application and payment of the administration fee and deposits.

4. If the parties have agreed on the seat of the arbitration, such seat shall be the seat of the proceedings for emergency interim relief. Failing such an agreement, the seat of the proceedings for emergency interim relief shall be Singapore, without prejudice to the Tribunal's determination of the seat of the arbitration under Rule 21.1.

5. Prior to accepting appointment, a prospective Emergency Arbitrator shall disclose to the Registrar any circumstances that may give rise to justifiable doubts as to his impartiality or independence. Any challenge to the appointment of the Emergency Arbitrator must be made within two days of the communication by the Registrar to the parties of the appointment of the Emergency Arbitrator and the circumstances disclosed.

6. An Emergency Arbitrator may not act as an arbitrator in any future arbitration relating to the dispute, unless otherwise agreed by the parties.

7. The Emergency Arbitrator shall, as soon as possible but, in any event, within two days of his appointment, establish a schedule for consideration of the application for emergency interim relief. Such schedule shall provide a reasonable opportunity for the parties to be heard, but may provide for proceedings by telephone or video conference or on written submissions as alternatives to a hearing in person. The Emergency Arbitrator shall have the powers vested in the Tribunal pursuant to these Rules, including the authority to rule on his own jurisdiction, without prejudice to the Tribunal's determination.

8. The Emergency Arbitrator shall have the power to order or award any interim relief that he deems necessary, including preliminary orders that may be made pending any hearing, telephone or video conference or written submissions by the parties. The Emergency Arbitrator shall give summary reasons for his decision in writing. The Emergency Arbitrator may modify or vacate the preliminary order, the interim order or Award for good cause.

9. The Emergency Arbitrator shall make his interim order or Award within 14 days from the date of his appointment unless, in exceptional circumstances, the Registrar extends the time. No interim order or Award shall be made by the Emergency Arbitrator until it has been approved by the Registrar as to its form.

10. The Emergency Arbitrator shall have no power to act after the Tribunal is constituted. The Tribunal may reconsider, modify or vacate any interim order or Award issued by the Emergency Arbitrator, including a ruling on his own jurisdiction. The Tribunal is not bound by the reasons given by the Emergency Arbitrator. Any interim order or Award issued by the Emergency Arbitrator shall, in any event, cease to be binding if the Tribunal is not constituted within 90 days of such order or Award or when the Tribunal makes a final Award or if the claim is withdrawn.

11. Any interim order or Award by the Emergency Arbitrator may be conditioned on provision by the party seeking such relief of appropriate security.

12. The parties agree that an order or Award by an Emergency Arbitrator pursuant to this Schedule 1 shall be binding on the parties from the date it is made, and undertake to carry out the interim order or Award immediately and without delay.

The parties also irrevocably waive their rights to any form of appeal, review or recourse to any State court or other judicial authority with respect to such Award insofar as such waiver may be validly made.

13. The costs associated with any application pursuant to this Schedule 1 may initially be apportioned by the Emergency Arbitrator, subject to the power of the Tribunal to determine finally the apportionment of such costs.

14. These Rules shall apply as appropriate to any proceeding pursuant to this Schedule 1, taking into account the urgency of such a proceeding. The Emergency Arbitrator may decide in what manner these Rules shall apply as appropriate, and his decision as to such matters is final and not subject to appeal, review or recourse. The Registrar may abbreviate any time limits under these Rules in applications made pursuant to proceedings commenced under Rule 30.2 and Schedule 1.

Bibliography

Books and Articles

Ali, Shahla F, 'The Jurisprudence of Responsive Mediation: An Empirical Examination of Chinese People's Mediation in Action', (2013) 45 *Journal of Legal Pluralism and Unofficial Law* 1 (University of Hong Kong Faculty of Law Research Paper No. 2013/023)

Allison, Graham, Robert D Blackwill with Ali Wyne, *Lee Kuan Yew: The Grand Master's Insights on China, the United States, and the World* (MIT Press 2013)

Blackaby, Nigel, Constantine Partasides, Alan Redfern & Martin Hunter, *Redfern and Hunter on International Arbitration* (Oxford University Press 6th edn student ver 2015)

Bodde, Derk & Clarence Morris, *Law in Imperial China* (Harvard University Press 1967)

Bond, Stephen R, 'The International Arbitrator: From the Perspective of the ICC International Court of Arbitration', (1991-2) 12 Northwestern Journal of International Law & Business 1

Born, Gary B, *International Arbitration: Law and Practice* (Kluwer Law International 2012)

-----, *International Arbitration: Cases and Materials* (Kluwer Law International 2 edn 2015)

Chen Fuyong, 'Striving for Independence, Competence, and Fairness: A Case Study of the Beijing Arbitration Commission', (2009) 18 *American Review of International Arbitration* 313

Chen Fuyong & Sun Wei, 'Looking Beyond Rules: An Analysing Insight into the Competitive Attractions of BAC', (2014) *LexisNexis Dispute Resolution Law Guide*

Chen Youxi, 'A Tale of Two Cities: The Legal Profession in China', (Mar 2013) *Thematic Papers No 2 International Bar Association's Human Rights Institute (IBAHRI)*

Chi Manjiao, 'Time to Make a Change? A Comparative Study of Chinese Arbitration Law and the 2006 UNCITRAL Model Law and the Forecast of Chinese Arbitration Law Reform', (2009) 5 *Asian International Arbitration Journal* 142

Cohen, Jerome A, 'Settling International Business Disputes with China: Then and Now', (2014) 47 *Cornell International Law Journal* 555

Collier, John & Vaughan Lowe, *The Settlement of Disputes in International Law* (Oxford University Press 1999)

Confucius (trans DC Lau), *The Analects* (Penguin Books 1979)

Derains, Yves & Laurent Lévy (eds), *Is Arbitration Only as Good as the Arbitrator? Status, Powers and Role of the Arbitrator*, (International Chamber of Commerce 2011) ICC Publication No. 714E

Dezalay, Yves & Bryant G Garth, *Dealing in Virtue: International Commercial Arbitration and the Construction of a Transnational Legal Order* (University of Chicago Press 1998)

Ellenbogen, G, 'English Arbitration Practice', (1952) 17 *Law and Contemporary Problems* 656

Fan, Kun, 'Arbitration in China: Practice, Legal Obstacles, and Reforms', (2008) 19 *ICC International Court of Arbitration Bulletin* 25

Fei, Jessica & Richard Hill, 'Enforcement of Arbitral Awards in the PRC', in Michael J Moser (ed), *Dispute Resolution in China* (JurisNet LLC 2012) 157

Fu Hualing, 'Access to Justice in China: Potentials, Limits, and Alternatives', in John Gillespie & Albert HY Chen (eds), *Legal Reforms in China and Vietnam: A Comparison of Asian Communist Regimes* (Routledge 2010) 163

Gaillard, Emmanuel, 'Sociology of International Arbitration', (2015) 31 *Arbitration International* 1

Gelatt, Timothy A, 'Lawyers in China: The Past Decade and Beyond', (1991) 23 *New York University Journal of International Law & Politics* 751

Gu Weixia, *Arbitration in China: Regulation of Arbitration Agreements and Practical Issues* (Sweet & Maxwell Thomson Reuters 2012)

-----, 'Arbitration in China', in Shahla F Ali & Tom Ginsburg (eds), *International Commercial Arbitration in Asia* (Juris Publishing 3rd edn 2013) 77 (University of Hong Kong Faculty of Law Research Paper No. 2013/022)

-----, 'The China-Style Closed Panel System in Arbitral Tribunal Formation: Analysis of Chinese Adaptation to Globalization', (2008) 25 *Journal of International Arbitration* 121

Gupta, Anil K & Wang Haiyan Wang, *Getting China and India Right* (Jossey-Bass 2009)

Heilbron, Hilary, Jonathan Hirst & Klaus Reichert, *SIAC Rules: An Annotation* (LexisNexis 2014)

Hofstede, Geert, Gert Jan Hofstede & Michael Minkov, *Cultures and Organizations: Software of the Mind* (McGraw-Hill Education 3rd edn 2010)

Hunter, Martin, 'International Commercial Dispute Resolution: The Challenge of the Twenty-first Century' (2000) 16 *Arbitration International* 383

Jacques, Martin, *When China Rules the World* (Penguin Books 2nd edn 2012)

Joseph, David & David Foxton, *Singapore International Arbitration: Law and Practice* (LexisNexis 2014)

Kaufmann-Kohler, Gabrielle & Fan Kun, 'Integrating Mediation into Arbitration: Why It Works in China', (2008) 25 *Journal of International Arbitration* 479

Kim, Tae-Yeol, Wong Chongwei Wang, Mari Kondo, & Kim Tae-Hyun, 'Conflict Management Styles: The Differences Among the Chinese, Japanese, and Koreans', (2007) 18 *International Journal of Conflict Management* 23

Kissinger, Henry, *Henry Kissinger on China* (Penguin Books, 2012)

Kun Fan, 'Arbitration in China: Practice, Legal Obstacles and Reforms', (2008) 19 *ICC International Court of Arbitration* 25

Lalive, Pierre, 'Towards a Decline of International Arbitration?', (1999) 65 *Arbitration* 252

Lee Kuan Yew, *One Man's View of the World* (Straits Times Press 2013)

Liebman, Benjamin L, 'China's Courts: Restricted Reform', (2007) 21 *Columbia Journal of Asian Law* 1 (Columbia Public Law Research Paper No. 08-180)

Luttrell, Sam, *Bias Challenges in International Commercial Arbitration: The Need for a 'Real Danger' Test* (Kluwer Law International 2009)

Lynch, Elizabeth M, 'China's Rule of Law Mirage: The Regression of the Legal Profession Since the Adoption of the 2007 Lawyers Law', (2011) 42 *George Washington International Law Review* 535

Menzies, Gavin, *1421: The Year China Discovered the World* (Bantam Press 2001)

Merkin, Robert & Johanna Hjalmarsson, *Singapore Arbitration Legislation Annotated* (Informa Law 2nd edn 2016)

Minzner, Carl, 'Legal Reform in the Xi Jinping Era', (2015) 20 *Asia Policy* 4

Lew, Julian DM, Loukas A Mistelis & Stefan M Kroll, *Comparative International Commercial Arbitration* (Kluwer Law International 2003)

Moore, John Bassett, 'International Arbitration', (1917) 7 *Proceedings of the Academy of Political Science in the City of New York* 21

Paulsson, Jan, *The Idea of Arbitration* (Oxford University Press 2013)

Peerenboom, Randall, *China's Long March Toward Rule of Law* (Cambridge University Press 2002)

Reisman, Michael W, W Lawrence Craig, William Park & Jan Paulsson, *International Commercial Arbitration Cases, Materials and Notes on The Resolution of International Business Disputes* (Foundation Press 1997)

Rivers, Cheryl, 'Negotiation Ethics Across Cultures: An Examination of the Influence of Law and Codes of Ethics' (IACM 23rd Annual Conference Paper (July 2010))

Rosenbaum, Samuel & Herbert Harley, 'Commercial Arbitration in England', (1917) 3 *American Bar Association Journal* 21

Savage, John & Emmanuel Gaillard (eds), *Fouchard Gaillard Goldman on International Commercial Arbitration* (Kluwer Law International 1999)

Shen Sibao & Shen Jian, 'The Characteristics of Business Mediation System in China' (2012) *Opinio Juris in Comparatione* No. 1/2012, Paper No. 9

Sun Wei & Melanie Willems, *Arbitration in China* (Kluwer Law International 2015)

Sun Tzu (trans John Minford), *The Art of War* (Penguin Books 2002)

Szto, Mary, 'Gender and the Chinese Legal Profession: From Heaven and Earth to Rule of Woman?', (2009) 18 *Texas Journal of Women & Law* 195

Tang, Houzhi, 'Arbitration: A Method Used by China to Settle Foreign Trade and Economic Disputes Lecture', (1984) 4 *Pace Law Review* 519

Tao Jingzhou, *Arbitration Law and Practice in China* (Kluwer Law International 3rd edn 2012)

Wunschheim von, Clarisse & Kun Fan, 'Arbitrating in China: The Rules of the Game: Practical Recommendations Concerning Arbitration in China', (2008) 26 *ASA Bulletin* 35

Yu, Peter K, Gordon G Chang, Jerome A Cohen, Elizabeth C Economy, Sharon Hom & Adam Qi Li, 'China and the WTO: Progress, Perils, and Prospects', (2003) 17 *Columbia Journal of Asian Law* 1

Newspapers, magazines and online

'Chinese legal mergers: Rules and laws', *Economist* (London 31 Jan 2015) <http://www.economist.com/node/21641291/print>

'Supreme People's Court of China judge speaks on arbitral awards', Columbia Law School (New York 19 Feb 2013) <www.law.columbia.edu/media_inquiries/news_events/2013/february2013/chinese-arbitral-awards>

Beck, Susan, 'It's official: Dentons merger with Dacheng creates global giant', *Law.com* (New York 10 Nov 2015) <http://www.law.com/sites/articles/2015/11/10/its-official-dentons-merger-with-dacheng-creates-global-giant/>

Cao Lijun & Lu Leilei, 'To be or not to be: The practical implications of choosing foreign arbitration for purely domestic contracts', *Kluwer Arbitration Blog* (6 March 2015) <http://kluwerarbitrationblog.com/2015/03/06/to-be-or-not-to-be-the-practical-implications-of-choosing-foreign-arbitration-for-purely-domestic-contracts/>

Eberhardt, Pia, Cecilia Olivet, Tyler Amos & Nick Buxton, 'Corporate Europe Observatory 'Profiting from injustice: How law firms, arbitrators and financiers are fuelling an investment arbitration boom', (2012) Corporate Europe Observatory and The Transnational Institute <https://corporateeurope.org/international-trade/2012/11/profiting-injustice>

Harris, Dan, 'China lawsuits as a growth industry', *Above the Law* (New York 1 Feb 2016) <http://abovethelaw.com/2016/02/china-lawsuits-as-a-growth-industry>

Jones, Leigh, 'What's in a name? For Chinese law firms, Bright is often right', *Reuters* (New York 8 Feb 2012) <www.reuters.com/article/lawfirms-china-names-idUSL2E8D87Y320120208>

Li Shangjing, 'Wu Mingde of Allbright Law Offices: Corporate structure not the future for law firms in China', *Asian Legal Business* (20 Apr 2016) <www.legalbusinessonline.com/features/wu-mingde-allbright-law-officescorporate-structure-not-future-law-firms-china/72132>

SIAC Annual Report 2015 <http://siac.org.sg/images/stories/articles/annual_report/SIAC_Annual_Report_2015.pdf>

Vanderklippe, Nathan, 'East meets West: Dentons-Dacheng merger raises host of questions', *Globe and Mail* (Toronto 27 Jan 2015) <http://www.theglobeandmail.com/report-on-business/industry-news/the-law-page/east-meets-west-dentons-dacheng-merger-raises-host-of-questions/article22647980/>

Zhang, Anna, 'How do Chinese law firms operate?', *Asian Lawyer* (New York 6 June 2016) <www.international.law.com/id=1202759347077/How-Do-Chinese-Law-Firms-Operate?mcode=0&curindex=0&curpage=1>

Zhou, Tina, 'Supreme Court of China issues interpretations governing foreign-related civil relationships', *Lexology*

(London 30 Apr 2013) </www.lexology.com/library/detail.aspx?g=827521b3-94c8-495b-bbd0-e35c73241a39>

Index

www.ingramcontent.com/pod-product-compliance
Lightning Source LLC
LaVergne TN
LVHW102010210926
848483LV00010B/246
* 9 7 8 1 9 1 2 1 4 2 0 7 1 *